Prison Correctional Officer

The Use and Abuse of the Human Resources of Prisons

compiled and edited by
Robert R. Ross
Department of Criminology
University of Ottawa

BUTTERWORTHS
Toronto

Prison Guard/Correctional Officer
© 1981 Butterworth & Co. (Canada) Ltd.

All rights reserved. No part of this publication may be reproduced, stored in a retrieval system, or transmitted, in any form or by any means, photocopying, electronic, mechanical, recording, or otherwise, without the prior written permission of the copyright holder.

Printed and bound in Canada

The Butterworth Group of Companies

Canada:
Butterworth & Co. (Canada) Ltd., Toronto
Butterworth & Co. (Western Canada) Ltd., Vancouver

United Kingdom:
Butterworth & Co. (Publishers) Ltd., London, Borough Green

Australia:
Butterworths Pty. Ltd., Sydney, Melbourne, Brisbane, Perth, Norwood

New Zealand:
Butterworths of New Zealand Ltd., Wellington

South Africa:
Butterworth & Co. (South Africa) Ltd., Durban

United States:
Butterworth (Publishers) Inc., Boston
Butterworth (Legal Publishers) Inc., Seattle
Butterworth & Co. Ltd., Ann Arbor
Mason Publishing Company, St. Paul

Canadian Cataloguing in Publication Data

Main entry under title:
Prison guard/correctional officer

Bibliography: p.
ISBN 0-409-86320-3

1. Correctional personnel. 2. Prisons - Officials and employees. I. Ross, Robert R., 1933-

HV8759.P74   365   C81-094073-6

Dedicated to those correctional officers who dignify their job by doing it well.

About the Editor

Bob Ross is a Professor of Criminology at the University of Ottawa. He received his Ph.D. in Psychology from the University of Toronto. Dr. Ross has been a Research Associate for the Human Justice Program at the University of Regina; a Lecturer at Wilfred Laurier University; and an Associate Professor of Psychology at the University of Waterloo. His experience in criminal justice includes more than ten years as a clinical psychologist in a wide variety of correctional institutions for juveniles and adults and twelve years as Chief Psychologist for the Ontario Government's Ministry of Correctional Services. He has also been a faculty member for the Ontario Department of Education's programs for special education teachers, and Consultant to the Department of Educational Television. Dr. Ross's publications include articles in professional journals in psychology, criminology and corrections, and chapters in several books on corrections and on behavior modification. His other books include: *Self-Mutilation* (with H. B. McKay), D. C. Heath Co., and *Effective Correctional Treatment* (with P. Gendreau), Butterworths Co.

Table of Contents

	Page
Contributors	vii
Preface	ix

I Introduction 1

II The Job: The Guard's View 7
    1. A Day on the Job — In Prison 9
        Edgar May
    2. Prison Guards in America — The Inside Story 19
        Edgar May
    3. What Prison Guards Think: A Profile of the
       Illinois Force 41
        James B. Jacobs
    4. Prison Guard 55
        James B. Jacobs and Harold G. Retsky

III Social Service Role of the Prison Guard 75
    5. Changing World of the Correctional Officer 77
        Elmer H. Johnson
    6. Is a "Correctional Officer" by any Other Name,
       a "Screw?" 87
        Hans Toch
    7. Informal Helping Network in Prison: The Shape of
       Grass-Roots Correctional Intervention 105
        Robert Johnson
    8. Correctional Officers with Case Loads 127
        Richard J. Ward and David Vandergoot

IV Pseudo-Guards 135
    9. Interpersonal Dynamics in a Simulated Prison 137
        Craig Haney, Curtis Banks, and Philip Zimbardo
    10. Changing of the Guard: Citizen Soldiers in
        Wisconsin Correctional Institutions 169
        League of Women Voters of Wisconsin

V Female Correctional Officers 191
    11. The Sexual Integration of the Prison's Guard Force:
        A Few Comments on Dothard v. Rawlinson 193
        James B. Jacobs

		Page
12.	The Upward Mobility of Women in Corrections *Sandra Nicolai*	223

VI Correctional Officer Selection 239

13. Psychological Tests for Correctional Officer
    Selection: Research and Issues 241
    *Barbara Krug-McKay, H. Bryan McKay and
    Robert R. Ross*
14. Correctional Officers: Selection Through Training 259
    Robert R. Ross and H. Bryan McKay

VII Organization, Management and Rights 273

15. The Correction Officer Subculture and
    Organizational Change 275
    David Duffee
16. Drop-Outs and Rejects: An Analysis of the
    Prison Guard's Revolving Door 297
    James B. Jacobs and Mary P. Grear
17. Correctional Employees' Reactions to Job Characteristics:
    A Data Based Argument for Job Enlargement 313
    Arthur P. Brief, Jim Munro and Ramon J. Aldag
18. Guard Unions: The Search for Solidarity 321
    Joan Potter
19. A Bill of Rights for the Correctional Officer 337
    Stanley L. Brodsky

Contributors

Ramon J. Aldag, Graduate School of Business, University of Wisconsin.
W. Curtis Banks, Educational Testing Services, Princeton, New Jersey.
Arthur P. Brief, Department of Management Sciences, College of Business Administration, University of Iowa.
Stanley L. Brodsky, Department of Psychology, University of Alabama.
David Duffee, School of Criminal Justice, State University of New York at Albany.
Mary P. Grear, Lord, Bissell and Brook, Chicago, Illinois.
Craig Haney, Adlai Stevenson College, University of California, Santa Cruz.
James B. Jacobs, Cornell Law School, Ithaca, New York.
Elmer H. Johnson, Center for Study of Crime, Delinquency and Corrections, Southern Illinois University.
Robert Johnson, School of Justice, The American University, Washington, D.C.
Barbara Krug-McKay, Research Consultant, Ottawa.
League of Women Voters of Wisconsin, Madison, Wisconsin.
Edgar May, Contributing Editor, Corrections Magazine.
Bryan McKay, McKay Trost Associates, Inc., Toronto.
Jim Munro, University of West Florida.
Sandra Nicolai, CONtact, Inc., Lincoln, Nebraska.
Joan Potter, Contributing Editor, Corrections Magazine.
Harold G. Retsky, Alcoholism Center, Comprehensive Health Council of Metropolitan Chicago.
Robert R. Ross, Department of Criminology, Faculty of Social Sciences, University of Ottawa.
Hans Toch, School of Criminal Justice, State University of New York.
David Vandergoot, Human Resources Center, Albertson, Long Island, New York.
Richard J. Ward, U.S. Department of the Navy, Naval Military Personnel Command, Washington, D.C.
Philip G. Zimbardo, Department of Psychology, Stanford University.

Preface

Training programs for prison guards have proliferated in correctional agency staff development programs, in university undergraduate and extension programs, and in hundreds of community colleges throughout North America. This book is intended to serve as a text–reader for such courses and for other courses in criminal justice, corrections, sociology, criminology, and psychology which purport to teach about the world of prisons. Teachers and students in these courses have heretofore had to rely on academic literature which systematically neglected a crucial part of the prison — the correctional officer.

This anthology consists of a collection of articles by contributors who have considered the correctional officer an important and legitimate subject for objective study. They have gone against the grain by asserting and demonstrating that the prison guard is a key figure and that the prison cannot be fully understood, or even adequately described, without careful study of the role of the correctional officer. It is intended to serve as a long overdue substitute for more widely publicized and oversimplified descriptions of prison guards, found in media reports and in the biographies of ex-inmates which have created a negative and sensationalized impression of guards. In contrast, the articles in this book are based on objective study of the men and women who guard our prisons. I think that *Prison Guard/Correctional Officer* does justice to the importance and the complexity of the guards' work, and adequately stresses their potential for contributing to prison disruption or to harmony.

The articles were selected to provide the reader with the most penetrating and objective analyses of correctional officers — who they are; what they do; how they are selected; how they control and are controlled in the unique social environment in which they work; why and how they respond to and seek change in their working conditions, their power and their status; and why they leave their jobs.

I make no apology for using the terms "prison guard" and "correctional officer" interchangeably. I recognize that *guarding* is what many officers actually do and my use of the term is intended to convey that I do not consider this essential task to be ignoble. I use the correctional officer title with full realization that in some settings it is only a euphemism, but with sufficient optimism that the term makes explicit some recognition of their wider contribution. Perhaps the new title may signify that there is at least a possibility that their status in the prison hierarchy may be improving.

I wish to thank the contributors and publishers who have allowed their works to be reprinted, particularly those who prepared original materials expressly for this book, those who provided previously unpublished materials, and those who kindly tolerated my editorial suggestions for modifications of their articles.

I particularly wish to thank Dr. Andy Birkenmayer who stimulated and encouraged my research in this and many other areas, and the Ontario Ministry of Correctional Services for continuing support.

I am grateful for the initiative and competence of my secretary, Chi Hoang. The assistance of C. Currie and J. Proctor in compiling reference materials is appreciated.

Finally, I thank countless correctional officers who, while tolerating my pontifications on offenders and their care, helped me to learn about aspects of prison that few who have not walked in the guard's shoes can understand or appreciate.

Part I
INTRODUCTION

There is extensive literature on prison riots, prison architecture, prison reform, prison management, and on prison programs. There are also many books on prison inmates and prison wardens, but the individual attempting to gain an understanding of prisons by examining the criminological literature would have to search very carefully and very long before he would find much material on prison guards. If knowledge of prisons were to be based exclusively on a sample of the academic literature, even a very large sample, the reader might very well come to believe, so seldom are they discussed, that in prison there are no guards.

Prison guards have long been ignored by social scientists and others who have described the world of prisons. Academic and professional journals in criminology or corrections rarely include articles on correctional officers. Most books on prisons mention the guard only in passing, if at all.

It is remarkable that so little study of the correction officer has been made when one considers how often, and how eloquently, eminent spokesmen on corrections have acknowledged the critical importance of the guard in the functioning of correctional institutions. For example, Sykes (1958: 53) referred to the guard as "the pivotal figure on which the custodial bureaucracy turns." Glaser (1964: 133-134) concluded that "custodial officers can be said to have the greatest total impact everywhere . . ." and are "a major factor in determining the nature of the prison experience of most offenders." The President's Commission on Law Enforcement and Justice in its 1967 *Task Force Report on Corrections* asserted:

> They may be the most influential persons in institutions simply by virtue of their numbers and their daily intimate contact with offenders. It is a mistake to define them as persons responsible only for control and maintenance. They can, by their attitude and understanding, reinforce or destroy the effectiveness of almost any correctional program.

A conclusion of Thomas' study of the prison officer in the English prison system is that:

> . . . the central figure in any prison system is the basic grade uniformed officer and the collective views of officers have a direct

and supreme effect on the working of the system . . . the uniformed officer *IS* the English Prison Service. (Thomas, 1972: 22)

The correctional officer has not always been ignored. In times of trouble he has been the focus of considerable attention. Investigatory committee reports on prison riots and disruptions and journalistic descriptions and analyses of such events frequently focus on the role of the correctional officers. Typically, these lament their lack of training, bemoan the inadequacy of the procedures by which they are selected, and demand improvements in their salaries, their management, their career opportunities and their supervision. Then the dust settles and, once again, they become the invisible men.

There are probably many reasons why the correctional officer has been overlooked. Perhaps the neglect reflects our disdain for people who would work in what is often considered a low paying lack-lustre job in an unattractive work-setting in which one must live in unavoidable proximity to individuals who are often hostile, belligerent, abusive, and sometimes destructive and assaultive. Their job offers little upward mobility, not inconsiderable personal danger, and much boredom. Surely, one might reason, there must be something lacking in a person who would accept such a position. Surely, one might reason, a person who would accept such a job is undeserving of much attention. Perhaps the neglect of the prison guard has been fostered by the fact that, until recently, social scientists who have studied the prison guard have typically focused on the guard's negative qualities — their limited education, inadequate training, and poor salary — and have painted a bleak picture of the possibility of improvement (e.g., Barnes & Teeters, 1943; Tannenbaum, 1922). Perhaps the lack of research reflects the correctional officer's suspiciousness of researchers and their lack of enthusiasm for subjecting themselves to the highly critical scrutiny they have come to expect from "outsiders." Perhaps the lack of research reflects the uncooperativeness of correctional managers who are reluctant to have much attention paid to those who may be eager to condemn them.

When they are not ignored, they are maligned. Investigatory committee reports seldom provide a flattering picture of the correctional officer. Perhaps this is, in part, because their information derives either from inmates who are unlikely to be excessively complimentary in their remarks about those who control them against their will, or from "front-office politicians who are the most articulate spokesmen of anti-staff values" (Glaser, 1964: 116). Correctional officers provide a convenient scapegoat for those who might wish to deflect interest from other salient riot-engendering factors such as inefficient or inappropriate management practices.[1] This is not to suggest that correctional officers have no role in prison disturbances, but only to point out that the literature may present a rather distorted and melodramatic picture of the correctional officers' work and a somewhat biased sample of opinion about their skills and values.

They are noticed also in treatises on the treatment-custody conflict in which, typically, they are viewed as undereducated, ill-informed, oppositional malcontents and cynics — the Achilles Heel of progressive correctional rehabilitation programs. Often they are blamed for the failure of programs which would have had little chance of success in the first place with or without their support.

The guards have not been ignored by inmates. Most of the written material on prison guards consists of descriptions by inmate and ex-inmate authors. It is fair to say that few of these descriptions present a kind picture of the correctional officer.

> For a prisoner, of course, a guard is possibly the lowest imaginable form of humanoid life . . . The intriguing aspect of this view of guards, however, is that no inmate I've ever met came by it through his own experience . . . It's an opinion a prisoner automatically picks up at the door along with his issue of prison clothes and his government-issued toothbrush . . . he understands instinctively . . . that it's wise to establish one's loyalties clearly and that guard-hating is an act which clearly confirms such a loyalty to the inmate cause. It's expressly part of the function of being a prisoner. (Schroeder, 1976: 151-152)

Much of the material that is available presents a stereotypical picture of the guard as a harsh (if not sadistic), power-hungry illiterate — an ignorant, rigid, authoritarian individual who is vigorous only when demanding inmate compliance, when opposing inmate's rights, when criticizing management policies or when scuttling rehabilitation programs. Whereas some prison analysts have described them as thugs, others have viewed them as clones or zombies — an amorphous mass of uniformed automatons, indistinguishable one from the other, performing routine mundane and mindless tasks which anyone could do, which permit no individual excellence, and require no notable skills.

There is another body of literature. It is smaller and much less publicized than the prison exposés and riot autopsies, or the autobiographical accounts of prison life written by prison wardens or prison inmates. This literature has developed through the efforts of a small number of social scientists and others who have paid more than lip-service to the view that correctional officers are an important element in prison management and not merely cogs in the cumbersome machinery of justice. They have judged the correctional officer to be a fitting subject of research in his own right and not merely incidental to the study of inmates. Moreover they have seen fit to look beyond the routine surveillance functions of the guards to examine other equally important aspects of the correctional officer's work which involve exceedingly complex interactions with inmates, managers, and peers. Rather than merely describing the behavior of the guards in pejoratives, they have gone beyond explanations in terms of "the guard mentality" and tried to understand their behavior by examining it in terms of how it is shaped by the unique social environment of the prison, by "the system," by the contempt or indifference of the public, by the shifting, often conflicting and seldom clearly articulated goals and policy of prison management, and by the behavior of the inmates they are required to guard.

The following chapters comprise a collection of articles selected from that body of literature. The articles were chosen to portray the current state of knowledge about correctional officers — their functions, their selection and training, their organization and their management. It was considered particularly important to include articles which describe the influence that correctional officers exert in the prison environment, how that influence is effected, and what factors determine its direction. A major concern was to include materials which reflected the views of the correctional officer — how *they* perceive the prison world and their role in it. The contributors studied not only the inmates' views, not just the sensationalized Hollywood version, and not just the official management perspective. Part II presents a description of the day-to-day work of the prison guard and how he views his job, his career and the unique environment which imprisons him, shift after shift. Contrasting to the more popular view that the guard is only a "turn-key" performing routine tasks, the articles in Part III document the complexity of the job and emphasize the social service role that correctional officers can, and do perform in their work with inmates. In Part IV two articles are presented which raise questions about what guard-inmate relations would be like if the prisons were manned not by real correctional officers but by laymen. The recent entry of women into the correctional officers corps and the many issues which their participation has raised are discussed in Part V. The selection and training of correctional officers is discussed in Part VI. The final section discusses the impact on correctional officers of various organizational and management approaches in prisons, the unionization of guards, and the establishment of collective bargaining.

Most of the important literature on the correctional officer is either presented as a chapter or is summarized and discussed by one or more of the contributors. Moreover, the reference sections which are provided in many of the following articles provide the interested reader with a comprehensive bibliography on the correctional officer. It is encouraging to be able to assert that, at last, one edited volume cannot exhaust the growing body of literature on the correctional officer.

Notes

1. The role of the correctional officer in riots and the management practices which engender that role has been provocatively discussed in Stotland's (1976) analysis of the Attica riot.

References

Barnes, H. E. & Teeters, N. K. *New Horizons in Criminology.* New York: Prentice-Hall, 1943.

Glaser, D. *The Effectiveness of a Prison and Parole System.* New York: Bobbs-Merrill, 1974.

President's Commission on Law Enforcement and Administration of Justice. *Task Force Report: Corrections.* Washington, D.C.: U.S. Government Printing Office, 1967.

Schroeder, A. *Shaking It Rough.* Garden City, New York: Doubleday, 1976.

Stotland, E. "Self-esteem and violence by guards and state troopers at Attica." *Criminal Justice & Behavior,* 1976, *3*(1), 85-96.

Sykes, G. M. *The Society of Captives.* Princeton, N.J.: Princeton University Press, 1958.

Tannenbaum, F. *Wall Shadows: A Study in American Prisons.* New York: Putnam's Sons, 1922.

Thomas, J. E. *The English Prison Officer Since 1850: A Study in Conflict.* London: Routledge & Kegan Paul, 1972.

Part II
THE JOB: THE GUARD'S VIEW

... he knows he is one of 40 men whose function is to suppress thousands.

George Jackson, 1970

The articles in this section present a description of the *actual* work of the guard which is distinctively different from the more popular fictional or sensationalized accounts. The description is based on the perceptions of the guards themselves.

In Chapter 1 Edgar May provides a clear picture of the variety of activities and stresses that comprise one guard's day on the job. The second chapter, also by Edgar May, provides the reader with an unusual view of the guard's work derived from interviews with a number of guards who were invited to express their feelings about inmates, administrators, treatment, brutality, and other topics on which there is a wealth of information on the views of academics, managers, and inmates, but a dearth of information on the guards' conceptions. In the third selection James Jacobs, based on his survey of Illinois prison guards, describes the demographic characteristics of guards, their attitudes toward their job, their future, their supervisors, and their views of the causes of imprisonment and crime. Jacobs' research challenges popular conceptions of guards and their attitudes to offenders and raises some important questions and issues for correctional management.

In Chapter 4, James Jacobs and Harold Retsky (a former guard) discuss some of the factors which influence how the guard views his work and himself, including the lack of promotional opportunities available to him in the paramilitary organization within which he is managed, the conflicting roles he is expected to perform, the nature of the physical environment in which he must work, and the lack of public respect for his job.

Reference

Jackson, G.: *The Village Voice,* September 10, 1970, as cited in L. Orland, *Justice, Punishment and Treatment: The Correctional Process.* New York: The Free Press, 1973.

Chapter 1
A Day on the Job—In Prison*

Edgar May

The buzzer of the white clockradio drones through the bedroom. The hands of the luminous dial point to 5:20 a.m.

For Philip Martin Carvalho, the jarring sound is the same prelude to the morning ritual that millions of Americans call "going to work." But unlike most other job-bound early risers, his work place is different: it's behind eight steel and barred doors within the walls of the Massachusetts maximum-security prison at Walpole.

Phil Carvalho holds the rank of senior correctional officer. He has covered virtually every custody assignment in the eight years he has been in a prison that has been jarred by inmate riots and strikes by its personnel. Since last January, his post has been Ten Block, the segregation unit where Massachusetts houses up to sixty of its toughest and most incorrigible inmates.

It is a quantum jump from the bedroom of the modern brick and shingled Cape Cod house to the refuse-littered Ten Block twenty-seven miles away . . . from the oak trees on his lawn and the river view to the nine-by-six-foot cells where inmates build makeshift cardboard floor barricades to keep out mice and rats. On work days, Phil Carvalho doesn't use the handsome valet dressing stand in the corner. He slips into his khaki shirt and trousers, the same style uniform worn fifteen years ago by the bus drivers of the Massachusetts Street Railway Co. on the Boston to Providence run. After toast and coffee with his wife, Shirley, he grabs his brown bag lunch, a tall thermos with coffee and climbs into his van for the fifty-minute drive to the prison.

Phil Carvalho is not necessarily the prototype of the American correctional officer. There probably is none. There is no mold that stamps out the "average" officer. But Carvalho, at thirty-four years of age, has biographical bench marks that are similar to his counterparts who guard America's quarter million adult prisoners. High school graduate . . . a couple of jobs in industry before he moved into the "steady work" offered by the state prison system . . . married . . . to the girl who lived four houses down from his own in the tight-knit Portuguese-American community in nearby Fall River . . . She was eighteen . . . he was nineteen.

---

* Copyright 1976, Criminal Justice Publications, Inc. Reprinted with permission from *Corrections Magazine* (December, 1976).

For Phil Carvalho and thousands like him, reporting for the seven to three shift in America's maximum-security prisons, the work day begins with the small ironies that sometimes blur the distinctions between the guard and the guarded.

"All persons entering the lobby," the sign on the prison doorway says, "must have their packages, pocketbooks, etc. inspected. Failing to do so, the officer on duty will refuse entry to the lobby. *This applies to employees of the institution also.*"

Phil Carvalho punches the time clock, moves through the first of the electronically controlled steel doors, opens his lunch bag for inspection by another officer, empties his pockets of keys and small change, and removes his buckled belt before stepping through the archway of the metal detector. The unseen electronic eye doesn't flicker any alarm.

Door after door opens and closes. Click, bang, click, bang . . . some are operated by unseen hands secluded in the tower above the wall. The last two doors are at the end of the long corridor beyond the inside control room, with its barred, bullet-proof glass protective shield. Keys unlatch those last doors . . . click, bang, click, bang . . . and Carvalho is at his work place.

"They're not too many officers who beat a track to get down here," he says to a visitor who follows him through his work day.

Ten Block is a steel barred island within the walled continent of the prison . . . insulated and isolated for those who live there and those who work there. It is an island cut off from the institutional mainland by more than the click, bang of steel. Because it confines or segregates those who have assaulted guards and inmates, it is often territory that is ostracized by other guards and inmates. "Nobody is going to be in a hurry to do anybody any favors down here," Carvalho says.

Ten Block also is an island marked by the paraphernalia of violence. Handcuffs dangling from a peg board . . . a trio of fire extinguishers within easy reach on the floor . . . a convex plexiglass riot shield resting in the corner. Its sixty cells are divided between two floors, fifteen to a corridor. Some of the cells on the first floor have solid steel doors, in front of the bars, that are clanged shut when an inmate does punitive isolation time.

When Carvalho arrives, nine young officers already are beginning to fill cardboard trays with muffins, cereal and paper cups of coffee from the kitchen wagon. Like Carvalho, all are volunteers for Ten Block.

"Yeah, you gotta be crazy to work here," one of them says, "but it's got good days off." Most of the officers have been spit at by some of their charges. Some have been hit by urine and excrement.

Before Carvalho has a chance to move through the door of the cubicle that serves as an office, one of the three phones inside rings.

"Ten, Carvalho."

CHAPTER 1 A DAY ON THE JOB

The phone is sandwiched between the cheek and the shoulder of the 220-pound, six-foot, two-inch Carvalho. For the next eight hours, it will ring incessantly, with rare moments of silence. For Carvalho, the telephone is something more than an electronic instrument.

He growls at it, purrs into it, persuades, cajoles, allowing the cadence of his voice to vary with the purpose of his message. "Yeah, right. Hey, sweetheart, do me a favor. . . ."

Carvalho shares the responsibilities of running Ten Block with Arthur Latessa, the most recently promoted supervisor of the Walpole prison. Ten Block is the lowest rung of desirable supervisory assignments and the newest man usually is in the job. When Latessa is absent, Carvalho runs the block by himself.

For his efforts, Carvalho takes home $199 a week, some $17 more than the younger officers.

"Guard House, Guard House . . ." the inmate's voice comes from midway down the corridor. "Hey, Phil. . . . Phil . . . Phil Carvalho."

One of the other officers unlocks the corridor's steel entry gate. He never lets his eyes wander from Carvalho's back as he moves down the hallway.

Carvalho kicks aside an empty milk carton as he moves down the narrow aisle between the cells and the wall. The floor is littered with yellow paper food trays, used plastic forks and spoons, and the remnants of yesterday's evening meal.

The corridor is temporarily without an inmate porter. He lost his job after officers found a jug of home brew in his cell. The notice on the office bulletin board says it's the responsibility of the 3 PM to 11 PM shift to sweep the corridor.

"Yeah, Charlie?"

"Listen, Phil, you gotta get that son-of-a-bitch out of here. . . ." The voice in the dimly lighted cell details a complaint against an officer on the 3 to 11 shift.

Other inmates shout their own litany of complaints. Hands holding mirrors protrude from the other fourteen cells in the section, giving their owners a glass-reflected picture of the officer and the visitor.

"The only thing I can tell you," Carvalho responds, "is that I've got to get McLaughlin down here."

Thomas McLaughlin is deputy superintendent at Walpole. He is one of the key reasons why Phil Carvalho volunteered for Ten Block. "He backs you up. And he's there when you need him. . . . All these guys," Carvalho says pointing to the young officers, "they're there when you need 'em."

"Who's that guy?" a voice queries from one of the cells.

"He's writing an article. . . ."

"Yeah, the mother f. . . . . looks at you like you was a f. . . . . lizard."

Back in his cubicle office, Carvalho's fingers dial the extension number.

"Hey, Mac. . . . Phil. You gotta get down here. I need you. Yeah, fifteen minutes. No more. O.K.? Thanks."

The office in its clutter and congestion offers another reminder of the similarities between the guard and the guarded. Like the cells, it, too, is cramped. It is only an hour into the shift and the half-empty coffee cups are beginning to accumulate. Cigarette butts are piling up in the ashtray, and some from days and weeks before are in the corners. A calendar with a picture of a nude girl dangles from a peg board holding twenty-one keys.

When McLaughlin arrives, Carvalho takes him through the corridor where the inmates are complaining about the officer. They move from cell to cell like army medics making rounds in a crowded hospital. The deputy superintendent is a listener. Occasionally, he asks a question, sometimes he nods, but his face shows neither a flicker of sympathetic agreement nor cynical disbelief. Later, he tells Carvalho there will be a meeting with the night officer at the end of the shift.

"Hey, Phil . . . Phil. . . ." Another voice from the cell in the corridor. Carvalho again moves into the narrow hallway.

"Hey, Phil, I need a legal visit. My case comes up on the fourteenth."

"O.K. I'll take care of it."

From a hall phone, Carvalho dials an extension. "Yeah, Phil Carvalho. I need a legal visit for. . . ."

The demands made on Carvalho are not phrased in convoluted euphemisms. They are direct. They deal with basic wants in the limited, cramped world of the segregation unit . . . an appointment for a visitor, a phone call to a relative . . . some writing paper. Sometimes the demands attempt to stretch the narrow boundaries of Ten Block. Either way, the answers are equally direct. Carvalho's booming voice, intoning, "I'll try," or "Yes," or "No," leaves little room for doubt.

The conversations are always on a first-name basis, sometimes flecked by touches of jail house humor that softens the harshness of where they take place. There is a subconscious line between Carvalho and the inmates that marks the perimeter between levity and insolence, between what is permitted and what is not. Since he arrived in Ten Block, Phil Carvalho never has been spit at or assaulted by anything more than a barrage of four letter words.

In the office, the phones are ringing again.

"Ten. Carvalho."

"Yeah, O.K. Sullivan's visit cancelled. O.K. Thanks."

"Ten. Carvalho."

"No. I can't do it. I don't have a place to put him. Look, sweetheart, he can have a legal aid visit. Yeah, but not today. I got visits at

11, at 11:30, 1:30 and a disciplinary board. Yeah, try tomorrow. Sorry. You're doing a great job . . . a great job."

Carvalho recalls that a few weeks earlier a lawyer had to interview his client in the elevator that is used to transport the food cart between the two floors of the block.

"It's confined, this block. It's too small a place. After a while, even the officers start arguing with themselves. It happens every day. Any old thing sets the officers off. Out in [the general prison] population at least you're walkin' around, you got space out there. Or you have the yard duty or you go on transportation, or hospital detail or something. But down at Ten. Where you goin'? Upstairs, downstairs, that's it. We're bangin' into one another."

An officer comes into the cubicle with a handful of small brown envelopes. Carvalho counts them, records the total and the time in the dog-eared log book in front of him.

"Medication," he says. "O.K. give 'em out."

Ten Block distributes medication more frequently than meals. Four times a day, inmates may receive prescriptions that include sedatives, tranquilizers and sleeping pills. During the morning distribution, fourteen of twenty-eight inmates on the first floor receive pills. Five milligrams of Valium four times a day plus a sleeping pill at night is not unusual.

"I can't understand it," says Carvalho. "These guys [when they're] on the street can't be gettin' that medication. Impossible. Some of 'em need it for their nerves. Being in this situation they need something to calm them down. But the pain pills they put out, the depressants . . . it's unbelievable. In the street, these guys don't go, 'Hey, wait a minute, I got to take my pill. I'll be right back to help you rob the bank or somethin'.' Everyday they've got to get their pills. Now they're dependent on it. They need it or they're goin' to crash."

"In a way, we're making pill addicts out of 'em. Yeah, and I've heard a medic say that, too."

Ring. Again, the phone.

"Ten. Carvalho."

"No, We can't take 'em. We haven't any room. Yeah, I'll call you back."

Carvalho slams the phone back and ticks off the names of inmates the administration wants to send to Ten Block. One prompts a groan from the officers in the room. All are known to them, but the last one is a particularly troublesome prisoner who shuttles back and forth from Ten Block and the state mental hospital at Bridgewater.

Carvalho dials again. He's thinking about making room for the newcomers, but he needs approval from a deputy superintendent before he can move any segregation block inmate to another unit or even to another corridor and cell within Ten Block.

"Hello, Mac. Suppose we move him up to forty-five? Yeah, we're playing checkers down here. You've got to talk to them and get some of these guys out of here."

Ten Block is nearly always at or pushing toward its sixty-cell capacity. Some have been in the unit for as much as two years. It is two years spent almost entirely in a nine-by-six-foot cell. Each man is let out for about a half-hour a day for a shower and some exercise in the narrow corridor. But there are never more than two men free in the corridor. On clear days, an inmate may be permitted as much as an hour in an outdoor exercise cage.

Within a half-hour, McLaughlin calls Carvalho to tell him that he has "front office" approval to move four inmates out of Ten Block. Carvalho instructs other officers to inform three of them that they will move out of the most restricted and confined cellblock in Walpole prison. Carvalho goes down a corridor to tell one of the inmates himself.

"Hey, Phil. I don't want to go. I got problems in Block three."

"Hey, this ain't the Holiday Inn. This is Walpole."

Back in the office other officers return shaking their heads. Carvalho reaches for the phone again.

"Hey, Mac. Nobody wants to go." He ticks off the names and adds, in an almost sorrowful monotone after each of them, "don't want to go."

"Oh, God! I've never seen anything like it. Guys refuse to move . . . one big happy family. . . ."

"Yeah, I know. Those guys on Top Right, they've got nothin'. No cans (canned snacks), no fans, no hot pots (to heat soup or coffee). These guys should be dying to get out of here. O.K. We'll talk to them again."

Carvalho shakes his head. "Ain't that a bitch when a guy doesn't want to move from Ten Block?" He explains that a forced move is pointless. The inmate will commit an infraction in his new block assignment and five minutes later will be returned to the segregation unit.

"They feel safer here. They'd rather be here than in that zoo at the max [maximum security] end. They get more attention here. They've got ten officers for sixty guys. Down there [in the general prison population] there's one officer for forty-five guys. It's filthy. Stuff all over the walls."

The conversation is interrupted by more phone calls. Visitors to be escorted. A three-man disciplinary board to be brought into the block. Appointment requests from social workers, medical personnel.

After each conversation, Carvalho makes notations in the log book or on a separate schedule he keeps for visits and appointments. Ring, Ring, Ring.

Carvalho laughs. "Yeah, my wife says: 'how come you never answer the phone when you're home.' "

An officer returns from the second floor and reports one man thinks he's willing to make the move to another block.

"Great, O.K., O.K. Get him out of here now before he changes his mind."

Moments later the inmate's replacement is led into the block, handcuffed and chained. He is searched before he is led into his cell. An officer reaches into the prisoner's pocket and gingerly pulls out a broken half of razor blade.

"This guy shouldn't even be here," he says, shaking his head. "They should keep him in Bridgewater. He's just goin' to flip out again."

Carvalho is on the phone again.

"Good. We're not going to get him. Fine."

Carvalho reports to the junior officers that a second inmate scheduled for Ten Block just cut himself while he was in the hospital. "They've got blood all over the floor over there. They've got him in a hospital security room."

WHY THIS JOB?

The pressure is momentarily off. Carvalho lights another cigarette and tilts back in his chair.

Why did you become a correctional officer?, he is asked.

"One word, Security. That's what I was looking for. Not in two years, five years, but overall. In twenty years when you were ready to retire. The benefits are there. The job has its bad points and its good points."

What are those good points? What do you get out of this job besides security?

"Well, I try to accomplish something . . . personal satisfaction. If I've done somethin' to help 'em. Me, I can go home and use the phone, watch TV, go out to my neighbor's house, buy a drink if I want to . . . these guys can't. Their only line of communication is through me. So if they want to use the phone I'll say, 'I'll see what I can do.' "

"It's somethin' like that that makes you feel good — that would be the word for it. Especially when a guy is having trouble. His wife hasn't written him or come up to see him and you let him make a phone call and he goes back and he thanks you. Things are cooled down.

"You can't do it to them all because some of them don't even let you get near 'em. They're just cold. You don't make waves there either. You don't go out of your way to gaff this guy or stick him. Hey, you can't. It's impossible to go in there with that attitude. You're not going to last. I don't care if it's Ten Block or the rest of the institution. You're not going to last. Because one of 'em will definitely get you. A pipe, a knife or somethin' like that, but they'll definitely get you. Or if they don't do it that way, they'll make it miserable for you.

"Even though they're the toughest, hey, they're human beings, you know. I don't care what they did. Well, I shouldn't say that because we know what they did on the outside or what they did to other corrections officers, but when he comes into Ten Block I'm not going to mess with a guy's meal or throw letters away. You've got to communicate. These guys are livin' with you. It's going to be an easy day or it's going to be a tough day."

The noon food wagon arrives and the officers dish out the meal onto the paper trays. After the inmates are served, the officers grab a tray and bring it into the office, a few at a time. Some have brought their lunch and eat it piecemeal between running upstairs or into the cell corridors. Elsewhere in the prison, most corrections officers eat in the staff mess hall. In Ten Block, there is no formal sit-down dining.

Carvalho, between bites, dials the phone again. "Yeah, Rus. . . . He's back in Block three. Yeah, he's back. My count is fifty-eight." The count of inmates is reported to control at the beginning of the shift, at noon or whenever any inmate leaves or returns to Ten Block.

The frequently interrupted lunch break conversation is devoted to shop talk. It is the small talk of infantry GI's dissecting the foibles of the higher echelons back at division headquarters.

"If the people out front who make up the rules had to come in here and enforce them, they'd never make them up. . . ."

". . . Yeah, they ought to have an officer out there with 'em when they make up those damn things. . . ."

"Yah, yah, yah, but then they'd pick some guy who never worked in population . . . you want to bet on it . . . that's what they'd do. . . ."

"If you run this institution by the book they give you you'd have a riot. You can't do it. It's impossible. Hey, they tell you a guy can't go to another tier to see another guy even if that guy's his brother."

A young officer comes in and hands Carvalho another packet of brown envelopes. Medication. Second distribution. Carvalho registers them in the log.

The log book is something of a barometer for the shift. It records the traffic like a counter at a busy intersection. And it offers some distinctions between the shifts.

The preceding 9 PM to 11 PM shift had seven entries for its entire eight-hour segment. The 11 PM to 7 AM shift showed three entries. By noon, Carvalho had written twenty-one separate items into his log.

"Hey, Phil," an officer says. "Listen, I can't get that canteen order. They say they just aren't going to fill it for him." The dispute is over how much credit an inmate has at the canteen. Carvalho's hands move back to the phone.

"Yeah, Phil Carvalho. Look, on that canteen order, . . . do me a favor . . . I know, I know. But I need it. Yeah, I do . . . do me a favor . . . I'll be down to get it . . . you're doin' a great job . . . a great job."

Carvalho tells one of the officers to unlock the double doors to Ten Block and let him out. He makes his way down through a series of corridors and cell blocks until he comes to the canteen. The officer in charge makes it clear that he has no particular love for the inmate whose order hasn't been filled.

Carvalho's litany of praise begins again as he grabs a paper sack and starts filling the order himself. The inmate's canteen ticket is punched for the items and Carvalho reaches for four lollypops and throws them in the bag. "That's his change, right? Thanks, sweetheart, you're doing a great job . . . a great job."

"So I get the order myself. So? What the hell, it takes five minutes to get down there. You bring it back. You keep him happy and he thinks he beat you. Right? That's his job. To beat me. But I know better. He went into his room [cell] and he was happy. And it avoided a lot more b.s. Because with this guy, there would have been trouble. I know. I know him from the past."

The clock on the office wall ticks the shift slowly to an end.

Carvalho leaves a little early to attend the "front office" meeting with the administration and the officer of the incoming shift about whom the inmates complained. The decision: Keep him at his post.

Fifty minutes and twenty-seven traffic-congested miles later, Carvalho is back in his private world on the outer fringes of suburbia. He is greeted by his wife and his fourteen-year-old daughter, Cheryl. A miniature poodle and a tiny Yorkshire terrier come bounding across the lawn as the advance contingent of the welcome. Supper is on the table a half-hour later. The small talk is about an afternoon shopping trip in search of parochial school uniforms for Cheryl. There is no small talk about Ten Block.

"He doesn't talk about the job," his wife, Shirley, says. "He tells his father about the job and his father tells his mother and she tells me some things. That's how I get information about the prison. If he comes home and he's in a good mood, I'll know he had a fine day. If he comes home a little bit aggravated, then I know he had a bad day and I'll just go about my business.

"But I worry about him all the time. The last time there was a riot it was on the late news. I didn't know a thing about it. I was lying on the couch, watching the news, and that came on in a big way. I thought I'd die. I tried calling the prison but all the lines were tied up. He finally called me about an hour after and said that he would be home early in the morning. But, oh, my God. Who could sleep?"

When Shirley is out of earshot, Carvalho acknowledges her worrying. "I know it affects my wife. I'll tell her, 'I'm not going in today.' and she'll say, 'Oh, good, good. Call in sick.' And then I tell her I'm only kidding. And I trudge in there. But I must like it because I keep goin' back."

"It has its good days and its bad. Today, was a good day," he says.

The plexiglass protective shield remained unused. No inmate had refused to return to his cell. None of the young officers had urine or excrement thrown at them. The fire extinguishers remained in their places.

Shirley nods in agreement. Today, Phil Carvalho came home in a good mood.

Chapter 2

Prison Guards in America— The Inside Story*

Edgar May

The motion picture camera pans down the seemingly endless tier of cells. The lens zooms in on inmate hands banging tin cups. Above the din there are gravel-voiced shouts of authority.

The camera lens shifts to the perspiring face of a menacing guard with a shotgun. A well-chewed cigar is clenched between his teeth and an ample portion of belly flops over his belt. At his side, a black polished billy club dangles from a leather holster.

In a few minutes, the camera will flit to another scene . . . elsewhere in the prison . . . in a prosecutor's office . . . or a police station. There it will focus on the tough-talking star — someone like James Cagney, Edmund O'Brien or Humphrey Bogart.

It is vintage Holywood. And it is a stereotype, a cliché-ridden portrait of the prison and its guardians. It is current because frequently millions of Americans can find variations of these scenes on the Late Late Show of their local television stations.

For the contemporary correctional officer, who may well be enrolled in the criminal justice program of a community college, the TV image has a strange reality. He is convinced that this is how outsiders see him in his job.

"The average person, the only connection they have with prisons," says Conneticut's maximum-security officer Raymond A. Zapor, "is what they've seen in the movies . . . 1938, James Cagney, you know. The officers walk around with clubs and they do nothing but beat on these people or look to get 'em into trouble. When you say prison, prison guard, even to my neighbors, the only thing that comes to mind is the movies."

The celluloid stereotype haunts correctional officers throughout the nation. Convinced that the image is firmly in the public's mind, they see themselves on the lowest rung of the law enforcement pecking order. And they have this standing confirmed by small irritants that are like pebbles in a shoe.

In Illinois, for example, the Department of Corrections staff doesn't get new state cars for official business. Guards transport inmates in

---

* Copyright 1976, Criminal Justice Publications, Inc. Reprinted with permission from *Corrections Magazine* (December, 1976).

hand-me-down State Police cruisers that have too much mileage to be considered suitable for troopers.

When off duty at a social gathering, where no other correctional personnel are present, many officers resist volunteering where they work.

"I just avoid mentioning the fact that I'm just . . . you know . . . just a correctional officer," says another Connecticut officer. "It would be: 'Oh, you're a guard, oh!' and then they sort of would look down on you. 'Not really,' I would say, 'I'm a correctional officer.' Now, see if I use that word it would sort of soften the situation a little bit, just a little. If I would say that I was striving to be a treatment officer, that would even bring me up another level. But the idea that I'm just a guard embarrasses me because I know what the connotation is."

This embarrassment, rooted in lack of public acceptance and lack of understanding of what the job is, ranks high on the national problem list of those charged with guarding a record quarter of a million adult inmates in state prisons throughout America.

With more men and women in prison than ever before, the correctional officer is in a growth industry. Including the prisons and the nation's jails, there are now an estimated 100,000 men and women in custody jobs alone. A *Corrections Magazine* national survey shows that of the total, 42,324 are in state-operated institutions, and their numbers are increasing.

But even during recent difficult economic times, when national unemployment statistics hit new post-Depression peaks, some prison jobs have gone begging. Correctional officer turnover in some places continues at such a rate that some administrators say it is almost impossible to run their institutions with any kind of consistent policy. Officers aren't there long enough to understand the policies. In Louisiana, the annual turnover of correctional officers is 74 percent; in New Mexico it's 65 percent. In states with far lower system-wide turnover percentages, the maximum-security institutions report that it's not unusual for them to lose at least half of their new officers in the first year.

But there are exceptions and a few are spectacular. Illinois' Vienna Correctional Center — a tranquil, college-like minimum-security institution — has file cabinets bulging with job requests. Last October it had 1,428 applications on file for the security force alone.

For most shift supervisors and personnel directors, however, the manpower dilemma is not surplus, but shortage. "Supervisors think more in terms of bodies rather than quality — are the job stations going to be filled is the overriding question," says Massachusetts' Frank Gunter, who until recently was superintendent of the maximum-security prison at Walpole.

Because of the almost constant problem of empty slots on various shifts, the burden of filling them falls on officers who stay. At San Quentin in California, some members of the custody force complain about being ordered to work on their days off. They grumble about the inability to schedule vacations. At Walpole, staff shortages this summer resulted in a mandatory sixth work day for every officer.

THE GUARDS: A NATIONAL PORTRAIT

Why are the men who watch the men in America's prisons so often their turnstile guardians?

How do those who stay, year after year, see themselves and their work?

How valid is the often held public perception that guards rule by force, with a club and blackjack that foreshadow implied or real head-cracking violence?

There are no simple answers. To study the correctional officer, *Corrections Magazine* spent several hundred hours tape recording the thoughts, concerns and the hopes of guards in six states — California, Connecticut, Massachusetts, Illinois, Rhode Island and Arkansas. Questionnaires were sent to and returned by all fifty states and the District of Columbia.

Unlike the picture of the Hollywood formula guard, his real life counterpart does not lend himself to a capsule portrait. There is no national model. There is none even within a single state or, for that matter, within different prisons under the jurisdiction of the same department.

The inability to generalize about the contemporary correctional officer even is apparent inside one single institution. Attitudes, behavior, enforcement of regulations differ markedly from shift to shift. It is a common observation made by both custody officers and inmates in maximum-security prisons.

> "There are two completely different prisons here" says Supervising Correctional Officer Leo Bissonnette at Massachusetts' Walpole facility. "It changes the minute the night shift comes on. The tensions on that three to eleven shift . . . you can cut them with a knife. I was on the three to eleven for thirteen years, and I never left a cup of coffee where an inmate could get at it. The three to eleven . . . they have rules that don't bend. It's weird. You could research this for the rest of your life and you'd never get an answer."

Nationally, America's correctional force is marked by disparity . . . disparity in everything from training to paychecks, from guard-inmate ratios to uniforms and equipment. Even the dangers connected with the job fluctuate widely among different prisons.

In Maine, the officer injury rate is so low that the department doesn't bother to keep statistics. In California, in 1975, there were 414 injuries among a state-wide custody staff of 2,888. Even there some officers suggest that sometimes the public perception of the dangers of the job is exaggerated. In Rhode Island, a maximum-security officer suggests that "if you think you're going to go twenty years in an institution without getting a rap in the mouth, you're kidding yourself. That's part of the job. That's part of what you're getting paid for."

The number of inmates a guard is responsible for varies dramatically among maximum-security prisons. Some may have fewer inmates than other institutions, yet have three and four times the number of guards. New Jersey's state prison at Trenton has a custody staff of 330 and an inmate population of 870. In Arkansas' Cummins unit there are 1,505 inmates. The total security force number 97.

In many prisons, officers grumble about the public image of guards carrying clubs and mace. In the Arizona State prison, however, officers still carry nightsticks on virtually every post. Some sergeants are armed with small cannisters of mace. But in other institutions there are no clubs and even traditional uniforms have been discarded.

At the Vienna Correctional facility — reported to be the largest minimum-security institution in the nation — correctional officers wore civilian clothes during a two-year test period. Now, with a population pushing toward the 550 capacity mark, the security force has gone back to uniforms. They wear smartly tailored forest green blazers that do not have the aura of the more traditional law enforcement garb.

Salaries, too, range across a broad spectrum (See Table 1). In some urban states a few correctional officers working double shifts have parlayed their overtime and regular salary earnings into $30,000 annual incomes. In rural states, many of which don't pay any overtime, take-home pay for a new officer sometimes is around $100 a week.

Arkansas is near the bottom nationally in starting salaries — $6,942 a year. Ray Mathew, a young officer who began work there last February, took home $96.50 every week for his first six months. In New Jersey, his counterpart at the state prison two years ago received almost that much money in overtime pay alone. Although overtime has been cut back at the Trenton State Prison, it still totals about $1.3 million a year, or nearly $4,000 per man.

In Rhode Island, where some officers work double shifts at the state's maximum-security prison, a union spokesman said that their yearly earnings would be just around $25,000.

The beginning salary leaders in the continental United States are California, $13,164; New York, $11,410; and Michigan, with $10,795. Alaska, with very high salaries in all fields, leads all the individual states with beginner's pay at $15,744. The lowest starting pay is in Maine — $6,240.

But if there are disparities within and among individual corrections systems, there are similarities that transcend departments in large and small states alike. They are the similarities of attitudes, worries and, often, frustrations. Superimposed on them all are the similarities shared by both guards and inmates.

"Look, we live with these guys," is a common refrain from officers. The cellblock for the officers' eight-hour shift is no different than the block for the inmate who does a twenty-four-hour shift. The food served officers and inmates, whether good or poor, is the same. The language of the prison, a shorthand idiom flavored with heaping portions of four-letter Anglo-Saxon words, is spoken by both the guards and the guarded. In Walpole, a cell is "a room" for both prisoner and officer. In Arkansas, someone can "short hair you" (lie to you) whatever side of the bars he's on. For the inmates in the nation's prisons, those who watch them are "cops, hacks and screws." In their own conversations, guards who may prefer to be called "officers" sometimes refer to each other as cops, hacks and screws.

The similarities shared by officers in one prison may belong to inmates in another. In Massachusetts, the guards' chino khaki summer pants and shirt are the same color and material as the mandatory clothing worn by inmates in neighboring Connecticut. At New York's Attica, an armed tower guard does an eight-hour shift surveying the yard and earns about $200 a week for his watchfulness. At the maximum-security Cummins unit in Arkansas, the unarmed men surveying the yard from all but two guard towers work twelve-hour shifts. They are unpaid. They are inmates.

THE JOB

What is the job of a correctional officer?

For most officers, the technical language of their job description can be found in the rule book, or in the advertisements for new recruits. But the realities of their task remain blurred. "Never mind what the rule book says," one guard remarked, "the fact is that you've got to work it out for yourself." The lack of clarity and, particularly, consistency regarding what is expected of them is a frustration that links officers from one part of the nation to the other.

> "The idea of what a prison should be like," says Albert (Bud) Gardner, a maximum-security officer and acting president of Rhode Island's Brotherhood of Correctional Officers, "has swung from one end of the pendulum to the other. No one really knows what the answer is. A lot of people think they do. One day this is o.k. and the next day it's not o.k. And the next day . . . well, maybe it's o.k. There are no rules, no regulations for the correctional officer himself . . . there is no direction and he more or less fends for himself.
>
> "One thing that I remember, a couple of years back we had a small confrontation in the gym area. I called one of my superior officers and asked, 'What do you want done?' and he says, 'well,

Table 1
NATIONAL SURVEY OF STATE CORRECTIONAL OFFICERS

State	Number of state correction officers as of 7/1/76	Annual turnover rate for correction officers	Starting Salary	Do correction officers receive overtime pay?	Minimum entrance requirements for correction officers**	Percentage of racial minorities among officers	How many violent deaths among correction officers from 1/1/74 to 7/1/76
Alabama	482	25%	$ 7,111	No	21, H.S.*	22%	2
Alaska	105	-	15,744	Yes	H.S., 4 yrs. work exp.	-	0
Arizona	651	25%	9,771	Comp. Time	none, personal evaluation	17%	1
Arkansas	315	30%	6,942	No	18, H.S.	33%	0
California	2,888	10%	13,164	Yes	Equiv. H.S., 2 yrs. work exp.	28%	1
Colorado	157	9-12%	10,368	Yes	None	-	0
Connecticut	819	4%	9,383	Yes	None	30%	0
Delaware	187	25%	7,218	Yes	H.S.	28%	0
Florida	2,620	29%	7,976	Yes	18, H.S.	-	-
Georgia	1,161	-	7,278	No	H.S.	13%	-
Hawaii	253	32%	10,476	Yes	Equiv. H.S.	-	0
Idaho	142	20%	8,940	Comp. Time	2 yrs. work	3%	0
Illinois	1,162	32%	9,912	Yes	Equiv. H.S.	17%	3
Indiana	980	17%	8,918	Yes	H.S. or GED†	13%	0
Iowa	482	40%	8,476	Yes	H.S. or GED	4%	-
Kansas	439	-	8,016	Yes	21, H.S. or GED	9%	0
Kentucky	500	30%	7,914	Yes	H.S.	12%	0
Louisiana	1,206	74%	6,348	Yes	18, exam	20%	0
Maine	244	20%	6,240	Yes	H.S.	0%	0
Maryland	1,233	7%	9,300	Yes	H.S. or GED, 3 yrs. work	29%	0
Massachusetts	1,198	12%	10,228	Yes	19, H.S. or equiv.	6%	0
Michigan	1,169	15-20%	10,795	Yes	21, H.S.	14%	0

Minnesota	675	40%	10,476	Yes	None, oral exam	7%	0
Mississippi	390	54%	7,716	No	21, H.S. or GED, 1 Yr. wk.	48%	0
Missouri	485	27%	7,536	Yes	H.S., 2 yrs. work	8%	1
Montana	92	60%	9,022	Yes	H.S.	4%	0
Nebraska	294	34%	7,956	Comp. Time	H.S. or equiv.	6%	0
Nevada	210	24%	8,801	Yes	H.S., 2 yrs. work	7%	0
New Hampshire	100	20%	7,098	Yes	20, H.S. or GED	-	0
New Jersey	1,351	20%	9,813	Yes	18	28%	0
New Mexico	107	65%	7,476	Yes	H.S. or GED	78%	0
New York	5,209	4%	11,410	Yes	20, H.S.	18%	0
North Carolina	1,723	-	8,016	Yes	20, H.S. or GED	27%	0
North Dakota	64	20%	8,364	Yes	H.S. or GED	3%	0
Ohio	1,603	14%	8,819	Yes	4th grade	6%	0
Oklahoma	662	29%	7,680	Comp. Time	H.S. or GED	11%	-
Oregon	262	36%	10,152	Yes	H.S. or GED	10%	0
Pennsylvania	1,318	7%	9,869	Yes	H.S. or equiv.	9%	0
Rhode Island	250	-	9,386	Yes	H.S.	-	0
South Carolina	835	31%	7,355	No	H.S. & certificate	43%	0
South Dakota	80	2.5%	8,322	Yes	18, H.S. or GED	4%	0
Tennessee	1,200	40%	6,852	No	18, H.S.	30%	0
Texas	2,123	36%	8,640	No	18, H.S. or GED	24%	0
Utah	135	30%	9,252	Yes	21, H.S. 4 yrs. work	5%	0
Vermont	74	63%	7,072	Yes	H.S. & 2 yrs. work	0%	0
Virginia	1,819	30%	7,680	Yes	H.S. or 8th grade with exp.	23%	1
Washington	611	25%	9,612	Yes	H.S. or GED	20%	0
W. Virginia	378	-	7,295	Comp Time	10 yrs. ed. & work exp.	2%	0
Wisconsin	624	-	9,506	Yes	18 or H.S.	-	0
Wyoming	57	30%	8,796	Yes	None	3%	1
Washington DC	1,220	18%	9,946	Yes	College grad., or 3½ yrs. counseling supervising	57%	0

* High School † High School Equivalency ** *Some states may not have listed all requirements* you've been here longer than I have, do what you think is right.' I kind of laughed. Everything worked out all right, but I wonder how many times this has been told to other people. . . .

"You're expected to think for yourself in certain situations. If it turns out fine, all's well and good. If you make a decision they expect of you and it doesn't turn out right . . . even if it might not have been the wrong decision but it just didn't work out right . . . then you're an asshole. After a while, if you're called an asshole enough by the inmates, and you're called an asshole enough by the brass and, from what you read in the newspapers, [by] the vocal minority [those fighting for prison reform] . . . well, after a while you begin to feel like one. Who's the asshole? Me for staying, or the guy who left?"

Often at the nub of officer confusion and uncertainty is department policy governing relationships with inmates. Most prison staff handbooks have attempted to spell it out. The language is there, but the words are subjective and open to individual interpretation; meanings differ from one officer to another.

In California, it's Departmental Rule 3400: "Familiarity. Employees must not engage in undue familiarity with inmates. . . . Whenever there is reason for an employee to have personal contact or discussions with an inmate . . . the employee must maintain a helpful but professional attitude and demeanor."

"It's hard to draw a line between fraternization and being friendly," says Anthony P. Travisono, executive director of the 8,000-member American Correctional Association. "That line still is a large, monumental dilemma for the correctional officer."

Sometimes the uncertainty over where that line is creates friction among the officers themselves. Frederick Forté, who has been a correctional officer at San Quentin since July, 1973, says he was criticized because he was "too friendly with the inmates."

"That kind of bugged me. It was just because I stopped and took time to listen to a guy, I didn't see that as being overly friendly. . . . At first, I was concerned about what they were saying about me. But as time went on when I knew I was doing the job right — I wasn't breaking any institutional rules — and I felt I was right. . . . I have to live with myself. I don't have to live with those people. I'm not going to change myself so they'll say 'Forté's a good guy.' I won't do that for staff or inmates or anybody. . . ."

The different views of what rules mean to both administrators and officers have made the guards' job more complex. As short a time as ten years ago, most officers say they were not troubled with making such interpretive decisions. Most prisons had a clear policy and tradition that discouraged anything more than minimum verbal contact with inmates.

"In the old days," a more than twenty-year veteran on a New England prison staff said, "we watched them, we locked 'em in and we counted 'em. That's all there was to it."

In Illinois' Vienna facility, Sergeant Hartley Hilton concurs, recalling his assignment in the maximum-security prison at Pontiac in the mid-sixties. "If you stopped and talked to a convict for more than one or two minutes, you were being watched. And someone would write you a pinky." (A reprimand that meant days off without pay.)

While there may be confusion sometimes about what administration policies really mean in officer and inmate relationships, there is near unanimity in the essential standards that America's correctional officers set for themselves. In corrections departments large and small, distant or adjacent, the same words keep cropping up. They, too, are subjective, open to individual interpretation: "firm," "fair," "down the middle." Officers at opposite ends of the country use them to respond to the question: What is a good officer?

Ronald J. Englund, a nine-year veteran at San Quentin, answers by pinpointing the two extremes of the job.

> If you come in here and feel a man is worthless because he's a killer . . . or if you start feeling sorry for these guys, you've lost all your perspective . . . you won't last six months. Convicts will run him off the yard if he tries to be a hardnose . . . I've seen it happen. You can't come in here and be one extreme or another. You've got to walk right down the middle of the road.
>
> I think a lot of people come in here with the concept that this is a place full of hardened criminals and they're going to have to show them that they're going to be a lot tougher. It doesn't work that way.
>
> I treat every guy as a human being. Now, if he wants to carry that a little bit further and treat me with a lot of disrespect, . . . I'm going to give that right back to him, except I may give it back to him just a little bit heavier. I don't want him to come up to me and say "yes sir," "please, sir," No, I just want him to treat me with the respect I have coming, and I'll treat him with the respect he has coming.

In Rhode Island, a similar assessment is made by Bud Gardner:

> The hardnose, thick-headed, bull correctional officer of the movies in the Jimmy Cagney era doesn't exist. And if he comes in here, he doesn't last very long. Your first goal ought to be to gain the respect of an inmate.
>
> You can't gain respect from an inmate from being an easy mark. They don't respect easy marks. You don't gain respect through bully tactics, then everyday he comes into the joint it's going to just wear him down a little bit more. Things just don't work that way anymore.

> You gain respect by attempting to treat everyone the same . . . equally . . . no matter what they're in for. As a matter of fact, myself, I try not to find out what a man's in here for. It might change me a little bit . . . I might not feel that it showed, but it shows. Now, someone will ask me to do something, send a request out to the visiting desk or something like that . . . his request might sit in my pocket where someone else's request would be expedited right off the bat because of maybe what he did on the street . . . so I try not to even know what he's here for. . . .

If there is agreement on what the officer's standard should be, there often is agreement, too, that sometimes, with high turnover, inadequate training, low salaries and ever-pervasive public image of the guard, the standard may not be met. Officer Donato DeRobertis, with thirteen years in Connecticut's maximum-security prison, acknowledges the gap that sometimes exists between what a guard is and what he should be.

> There are some who think their word is law and they feel this sense of power maybe because they couldn't have power anywhere else. I think that's part of it. They go home and they tell the wife "to get me a glass of water, and she says get your own glass of water." Now he's all frustrated because during the day he can have a 350-pound muscleman to whom he says "do this" and the man jumps. He goes home and his little wife says "go to hell."
>   An officer may try to live up to a certain image, that he's the authority. The minute he does that and an inmate questions his authority . . . now there's an image to attack and he's got to come on strong. Now if you're just yourself, I don't care if you're a bastard, if that's the way you are, hey, these inmates don't mind. As long as you're constant. They'll know what to do. They'll leave you alone. This idea of smiling today and stabbing them in the back tomorrow . . . because your eggs were burned you come in with a grudge, this don't go.

The words "consistent" and "respect" are not only focal points for officers describing the qualities of their job, but they also are used frequently by inmates when questioned about what they expect from their guards.

"I act respectable and they give me respect. That's what I want," says an inmate in an Arkansas maximum-security cellblock. "I want an officer that has understanding . . . knows how to talk to inmates . . . help the inmate as much as he can . . . an officer who does his job."

For an inmate, is there a "good" guard?

While many grouse about the quality of guards as a group, most inmates will point to an individual officer whom they consider fair, who has helped clear bureaucratic hurdles, encouraged them to apply for school . . . who has made a difference in their personal lives.

"Yeah. There's a fair guard," says the Arkansas inmate. "There's officers that would try to help you . . . quite a few of them. There's a fair guard just like on the street there's a fair cop."

COMPLAINTS ABOUT LOYALTY

Older officers in maximum-security prisons today, however, talk of more than "respect" and "fairness" when you ask them to define the qualities required of their job. They talk of loyalty to the institution and to the other officers who work with them. They grumble about its decline. "The new guys here," one veteran said, "they come here for the money. Just the money. That's all."

Like older workers in other fields far beyond the prisons, they complain about shrinking loyalties to the job, the decline of authority, the indifference to excellence. Their criticisms are parcelled out to inmates and their younger colleagues alike. In Massachusetts, a veteran officer complains about the slovenly dress of the younger officers, the hair styles that run over shirt collars. At San Quentin, older officers complain about the lack of dress requirement for inmates. . . . "Now, he can wear the dirty old clothes he's been working in all day to dinner," fifty-four-year-old Lieutenant William Faust observes. "I think with this freedom of expression thing he's infringing on the freedom of the other guys."

In both Massachusetts and California, the older officers quarrel with the decline of authority, a quarrel they have not only had within the prison, but also outside of it as well.

"Today, a man would question an order . . . if I was given an order when I first came to work here, I did it," says Captain Norman Carver, a twenty-three-year man in Massachusetts' prison system. "If there was any question in my mind, then I might have said 'how come I had to do that?' Today, when you give a man an order he asks: 'how come I have to do that?' . . . before he carries it out.

"If you go to work for a company, and this includes the Commonwealth of Massachusetts, I don't think you should steal from them. I think you should put your time in, do your job, just as you would if you were sitting on a production line making automobiles. . . . You take automobiles today. How many automobiles have you heard about where the rear end drops off because there's a loose screw somewhere or something else happens to it. A brand new car. You've paid four thousand dollars! They don't do their jobs, those fellows on the production line. Well, it's the same type of thing in this institution."

In California, Bill Faust is in charge of a special security squad which cover the gunrails, does searches, and is on standby for emergency situations. He is one of 390 custody officers, sergeants, and lieutenants at San Quentin. He, too, talks about the decline of authority, about permissiveness, and the changes since he started as a guard for $231 a month twenty-six years ago.

"When I was a sergeant of that yard out there, we'd blow a whistle at 4:25 and they'd know it was time to lock up. They'd line up in four lines, for (each) cellblock and file in. But now, everything seems to be a mass movement. This is an expression of 'move yourself.' We're just seeing the same things that are happening outside filtering in here," he says.

Some of the older convicts, those who have served lengthy prison terms spanning both the old, more rigid and the new expanded rights regimes, sometimes also look back with some of the same nostalgia.

"The old screws were hard and fair," says a forty-one-year-old Walpole lifer who has spent most of his years in prison. "I'd like to have the old screws back. If a guy is doing a lot of time, he's got to know where he stands. There was no ——— game playing. With them (it was), 'This is the way I want it' and 'this is the way it's going to be.' You knew where you stood."

But if there is nostalgia, it is selective and does not enshrine all the old ways. Most veterans interviewed by *Correction Magazine* said that longing for the past was more a longing for the simplicity of discipline for both the guarded and the guards, rather than for the arbitrary, lock-step prisons of the past.

"Hey, years ago an inmate would come in and say 'the officer lied.' The deputy superintendent would say: 'My officers don't lie.' Hey, I know some officers lie," said Albert B. Carr, associate deputy superintendent at Walpole.

In Connecticut, Ray Zapor, who complains of the James Cagney film stereotype of guards, has one more year before he qualifies for his twenty-year retirement. He is regarded by his fellow officers as a model of the old school correctional officer.

> The only thing I liked about the old school is I think we had more control. I think we had more respect from the inmate. They wouldn't dare talk in front of the officers the way they do today.
>
> We had the silent system, you know, when the inmates weren't allowed to talk. It was just in the mess hall. I don't see where that helped anything. When an inmate goes to eat, it's a big time of his day. It's socializing. It's an event in their day to break up the monotony. So I think that the talk back and forth is good for them. If they have something that's bothering them, they can talk it over with their buddy. I think it takes a lot of pressure off the inmate so I'm not in favor of the silent system. Never was.
>
> We carried clubs when I started. And they were of no value to us. You ran the risk of having it taken away from you and having it used on you. If you went and broke up a fight and there were two

inmates fighting and you went to use the club, you had two hundred inmates fighting . . . the first thing we'd do is throw the clubs over the wall. They only got in our way.

If [you] saw a man walking back and forth wearing a club, you know every time you saw the club . . . I have no doubt that these people have been hit sometime in their life by a cop . . . even the badge . . . they look at the badge. All their life they've had trouble with the police officer. They go to prison, the correctional center as you call them, and they see the badge and, hey, what do they see? The cop they had trouble with all their life. They don't see a correctional officer, just another cop . . . it all depends on what you want to do. Do you want to help the inmate? And that's really a tough thing to do, to help somebody who doesn't really want to be helped. But I don't think you're going to do it with badges on.

Like I say, I'm considered about the hardest . . . what is the word for the most hard-nosed person who is here? Hard Rock. Yeah, this type of thing. Perhaps the jacket [reputation] that I carry is, you know, a little heavier than I deserve.

I've talked to inmates who come in and figure the guards are going to make them toe the line . . . and they're really disappointed . . . it's like they're looking for their masculinity. Their conception of a man is tough, physically tough. My conception of a man is a guy who pays the mortgage every month. That's tough.

IS THERE BRUTALITY TODAY?

Veteran correctional officers acknowledge that the "old school" had more ramifications than just tougher discipline. Prisons were tougher physically. While clubs may not have been used in day to day institutional security chores, they were used selectively, in a segregation wing, in the privacy of an inmate's cell. "The ultimate method of control was a rap in the head," says a veteran maximum-security guard who was, by his own admission, part of what he called "the head knocker period."

How much is violence part of the arsenal that maintains contemporary prison order today?

The answers are elusive. They are often limited. Rarely are they made for attribution to a particular officer, inmate or administrator. After a serious prison disturbance and in the investigations that follow, they sometimes crop up in testimony of witnesses.

Some inmates and ex-offenders interviewed by *Corrections Magazine* had individual vignettes of what they considered guard violence. An unruly inmate hurled — unnecessarily, they said — down a stairway . . . beatings in an elevator stopped between floors — "they called it the bucket of blood" — force used against an inmate when they believed force was unnecessary.

One ex-convict who had been held in a number of maximum-security prisons within the last five years said that in one of them, beatings were considered routine. In others, physical attacks by officers were more muted and less frequent.

"There is a correlation between how unstable an institution is and how much head-cracking goes on," says the commissioner of an eastern state. "When it's unstable then everybody's frustrated and heads get beaten."

It still happens today?

"Yes," in a few places.

"None of my colleagues would admit to me that they look the other way. But I know a couple do. When I started in this business fourteen years ago, captains and lieutenants clearly said to you the way they maintained control was to crack a head or two now and then. Now, at least, they don't talk about it anymore."

Physical attacks by guards on inmates, he said, have been sharply reduced because prisons everywhere are far more open to outsiders than ever before. "Probably the most important factor has been the legal movement into the prison. Systematic beating to maintain control just isn't there anymore."

The few officers who would discuss their own part in the head-knocker era concur with the commissioner's assessment. Some, too, suggest that they have changed their minds about the usefulness of beatings as a method of prison control.

> If you have to thump a guy's head and you have to do it again in two months, and again two months later, you're not doing any good," says a supervisor who for five years has been in the segregation unit of a major midwestern maximum-security prison. He allowed that the club was used regularly as a persuader, sometimes landing on the inmates regardless of their guilt or innocence.
>
> I thought it helped at the time. I thought it helped even after I left. In fact, if you had told me up there that it wouldn't do any good to beat a guy's head, I would have probably escorted you right out of there. I would have told the warden you was crazy and he would have believed me.

Among America's professional prison monitors, the ombudsmen for corrections, cases of overt guard violence are reported infrequently. Minnesota's Theartrice Williams, the nation's senior prison ombudsman, and James T. Bookwalter, his counterpart in Connecticut, believe that unprovoked beatings don't occur in their state prisons.

"I don't believe that in Connecticut people are taken out of their cells and worked over anymore. It happened in the past, but it doesn't happen anymore," says Bookwalter.

"What does happen when there is a physical conflict between an inmate and an officer and force is required to bring an inmate under control, the inmates believe that the guard gets in a few extra licks."

In three years as Connecticut's ombudsman, Bookwalter has received 1,062 different complaints from the state's maximum-security prison at Somers. Between ten and fifteen of these, he said, involved charges of guard violence. He has been unable to document any of them. "There are certainly incidents where an inmate has been injured while physically resisting an officer, but it's impossible to document if an officer used necessary or excessive force, but no inmate ever has said to me that he has been slugged without any reason."

"I would be very close to that," says Minnesota's Williams, who in four years has pursued about 4,500 inmate complaints. Fewer than half a dozen, he says, have involved charges of officer violence.

"We've had accusations made in the maximum-security prison that officers have attacked inmates, but when we began to check it out, it began to fall apart. I know we don't have a documented case of so-called brutality. What we have had is a case where the question was how much force is enough force."

Williams recalls an incident where an inmate filled a cup with urine and threw it at a passing guard. The officer happened to be carrying a pot of coffee and the inmate got the coffee. "Now if he had done that three days later, making sure that the coffee was good and hot, I would have considered that brutality," he said.

"The officer — at least in the Minnesota system — who provokes a situation where he is the aggressor, he'll be in trouble on two counts: The inmates wouldn't tolerate it, and the administration would want to deal with it quickly because that's a situation that leads to a riot."

THE QUESTION OF JOB COMPETENCE

While opinions about current violence may vary among inmates, there is near unanimity on another question: the inmates claim that many correctional officers are not prepared for their jobs. They tick off a litany of complaints that, in less-harsh language, often parallels the complaints of officers and prison administrators as well: There isn't any real screening to weed out the psychologically unfit . . . officers sometimes bring their personal "hang ups" into the prison . . . rural guards from the small towns where prisons generally are located do not understand the inmate who generally comes from the city . . . and, most often heard, they are untrained.

Entry requirements for correctional officer jobs are minimal and vary from state to state. Many now demand a high school diploma. In Ohio, however, the minimum is a fourth-grade education or its equivalent. In some states an applicant must be twenty-one, in others only eighteen. Many now give standard state civil service tests, others have no tests at all. Some give physical examinations, some don't.

In 1974, a study of the Commission on Correctional Facilities and

Services of the American Bar Association found that only seven of forty-six states that participated in the survey made background checks on applicants. Few states have detailed psychological fitness standards, the survey said. A dozen states acknowledged that the screening methods for emotional and psychological fitness they did have were "not very effective."

"Since correctional agencies commonly administer a battery of tests to aid in classifying inmates, which result in rather specific indications of strengths and weaknesses," the ABA report said, "the primitive 'state of the art' as regards staff selection was not fully anticipated."

Once an applicant is accepted, training, too, differs from state to state. Sometimes an individual department will curtail a training program in mid-year because educational funds are running low or are needed elsewhere. With increased availability of federal Law Enforcement Assistance Administration (LEAA) training funds, more states have organized at least some formal programs. These range from pre-service, full-time academies, to a smattering of basic courses sandwiched between or ahead of work shifts.

In New York State, a new man goes to an academy for thirteen weeks before he is assigned his first prison post. In other states, however, the recruit still learns most of his trade by doing it — on-the-job training, labeled by one officer as a euphemism for "flying by the seat of your pants."

"I've worked in places," says former Massachusetts penitentiary superintendent Frank Gunter, "where the inmates showed the new man how to use the key."

In Arkansas, Arthur L. Lockhart, superintendent of the maximum-security Cummins unit, tells a similar story of his early days as a correctional officer in the Texas system. "I had OJT (on-the-job training) from a convict. He showed me how to shake down and do the count."

The Arkansas Department of Corrections, in many ways, is among the newest in the nation. It has virtually no veteran correctional officers. Until 1971, custody at the maximum-security Cummins unit was in the hands of trusty inmates. Six years ago, Cummins contained about 900 inmates. The total staff, from secretary to the superintendent, was 28. The custody staff alone is now close to 100.

With the help of an $80,000 LEAA grant, the department is now beginning to develop a series of in-service training courses. A formal, pre-service academy program is about two years away, said Lockhart.

Ray Mathew is a soft-spoken twenty-year-old who will complete his first year as a correction officer at Cummins in February. Before he came to the maximum-security unit, he was unemployed for three months after he lost his job as a cafeteria worker in Little Rock. He said that he had never seen a prison before.

My idea was that they all would be locked up. When I saw 'em all walking around it made me scared at first. During the first two days, I walked down the barracks and there was about 100 inmates. I thought "there I was alone and any one of 'em could jump me." But then I realized they could just as easy get out the door.

The employment office sent me over. I talked to the personnel manager at Cummins on a Monday. He looked over the application and at the end he said there was no reason why I couldn't start Wednesday night.

I got here Wednesday night and they told me they didn't need me . . . that I should come back the next day at 2:30 . . . We all met in the officers' mess. We had our (shift) briefing and they told me to work the hospital door. I had to ask another officer where the hospital door was.

There were two of us at the door. The other officer explained to me what we were supposed to do. He showed me how to shake down. During the first two weeks, sometimes, I took it over alone. Some weeks — on Tuesdays and Thursdays — they had me come in at 1:30 PM instead of 2:30. They'd choose a certain assignment and they explained what you were supposed to do.

Minimal or virtually no training is not unique to Arkansas. Dr. John E. Grenfell, professor of rehabilitation at Southern Illinois University at Carbondale, has been training officers and their training supervisors for more than ten years. He has produced training handbooks for LEAA. He says that some training programs in the Midwest and South still are rudimentary and offer only a few basics. "Some years ago I interviewed guards in Tennessee who were on the wall with guns they didn't know how to use," he says.

In a survey of midwestern correctional officers conducted by Grenfell ten years ago to find out what kind of training the guards wanted, they listed a combination of academic courses and instruction in security techniques. "What they wanted most was a course in human relations . . . how to predict inmate behavior . . . when somebody was going to blow his top and how to prevent it. . . ." Professor Grenfell believes that those training priorities still are wanted today. They were mentioned frequently by young officers interviewed by *Corrections Magazine*.

In departments throughout the nation, some officers are obtaining these courses on their own. They are enrolled in psychology and sociology classes in four-year colleges as well as in community colleges.

In Rhode Island, Bud Gardner obtained his degree in criminal justice by going to college after his day shift ended at the maximum-security prison. He found the psychology and sociology courses particularly helpful.

I grew up in a suburban community. I went to suburban schools. Up until I went into the service, I had very little contact with people from other backgrounds. The education taught me a little about what it's like for other people. I find myself not bothered as much . . . somebody directs a remark to you, a hostile remark, and you start to take it personal. But I began to realize that it's not Bud Gardner they're talking to, they're talking to the uniform, the symbol that's standing in that spot . . . they're venting their frustrations there because there's no other place to vent them. . . .

EMPLOYEE ORGANIZATIONS

Those who administer today's prisons have more woes than coping with untrained manpower. Beyond the often high correctional staff turnover, those who stay are making stronger employee demands in many states. Unions and their drive for collective bargaining agreements are on the rise.

Only a handful of states now have no employee organizations representing their correctional officers. The groups vary from in-state associations to international trade unions that range from the American Federation of State, County and Municipal Employees (AFL-CIO), to the Teamsters. In Ohio in 1974, the Director of Rehabilitation and Corrections signed ageements with forty separate collective bargaining units representing five different employee groups.

A study of management-employee relations in corrections now being conducted by the American Justice Institute, of Sacramento, California, shows not only unionism in prisons on the increase, but also an upswing in demands for collective bargaining. Preliminary information collected in 1975 indicated that fourteen states had collective bargaining agreements.

Some state corrections departments reported breakdowns in negotiations that led to strikes and organized sick outs. The Ohio Department of Rehabilitation and Correction has had ten strikes in the past five years. In Pennsylvania, correctional officers have boycotted their prisons thirteen times via waves of sick calls.

A veteran corrections administrator with experience in labor relations believes most prison administrators are not equipped to deal with union-management negotiations. "They are babes in the woods," he said, adding:

"Management in many of these states have had very little experience with collective bargaining and have gotten themselves into some incredible messes. They've been giving them things they didn't have to give them because they didn't know how to negotiate."

Many urban state prison administrators are caught sometimes between increasingly militant union demands and cumbersome civil service systems that can delay routine decisions for months. The Massachusetts Corrections Department recently waited more than half a year to obtain the scores of Civil Service exams. A written test was given in November, 1975, and the oral component was held last March. By the end of this summer, the results had not been reported to the prison. At Walpole, twelve of eighteen supervisors held provisional appointment because the scores from supervisory examinations had not been furnished by the state system.

While these administrative headaches are mounting for shift supervisors in many prisons, the immediate overriding concern often is absenteeism. It is so pervasive in some institutions that job assignments are juggled daily and last-minute calls are sent out for men to give up their days off to replace an absent co-worker.

At San Quentin last May, the work force of 451 employees of the Security Division — including secretaries, counselors, sergeants and lieutenants — compiled 4,464 hours of sick leave. It averaged nearly ten hours per employee for the month. At Walpole, the sick leave totals during the same month averaged three hours for members of the custody force. In New Jersey's maximum-security prison at Trenton, the average member of the custody force took three weeks of sick time per year, just about the allowed maximum.

In institutions with less stress, the "illness" frequency is dramatically reduced. In the minimum-security facility at Vienna, Ill., the sick leave totals were half of those at San Quentin for the same month. The custody force of 171 averaged five hours per man.

"Sick leave has turned into a right rather than a privilege," says ACA director Anthony Travisono, the former head of the Rhode Island prison system. "When they gave that away, we lost a helluva lot. The job is so rotten, they look for any way to get out of the prison even if it means fudging it."

Job dissatisfaction increases where turnover and absenteeism are higher, frequently in the overcrowded maximum-security institutions. Both older and younger correctional officers acknowledge that often they accepted their jobs in the first place largely because of the security it offered, the steady work, the retirement plan. "This place is just not about to pack up and move some place else," one of the officers said.

But many correctional officers emphasize that they want and look for more than a steady paycheck. Officers with less than a year of service and those with more than two decades behind them share common job-goal frustrations. Many resent what they believe is their too limited role as jailors of America's convicts as well as the lack of encouragement from administration to work more actively with inmates. There is also resentment over what they see as the gap between themselves and the treatment staff.

"You've got to show that he (the officer) is needed," one of them says. "You've got to show that we're doing something that's worthwhile . . . but how in the world can you feel worthwhile if you're just opening and closing doors?"

Everywhere *Corrections Magazine* interviewed officers, they defined the "worthwhile" aspects of their jobs in highly personal anecdotes of inmates they believe they may have helped: Unscrambling administrative snarls for an inmate who may not have received what was due him . . . the isolated success stories of those who "made it on the street," job assignments they urged for a man who later used the newly learned skill "on the outside."

In Arkansas, a young black sergeant in a segregation unit talks about being the link between the inmate and the world beyond the fence. He points to examples that would be trivial outside of prison — some writing paper, a phone call. "I try to get things for the inmate that he's supposed to have. If I can do that, that makes me feel good."

In Connecticut, a lieutenant talks about an inmate in the maximum-security prison who recently took his college entrance exams:

> He came in first in the state of Connecticut . . . twenty-eighth in the United States. Things like that make you feel good . . . We get judged on our failures. Corrections always gets judged on its failures . . . we do . . . never on the positive things that happen. When something like that happens it really makes you feel good if you're really into what you're doing . . . I couldn't get over that. The guy came in No. 1 in the State of Connecticut.

In Rhode Island, Bud Gardner talks of satisfactions, ". . . seeing them a year or so later on the street and having them go out of their way to say hello to you. You'll be in a store somewhere and not even notice that they were there and they would spot you and cross the store to say hello and sit down and have a cup of coffee together. . . . This helps on the other end of the scale for some of the things that go on in the institution."

In California, San Quentin's Fred Forté suggests "there's a lot more to this than just locking a guy up and unlocking him. You get into a lot of heavy personal things that you wouldn't think a guard would be concerned about. The majority of the officers I've seen do take some concern in where a guy is, what his problems are. I would like to think that most consider it at least a part of the job."

Some officers believe that they and their colleagues often have been an unused resource within the prisons. They insist that they should have had a part in staffing the raft of new programs that have been brought into institutions in recent years.

Ronald W. Phillips is a lieutenant on the custody dayshift of Connecticut's maximum-security prison. A former president of the correctional officer's union, he was one of the "Young Turks" who fought not only for greater benefits, but also for increased professionalism among guards. Five years ago, at age thirty-eight, he was promoted to lieutenant, one of the youngest men to make that rank in the Connecticut system. Phillips today is concerned about what he fears is a retrenchment of prison programs because of a belief that they don't work.

I think if they had gone to the people that they already had in their system and put them in to run those programs, they would have made them work. Everyone who came from outside had to learn what this was all about first. They had expertise here that they didn't use.

If they had made it graceful for those men (older correctional officers) to throw away the stereotype . . . you know you just can't blast people . . . there's an amount of personal pride in everyone, whether they're wrong or they're right. If they would have allowed them to put down that stereotype that they had armored themselves with, then these programs they're now complaining are not working would have worked. The people they brought in are very intelligent people, well educated people, good people, o.k.? But it took them so long really to grasp the situation about the types of people that we work with . . . why didn't they make a little effort to give them (the guards) the academics that were needed and work it that way instead of bringing in new people?

Now what you have are two groups of people who are disillusioned. You have those who you brought in. They're saying "shit, you know, it's not working." And you still have the people we've been talking about, the officer who feels, "I can't move myself, I can't do anything for myself in this business. I've got a lot to give and they're going outside to get people to give it." He's still disillusioned.

Lieutenant Phillips has allies for his views among some prison administrators. Dr. David Fogel, formerly the commissioner of the Minnesota Department of Corrections and frequently an outspoken critic of prison policies, also suggests that the guard had been overlooked in the nation's prisons. Now executive director of the Illinois Law Enforcement Commission, he wants officers to be at the center of an institution's treatment system. "The talent is there," he says, "or it can be developed if we bite off manageable pieces."

The officers can deliver treatment, he insists. "They can either embarrass the best effort, they can sabotage it or they can outright do it. What's the use of sending an inmate for an hour to the pressurized cabin of a treatment situation with a psychotherapist and then have him return to a concentration camp atmosphere where he's spending virtually all of his time.

"It's not hard to figure out that these guys would like to be involved. Why can't the guard be in the helping profession and still make sure that nobody runs away?

"Stop the rhetoric and send me your tired and your sick. Stop the rhetoric that we can cure them. Just start talking about fairness. The guards know that. They know it because they've been treated just like the inmates, often unfairly."

In Connecticut, Ray Zapor, and others like him who are nearing retirement, doesn't think he will see those changes. When he quits within a year, he says he will take with him "very little satisfaction" from the job he did for twenty years.

> My whole family is in construction. They're masons. They take me to show me a building they finished. They're proud of it. They come home at night and they get a feeling of accomplishment. You can show it to somebody.
>
> But you come out of a prison . . . and what can you show somebody?

Chapter 3
What Prison Guards Think: A Profile of the Illinois Force*

James B. Jacobs

Prison-related scholarship has focused almost exclusively on the culture and social structure of prisoners. Countless studies report prisoners' attitudes about themselves, fellow inmates, prison staff, and society in general. However, there is no comparable body of research[1] on the demography, attitudes, values, and ideology of correctional officers, as prison guards have come to be known since World War II.[2] This is unfortunate and surprising, since prison scholars and reformers have, from the beginning of the penitentiary movement, emphasized the guards' decisive importance in carrying out penological goals.[3] Furthermore, the way guards are recruited, the segment of society from which they are drawn, and the attitudes and values embodied in their subculture should be of great interest to those seeking to understand the role of the prison in society as well as the prison's internal organization.

The descriptive data reported here are a first step toward a comprehensive assessment of American prison guards. Questionnaires were administered to 929 Illinois prison guards at Illinois' Correctional Training Academy between July 1974 and October 1975. Anonymity was preserved at all times. A comparison of guards' responses in the early months with questionnaires completed several months later shows no systematic variations.

DEMOGRAPHIC PROFILE

The median age of this sample of Illinois correctional officers is forty-five; slightly more than 25 percent of the force are under thirty, and 15 percent are over sixty years old.[4] Despite substantial efforts in the last several years to increase minority representation, 85 percent of the guards are white, while a majority of the prisoners are black or Latino. Average time on the job is sixty-five months; 16 percent of the guards have two years experience or less, and 23 percent have worked on the job more than ten years. Seniority is not distributed evenly across the nine adult prisons in the state: At one institution (Vandalia), only 35 percent of the force

---

* Copyright 1978, National Council on Crime and Delinquency. Reprinted with permission from *Crime and Delinquency* (April, 1978).

have less than five years' experience, while at another (Vienna), 83 percent have been on the force less than five years.

Thirty-five percent of the Illinois guards grew up on farms, 12 percent were raised in the country, 36 percent came from small towns (less than 25,000 people), 9 percent grew up in moderate-sized cities (25,000-250,000 people), and only 7 percent lived in metropolitan areas. Even at the Stateville and Joliet prisons, located thirty-five miles from Chicago, only 36 percent of the black guards and 11 percent of the whites grew up in a metropolitan area.

Approximately half (54 percent) of the guards have a high school diploma or its equivalent. Forty-nine respondents received degrees from junior colleges, but only eleven guards in the entire state have a four-year college education. Despite such modest educational achievement, and contrary to public opinion, slightly more respondents describe themselves as "very liberal" or "somewhat liberal" (10 percent and 21 percent, respectively) than as "moderately conservative" or "very conservative" (21 percent and 5 percent). Blacks are much more likely than whites to consider themselves politically liberal, but the largest percentage of the entire force characterize themselves as "middle of the road."

ATTITUDES TOWARD WORK, OCCUPATION, AND CAREER

Why did these front-line correctional officers choose this occupation in the first place? More than one-half (57 percent) did so for reasons unrelated to correction: They "just needed a job." Forty-one percent reported that they were unemployed at the time they joined the force. In contrast, however, one in ten respondents mentioned having specifically aspired toward becoming a guard, and one in three gave both reasons — looking for a job and thinking guard work would be interesting.

There are striking differences between blacks and whites with respect to reasons for joining the force. At the Stateville and Joliet prisons, where most (63 percent) black guards in the state work, 49 percent of the whites and 70 percent of the blacks gave some indication of having specifically sought careers as guards. The greater commitment of black guards to the career confirms a companion study of guard "drop-outs and rejects,"[5] which found that at the time they were hired more than half the blacks, but only one-third of the whites, intended to remain on the job for at least five years. The present study reveals that, regardless of their original intentions, most guards expect to continue in their jobs for at least five years, the only exception being those anticipating retirement. This finding is contrary to traditional thinking which pictures the guard as interested only in interim employment until something better comes along.[6]

Ninety percent of the respondents described themselves as either "very happy" (40 percent) or "somewhat happy" (50 percent) in their job. This finding confirms the 1968 survey by the Joint Commission on Correctional Manpower and Training, which revealed that 92 percent of the line workers considered their jobs "almost always satisfying" or "usually satisfying."[7] When asked to describe how interesting their work is, 58 percent of the Illinois guards answered "quite interesting"; only 8 percent said "somewhat boring" or "very boring." "Job security" and "stimulation" were cited as the main advantages of the job. (See Table 1.) However, this response does not mean that Illinois prison guards are completely content. Apparently, most American workers answer survey questions about job satisfaction similarly,[8] but in-depth interviews often reveal considerably more dissatisfaction.[9] It does indicate that there is no widespread or deeply held disaffection with the job. Prison guards seem no more discontent than fellow workers in other occupations. This conclusion is confirmed by several of the questionnaire responses discussed below.

To assess the strength of each respondent's commitment to his occupation we asked whether he would prefer any or all of six alternative jobs if offered at the same rate of pay. Table 2 demonstrates that most guards preferred their job over every alternative. The next most attractive job was private security, the occupation most similar to the present one. A position on the police force was the only other job in which the guards exhibited substantial interest.[10]

Perhaps a more suitable indication of the prison guard's attitude toward his occupation is his reaction to his son's following in his footsteps. Only one-fourth of the respondents acknowledged that they would like to see their sons become correctional officers. However, whether the majority prefer that their sons follow a different career because of specific characteristics of the job or because they simply wish their sons to attain a

Table 1
"What, in your opinion, are the three main advantages of being a correctional officer?"*

Interesting work	59.0%
Job security	59.0
Money	39.8
Easy work	11.6
Promotion opportunities	6.8
No advantages	2.7
Non-prison-specific reasons	40.8

N = 805.
* Multiple responses permitted.

Table 2

APPEAL OF ALTERNATIVE OCCUPATIONS

"Suppose you were offered a job as a _____ at the same salary as you are now making as a correctional officer. Would you take the job?"

	I Would Definitely Not Take It	I Don't Think I Would Take It	I Don't Know	I Would Probably Take It	I Would Surely Take It
Construction worker	52.0%	23.6%	12.3%	4.8%	7.3%
Policeman	45.2	21.3	9.1	11.1	13.5
Garbage collector	69.0	17.6	4.9	4.8	3.7
Factory worker	65.3	20.1	5.3	6.0	3.3
Auto mechanic	61.6	20.3	6.4	6.2	5.4
Private security guard	33.5	19.8	12.0	17.4	17.3

N = 924.

higher status occupation is not known.[11] Another subject for future research is the extent to which correctional officers feel stigmatized by their occupation. Two-thirds of the respondents agreed or strongly agreed with the statement that "people are more sympathetic to inmates than to correctional officers." On the other hand, when asked how they felt about telling people what their occupation was, almost half the respondents described themselves as "very proud" or "somewhat proud"; only 5 percent reported being "embarrassed."[12]

Confronted with an unstructured question requiring them to list the "main disadvantages" of the job, the guards most often noted "danger" and "superior officers." (See Table 3.) Since the guards spend their working lives locked in a tense environment under a constant threat of individual or collective violence, it is not surprising that they are most concerned about personal security. We asked the guards to rate, on a seven-point scale, how dangerous they perceived their job to be, with "1" indicating "extremely dangerous" and "7" indicating "not dangerous at all." The mean score for all guards was slightly less than 3; 29 percent marked 1 and 20 percent marked either 5, 6, or 7. The mean score for blacks at Stateville and Joliet was significantly lower than the mean score for whites at the same institutions; blacks feel more threatened.

With respect to complaints about superior officers, 44 percent of the guards either strongly agreed (15 percent) or agreed (29 percent) that "in general lieutenants are more sympathetic to the problems of inmates than to the problems of correctional officers." Younger officers reported more positive attitudes toward superiors than did their older colleagues. Two in five respondents disagreed with the statement: "When a problem

Table 3

DISADVANTAGES OF GUARD WORK*

Danger	49.0%
Superior officers	32.1
Hours	27.2
The inmates	20.0
Money	15.7
Understaffing	4.4
Other officers	4.2
No disadvantages	3.3

N = 750.
* Multiple responses permitted.

arises between an officer and an inmate, the Warden and other administrators usually support the officer." Thus, there is substantial feeling that the guards do not get sufficient "backing" from the administration. The greatest organizational strain, however, becomes evident in the attitude of the Illinois guards toward civilian counselors.[13] Thirty-one percent of the guards strongly agreed and 49 percent agreed with the statement: "In general, counselors and treatment personnel are more sympathetic to the problems of inmates than to the problems of correctional officers."

Respondents also sharply criticized the promotion system. Seven out of ten guards found it "very unsatisfactory" or "somewhat unsatisfactory." In part, this discontent reflects the absence of opportunities for upward mobility in the paramilitary penal organization where there are only a few

Table 4

PERCEPTIONS ABOUT PROMOTIONS

"What are the two main criteria used in determining who gets a promotion?"*

Politics (e.g., who you know, friendship, connections)	67%
Specific qualifications (how well you do the job)	35
Reliability or work record	11
Seniority	10
General qualifications (e.g., education)	8
Ability to get along with inmates	3
Other	2

N = 813.
* Sixty-four percent of the respondents provided only one response.

Table 5

HOW GUARDS FEEL PROMOTIONS SHOULD BE MADE*

Special qualifications (how well you can do the job)	92%
Seniority	42
General qualifications (e.g., education)	25
Reliability or "work record"	24
Ability to get along with inmates	9
Other	1

N = 821.
* Multiple responses permitted.

top officer positions. Of greater concern is the claim that promotion decisions are tainted by nepotism and arbitrariness. Table 4 shows that two-thirds of the Illinois guards believe "politics" to be one of the two main factors determining who is promoted.

In a human services organization like a prison, where objective criteria of productivity and standards of accomplishment seemingly defy definition, what promotional criteria would the guards themselves prefer? Table 5 illustrates that an overwhelming majority favor a promotion system based upon merit. However, finding objective criteria to measure "who is a good guard" is difficult. Any evaluation of job performance by superiors is likely to be condemned as subjective and political. Forty-two percent of the guard force endorsed seniority as an alternative standard. This support for a seniority system may reflect the growing influence of the prison officers' union.

ATTITUDE TOWARD IMPRISONMENT AND PRISONERS

The Joint Commission on Correctional Manpower and Training found in 1968 that almost three-fourths of the American public accepted "rehabilitation" as the primary justification for imprisonment.[14] Another Joint Commission survey revealed that 98 percent of correctional line workers felt that "rehabilitation" should have primary or secondary emphasis in correctional agencies, while 48 percent believed "protection of society" should be emphasized; only 12 percent thought that "punishment" should be a primary or secondary goal.[15] The Illinois data are consistent with the earlier study: 46 percent of the guards considered "rehabilitation" the purpose of imprisonment, although 26 percent of the guards believed that punishment "is the main reason for putting the offender in prison." (See Table 6.) Six out of ten officers disagreed with the statement that "rehabilitation programs are a waste of time and money."

Table 6

THEORIES OF IMPRISONMENT

"What, in your opinion, is the main reason for putting the offender in prison?"*

To rehabilitate him	46%
To protect society by making sure that he does not commit any more crimes for a while	28
To punish him for what he did wrong	26
To deter him from committing crime in the future	14

N = 916.
* Multiple responses permitted.

The Illinois guards also favor deterministic — sociological and psychological — explanations of crime causation. In response to the question, "Why do inmates commit crimes?" the respondents adopted a multicausal theory of criminality, giving some support to all the social science theories of criminality and rejecting decisively only the theory that people are born to be criminals. (See Table 7.) When asked why so many members of minority groups are in prison, the guards again evidenced a distinct preference for general sociological explanations — poverty and lack of jobs. (See Table 8.)

This is not to say that the guards necessarily accept the inmates or feel comfortable with them. Eighty-six percent believed that "prisoners try to take advantage of you whenever they can," but 75 percent agreed with the statement that "only a few inmates are troublemakers; most of

Table 7

CAUSES OF CRIME

"Why do inmates commit crimes?"*

Because they are poor	58%
Because they come from broken homes	56
Because they freely choose to	55
Because they are sick or have mental problems	53
Because they are born criminals	13

N = 913.
* Multiple responses permitted.

Table 8

"Why are there so many minority group members in prison?"*

Lack of opportunity	
Society, lack of jobs, poverty, lack of money	45%
Subculture of violence	
Gangs, the ghetto, brought up breaking the laws	30
Psychological reasons	
Sick, mentally ill	1
Choose to commit more crime, "they want to,"	
they are lazy, shiftless, etc.	22
The society's racism produces greater rates	
of imprisonment among minorities	9

N = 694.
* Multiple responses permitted.

them are decent people." There seems to be a sharp division on the prisoner's moral worth. In response to the question, "In your opinion, when considered as people, how similar are correctional officers and inmates?" a bare majority of all Illinois correctional officers answered, "very similar" or "somewhat similar." Yet a slight majority supported the statement that "inmates lack morals."

With respect to homosexuality, the guards shifted away from the vocabulary of liberal responses which stress environmental determinism. Slightly less than half (42 percent) of these respondents believe that prisoners are "sick and in need of medical treatment." Approximately the same proportion said that prisoners "lack morals and self-control." A significant minority (14 percent) assume that prisoners engaging in homosexuality are "acting normally under the circumstances."

IMPLICATIONS FOR PENAL PRACTICE AND POLICY

The Illinois prison guard survey data presented here do not support stereotypical depictions of the guard as a stern — even brutal — disciplinarian. No extreme desire to punish prisoners is evident. Indeed, the guards' opinion as to the causes of crime and the purposes of imprisonment parallels the liberal sociopolitical position. The recent trend toward punitive justifications for imprisonment may leave the guards in the anomalous position of having greater commitment to rehabilitation than the academic penologists and prison administrators.

As the academic commentators and professional administrators move toward abandoning the rehabilitative ideal, what effect will this have on the line officer and other prison staff? Even if no rehabilitation programs worthy of the name were ever actually in operation in the great mega-prisons, still, the organizing philosophy of rehabilitation may have provided some of the most idealistic staff members, including line officers, with a sense of mission that sustained their commitment to their career. The impact on guards' morale and dedication of defining the prison as a warehouse institution is worthy of future research.

One thing is clear: Guards continue to be recruited from the lower levels of the work force, and very few have been exposed to higher education, even with the opportunity provided by the Law Enforcement Education Program. Despite the call for a better-quality guard force, the prison is unlikely to appeal to idealistic college graduates. With the facade of idealistic purpose stripped away, the attraction of prison work will probably decline.

Given the demise of idealistic purpose, the recent trend toward increased contact between the prison and the rest of society may be reversed, and the prison may become more segmented from society. The staff may become more parochial and inbred. Only in the unlikely event that Congress passes some kind of voluntary national service might this parochialism of the line staff be significantly challenged.[16] If some portion of line positions were filled by young volunteers serving a period of national service, the prison would be exposed to persons who could not otherwise be recruited. In addition, such a program would establish important institutional bonds between mainstream society and the prison.

The only major demographic change in the character of the guard force over the past several years has been the increase in minority guards. In the "northern" Stateville and Joliet prisons, minority guards now make up approximately half of all recruits. We must be careful, however, not to exaggerate or overstate the significance of this directed social change. Reformers have consistently argued that minority guards would bring to the prison empathy and understanding, which the white rural veterans, often charged with being sadistic and racist, lacked completely. But a separate analysis of the attitudes of black and white officers at Stateville and Joliet fails to reveal any consistent divergencies.[17] Responses to several questionnaire items indicate that the minority guards are even more punitive than their white colleagues. Several factors may account for this: (1) the existence of a pervasive guard subculture which overwhelms even racial differences; (2) the situation of structured conflict, which shapes the roles and working personalities of all officers; or (3) the special position of "double marginality" experienced by the minority officer, who is accepted by neither his white colleagues nor the prisoners.[18] In any case, it appears that the recruitment of minority guards, while an important change in its own right, may not greatly ameliorate the tension and stress characteristic of the great maximum security prisons.

These survey data certainly do not point to any "crisis" among Illinois' correctional employees. To know whether this state is atypical requires similar studies elsewhere in the country. It is true that turnover, at least in some Illinois penal institutions, remains very high at the lower levels; but most officers, who have been on the force long enough to have attained civil service certification, are not dissatisfied with their work. Indeed, the great majority would choose to remain on the force even if they had other job opportunities, and they expect to stay on the job indefinitely.

There is, however, widespread dissatisfaction with the promotional system, and certain strains are evident in the relationship between line officers and their superiors. The promotion question remains troublesome. There are few, if any, objective standards for identifying a "good prison guard," and any system of promotion will probably be criticized as arbitrary. In addition, as management becomes more complex, we can expect more top administrative positions to be filled by college-trained professional administrators recruited laterally into the prison organization. While this is probably a healthy development for correction, it increases the line officer's frustration over the lack of career opportunities.

In the last decade or so the prison has witnessed a clear movement toward specialization, and activities such as counseling, education, and vocational training have been taken from the uniformed officer. This means that the correctional officer is specifically defined as a specialist in security and discipline. Training programs should recognize and build upon this fact by emphasizing the development of detached, efficient, and rational security skills. By following the example of the state police, it may be possible to instill an esprit de corps and a strong, positive self-image in a force of professional security specialists. Indeed, work in correction may be perceived as a stepping-stone into other law enforcement agencies to increase career mobility.

During the last several years, "correction academies" have been established across the country. Although there is little information about these new institutions, one study indicates that the academies have gradually evolved from "academic centers" to "basic training centers."[19] This trend reflects the desire of academy personnel to appear "realistic," but it also indicates a failure to establish ties with higher education and an inability to develop a conception of "correction" that can be easily assimilated by students with very low educational qualifications. On the other hand, if the academies push security skills beyond the mere reiteration of folklore, ideology, and ritual, they may stimulate systematic concern with running maximum security prisons safely, efficiently, rationally, and legally. The new correction academies may also ameliorate the strain between line staff and supervisory personnel, for they may provide a "neutral" setting where the various levels of the prison organization can meet to discuss their work perspectives, opinions, and frustrations.

THE NEED FOR FUTURE RESEARCH

This article is offered as a first step toward building a knowledge base about prison guards and as a plea for more studies of this seriously neglected occupation. There is no reason why prison guards should not attract the same kind of scholarly attention that has been directed toward the police. Without such attention an adequate understanding of prison organization is difficult if not impossible, to achieve.

Systematic studies of prison guards could both draw upon and contribute to the rich tradition in the sociology of occupations.[20] We should like to know far more than what has been presented in this paper about the recruitment and career adjustments of the guards. Longitudinal as well as cross-sectional data are vital for understanding the evolution of the occupation and its relationship to different models of correction. Of paticular theoretical interest is whether recruitment patterns, attitudes, and values vary according to penal goals and types of prison organizations. In general, it will be important to know whether the guards' attitudes, values, and behaviors are better explained by such background characteristics as age, race, and social class or by such occupationally specific variables as time on the job, work assignment, and rank.

From the perspective of the sociology of work, we should be interested in identifying career contingencies. Are there "crises" and crucial tests which the guard must overcome if he (or she) is to adjust to the special demands of the job? At the social-psychological level it is important to ask how a prison guard comes to neutralize the environment of fear that surrounds him. Do different kinds of adjustments lead to identifiable informal roles, parelleling the roles which have been so well described among the prisoners? Future research offers promising opportunities for finding answers to these many questions.

Notes

The author wishes to express his gratitude to the Illinois Correctional Academy, and particularly to its director, Jesse Maughan, for providing the support and opportunity that made this research possible.

1. One notable exception is a Louis Harris survey, conducted for the Joint Commission on Correctional Manpower and Training, which examined the demographic, sociological, and social psychological characteristics of a sample of prison guards. The Joint Commission interviewed 189 line workers from six departments of correction, using both structured and unstructured items. The 189 line workers, however, were not all drawn from adult prisons. The sample included both juvenile and adult correctional officers, cottage parents and counselors, group supervisors and child-care staff. Responses to the survey items were not differentiated for each group, thus, the attitudes of prison

guards in adult correctional facilities cannot be determined. Joint Commission on Correctional Manpower and Training, *Corrections 1968: A Climate for Change*, Washington, D.C., 1968.

2. Most of the scholarship on prison guards is discussed in David Fogel, *We Are The Living Proof: . . . The Justice Model for Corrections* (Cincinnati: W. H. Anderson, 1975), ch. 2; and Gordon Hawkins, *The Prison: Policy and Practice* (Chicago University of Chicago Press, 1976), ch. 4.

3. For example, E. C. Wines and Theodore W. Dwight, Report on the *Prisons and Reformatories of the United States and Canada* to the legislature of New York, January 1867 (Albany, N.Y., Van Benthuysen and Sons' Steam Printing House).

4. The Joint Commission found that the median age of line workers was 40.8. Joint Commission, *Corrections 1968*, 27.

5. James B. Jacobs and Mary P. Greer, "Drop-outs and Rejects: An Analysis of the Prison Guard's Revolving Door," *Criminal Justice Review*, Fall 1977.

6. This does not mean that turnover in the ranks will be low, since most turnover occurs during the six month probationary period, before civil service certification. No respondents in this survey were drawn from the probationary personnel.

7. Joint Commission, *Corrections 1968*.

8. Special Task Force to the Secretary of Health, Education and Welfare, *Work in America* (Cambridge, Mass.: MIT Press, 1973).

9. Studs Turkel, *Working* (New York: Avon, 1975).

10. In New York, correctional officers have consistently fought to maintain their legal designation as "peace officers" in order to continue carrying handguns. The Joint Commission reports that line workers in correction give strongest approval to the police. "The police receive a positive rating from over eight in ten of the line workers and about seven in ten from each of the other job groups," Joint Commission, *Corrections 1968*, 12.

11. The Hodge-Siegle-Rossi Occupational Status Index does not even include prison guards.

12. In an ethnographic study of Stateville Penitentiary prison guards, my coauthor and I concluded: "If, as [Egon] Bittner suggests, 'police work is a tainted occupation,' then prison guard work is utterly polluted. While Secret Service Agents and Brinks guards may achieve esteem from their contact with the objects they are guarding, close contact with convicted felons seems morally profaning for the guard. Even close friends do not know what to make of the prevailing belief that prison guards are sadistic, corrupt, stupid, and incompetent." James B. Jacobs and Harold G. Retsky, "Prison Guard," *Urban Life*, April 1975, 10. A later empirical study found that only 20 percent of the guards who left prison work, voluntarily and involuntarily, were "embarrassed" by their work. We conclude that "our data indicate that the effect of stigma attached to the guard role may be exaggerated." Jacobs and Greer, "Drop-outs and Rejects."

13. See James B. Jacobs, "The Stateville Counsellors: Symbol of Reform in Search of a Role, *Social Service Review*, March 1976.

14. Joint Commission on Correctional Manpower and Training, *The Public Looks at Crime and Correction*, Washington, D.C., 1968.

15. Joint Commission, *Corrections 1968*, 16.

16. See Donald J. Eberly, "National Service: Alternative Strategies," *Armed Forces and Society*, May 1977.

17. James B. Jacobs and Lawrence S. Kraft, "Integrating the Keepers: A Comparison of Black and White Prison Guards in Illinois," *Social Problems*, February 1978.

18. The double marginality of black New York City police officers is documented in Nicholas Alex, *Black in Blue* (New York: Appleton-Century-Crofts, 1969).

19. Jay Cohen, "The Corrections Academy: The Emergence of a New Criminal Justice System Institution," mimeographed (Cornell University, 1977).

20. For a start in this direction, see James B. Jacobs and Harold G. Retsky, "Prison Guard."

Chapter 4

Prison Guard*

James B. Jacobs
and
Harold G. Retsky

Unlike the police who have been the subject of considerable attention in recent years, the role and person of the prison guard systematically have been ignored. Neither Clemmer (1958) nor Sykes (1966) in their classic studies of prison communities pauses long to consider the *career* of the guard. What others have said about guards is mostly by way of lament over their meager education, poor training, provincial world view, and sometimes sadistic personality traits. The more complimentary treatments cite the difficulties of the work and the subsistence wages, recommending that censure be withheld in the light of the circumstances (see Roucek, 1935).

Surely there is a need to develop a fuller literature on the prison guard, not only because of their crucial importance to all questions of prison reform, but also because of their significance as social control agents organized within a paramilitary regime. In addition, close attention to this occupation may sensitize us to the moral division of labor as well as to the organization of "dirty work" (Hughes, 1958) within formal organizations. We offer an ethnographic picture of the prison guard gained from the scarce literature on the subject, our own substantial contact with maximum security prisons, and formal interviews with more than thirty prison guards at various stages of their careers at Stateville Penitentiary, Joliet, Illinois.[1]

THE ROLE

While it is a central theme of this report that guards can be distinguished according to the kind of work they are assigned, their rank within the paramilitary organization, and their length of service, it is necessary to examine the dimensions of the role common to all prison guards.

The prison guard's role immediately can be distinguished from the role of those who guard objects in order to protect them. Brinks guards, military sentinels, Secret Service Agents, and those who guard nuclear materials are concerned with external threats to the objects they are

---

* Copyright 1975, Gage Publications, Inc. Reprinted with permission from *Urban Life*, Vol. 4, No. 1.

protecting. The situation is radically different for the prison guard whose task involves protecting the surrounding community from the possibility of contamination by exposure to convicted men. While the Secret Service Agent enjoys a community of interest with the individual whom he is guarding, the prison guard from the outset owns an interest diametrically opposed to the inmates left to his charge.

The inmate rarely will see restrictions on his freedom within the prison as necessary or legitimate, while such measures as counts, shakedowns, and controlled inmate movements may be essential if the small number of guards is to successfully manage the vastly greater number of inmates among the hodgepodge of buildings, tunnels, corridors, yards, and gates that characterize mega-prisons like Stateville.

The prison's primary goal is to contain securely those convicted men assigned to its charge. The plain fact is that the inmate does not want to be in prison. Indeed, a small number are likely to be frequently reassessing opportunities for escape. Prisoners cannot be treated or trained if they cannot be held. The public will not tolerate escapes. In fact, escapes and riots are the only two occurrences likely to focus momentary public attention on the prison.

Prevention of escape and riot is the primary task around which the role of the guard is organized. Closely related is maintenance of a modicum of internal order and security. In recent years chilling stories of gang rapes and assaults among inmates have been reported in the press and before Congress. Such developments call attention to the fact that the guard is involved in adjudicating claims over residual freedom among conflicting groups (Werthman and Piliavin, 1967).

Aside from these primary goals the prison as a total institution necessarily generates several subsidiary goals connected with people-processing (Goffman, 1961). In any large-scale total institution, there is a whole range of maintenance tasks that must be carried out under staff supervision of inmate laborers. In the prison, new inmates must be processed, clothing must be laundered, medicine must be distributed, food must be prepared, lavatories must be kept clean, dining rooms and living quarters must be cared for; in short, the institution must be kept running. In the great mega-prisons plagued by low budgets and high turnover this requires no small amount of organization and coordination of human energies.

To the primary goal of preventing escapes, riots, and predatory behavior, rehabilitation has been added. That these primary and secondary goals are fundamentally incompatible is the subject of considerable comment (for example, Janowitz and Vinter, 1959). It is not surprising that contradictory organizational goals have caused conflict in such organizational micro-units as the guard role. Under the role prescriptions dictated by the rehabilitative ideal, the guard is to relax and to act spontaneously. Inmates are to be "understood," not blamed, and formal disciplinary mechanisms should be triggered as infrequently as possible. These are vague directives. Cressey (1960) argues that no more precise rules concerning the "how" of rehabilitation can be formulated since the essence of rehabilitation work, as practiced by "professionals," lies in treating each individual as unique according to professional judgment, which belies adherence to hard and fast rules. What is allowed one prisoner may be denied another depending on evaluation of individual needs.

Where guards have attempted to follow these vague role prescriptions, they have often met with frustration. Inmates themselves believe that differential treatment based on individual needs requires professional competence. While competency and proficiency may be imputed to psychologists and social workers based on academic credentials, inmates are quick to point out that they will grant no such discretionary authority to "screws." The very essence of the professional's authority lies in his claim to charisma while the guard's only basis for authority is his rank within the caste system.

The rehabilitative ideal has no clear directives for the administration of a large-scale people-processing institution. In order to carry out primary tasks and to manage large numbers of men and materials, bureaucratic organization and impersonal treatment are necessary. Furthermore, to distinguish between inmates on the basis of psychological needs leaves the non-professional open to charges of gross bias, discrimination, and injustice.[2]

Treatment personnel in their administrative capacities are likely to hold guards responsible for preventing escapes and riots, ensuring order, and maintaining the prison as a smoothly functioning institution. The consequence of these contradictory demands on the guard is evidenced by the extremely high rates of staff turnover. At Stateville the turnover is greater than 100% per year and much higher among new guards since there does exist a sizeable proportion of guards with long years of service.

The old-timers complain about not knowing what is required of them and look back nostalgically to the "old days" when they knew what their job entailed and how they would be evaluated.[3]

> During Ragen's days you knew every day what you were suppose to do and now you are in a position where there are too many supervisors and too many changing rules. First one will come and tell you its got to be done this way and then somebody else comes along and says to do something different. In the old days we knew what our job was.

Guards are more likely to fall back on their security and maintenance role because it is the only one on which they can be objectively evaluated. No guard will be reprimanded or dismissed for failure to communicate meaningfully with inmates. On the other hand, the guard whose carelessness smooths the way for an escape or whose lack of vigilance contributes to opportunity for a stabbing or rape will most likely find himself out of a job.

THE CAREER

Individuals do not grow up aspiring to become prison guards. Only 1% of teenagers surveyed by Lou Harris indicated that they had given any consideration to a career in prison. Our data indicate that the decision to seek employment as a guard usually came after a period of unemployment (the State Office of Employment Services regularly refers applicants), a layoff, or a physical accident that made previous work (e.g., mining) impossible.

> Well they had this piece in the paper, see I'm from Hamilton County; that's about 300 miles south of here. And they was wanting guards. I knew several fellows used to work here from down there at the time. The dust — the corn dust — I'm allergic to it and the lint off a cattle. So there's this place to go to Vermont to take a civil service examination. So I just drove up there that day and I took that civil service examination and in about 3 weeks, why they called me up to the Menard Penitentiary.

In spite of the fact that the State of Illinois has no residency requirement, does not demand a high school diploma, will accept men from 18 to 55 years of age, has even dropped the written civil service examination (substituting an oral examination to determine ability to communicate rules and orders), and has substantially increased its pay scale (approximately $10,000 after certification) there remains a chronic shortage of applicants. If, as Bittner suggests, "police work is a tainted occupation" (Bittner, 1970), then prison guard work is utterly polluted.[4] While Secret Service Agents and Brinks guards may achieve esteem from their contact with the objects they are guarding, close contact with convicted felons seems morally profaning for the guard. Even close friends do not know what to make of the prevailing belief that prison guards are sadistic, corrupt, stupid, and incompetent.

The stigmatization of the job, the peculiar working hours, and the frequent isloation of the prisons in out-of-the-way places make for a certain esprit and solidarity among the guards. Like the police, guards may sometimes view themselves as a society apart. This is especially true where the prisons have supplied dormitories and other facilities for living quarters. Stateville Penitentiary maintains both a dormitory for bachelors and a trailer park for married couples on prison property beyond the walls. The subculture which develops in these closed communities promotes a parochial and defensive world view.

The shortage of guards and the high turnover rate have important consequences. The chief guard needs bodies to fit into work slots around the prison and tends to see those who do not show up for work for any reason as spiting him and the institution. The constant pressure to fill the gaps in the various institutional assignments out of an unreliable work force causes the captains to view subordinates as objects. At Stateville absenteeism is staggering, sometimes approaching 40%. In a job that has few objective criteria for evaluating performance, simply reporting for work is likely to become the most important factor on which the new guard will be rated.

Being a prison guard is a dead end. To date no career ladders have been built to reward those guards who have shown particular promise on the job. The skills necessary for guarding usually are not transferable to other situations except to lower-paying jobs in private security. While a few individuals have been promoted through the ranks to sergeant, lieutenant, and captain (and even warden), these opportunities often close early in the guard's career and the increasing professionalization of prison administration makes the availability of such administrative opportunities in the future even less likely. Without an outside sponsor or an immediate acceptance into the dominant clique, the guard will have to wait many years for promotion to sergeant, if indeed he is ever promoted at all.

Claims of favoritism in promotions are a common complaint and another cause of resentment.

> I think most of the supervising personnel is unqualified, they got their position through friendships, and I think some example of what I am talking about is you have a man over you. You've been here three weeks and you can see the man is inefficient. Why can't his supervisor see that he is inefficient? And you can see it. And if you will check some of the supervisors' educational background and go to their personal files, you will come up with something else. I've met a lot of people who've started here from the time that I've been here and I think we've wasted a lot of time and the main gripe that we've had is that supervisory officers have a way of degrading men; treating men like they're beneath them and causing difficulty.

The social distance between higher-echelon guards and the new recruit parallels the social distance between the recruit and the inmates he is assigned to guard. At Stateville this organizational distance is reinforced by the different backgrounds of the high-ranking guards and old-timers and the vast majority of new recruits. The former have traditionally been recruited from rural southern Illinois while the latter increasingly are being drawn from the minority population of Chicago. There are many illustrations in the literature of the difficulties in becoming accepted in the closed prison community (Cronin, 1967: 114). Because most guards do not stay beyond the first year or two, old-timers will tend to remain aloof until the end of this period.[5] This informal probationary period may be more trying than the formal one.

The social distance between lower- and higher-level guards is further reinforced by the paramilitary organization which passes information upward while initiative and decisions flow in the reverse direction. The line officer is often under the same kind of scrutiny as the inmate under his surveillance. Alleged trafficking in contraband is held to justify periodic shakedowns of the line officers. In addition, it is not unusual to have a lieutenant inspect both guards and inmates at an assignment to see that they are working. Just as guards are required to write tickets (disciplinary reports) on inmate rule violators, so too do superiors (and sometimes inmates) make written reports on guard infractions of the rules. Guards also are encouraged to write tickets on each other. The disciplinary board for guards is quite similar to the tribunal that hears inmate cases.

> I was disciplined once because I took a shoeshine in the barber shop and which only takes about six minutes. There was a sign in the shop which had fallen down forbidding this. But I did not see it. A captain spotted me and wrote me up, which was only his job and for which I hold no grudge, but I do feel he could have warned me that he was writing me up. I had no knowledge this had happened until I got a letter two weeks later telling me I had to go before the review board. They gave me three days off without pay. I think I was dealt with harshly. One man shouldn't take food from you.

The advent of the union movement has served to strengthen the line officer in his position relative to higher-echelon guards, although this has been attenuated by the membership of all levels of guards in the union and by the difficulties of developing a viable collective bargaining procedure in the public sector. Unlike the police union which is closed to supervisory personnel, the guards' union (although not the bargaining unit at the present time) includes all uniformed guards and civilian counselors as well. According to one informant, the attempt to limit union membership to line personnel was unsuccessful because without top-echelon guards there was an insufficient number of men with adequate qualifications to run the union. When one of the line officers who had served as secretary was promoted to sergeant, there was no one else with the educational skills to handle the job, so a decision was made to retain the secretary and to open the union to all.

Not only does the prison guard occupy a low social status in the outside community, he also experiences the disdain and sometimes open contempt of prison professionals. Thomas (1972) argues that in England over the past two decades, the prison administration formed a kind of alliance with inmates. While this has not occurred so dramatically in the United States, it would not be an exaggeration to say that administrators and professional treatment personnel feel more respect and greater affinity for the inmate than they do for the guard.

Increasingly top prison administrators have come to justify their careers in terms of an ethos of public service. Whether professionals and administrators will be evaluated as successful in their jobs depends to some degree on the statements that inmates make to lawyers, visitors, and the press. Recent court decisions have made administrators doubly conscious of the importance of staff/inmate relations. If riots, work stoppages, and demonstrations are to be avoided, inmates must be somewhat placated. Their demands must be taken, to some degree, into account.

Professionals from the domains of social service and psychology often hold to a view of inmates as individuals with deficiencies that need to be erased so that successful readjustment to the society will be possible. In effect, the success of their career depends on their ability to get along with and to "convert" inmates. Relationships with guards are in no way essential to the careers of treatment personnel. On the contrary, the guards serve as a convenient scapegoat for the lack of success that has attended most efforts at rehabilitation. It always can be argued that the guards have been engaged in subverting the program and plotting against the best efforts of modern penology.[6]

The Work

Many of the principles used to describe continuous mass-production organizations are also applicable to the prison where argot refers to inmates being "worked," "fed," and "housed." The most obvious characteristics about prison work are its routine and boredom. The prison is to a great degree an institution isolated from the day-to-day exigencies of the outside world. It is a closed and timeless society where days, weeks, and months have little to distinguish them. With the exception of infrequent riots, few exceptional happenings are likely to occur. One day's routine is like the next. "Most guards having nothing to do but stand guard; they do not use inmates productively any more than they themselves are used productively by prison managers. Guards manage and are managed in organizations where management is an end, not a means" (Cressey, 1965).

DIVISION OF LABOR

Just as an understanding of the division of labor in the police department is vital for the study of that organization and of the police as an occupation (see Skolnick, 1966), so too it is necessary to note that prison guards are not a monolithic work force, but engage in a variety of tasks that bring them differentially into contact with administrators, inmates, and outsiders. That a single individual may be called on over time to perform many work tasks does not belie the significance of each work assignment in generating unique problems requiring different skills. While prison guards carry on numerous activities ranging from transporting inmates to and from court to sitting on disciplinary boards, we will concentrate here on three broad areas of guard work carried on in living units, work units, and security units.

The cell house is the basic living unit of the traditional maximum security prison. At Stateville Penitentiary, each circular cell house holds approximately 250 inmates, supervised by two, three, four, or five guards, depending on the shift and who shows up for work. In the course of a day's work the cell house guard, stationed at the gate, is required to open and to close the steel-barred door allowing entrance and exit to inmates whose work or visits require movement in and out of the cell house. Another guard may distribute medicine, mail, and laundry, answer telephones, and supervise maintenance activities. A third guard is positioned in a tower in the middle of the cell house from where he can see into every cell. The most important responsibility of the cell house guard is conducting the "count" whereby the staff determines several times a day if all inmates are present and accounted for. A proper count in a cell house is the most important single activity of the daily routine. If there is a miscount (either short or over), all operations and movement cease. Depending on the time it takes to rectify the mistake, the guard may suffer punishment, from reprimand to dismissal.

After the escape of three prisoners in 1972, four Stateville guards were fired. One of these men did not report for work until 3:00 p.m. and the escape had occurred at 1:30. He discovered the escape at the 6:00 p.m. count, but was fired for not alerting the institution to the escape earlier by checking out the movement chart in the cell house.

Not unmindful of the significance of the count, inmates can withhold cooperation in order to place an unpopular guard's job in jeopardy. They may attempt to elude the counting officer by hiding in their cell or by shuffling back and forth if the count is taken while the inmates are in line entering the cell house. In either case, the delay and disruption of the prison routine will be attributed to the guard who is responsible, and he will earn both formal censure and informal derision from his colleagues.

The guards who work the cell houses are the busiest in the institution. The need for cooperation in carrying out maintenance tasks (distribution of mail and medicine, running telephone lines, feeding, overseeing maintenance, and so forth) and in conducting the count brings the guard to increasing reliance on his clerk and other key inmates.

> I was lucky in that I had a sharp, smart and concerned inmate working for me. Whatever benefits he received from our relationship, it was understood that he had to pay for by helping maintain a correct count. He knew how many left the cell house; how many returned and where every man was at a given time. When I finished

the count of each gallery and called the number to him he could verify this with his figures. At one particular count, after I had been working with him for 18 months, I miscounted and he verified the count as correct when in fact it was incorrect. This continued three more times so that I delayed the count over three hours until at the fifth count, I came up with the correct answer. Needless to say, I heard from my clerk, who in spite of the advantage the job offered him, immediately offered to resign and when I turned this down, was apologetic about the affair for months afterward. He made many overtures to keep my good will and prove to me that his error was only a ridiculous one time error that could never happen again. And, in fact, it never did as long as we worked together.

The cell house is the most dangerous place for the guard. Inside the cell house of a mega-prison guards are clearly at the mercy of the inmates. In case of emergency there is no fast exit. At any time the guard knows that he could be siezed and held hostage. Not only might an unpopular cell house guard be treated roughly during a riot, he might at any time be assaulted, thrown off a gallery, or pelted with objects thrown from the upper tiers. During the 11:00 p.m.-7:00 a.m. shift, when lights are out, objects such as steel bearings, bed springs, or paper clips are thrown or shot with the aid of rubber bands or spring devices at the guards.

The majority of guards during the day shift are assigned to work areas — the mechanical store, the metal factory, or the yard gang. Some are assigned to maintenance crews in the cell house. These guards are somewhat analogous to factory foremen although, as Cressey (1965) points out, the guard really has no counterpart in the business or industrial world.

It is not rare to enter a prison workshop and see no activity whatsoever. The guard may be found sitting in an office or standing in a corner talking to a colleague. The guard at the work area does not need more than a very minimal amount of compliance from the men assigned to him. Even this, however, may place the guard in a position where he is likely to have his authority "corrupted by reciprocity" (Sykes, 1956). In order to meet minimum requirements (boxes have to be warehoused, furniture has to be repaired), the guard may be willing to overlook certain breaches of the rules.

This ultimately may prove an unstable accommodation if inmates continue to demand greater favors for the same conformity. The newly recruited guard's first orientation to the prison invariably includes the warning to remain aloof from inmates lest the cycle of corruption and blackmail destroy the guard's career.[7] Until a recent policy change, guards at Stateville were not allowed either to offer or to accept a light from an inmate on the rationale that any nonessential contact, no matter how superficial, ultimately would be corrupting.

It also seems that the guard in the work area establishes the closest relations with inmates. Perhaps men who work together for years often develop a camaraderie. Work assignments usually consist of a reasonably small number of inmates, and conversation between inmates and guards develops spontaneously. It also happens that there are guards assigned to workshops who have skills which they pass along to inmates. Those inmates who learn to weld or to repair a TV set may be grateful to their "teacher." At Stateville, Mr. V., the guard in charge of sheet metal, is among the few men who is held in great respect by the inmates. He is not only considered a good teacher, but is constantly seeking to place inmates in industry upon release.

It is not unlikely that work assignment guards and their subordinates will sometimes develop friendships and will come to see each other as individuals. One guard noted that it is not rare for a guard "to unburden things to an inmate that he would not tell his wife." It is under the conditions of small work groups in the industries and in the cell houses that it is most possible for the guard's authority to be "eroded through friendship" (Sykes, 1956).

The work unit guard often may become dependent on his men for the skill and expertise which they have developed over the years. As prisons are chronically understaffed, it seems natural that one small task after another will be delegated by the guard to inmates anxious to ingratiate themselves and to keep busy in an environment where lack of work and boredom are endemic. At times a locksmith, machine operator, or agricultural worker becomes indispensable to the prison regime. This is reinforced by the fact that the turnover rate in many prisons is so great that many work areas will find an inexperienced guard directing an inmate group in a task that he knows nothing about.

There are two security jobs in the maximum security prison that need to be distinguished: the tower and the gate. Traditionally, assignment to the guard towers along the prison wall had been reserved for recruits, old-timers who are partially incapacitated, and guards who are unable to manage inmates or who tend to harass them, although in recent years the increased violence in some prisons has led old-time guards to request transfer to the towers. The position is not likely to attract many volunteers. The loneliness, uncomfortable temperatures, and boredom are calculated to make this task more like a punishment than a viable job assignment.

The guard on the tower pulls a regular shift of 8 hours and often 8½ depending on when his relief arrives. At Stateville, his lunch is delivered in a metal cannister which is hauled up to the tower by rope. During the winter, coal for a 50-year-old, pot-bellied stove is hauled up in the same fashion. The stove is inadequate to heat the tower because of wind leaking through the windows. If you are close enough to the stove for heat, it becomes unbearably hot; if you watch the yard and road running alongside the wall, you have to move away from the stove, thereby exposing yourself to the bitter cold. In the summer, the towers are always intolerably hot; the only relief is being supplied an ice container hauled up along with the food.

The tower guard is alone. Except for telephone and walkie-talkie communication with the security headquarters, he has no contact with other individuals during the eight-hour shift. It is forbidden to bring either a radio or reading matter into the tower. The guard caught reading or dozing is dealt with quite harshly. Indeed, he is liable to be fired on the spot by the shift commander.

Tower work places the guard in a position of confrontation vis-à-vis inmates. If there be any doubt as to the nature of the institution or as to the purpose of the custodial staff, the inmate may merely glance at the walls. The tower guard symbolizes the stern hand of the community that has placed him in exile. The interaction between the tower guard and the inmate is continuous and uncomplicated. For the most part it consists merely in the positioning of the actors. No words are exchanged. The guard always has the inmate under surveillance while the inmate always must take the tower guard into account. One guard noted: "The guard on the tower is so far removed from the human element that it becomes impossible for him to see a man. He can only see a problem and has the immediate resolution for this in his hand."

The tower guard himself is placed in an uncomfortable position, both physically and existentially. The rules relating to the use of deadly force are ambiguous. In addition, there are those whose training and experience with firearms are such as to raise doubts about their ability to act decisively at the critical moment. However, with respect to the use of weapons, all guards indicated to us that they viewed this as just another aspect of the job.

> That doesn't bother me in the least. If I had to use the weapons, I would use them. Uh, if a person's whole life was in danger, like say you was in the yard, and if two or three or maybe just one would jump you, and was trying to take your life, I would put a few rounds off in the air to stop them for a warning and then I would do my best to wound him to bring him off of you but if it didn't do any good and I only wounded him and if he started at you again and then if I had to put him out for good, I would. If his intention is to kill you or any personnel then he's going to do it knowing that he's going to die, knowing that he might lose his own life. He's gotten to the point where he doesn't care. Because it may be me down there some time. And if someone's trying to kill me, I would definitely want to live. I'd want this person off of me. I wouldn't want my life drained out on the ground because somebody's sittin' in the tower and not doing anything about it.

On entering the maximum security prison as an outsider, one is frisked, stamped, and checked by guards standing at gates each successively closer to the heart of the prison. At Stateville, there are four iron gates; each has a guard assigned to it. The guard is not permitted to open the gate unless the visitor is with a staff member or has been approved. The gate is an attractive job for an ambitious individual. It gives one the opportunity to be in constant touch with top-echelon security people and administrators. Assignment to the gate is often a sure indication that sergeant stripes are forthcoming.

It is the guards at the gates and those stationed in the visiting room who actually present the face of the institution to the stream of outsiders (students, relatives, lawyers, legislators, and so on) who enter the prison each day. They have a high number of brief and superficial contacts with staff, inmates, and outsiders. Different social skills are required in this work role than in those roles requiring more sustained contact with inmates. Top staff are sensitive to the fact that the staff often may be judged by the behavior and appearance of those guards in these front-line positions. Conscious efforts are made to choose those who will make the best impression. Even then, however, tension is likely to develop between the guards and visitors who resent having their motives for entering the prison questioned by searches and other security measures.

Inmates passing through the gates are required to have a "pass" and are "patted down" at each gate. For some inmate runners who pass back and forth through the gates many times a day, the patting down may be a particularly humiliating dramatization of their lowly and unworthy status. In order to normalize the interaction between gate keeper and those inmates who move frequently through the gates, the patting down becomes a ritual in which the guard attempts by his detachment, inattention, and speed to show that this is a mere formality, not an impeachment of the inmate's character.

SERGEANTS, LIEUTENANTS, AND CAPTAINS

It is important to emphasize that the diversion of labor sketched above is applicable only to the lowest-ranking guard — the line officer. In Illinois there are three ranks of guard higher than the line officer — sergeant, lieutenant, and captain. The chief guard recently has been promoted to the new rank of major.

The work of a sergeant is almost identical to that of a sergeant in the army. He is not only directly familiar with the work of the line officer, but often fills in as a line officer, manages the unit he is assigned to, and participates in specific jobs that require special responsibility such as gate keeper at various key points in the institution. In addition, a sergeant is usually in charge of cell houses, work units, and the hospital.

Lieutenants function as a police force within the prison. When there is any kind of disturbance in a cell house or on a work assignment, the lieutenants immediately will be called to the scene to deal with the problem. If an inmate must be "walked" to isolation or forcibly removed from his cell, this task will be carried out by the lieutenants. When they are not responding to trouble, the lieutenants roam about the institution making checks and shakedowns on inmates and lower-ranking guards.

There are only a handful of captains among the guards. They rarely have time to exercise first-hand supervision of the general prison area, but instead are assigned either to full-time administrative responsibility or to shift commands. Increasingly, they have been saddled with greater and greater amounts of paper work regarding such matters as personnel evaluations and budgets. At Stateville, during the day shift, one captain sits as chairman of the assignment committee, a second is in charge of the disciplinary committee, and a third functions as head of the security force and operates out of a control room. The power of the captains has dwindled in recent years with increasing responsibility for the management of the prison being assumed by college-educated professionals and administrators. The very committee structure alluded to above signifies the loss of an authority that was once both unchecked and unquestioned.

The Guard's World

That man's work tends to shape his view of the world is a common notion in sociology. Similarly, the position of an individual within a social setting goes far in shaping his perceptions and behavior. The total institution is a pervasive organization for guards as well as inmates. The concrete walls which lock the inmate inside also lock society out; the guard's daily contacts are limited to inmates and a few staff members. In this situation, both inmates and guards become deeply committed to their organizational roles.

The guard's world has increasingly come to be pervaded by fear and uncertainty. Within the maximum security prison, guards carry no weapons because they might be overpowered by the great number of inmates and have the weapons turned against them. Ironically, many inmates are armed or have easy access to lethal weapons like shivs, razors, iron pipes, bats, and broken glass.

> I was back there on the job when it broke out. I was frightened. I think every officer out there was frightened because we had no weapons. The tower officers — they didn't know exactly what to do. They were firing warning shots. You couldn't see clearly what they were doing, so you didn't know whether to duck, run or stand still — and then you look at the inmates and they are coming with sticks, baseball bats, iron bars and all this stuff. Any man who says he wasn't afraid, I'd have to call him a liar.

Tension continually looms over the prison threatening to explode into assault or even riot. This is drilled into the recruit during his first training classes. The guard's manual stresses the need for vigilance and alertness lest the unexpected take one unaware. Not only is the new guard exposed to the word-of-mouth stories of fellow students and training officers, but at the prison he immediately may be exposed to situations which confirm his worst fears.

> When I arrived, I was almost immediately assigned to "B" house which contained a gallery known as 3-gallery lock-up. The inmates here had been under constant lock and key for almost a year. As a result of this, they were acting like animals and their verbal abuse scared the shit out of me. I decided then and there to turn in my resignation but was talked out of it by my supervising officer.

Similar to Skolnick's (1966) findings on the police, few prison guards speak openly about fear, although they attribute such concern to their wives and families. In recent years, assaults on prison guards have become more common. At Stateville in 1973, the first killing of a prison guard in decades occurred when a guard was thrown off a high gallery. Not only has this demoralized the prison staff, it also has made them chronically apprehensive. There are three apparent strategies for dealing with this fear: becoming increasingly repressive, courting acceptance with the inmates, or retreating from duty and responsibility. All three strategies are very much in evidence in Stateville. The first is most common among the lieutenants, the second among new guards, and the third among old-timers.

Not only guards, but inmates too, live with an anticipation of violence. Perhaps awareness of this contributes to a normalization of relationships and a day-to-day accommodation. Inmates and guards share a small, shut-off, physical space as well as common language, diet, and each other's constant companionship. The fact that so much distance separates line officers from top-echelon decision makers places guards in the same position as inmates with respect to a feeling of powerlessness. Often line officers and the inmates in their charge will share a common definition of administration, and the lieutenants and captains will see their positions as being constrained by uninformed and ill-advised superordinates.

> I often put myself in the inmate's position. If I was locked up and the door was locked up and my only contact with authorities would be the officer walking by, it would be frustrating if I couldn't get him to listen to the problems I have. There is nothing worse than being in need of something and not being able to supply it yourself and having the man who can supply it ignore you: This almost makes me explode inside.

Guards and inmates also share similar socioeconomic backgrounds. Many black guards have known inmates on the streets. White guards, too, are not drawn from the more law-abiding middle class, but usually are drawn from delinquency-prone groups where scrapes with the authorities during teenage years were not uncommon. Where guards and inmates interact in living units and working units day after day, there may be subtle psychological pressures on the line officer to identify with the prisoners unless he can develop a theory to account for his differentness from the inmate population. One important function of the guard's uniform, for example, may be to sharply distinguish him from the inmates (Roucek, 1935).

Goffman (1961: 87) argues that within total institutions there is a tendency for ideology to develop to explain the nature of those under control. "This theory rationalizes activity, provides a subtle means of maintaining social distance, allows a stereotyped view of inmates and justifies the treatment accorded them." In general, prison guards tend to view inmates as morally inferior. Kirson Weinberg, one of the earliest students of the prison community, lends support to this assertion (quoted in Barnes and Teeters, 1943: 721).

> The officials, especially the guards, regard the convicts as "criminals after all"; as "people who can't and shouldn't be trusted", and as "degenerates who must be put in their place at all times". "You can't be too easy with them," states one custodian. . . . "They're on the go to put one over on you. They don't think about us when they try to get over the wall". "There must be something wrong with every man here," states another, "else he wouldn't be here. They're scheming all the time, soon as you give them an inch. That's because there's something wrong with every one of them." Convicts are considered "born bad"; as mentally or emotionally or morally deficient.

This stereotypical view of inmates is more prevalent among the lieutenants and captains, who must be thought of as the "tradition bearers" of the institution. Their distance from inmates and their long tenure within the institution seem to insulate them from seeing inmates as individuals. They have become most firmly committed to an emergent ideology.

This view of the inmate can be distinguished from the police officer's view of the felon. The latter views the felon as vicious and evil, while the former sees the inmate as sick, inadequate, disgusting, and degenerate. The difference is not due to a greater acceptance of the rehabilitative ideal on the part of the prison guard, but to the difference in the setting in which the policeman and guard interact with the criminal.

The police interact with the felon on the street. Unlike the guard, they are likely to have had a first-hand view of the victim and to have personalized society's quarrel with the criminal. The guard does not see the inmate until many months (or even years) after the crime, and he normally is unaware of the facts involved. In addition, the stripping of the inmate's identity, the drabness of his prison garb, the obliteration of his hair style all tend to make him less fearsome appearing in prison than he was on the street.

The prison organization is calculated to reduce the inmate to a child. With respect to medicine, for example, no more than one dose at a time is distributed even if the inmate will have to rely on the guard four times during the day for his pills. No matter what a man is occupied with in his cell, when count is called he must stand up and face front. If he is occupied in a bowel movement, he has to raise a hand and other inmates in the cell are required to point to him. The guard is likely to believe that the inmate is not a healthy, competent male, but stupid and inadequate. This view is reinforced by the behavior the inmate exhibits on entrance into the prison. No matter how street-wise the criminal is, commitment to prison will be somewhat of a disorienting experience. Dealing with the regimentation, lack of privacy, and new normative system, the prisoner may appear clumsy and unsure of himself. Certainly behaviors such as homosexuality go far in suggesting to the guard that the inmate is a moral degenerate.

> I think they (homosexuals) are sick. There are a lot of them in prison. . . . It's a disease the way I look at it. Maybe the man is sick and needs help from a doctor.

Guards do not view all inmates as degenerate. On the contrary, it is common to hear guards speak of good and bad inmates. Like all others in the criminal justice system, gradations of degeneracy are recognized. Some inmates thought to be wealthy or to have important ties in the professional underworld are respected, even admired.

At Stateville, guards make no distinctions among inmates on the basis of offense. Inmates are judged on how willingly they conform to authority. While the prevailing ideology prescribes abhorrence for the "no good son-of-a-bitch" inmates as a class, exceptions are made in individual cases. The "good inmate," like the "good nigger," cooperates with the guard, knows his place, and keeps to himself — in short, he does his own time. The "no good" inmate causes trouble for the guard by insisting on his rights and privileges: mail, medicine, telephone calls, and the like.

Stateville guards do not openly indicate racist attitudes. Whatever prejudices may exist are kept to one's self. This is in sharp contrast to studies of the police which have found an abundance of openly stated racist comments (Stark, 1972) and to other prison studies which have stressed the blatant racism among guards (Wright, 1973). Even in informal discussions, we have not heard guards refer to black inmates as "niggers" or in other racist terms, although whites continue to be disproportionately represented in better "up front" jobs. We suspect that much that has been explained as racist attitudes toward inmates in the literature stems from the organizationally sponsored conflict between guards and inmates.[8]

In a prison like Stateville, where blacks constitute 80% of the inmate population, racism may be a dead letter. There are too few whites to make white/black distinctions significant. The guards come to distinguish instead between the good and bad inmates among the blacks. On the other hand, evidence seems to indicate growing racial tension between white and black guards both in the barracks and sometimes on the job.

In general, prison guards are cynical about rehabilitation and the work of treatment agents within the prison. They feel that they see the prisoner 24 hours a day and are in a better position to judge the man's sincerity and true commitment to group therapy and other treatment programs. Inmates cannot be rehabilitated if that means that something is to be done to them by outside agents. Instead, they believe that a man can only change if he is motivated to do so — and this appears to be a characteristic of the individual and to have nothing to do with the organization and its therapists. Like the policeman and all those who must assume the capacity of clients to carry out their tasks, the guard adheres to a radical free-will theory of man and human behavior.

Notes

1. J. Jacobs has been conducting research at Stateville Penitentiary and at other maximum security prisons for two years. H. Retsky served two years as a guard at Stateville and currently is serving as a clinical counselor at that institution.

2. The same tension between equal treatment and recognition of the "special case" is discussed in the mental hospital context by Stanton and Schwartz (1954).

3. The Morrises (1963: 84) make a similar observation about nostalgia among the guards in their classic study of an English prison.

4. Attempts to ease the stigma by upgrading the job usually suggest placing more treatment responsibility on the guard according to a "collaborative model" of corrections. As prisons have been renamed Correctional Centers to improve their public image, so guards have been rechristened Correctional Officers, although they continue to refer to themselves as guards. The importance of the name as a symbol of the work is evident in the following communication received from Stateville's former warden, Joseph G. Cannon, after reading an early draft: "It bothers me a bit to see the term 'prison guard' utilized in reference to such a study. Most people, I am sure, understand who the correctional officer is and certainly, with the changing of terminology from

penitentiary to correctional centers, it would seem consistent to work on the image of the staff by adopting correctional officers as a reference to those men and women who wear the uniforms and play the initial roles which they do. Why does 'guard' die such a slow death. . . . The self concept we're trying to create at Stateville is certainly not of a 'guard' vintage."

5. There is an obvious schism among those prison guards who regard their job as a life's career and those for whom it is only a brief phase. Surveying all prison guards in the country, the Joint Commission on Correctional Manpower and Training found that 20% had three or less years of experience while 36% had more than ten years. For the student of the prison community this fact suggests the existence of distinct factions. Austin (1973) found that the length of time served as a guard correlates significantly with negative attitudes toward inmates. If this conclusion held up under more rigorous testing, it might illuminate a phenomenon similar to the cynicism attributed to veteran police. In addition, it is highly important to note the points in the career when guards "drop out." A comprehensive study of prison guards would require a concentration on drop-outs as well as on incumbents.

6. See, for example, McCleery's (1960) account of the revolt of the old guard power structure at Oahu Prison when a new liberal regime attempted to introduce reform principles.

7. Note the following sober warning presented as a model for guard training by the American Correctional Association (n.d.: 23). "Bribery usually begins as a result of being too intimate with inmates. They offer a cigar, cigarettes, or some trivial article. Each time this is done a closer contact is made and finally they come through with what they really want the officer to do. They may work the officer into a compromising position by securing information from him which may make it appear to his superiors that he has been passing on confidential or department information. Or it may be that an inmate is a witness to some incident involving the officer, and which, if known, would not add to his reputation for efficiency and reliability. Self-protection, being a powerful instinct, the officer might ask the inmate to keep quiet or to falsify his testimony when questioned. This is the beginning of bribery, and it may get the officer on the inmate's payroll from that time on."

8. That the hostility which characterizes interaction between guards and inmates results from the "inherently pathological characteristics of the prison itself" (Situational Hypothesis) rather than from the individual's evil motives (Dispositional Hypothesis) is supported by the well-publicized social psychology experiment by Haney et al. (1973) wherein they simulated the prison situation by creating a "mock prison" in the basement of the psychology building at Stanford University and assigned Stanford University student volunteers randomly to the guard and inmate roles: "many of the subjects ceased distinguishing between prison role and their prior self-identities. When this occurred, within what was a surprisingly short period of time, we witnessed a sample of normal, healthy American college students fractionate into a group of prison guards who seemed to derive pleasure from insulting, threatening and dehumanizing their peers—those who by chance selection had been assigned to the 'prisoner' role."

References

American Correctional Association (n.d.) Correction Officers Training Guide.
Austin, J. (1973) "Attitudinal variation in correctional officers." (unpublished).
Barnes, H. and J. Teeters (1943) *New Horizons in Criminology*. Englewood Cliffs, N.J.: Prentice-Hall.
Bittner, E. (1970) *Functions of the Police in Modern Society*. Washington, D.C.: National Institute of Mental Health.
Clemmer, D. (1958) *The Prison Community*. New York: Holt, Rinehart & Winston.
Cressey, D. (1965) "Prison organization," 1023-1070 in J. March (ed.) *Handbook of Organizations*. New York: Rand McNally.
——— (1960) "Limitations on organization of treatment in the modern prison," 78-109 in R. Cloward et al. (eds.) *Theoretical Studies in Social Organization of the Prison*. New York: Social Science Research Council.
Cronin, H. (1967) *The Screw Turns*. London: John Long.
Goffman, E. (1961) *Asylums*. Garden City, N.Y.: Doubleday Anchor.
Haney, C., C. Banks, and P. Zimbardo (1973) "Interpersonal dynamics in a simulated prison." *International J. of Criminology and Penology* (January): 69-97.
Hughes, E. (1958) *Men and Their Work*. New York: Free Press.
Janowitz, M. and R. Winter (1959) "Effective institutions for juvenile delinquents: a research statement." *Social Service Rev.* 33 (June): 118-130.
Joint Commission on Correctional Manpower and Training (1969) *A Time to Act*. Washington, D.C.: Joint Commission on Correctional Manpower and Training.
Morris, P. and T. Morris (1963) *Pentonville: A Sociological Study of an English Prison*. London: Routledge & Kegan Paul.
McCleery, R. (1960) "Communication patterns as bases of systems of authority and power," 49-75 in R. Cloward et al. (eds.) *Theoretical Studies in Social Organization of the Prison*. New York: Social Science Research Council.
Roucek, J. (1935) "Sociology of the prison guard." *Sociology and Social Research* 20 (November): 145-151.
Skolnick, J. (1966) *Justice Without Trial*. New York: John Wiley.
Stanton, A. and M. Schwartz (1954) *The Mental Hospital*. London: Tavistock.
Stark, R. (1972) *Police Riots*. New York: Focus.
Sykes, G. (1966) *Society of Captives*. New York: Random House.
——— (1956) "The corruption of authority and rehabilitation." *Social Forces* 34 (March): 157-162.
Thomas, J. (1972) *The English Prison Officer Since 1850: A Study in Conflict*. London: Routledge & Kegan Paul.
Worthman, C. and I. Piliavin (1967) 56-98 in D. Bordua (ed.) *The Police: Six Sociological Essays*. New York: John Wiley.
Wright, E. (1973) *Politics of Punishment*. New York: Harper & Row.

Part III

SOCIAL SERVICE ROLE OF THE PRISON GUARD

... *how hard it is for a normal person to be helpful while being hated.*

Barrington, 1980: 51

The articles in this section serve to debunk the myth that prison guards are only turn-keys who automatically, and almost unthinkingly, perform routine duties as simple cogs in a machine which is designed only to maintain custody and control. Whereas at some times in the past, and in some assignments in most correctional institutions in the present, such a description accurately describes some of the guard's role, it is no longer an appropriate description of the guard's work.

As Elmer Johnson indicates in Chapter 5, the role that the correctional officer is expected to perform has, for a variety of reasons, changed markedly in recent years and guards have been required to perform much more complex *human management* tasks in the social system of the prison. Johnson discusses the implications of this change in terms of its effect on the guard's duties and his job satisfactions and suggests some of the organizational issues which must be addressed if correctional officers are to be expected, or required, to be "change agents."

In Chapter 6 Hans Toch further indicates how a narrow definition of the guard's role overlooks important aspects of the contributions they can and do make in de-escalating conflict, preventing crises, and promoting behavioral change. He illustrates his comments by presenting excerpts from interviews with guards and discusses some of the administrative initiatives which are required if the guard's contributions to inmate welfare and prison tranquility are to be fostered.

The prolonged debate on the treatment-custody problem in corrections epitomized the view that correctional officers were only custodians and that, almost by definition, their work was incompatible with that of the treatment staff. Robert Johnson's article in Chapter 7, shows that the debate erroneously divides correctional officers and treatment staff into opposing territories and fails to do justice to the important work that many corrections officers *actually* do in counseling and treatment. He describes the social service role played by guards who have expanded their assigned duties to include working with their peers in unofficial teams providing counseling and other assistance to inmates. Johnson discusses how such roles could and should be encouraged by modification of the human resource management policies and practices in the prison.

The final selection in this section by Richard Ward and David Vandergoot briefly describes and rationalizes a program in which correctional officers work as case managers and counselors for inmates, not in the more common informal way, but in an official, systematic program. The authors' comments suggest that the guard's activities in helping inmates, which are justifiable on humanitarian grounds, may also be justifiable on empirical grounds in terms of reducing institutional behavior problems.

Reference

Barrington, R., "Correctional officers don't do time." *Corrections Today*, 1980, March-April, 50-51.

Chapter 5
Changing World of the Correctional Officer*

Elmer H. Johnson

INSUFFICIENT STUDY OF CORRECTIONAL OFFICERS

The correctional institution has been the subject of many research projects and investigations, especially in the last several decades. For a large proportion of these studies, the inmate has been the focus of attention. Certainly, there are many reasons to examine the experiences and thoughts of those human beings who have lost their freedom and responsible control over their daily activities because of conviction for violations of the law.

But, correctional officers — as are the many other employees — also are inhabitants of the correctional institution. They endeavor to gain personal satisfactions and to carry out their responsibilities within the deliberately contrived world of this institution. When given attention in the past, officers were likely to be described in negative terms. They have been accused of polluting the trust of inmates, causing the failure of rehabilitative endeavors, and resisting necessary penal reform. Although there is evidence of such faults in particular instances, these criticisms have been excessive and the result is that all officers have been "tarred by the same brush" regardless of their different attitudes and behavior and regardless of the different demands imposed upon them by their work functions.

An important result of these critical excesses has been the development of a belief among many officers that they are a minority group suffering unwarranted stigmatization, being denied proper benefits, and being systematically subjected to a poverty of means for carrying out the custodial duties given them. Correctional officers as a group are expected to perform the tasks of custody and restraint that most citizens would like accomplished but prefer the accomplishment of these tasks be out of the public eye. Then, criticized by many of the persons who tacitly support custody and restraint, the officers in general are placed in a "no-win" situation.

---

* Reprinted with permission from *Tools for Trainers*. Carbondale, Illinois: Center for the Study of Crime, Delinquency & Corrections, Southern Illinois University, 1978.

There is little profit in condemning *all* officers for the faults of some when this condemnation diverts attention from the effects that the prison organization has — regardless of the behavior of any single individual — on the work of correctional officers. Instead of looking only at the collection of individual officers, we should examine the unique world of the prison which determines what their duties are and shapes how most of the officers carry out these duties.

TRENDS AFFECTING THE WORK OF THE CORRECTIONAL OFFICER

The world of the prison has been fundamentally changed in the last some fifty years because of general changes in American society. The broad trend of penological history has been from simple retaliation against criminals and exploitation of the labor of prisoners, toward humanitarian consideration of prisoners' living conditions and a conviction that conditions conducive to criminality can be overcome through treatment. All four of these themes in public reaction to criminals continue to be present in public attitudes. However, a strange ambivalence has come to characterize attitudes directed toward the custodial prison. There is advocacy of suppressive crime control of which the custodial prison is the ultimate instrument. Yet, the suspicion directed toward the custodial prison has made guarding appear to be a tainted occupation. In early prisons, surveillance and repression were clearly mandated, but with the rise of the treatment purpose, the correctional officer has been receiving conflicting instructions, i.e., that he be an agent of surveillance and yet somehow utilize his relationships with inmates to change their behavior constructively. There is no guidance on how these opposing purposes are to be accomplished simultaneously in light of the reality of his work with the inmates and with other institutional personnel.

"CHANGING THE SYSTEM" AS A SOLUTION

It is inevitable that these discouraging conditions continue to be faced by those persons held responsible for working directly and continuously with residents of correctional establishments. The last century has accelerated the consciousness among human beings that they are subject to the influences of *man-made* social systems. Further, there is dawning recognition that, since the systems are man-made, they are also vulnerable to changes by human beings. The custodial prison, as a place for utilizing confinement and as a means of changing criminals through punishment or treatment, has been developed in the last 200 years — a relatively brief period in terms of the sweep of history. Then, as a man-made system, the custodial prison is vulnerable to changes and, as an element in that system, so is the "prison guard" role.

As a social system, the custodial prison presents relatively fixed ways for the various staff members and inmates to relate to one another. Both staff and inmates have their unique personalities and private interests. The custodial prison links these qualities of the individuals to a general scheme for organizing their activities to serve the intended purposes of the prison. This linkage is made through status roles. Each individual occupies a position (a status) in the prison's organization. This position represents the prestige and authority over other members that a given individual holds. Also, this position describes the relationship of the duties and work of the other members. Thereby, the whole set of duties and work tasks are coordinated so the several members fit together into a "team" serving the ultimate purposes of the organization. Intimately associated with each status is a role: a set of behavioral expectations (norms) which guide the status-holder in what he or she *should* do and which are a basis for evaluating the task performance.

The "prison guard" occupies a place at the bottom of the positions which collectively comprise the custodial prison's organization. Therefore, he receives instructions (role norms) from those individuals holding positions of authority in higher levels of the organization. Significantly, as the occupants of the lowest status in the official organization, the "prison guard" has the most direct and continuous relationship with the inmates who are the "material" of this system.

The term "prison guard" is employed in a special way to outline the status-role characteristics produced by the social system and rationale of the custodial prison. The difficulties of the "prison guard" role will be considered in more detail. But, because these difficulties come from the operations of the custodial prison, the conviction that man-made systems can be changed by human beings supports the view that changing the prison as a social system will remedy the difficulties being experienced by "prison guards." Later, this paper will present the role of "correctional officer" as a more promising alternative.

AMBIVALENT INTERPRETATION OF "PRISON GUARD"

The term "prison guard" is used popularly to refer to those prison employees who directly carry out custodial duties in an institution dedicated to safekeeping. Correctional personnel would prefer to avoid the term "prison guard" when considering the duties and work of the employees who occupy the lowest level of the prison's organization. Probably, this change in attitude mirrors public opinion and is motivated to alleviate general stigmatization of prisons and the persons who work within them. But the increased avoidance of "prison guard" by prison employees is even more significant in that it suggests dissatisfaction with the working conditions that go with being a "prison guard."

Here we will use "prison guard" as a term to describe objectively—free of any intention to stigmatize — the working conditions, duties and consequences of exclusive concentration on the surveillant and suppressive functions of the prison. Surveillance entails constant watching of confined persons, with the expectation that some of them will break the prison rules established to maintain order within "the walls," or will engage in escape attempts that threaten the psychological security and physical safety of the general public. When prison violence brings these duties to public attention in a major crisis, the public images of the prison guard are blurred by the competition between two opposing themes. The guard is sometimes portrayed as an heroic sentinel safeguarding the free community against the violence that festers among the "jungle" or "maladjusted" personalities within the walls, or he is portrayed as the victimizer of "helpless captives." Somehow, in the hyperemotional confrontation of these two opposing themes, the possibility of accurately assessing the work and duties of prison guards is lost.

These hyperemotional conceptions of the role of the prison guard overlook a major part of his work. Less apparent to outside observation are the guard's duties of supervising inmate work crews in preparing food, distributing supplies, and performing the many other routine tasks that are necessary to keep a prison in operation. These duties require that the guard motivate reluctant captives to carry out their work with minimum interference to the routines that enable a prison to meet the needs of its residents within the slender resources provided by budgets. Prisons do not fare too well in competition for tax revenues with other governmental activities — education, highways, mental health, and so on. So, "making do with what we have" falls heavily on the ingenuity of guards who are expected to maintain surveillance over inmates and yet get them to perform essential tasks.

DISSATISFACTION OF "PRISON GUARD" ROLE

The growing dissatisfaction with the guard role in prison circles stems from the poverty of socially rewarding incentives that go with this role. In fact, officers frequently complain that they "pull time" along with the inmates. With the exception of infrequent violence, their work consists largely of key-turning, counting and herding inmates, conducting searches, and manning a post when most persons are supposed to be asleep. Working hours may be peculiar, and the work site may be remote. Working within this seemingly mundane routine, the guard is subject to the rules of a paramilitary organization which give little opportunity for initiative and recognition.

Yet, there is always the possibility of danger in the strange world of the prison. Considering the "big house" image presented in the mass media, homicides and staff-inmate violence are remarkably infrequent.

Nevertheless, there is evidence of escalating violence in prisons as a whole. A policy of keeping more amenable offenders out of prison increases the relative presence of "toughs" in prisons and has reduced the stabilizing influence of less menacing personalities. The violence of street gangs has spread to some prisons. Not all prisons are dangerous, but in every prison the guard encounters the usually latent — but sometimes overt — hostility of reluctant captives.

Staff-inmate confrontations are being aggravated by a weakening inmate belief in the legitimacy of staff authority and by the interpretation of staff actions as racist-oriented. Under the conditions of inmate hostility in an overcrowded custodial prison, the "guard" experiences the organizational climate of a fortress under siege from enemies within its walls. "After you've had a certain amount of urine and feces thrown in your face," one guard said, "you tend to become more unified in your attitude."[1]

The guard appears to represent awesome power, yet he is merely in the position of dealing with symptoms rather than with the underlying sources of the prison disorder he is supposed to prevent and overcome.

Coercion as a sole control device is exemplified by the custodial prison; it requires surveillance and detailed instruction made possible only by the constant alertness of a relatively small number of custodial officers. Violent retaliation is ineffective in dealing with subtle forms of inmate opposition over the long term. Because the guard force on duty at any particular time is small compared to the inmate population, the custodial staff is insufficient for continual warfare.

The personal feelings of guards are another drain on the strength of coercion. Daily interaction between guards and inmates leads to what Sykes calls the "corruption of authority."[2] Because the officer's duties frequently require him to be both rule enforcing agent and a work foreman, to create work motivation he must reduce his aloofness as an enforcement agent. However, because the guard is placed at the lowest level of the official organization, he may develop reasons for resenting bureaucratic practices which give him a sense of common interests with inmates. Face-to-face contact is likely to lessen any tendency to regard prisoners as uniformly evil or deserving of arbitrary punishments. Since his superiors tend to rank his efficiency on his ability to handle inmates, the guard is vulnerable to inmate maneuvers that range from complete compliance to overt rebellion.

SUPPRESSION AND TASKS OF GUARDING

"Suppression" implies forced conformity to rules which the inmates — at least most of them — do not regard as consistent with their own interests or in accordance with their view of the prison world which they are experiencing. Suppression is part of custodial duties because inmates, having been involuntarily placed in penal confinement, are extremely unlikely to accept willingly the official rules framed without serious consideration of their interests and preferences. Instead, the rules serve the interests of the prison management and the interests of the community being protected against those confined.

Because within any organization individuals differ in their expectations and behaviors, inmates inevitably will vary in the nature and degree of their conformity to official rules. As a deliberately contrived organization dealing with a wide variety of inmate personalities, prisons cannot be expected to treat personally and with complete understanding the unique meaning of each inmate's deviation from the official rules.

It is very difficult for the prison guard to deal with each inmate's conduct by evaluating it against these highly general rules. The prison guard must follow the rules and their interpretations made by his superiors; the guard is not free to act toward inmates — either sentimentally or punitively — as he would personally prefer. So he is a "man in the middle" because he must enforce, directly and personally, rules not of his own making. He stands, without clear guidance from above, between the incompletely communicated instructions from his superiors and the inmates who present behaviors that could be interpreted, at least technically, as rule violations.

The tasks of the guard role are carried out within a set of punishments, constant surveillance, and narrowly defined patterns of inmate-guard relationships. The correctional facility depends heavily on the guards to impose scheduling of the inmates' routinized daily activities. In the free community, details of personal behavior do not come under intensive scrutiny unless something unusual occurs. In the prison, however, matters usually left to personal taste are subjected to regulations and judgments by staff. Regimentation of the details of daily living, which are usually regarded as trivial, disrupts the inmate's previous habits of balancing what he wants against what he can do in his normal life situation. Along with this regimentation of his personal life, the inmate is likely to resent these intrusions into previously private matters. The guard is left with the weighty problem of making decisions that distinguish proper control measures from unwarranted intrusion of privacy. As mentioned previously, formal regulations offer only highly generalized guidance for officers when they must decide whether or not an official reaction should be given in marginal situations.

Unwarranted actions will disturb the routines of prison life — routines which play a large part in making the prison usually free of overt violence and rebellion. Athletic events, decent food, various forms of counseling, and work activity are elements in humane prison administration, but they also forestall the buildup of frustrations that may lead to flagrant rule violations and even to violence. Assignments to preferred jobs and dormitories and good-time awards are positive incentives. Such assignments usually give inmates favorable opportunities to evade surveillance, but, appropriately administered, the assignments can also increase incentives for voluntary compliance to regulations.

The alertness and task performance of guards are crucial to the measures taken against inmates officially identified as "troublemakers." Shakedowns of inmates and their possessions are used to upset inmate conspiracies. Other methods include: rotation of inmate job assignments, the shuffling of cellmates, and intraprison transfers to keep "troublemakers" off balance. The deviant prisoner is sometimes assigned to another prison unit with sterner security practices and fewer privileges. Inmate cliques also may be broken up by reassigning members to different prisons.

CORRECTIONAL OFFICER: AN ALTERNATIVE ROLE

Because of the taint associated with the term "prison guard," correctional personnel tend to prefer "correctional officer." The preference sometimes expresses a kind of "white wash" which signifies no real change in the work and responsibilities. But the preference also indicates a resolve to strengthen the competence of personnel and improve their working conditions so that the "correctional officer" has a personally satisfying and socially constructive career. I will use "correctional officer" in a specific way to denote status-role characteristics likely to achieve this resolution.

Correctional officers would see themselves as agents of change dedicated to moving inmates toward acceptance of themselves as law-abiding citizens. The officers would prefer persuasive techniques of influence and would selectively utilize coercion only as a last resort for a short-term effect. They would convey messages of tolerance, initiative, and acceptance, instead of the messages of the custodial prison: repressive control, punishment of socially stigmatized criminals, and isolation from the free community. Impersonal carrying out of control duties *only* would be replaced by establishment of psychological *contact* with inmates. The officers would be full-pledged partners in the overall effort to restore inmates to the free community, prepared and ready for socially constructive lives. Role norms would require training of correctional officers in persuasive management, initiative and insight in recognizing the latent implications of spontaneous behavior, and a sense of partnership with treatment workers who would be expected to accept correctional officers as co-participants in change processes.

The latter point is significant in that revision of the officer role demands that treatment specialists abandon their usual refusal to accept correctional officers as colleagues and as potential agents of change. The fact of such refusals illustrates again the necessity to revamp the entire social system of the custodial prison if deficiencies of the "prison guard" role are to be overcome.

At the root of the matter is what Moos has called the "organizational climate" — the total effect over time of living and working within the organization. Both the setting and the interaction of persons within the setting are important for assessing behavior. The climates of correctional institutions would differ in provision for: *Support* — Are residents encouraged to be helpful to other residents? Are staff members helpful to residents?; *Practicality* — Is there a future payoff for the person?; *Affiliation* — Are persons separated or encouraged to be comrades?; *Order and Organization* — Do the residents' demeanor, the staff activities, and the facility's appearance indicate orderly life?; *Involvement* — Are residents active and energetic in the day-to-day functioning of the program, showing initiative and group pride in the program?; *Expressiveness* — Is open expression of feelings, including anger, encouraged?; *Orientation to Personal Problems* — Are residents encouraged to recognize and cope with personal problems?; *Staff Control* — To what extent are regulations used to keep residents under control?; And *Autonomy* — How much room is there for self-determination in planning activities and taking leadership?[3]

FINAL COMMENT ON IMPLICATIONS

These items will appear highly idealistic and excessively optimistic when compared with the realities of the environments many prisons present for correctional officers. However, note what a useful checklist these items — presented by Moos in regard to improvement of conditions for inmates — are for also evaluating the working conditions for correctional officers.

The nub of my proposition is that the working conditions of officers must approach these idealized conditions before corrections can capitalize on their great potential. This potential lies in the officers' particular direct and continuous relationships with inmates. The "correctional officer" role entails changes in the organization of the correctional institution as a setting for their work, changes in their working conditions, and changes in the rationale of the institution.

Existing correctional institutions come in a great variety. In presenting the "guard role," I have emphasized only one type — the custodial prison. We must avoid over-enthusiasm for the "correctional officer" role by recognizing that some inmates will never respond in ways making this role appropriate. Nevertheless, already there are correctional institutions which present the conditions implied in this paper to be necessary for implementation of the proposed "correctional officer" role. By delineating this role, I have endeavored to provide a context for practical discussion of how the potentialities of this role are being released by the changes that already have come about in correctional institutions.

Notes

1. Kenneth Lamott, "I Didn't Bring Anyone Here, and I Can't Send Anybody Home," *Saturday Review*, July 22, 1972, 12.
2. Gresham M. Sykes, *Society of Captives*. (Princeton, NJ: Princeton University Press, 1958).
3. Rudolph H. Moos, *Evaluating Correctional and Community Settings*. (New York: John Wiley & Sons, 1975), 37-41.

Chapter 6

Is a "Correctional Officer," By Any Other Name, a "Screw?"*

Hans Toch

No one confuses professionalization with semantic sleights of hand. Sanitary engineers with mops are transparently janitors. The Blue Knight and Serpico are not "peace officers," and a person who empties bedpans is not a "therapeutic" staff person. We are rarely fooled by quasi-professional role labels, and we know that the role occupant is liable to be less fooled than the rest of us.

Does the advent of the "correctional officer" augur an emerging role in penology, or is such an officer a rebaptized Keeper of Cons? Are there attributes that distinguish the "new guard" from his precursors? Does he have expanded functions? A reshaped mission? More discretion? New tasks to perform?

In specific cases, we know the answer is "no." A correctional officer assigned to tower duty is a residue of the dark ages. He requires 20/20 vision, the IQ of an imbecile, a high threshold for boredom and a basement position in Maslow's hierarchy. For most officers — who are better than this — a tower assignment is palatable as an undiluted sinecure. The tower guard "does his time" because we offer him a paycheck for his presence. He is paid not only to be non-professional, but to be flagrantly non-contributing.

Other officers operate under roughly equivalent mandates. They must count, lock, unlock, escort, watch, stand by. They must complete forms certifying to the obvious or recording the unusual. They are enjoined to eschew communication with inmates, to invoke supervisors where real decisions are called for, to refer problems of consequence to colleagues of consequence.

There is little in the literature (either on prisons or on total institutions) that offers much hope to the officer. The guard, we are told, is the natural enemy of the inmates; client contacts corrupt guards, and are offensive to inmates of integrity. Guard-inmate links pinpoint politicians, rats, square johns; denote areas of staff compromise and marginality, of emasculation and bartering.

There are new facts to consider, however, new voices, new drummers to heed. Areas of inmate freedom have expanded, living conditions have

---

* Reprinted with permission from *Criminal Justice Review*, Vol. 3, No. 2.

been ameliorated. "Total" institutions are less total, more permeable to the outside. The guard is enjoined to be humane, respectful of cultural plurality, sensitive to client grievances. We try to recruit the officer from a broader — and presumably more responsive — pool. He is trained, or retrained, in human relations, crisis management and the social sciences generally.

If such contexts furnish a potential for new officer role, this potential should be evidenced, or should be presaged, among the officers themselves. We should see *some* officers responding in *tentative, experimental* ways, beginning to shape more contemporary roles for themselves. For where winds of change blow, they affect some of us first, and others later. It takes innovators to convince the more brave among us before the rest of us are swept along. Do innovators exist among correctional officers? Are there guards on the prison scene thinking and acting in non-traditional ways?

INNOVATION GHETTOES

In responding to this question, we must exclude the realm of "innovation ghettoes." These are settings in which roles are contextually arranged as components of experimental programs. A prison with therapeutic community units, for example, may train officers to be group workers. Elsewhere, special programs may have officers with roles redefined to conform with other innovative practices.

The roles of "experimental" officers are similar to those of tower guards. Role components are different from those of the "average" officer, and are circumscribed to their settings. Like localized growths, they carry the potential of dissemination, but the probabilities of metastases are small. Experimental programs tend to be admired and unemulated, like platoon commanders who charge up hills under the watchful eyes of tired men encamped at the bottom.

Nondissemination is not inevitable, "new" officers may be used to train "old" officers to arrange spread-of-effect. But such activity is different from spontaneous role changes among a rank and file. It is *spontaneous* change (if it exists) that is most directly relevant to our concerns. If non-special officers are playing new roles on the prison scene, others may follow. For such officers are caught under similar cross winds, stand on similar thresholds, live in similar worlds. It is the officers' worlds we must enter, to view the possibilities they offer in the face of traditions that restrain.

PINPOINTING THE INNOVATOR

The vignettes we shall trace are excerpts of interviews.[1] The interviews from which the excerpts are drawn were aimed at one aspect of the guard role which is unambiguously non-traditional. This aspect relates to the officer as a dispenser of mental health services, as a person who resonates to adjustment problems of inmates-in-crisis, and seeks to respond to inmate suffering. Such activity falls into the human services realm and it is intrinsically non-custodial, though it may be clothed in a rationale of violence-prevention.

The interviews I shall use are representative in some respects, and atypical in others. They are representative because the samples are random and the officers are "mainline" guards in maximum security settings. But the officers are not representative of the samples. Quotes are drawn from a subsample of officers (comprising 20% of the sample) whom we adjudged "liberal" along a helpfulness-nonhelpfulness dimension.

Our purpose in this paper is to explore the emergence of new officer role components. The vignettes we have selected are relevant to themes we have predefined as highlighting significant elements of the helping role. They are intended to stimulate our thinking about (1) what is possible, and (2) how and why it is possible.

THE HUMANE EXERCISE OF DISCRETION

A custodial officer is a figure of power and dispenser of authority. When we think of a man in these terms, his exercise of discretion becomes monothematic. If he is a purist, he retains his authority and exercises power; if he is selective, he compromises authority and relinquishes power. Viewed in power terms, a man who cuts corners is corrupt.

Sociologists have viewed prison guards as corruption-prone. The view is tempered — though not modified — by contextual issues. Contextual exculpations produce a patronizing portrait: a guard must become corrupt to get along, to buy loyalty and goodwill. This picture is not reassuring. It leaves the guard juggling the roles of blackmailer and blackmail victim, facing impotence or compromise. Survival as a shell of authority hinges on continuing corruptibility.

Whatever the new *correctional* officer may be, he must be more than a custodial officer. This means that new themes, themes beyond the exercise of authority must enter into the definition of his role. The guard's behavior may subserve motives we have not encountered before, and these may have nothing to do with who's in charge, or who's running whom under what circumstances.

Among correctional officers, the power issue may emerge on its head. Power may be used on behalf of inmates rather than against inmates. Power may be used against superiors, or may be invoked to test their flexibility and resources. Where the custodial officer may give up power when he uses discretion, the correctional officer may stretch it. He manipulates power as a tool to get other (correctional) ends accomplished.

One correctional end is to provide support, to render assistance to inmates in need. This involves using guard power to supplement inmate power where the inmate is blatantly powerless. It involves testing resources, maximizing their "play" and flexibility, to get the job done.

Assistance-rendering is mobilized when there is a perception of need for assistance. Needs may take the form of manifest helplessness, misery, or anguish. The sufferer may request help, but (in prison) he may prefer not to. If there is no direct request from the person, his needs may emerge in symptomatic conduct. The officer diagnoses the man's symptoms by observing him. In doing so, the officer shows (1) "clinical" skill or sensitivity, and (2) empathy or willingness to care.

Where an officer is approached, he must assess the legitimacy of needs that underly the inmate's overtures. If the officer is support-oriented, he is unlikely to dismiss help-bids as superficial or "attention-getting." He takes care to review conduct for evidence of suffering.

> A 22: He never mentioned the fact that he slashed his wrists. Just the fact that if he didn't get his sleeping pills, that was it. "And please help me to get them." And come right out and actually trembling, crying — he didn't break right down, he had a certain amount of composure. But he was choking up and tears started coming. And more or less pleaded with me to make sure that he got that pill. So when he came back from observation, he looked like a 90 year old man. Drawn and pale, and he's grey-haired but it really stood out. He looked like he'd been a wino for 90 years with nothing to eat. Weight loss, the clothes he had on, he didn't care what he had on, how he looked, nothing.
>
> GH 1: I remember Timothy distinctly because he was the type of a person that wanted to be helped, and he was asking for it in a way that you really had to look for it. You could see that he was asking for help, but I mean when you went by his cell he didn't say "listen, Mr. K., would you help me?" Or "would you do this?" But you could see, he would come to you, he would seek a conversation with you, he would encourage it, stimulate conversation. And he would tell you things that he knew you would resent to get you into a conversation, so that he could — I think he felt so alone, so isolated from everyone else . . . he required so much attention that he used to do really strange things to gain attention. An awful lot like a child would. He would cut his hair off, I mean to the point where he'd shave his head . . . He would walk on the backs of his shoes, and he would put his slacks on and he wouldn't button them, he'd just kind of half-zip them so they hung on him. He was never an exhibitionist, he never exposed himself or suggested anything. But there was just a way about him, that you can tell it. Even if you weren't attracted to him, like keeping an eye on him security-wise, if he was just passing you in the corridor, you could tell there was something about Timothy that wasn't right.

I: I see. Now would he look to you like somebody that was depressed or confused or angry — what impression would be give you?

GH 1: Timothy was very, very confused. Very confused.

I: His confusion sort of stood out?

GH 1: It did. I think the thing about Timmy that really surprised me the most was the fact that I had taken such an interest in him.

Support-oriented guards not only respond to help-bids, but make independent determinations of needs. This means that the guard must be aware of inmate feelings, whether directly expressed, communicated to other persons, or revealed in conduct.

GH 4: He doesn't know how to handle the relationship and the feelings that come in. Because I hear that he sits in the visiting room and everyone can see the love in them. And it's indescribable. It's hard to tell how their emotions are coming out. He can't hide it. It's flowing out of him.

* * * * *

I: You felt that he was fearful about going out in the free world? He wouldn't make this clear, but that is what you picked up?

GH 10: This is what I picked up. Myself and the other inmates. You take your lead from the inmates. Many times they can give you a lot of direction, but you have to listen closely to what they're saying.

I: And some of the suggestions they made about what they'd observed —

GH 10: What they had observed, yeah.

I: Now did anyone give you an idea of what had happened to this guy over the two week period? Was it an overnight type shift or had this guy slowly fallen apart?

GH 10: He slowly worked his way into it. And it was a very shocking thing, because at that time I ran the — of porters at that time, they cleaned up throughout the whole area. And we were a rather close-knit group. And any man of us received this sort of recognition, everybody rejoiced in a sense. This in turn, gave us all a good feeling. And now 12 years behind him and suddenly they open the door, he just couldn't take it.

* * * * *

CB: He was a little guy who was afraid of everything and everybody and then all of a sudden in a day's time he started standing up, which he knew was foolish — but he started standing up to some of the roughest guys in the division. And it just wasn't him. And I was afraid that he was going to get hurt because these guys don't take that kind of stuff. It was a complete reversal.

I: So it just stood out to you — here's a meek guy acting like a tiger.

CB: And plus it was all in a day's time. One day he was a

meek guy and the next day he was on the move and he had just changed like that . . . The kid was actually serious. He wasn't putting it on. It was actually a serious thing. He actually, if it came right down to it, would have taken these guys on. Regardless of what the consequences would be. This is what I feel anyway and I knew he would get hurt.

Once an officer has diagnosed genuine needs, he is in a position to respond to these needs with supportive moves. Such moves can be routine practices, such as filing reports or making referrals. When an officer presses bureaucratic buttons, he is just doing his job. He exercises discretion where he transcends his mission.

Discretion may be exercised in a number of ways, including the exemption of inmates from obligations or restrictions. Such exemptions can be viewed as corrupt compromises, but they are really the very opposite. They are planned strategies of withholding pressure that is seen as stressful, and therefore as harmful to brittle inmates.

>GM 1: I have my clerk that I work with, he's a man in for murder, which means nothing to me, what he done out there. Now he's my clerk, I know he's a highly nervous person, he can't accept problems, he can't deal with them too fast. And he explodes, he doesn't mean to but he does. And a lot of times I tell him, "stay in your house, don't even bother coming out, just rest up."
>I: You can see he's on the verge.
>GM 1: Yeah. "Don't do your work today." I can see when he's nervous or upset. I got him now so he'll come and tell me, somebody's bothering him, he wants to stay in for a couple of days, "go ahead, stay in," we pay him, it don't make no difference. And he'll come back around in a couple of days, he's all right, works good. Actually he's a good inmate, but if you didn't recognize his problems, you would have him in keeplock, the next thing you know he'd be over in idle somewhere, or segregation. He wouldn't want to be, but it would break him right down. He can't adapt to the situation.
>I: So he's a guy that's easily made nervous and upset —
>GM 1: Yeah, and a lot of people try to make what we call a sweet boy or a punk out of him. He isn't that way, he actually is a very tough kid. As I say, he's in for murder, which doesn't help him any. And they pick on him, he's got a lot of time to do in jail.
>I: So even though he's a tough kid, this sort of upsets him.
>GM 1: Yeah, right. All of our reliefs know him and if they see anything with him, they let him stay in. Like when I come on duty, they'll leave me a note and say so-and-so has had a rough night, he was hollering, somebody was hollering to him. And I'll say okay, and I won't bother him. Finally he'll come around and say "hi," or "you don't mind if I stay in today?" "No, stay in, let me know when you want to come out."

* * * * *

CHAPTER 6 BY ANY OTHER NAME A "SCREW"

A 23: I had an inmate the other day, a big black inmate who is a known diabetic. He eats separate rations in the mess hall and he is a diabetic on a special diet here. He came out of the yard last week and went to C block to another officer and said "I've got to get to the hospital, I don't feel good." And it was about 35 degrees outside and he came in and he was totally saturated with perspiration. And they sent him back to the block and he said he didn't feel good, and I said "what's the matter?" And he said "I don't know, I think I'm having a spell." I knew the man was a diabetic, so I called the nurse, and I said "what can I do for him in the meantime?" And the nurse told me to give him about 5 teaspoons of sugar in a glass of warm water, mixed up and give it to him, and keep an eye on him for awhile, for at least an hour to make sure he doesn't have any reaction or anything. He may calm down, if he doesn't, give me another call. So I did, I gave the man the water and he said "thank you." And I told him to lay down. So I checked on him about every 15 minutes, and I said "are you sure you're going to be all right?" He said "yeah, I feel real good now." They were going to bring the medication later anyway, but he said he thought he would be all right. The man, the next day I was at work and he made a special point of breaking out of line for chow to thank me for giving him something to take care of his problem . . . This man definitely had a problem, he tried to get to a doctor, I talked to him afterward and told him that was the wrong thing to do, and he said he didn't know what to do. He didn't feel right. And you have to understand, you can't condemn a man for doing something wrong when he's in a position of feeling ill and he knows something could happen to him.

The officer may not only bend the rules on behalf of inmates-in-need, but he may explore the bureaucratic machinery for loopholes through which problems can be solved. This entails teaming up with other staff (who are problem-solving oriented) to find non-routine formulas or solutions.

A X: And this goes back quite a few years and this fellow had done something like eight years on a 15 year sentence and he had a child that was nine. And whatever the case was, he had never spent Christmas with the child. And he met the board and he got an open date for six months and he did not have an approved program and he had promised the child that they would be spending Christmas together, buying him presents and right on down the line. And he did not get out in time for Christmas and he was really down in the dumps. He was real low, about as low as you can get. And this is right after Christmas and he was bitter about a lot of things and he was very disappointed with everything and he worked for me and I talked with Mr. so and so who was in charge of the service unit at that time — and I asked him if he would at least call the guy off the block and let him get it off of his chest and he did . . . And something occurred to him that had occurred to nobody else and that was that the guy had worked in the plate shop for a good number of years and at that time he had saved half of his money. And so I asked the man how much they had in reserve for him and I told him and I said "let's take a chance and withdraw it and make a deposit in the bank in New York City and see if we can get you out on a reasonable assurance." And he did and he got it and he was out in ten days. And I think that it made an awful difference in that the man was let out and I think it could have been done before Christmas if someone had done more. If someone had taken the time.

Problem-solving conspiracies may not only involve the officer with other staff but also with inmates. The officer may combine forces with inmates to stretch prison rules on behalf of a troubled person.

A 23: And the other inmate came to me and said "let's put everything aside, you're an officer and I'm an inmate, but let's think of him as a man," and he had a very good point. But the only solution that I could come up with was the fact that I had already put in an observation report and it came back with the man, there wasn't that much involved in it. The main thing was they didn't have an interpreter with them at the time, I don't believe. So what I did, I went around the system a little bit and I told this inmate, "explain to him that he has to go on sick call in the morning to see the psychiatrist, and what you do, you put a slip in for sick call in the morning with the man. This way you'll both go to the psychiatrist together, you'll be there to interpret." I said "you may have a little bit of problems with the sergeant, but explain to the sergeant why you're there, if he has any questions, tell him to come to me because I'm the one that told you to do it." And he came back to me the next day and he thanked me, because they had moved the man out.

Discretion may border on advocacy where officers go out of their way to circumvent the system, or to fight it, on behalf of inmates. In the officer's eyes, the non-compliant bureaucracy is ritualistically and unreasonably obdurate, and he sees no point in conforming to it. This may cause resentment, and subject the officer to pressure.

A 22: There's times when the guys been out of pills, I don't have to do it, I could say piss on you, wait till fill-up day and get them yourself or go over and see the doctor and get them. I'll make the trip over and I'll go get them. One or two pills, whatever, to cover to hold the guy for the day. Because I've done it myself, I'm counting out pills or something and I'll drop them on the floor. I could shove it back in the bottle, but I destroy it, and I have to enter it in the book destroyed. There's times when the pharmacy will send over pills that says 28 in a bottle, there's 27, right off the bat I'm one short. So in the course of the week I have to go over and get that extra pill so that we're not short. Especially so that the night shift has got a pill to give the guy. Mainly this man with the sleeping problem and our epileptics. It's mandatory that they have the medication . . . You go over there to get some pills, they say "what the fuck you doing over here?" "I'm over to check this out." "That's what you got a hospital runner for." "Fuck it, I want to take care of it." . . . Four days ago, an epileptic, way down on the end, had fits, he hadn't been moved yet. So he come up, and he's given me static. This is the guy I was telling you, he's a Jew and he called me a Nazi and all this kind of shit. So I said "all right, I'll check into it." So I went over to the hospital, I was over there 2 hours, running this fucking thing down. Come to find out, the only thing that was holding it up was his job classification. You can't put a man on invalid company unless he's a grade 4, no job. He can't work, he's medically unfit to work. That was all that was wrong, because they had him marked as a grade one. Grade one, you're going to work. And that was all that was holding it up, and they had to have a written order on it. That the man was changed from one to four, it took me 2 hours to get it. And I got static over that. So the guy will be moving today, everything's kosher.

I: So in the process of helping this guy out you have to put up with a lot of abuse.

A 22: Yeah. Fuck them, I don't need it.

THE BUILDING OF RELATIONSHIPS

The custodial officer is not enjoined to be harsh or inhumane; he is presumed to be distant, vigilant, and firm-but-fair. Where an inmate gives the officer "no trouble," he is apt to be treated with nonintrusiveness; if the same inmate "acts up," he is dispassionately restrained and disciplined. In its positive stance, custody withholds negative power: it may even react with courtesy and politeness. It does not, however, get "chummy," because relationships complicate custodial functions. It is difficult to search, report or restrain an inmate tomorrow with whom one is personally involved today. If an inmate proves disruptive, the officer must react forcefully. He must do so because his principal function is to preserve order in prison.

The correctional officer may take a different view of inmates. He may see himself as "working" with inmates on a "person to person" basis. This may entail short-changing order maintenance to preserve or to create "working relationships."

A correctional officer has custodial assignments as part of his job. But he may give these assignments a human relations "twist." He may endeavor, for example, to de-escalate an impending officer-inmate confrontation to enable the inmate to establish reintegrative links. By taking a collaborative stance in a conflict situation, the officer may "defuse" an obdurate or rebellious inmate, and may establish a relationship with him.

GH 2: The sergeant called me in and said "go upstairs and move a man downstairs." So right away I assumed that the man was causing some problems because we had all these other officers with us. So we approached the cell, we had about 5 or 6 officers plus the sergeant. The inmate was a young Puerto Rican about 6'2", very, very angry, obviously scared to death. The sergeant says "come on, we'll take you downstairs." He said, "no man, I'm not going to come out, because as soon as I come out you're going to really kick my ass and I don't want anything to do with that." He says "I know I'm going to get hurt but I'm going to take some of you guys with me" . . . I asked if I could speak to him. The sergeant says "yeah, go ahead." So I walked in and said "hey, look, nobody wants to hurt you. I think I understand what your problem is." He says "what's that?" I said "you're putting yourself under a lot of peer pressure up here. Here you've been spouting off to all the other inmates in the gallery how tough you are. Now you want to prove something. You know and I know that we can take you out of here if we have to, but we don't want to hurt you. And why don't you just come along with me and I'll take you downstairs and nothing's going to happen to you." So after a few moments of saying I was lying to him and everything, I guess he really decided what the heck else did he have to lose? He says "you mean to tell me that you are going to take me out of here and nobody else is going to lay a hand on me?" I said "yeah, you got my word. You'll go down to my area and I'll keep you down there and see how you behave yourself." So he agrees to do so. When we walked out of the cell naturally he's waiting for somebody to jump on him and romp around on him a little bit, but to his surprise nobody laid a hand on him. So his anger turned into making me more or less a father-image in his behalf. So on a daily basis I talked to this guy, anytime he had a problem he'd come to me. He started telling me that his problems were really not due to prison, there was an outside source between his wife and that sort of thing.

A non-custodial or de-escalating approach can help to reduce inmate resentments and can disconfirm assumptions about the guard role. This may make it possible for the inmate to react to the officer as a human (non-merely-custodial) agent, so that "correctional" work can take place. The vignette we have quoted has sequels.

GM 2: I talked to him several times in the yard. He said "what about this peer pressure thing, explain that to me." So I tried to sit down and tell him the term and just what it meant to him and everybody else and he said "gee, that's very interesting, I never looked at it that way." So then we got talking, and we'd sit down and talk about marriage and the problems he had with his children and that type of thing. We got along pretty good.

I: So this peer thing, he came to see it as one of his problems too?

CHAPTER 6   BY ANY OTHER NAME A "SCREW"   97

GM 2: Yeah.
I: Did he ever admit to you that he was afraid and that's one of the reasons he put —
GM 2: Yeah, he said "I was scared to death. After all, you come to prison, you hear all kinds of stories." He said, "I've had a couple of occasions where they've kicked me around a little bit, I thought the same thing was going to happen to me." In fact he made a statement that surprised me the following day. He said "you know what, I'm afraid of you." I said "why are you afraid of me?" He said "you're too cool." I said "well, did I lie to you?" He said "no, I thought about that." He says "but you're either tough as hell or you got to be crazy." I said "why?" He said "well, you walked in the cell, obviously I was mad enough to hurt somebody." I said "well, I figured if you're going to hurt somebody you're not going to hurt me too bad because I had enough help there to back me up." But I said "I couldn't see you getting hurt from being stupid, and hurting somebody else." So he thought that was pretty good reasoning and we daily built a pretty good relationship.
I: Did he mention other things that had got him upset and made him act the way he was acting?
GM 2: Well, he said he was lied to.
I: By who?
GM 2: By other officers. I know another thing that upset him greatly too. I guess when he came in they took some personal property away from him he felt they shouldn't have taken. So I asked him what it was and I found that an officer made a mistake on two items and I got them back for him. So that sort of reassured him that everybody wasn't trying to be unjust to him.
I: He felt he was being treated unjustly.
GM 2: Yeah.

The custodial officer may cultivate links with a few inmates (such as informers) to advance security ends. For the correctional officer, relationships may be the medium through which he works. Trust, loyalty, communication, friendship allow the officer to provide psychological support when it is needed. Such commodities also help the officer stimulate activity without recourse to power. The correctional officer may see himself as working "with inmates" rather than as insuring their compliance. The inmate the officer "works with" may be described in surprisingly personal terms, approximating language used for members of one's family.

GH 4: He was pacing around and he didn't know where to turn. And I know more of the problem because when he has no one to turn to he turns to me. I don't know what he's in for. I don't know his crime. Although he has mentioned that one of these days he would like to sit and in length discuss it with me and he would like me to know. And we're very close, I'm his boss and his feeling for me is very close and he tells me almost every problem which he has. And we discuss it. And when he's uptight I talk about my own life and how my wife and I do this and that. And it kind of relaxes him and it's interesting for him. And how his feelings are for him he gets interested in the conversation. My aunt works here and we talk about the family all the time. And he was telling me about a dream the other night that he was on parole and he had married his girlfriend and she had gone to work and he was going out to have dinner and while he was out he ran into me and my wife and my aunt and her husband and we went out and he got his wife and the six of us went to Vegas just for the evening having a grand old time. And with a dream like this his feeling for me is more than just — we're very close friends.

Descriptions of this kind may strike us as strange, on two counts: first, our conceptions of officers may be custodial; second we conceive of inmates as resistant to officers, except for rats (who inform) or square johns (who are subculturally discountable). We know it takes two persons to form a relationship. If the correctional officer does not find counterparts among inmates, his potency is circumscribed. He can render services and defuse crises, but in work situations he must be compliance-oriented.

We forget that inmates adjust to concrete officers. The squarest of johns may find some officers uncongenial, and the most militant inmate may find an officer he trusts. Officers sometimes facilitate relationships, while inmates often need relationships. Where such confluences occur, subcultures are no deterrent.

It may help to quote a young inmate whose divisional officer happens to conform to the correctional mold and enjoys a good "rep" among inmates generally.

Cox V: When I first come to the division I had noticed that he was friendly toward the dudes that was on the floor, the tier boys. And he talked to them with respect, like you know, "how was your day today, did you do anything interesting?" It was different for a guard to ask inmates these questions. So when I got on the floor I started rapping to him about my main interest, which was cars, and he just happens to be another car freak, and we hit it off really good. And since then he's been a personal friend and not a guard to me . . . I talk to him about every problem. I go to him before I'll come to a chaplain or to a sergeant or something.

I: And he's usually pretty helpful?

Cox V: Very helpful. He's always got a suggestion. I mean it's not like "do this and this and this." He'll give me a suggestion and tell me the alternative, give me another suggestion and tell me another alternative . . . in June I had jumped in the silo and hurt my leg pretty bad. And they had left me up in the hospital for four whole days. That's about enough time for a cold to go away, and I had ripped all the muscles out of my leg, cracked a bone and so on.

CHAPTER 6 BY ANY OTHER NAME A "SCREW"

So they made me come back down to population and expected me to work. And I refused to work initially in the morning, but then I decided I'll go to work today and maybe I can talk to somebody tonight so I can get around it, get myself fixed up without getting locked up behind it. So I asked, "What should I do about this, these people want me to work, I can hardly walk." He said "who told you to go to work?" I said Sgt. so and so. He says "well listen, I'll get on the phone now and tell him you're having trouble with the leg, and I recommend you go up to reception. Because there's no sense you walking out of your limp a cripple because these people want you to go to work. We've got 700 inmates in here that can do your job." So he called up, talked to them and told them the situation, right from the beginning, how I hurt it, how long I was up in the hospital and so on. The lieutenant personally called on the deputy superintendents and got a direct order for me to stay up in reception until I was well enough that I could walk. This is from his personal interest.

I: Do you ever talk to this guy about very personal things, like your wife and your child, or what you think of the future, that type of stuff?

Cox V: Yeah, almost every night. We have a little chat session every night after lock-in. He stops by my cell, "hi, how you doing." And we start from there, you know. "Did you get a letter from your wife today?" Because he passes out the mail, he just asks as a joke type thing, you know. And I say "yeah, I got one." "What'd she have to say?" And I tell him this and that, and I won't hold nothing back. If she writes in there that she's having problems with the landlord or something like this, I'll tell it to him, he'll come up with either a suggestion or relate a story that happened to him and his wife, that would possibly help me out of my situation.

I: So this fellow really treats you as an equal?

Cox V: Right, he treats me as an individual, man, not as a group inmate . . . I believe out in the world most everybody's optimistic about what they want to do and so on. All right, when you come to jail, you're secluded from everything that's yours. Everything you love, everything you cherish, that you're used to doing, it's rough when you can't have it. And you figure "wow, I'm never going to get back out there again." And sitting in your cell and people bugging you, other inmates buggin you, this adds this much more badness on top of it. Losing hope is like just not even looking forward to getting back out there. I mean you're just institutionalized. And it's like every day is the same, it's just blah. You exist, you don't live. You eat your three squares a day, you take a shower at night and go to sleep and get up in the morning, and that's it. You don't think about ever getting back out there. No plans whatsoever. This happens I believe at one point to everybody who comes here.

I: And so when you say a guard shows concern for you, how does that give you that shot of hope?

Cox V: Well, it's like you remember like related incidents from the world to this man. Like if he says "hey look, when you get out there," you think back in the world, I remember a girl that used to say this, or my mother or father used to say this. And it brings you back closer to the world mentally. And when you're close to the world it makes you want to get back there because you remember the good things that happened. It's hard to explain . . . But it helps people, I don't know how, but when somebody's concerned about you, you've got the natural instinct to give them something back, whether it's affection or concern. You know, you've got to give them something back. And when you've got a contact like this, when you're concerned about somebody and he's concerned about you back, you've got a relationship going there that brings you above your environment. Brings you to be what you want to be. If you want to be back out in the world, you can put yourself to the point to remember when you were there. And how good it's going to be when you get back out there, not how long it's going to be, you know?

We have quoted our inmate at more length than seems necessary, (1) because of the "consumer" perspective the inmate can provide, and (2) because of his definitional or conceptual contribution.

The "traditional" officer is (in theory, at least) a custodial figure. As we meet new or emerging functions we see them first as departures from the custodial role, which tells us mainly about what they are not.

Our inmate defines the officer's role positively, because he highlights the concept "correctional" in "correctional officer." He tells us that the officer is helpful, but he also describes how he is being helped. His portrait deals with two major areas. The first is prison adjustment, which includes material assistance and stress-reducing counseling. The second entails enhancing the inmate's chances of reintegration into the community upon release. Our inmate includes the officer's contribution as a representative of the free world, with relevant experiences that help shape the inmate's expectations and attitudes. A custodial officer defines his job as order maintenance and this is a closed institution view. The corrections officer can deal with problems in the inmate's civilian past, in his links to the outside world, and in his future.

THE CORRECTIONAL LAG

Our "ideal type" portrait of officers is ideal in three senses: (1) the lines between "custodial" and "correctional" are less sharp than we have traced them: officers may be "mixed bags," and they may perform custodially in some situations, correctionally in others, and eclectically in others. Correctional goals may be custodially justified, or the other way around. (2) Thematic sequences are far from neat. Many officers were not "hacks" fifty years ago, and new men play anachronistic roles more frequently than we like. (3) Contextual pressures qualify trends, and may stunt or snuff them. The innovators may be brave without being masochistic or suicidal. If he has no institutional supports, his innovativeness may languish, his idealism turn sour and his alienation may grow. In the absence of inmate appreciation, of peer reinforcement, of rewards from above, his new role may be abandoned after brief rehearsals.

While success stories exist, so do failures. The latter have consequences which are at times serious. They give rise to doubt, guilt, discouragement, and a mounting sense of impotence. They convert some officers into "closet counselors" and others into men who "once tried."

Failures can be produced by the custodial frame of the officer's role. This context is a source of tangible pressures, such as bureaucratic or personal resistances. The context also contains definitions and interpretations of acts which can tarnish the officer's self-image and undermine his self-esteem.

A 22: And you have problems ever once in a while, like I have one man that during the noontime when everybody else is locked in, I let him out and he'll run a broom down the gallery. That's just a little extra, it keeps the dust down a little bit, cigarette butts and stuff. And he'll take a list at noontime for me and on weekends for movie, who's going to work, and it saves me from doing it because I've got a lot of other things to do. So I let him out. And he'll come up and maybe shoot the shit with me or go down and rap with somebody, and I had tabs dropped in on me that this guy is my pet, see.

* * * * *

A 22: I had a case and it backfired on me. A man got locked up. The man was always on the floor while I was here, very respectful, no problems. You told him to lock in and before you finished saying it he locked in. He wanted to get water, he come out, got his water and locked back in. Yes sir, no sir, if he wanted something, you'd get, thank you. To me he was a model inmate. At the time I hadn't known what he was in for. I had heard rumors but unless I see it myself, piss on it, I ain't worrying about it. So the guy got locked up supposedly for assaulting an officer. He got locked up on my days off, so when I come back I seen he was locked up, Jesus Christ, what the hell did he do? He was the last guy I figured would get locked up. So I go down and he runs it all down to me, the officer harassed him and all like this. And I said "you were supposed to have attacked this officer, took a swing at him." And I knew the guy knew a lot of the Japanese arts I guess you'd call them, kung fu, karate and all that. The man was fast, at times I'd seen him in the cell doing different jabs and stuff . . . And I knew the dude was fast and if he gets provoked enough where he takes a swing at a guy he's going to do a job on him because he's going to get busted one way or the other. So I said "all right, let me check." So come to find out that the officer more or less jived up the report a little bit to get this guy in the box. More or less "all right you cocksucker, you want to mouth off at me, I'm going to burn you good." So to make a long story short, when the guy came into court, I went to bat for him. Told him that the man was on my floor, he's all right, I can't understand. Plus the officer that wrote the report, he's wrote 90% of the reports that you get and they're all bum shit. He's a chronic report writer. And the reports are wrote like my son would write them. All busted up, nothing to the point, more or less hearsay, your word against mine. So this is the approach that I took, and I said I'm going to bat for the guy, I think he got a bum deal. Now they were all set to send this man right up to special housing. Anyway, they said all right, we're going to put it under investigation and I got to take care of it. "Do your end of it and we'll put a sergeant on it. Oh man, here we go." So I got static from my people. "What are you sucking his ass for and making another officer look like an asshole?" So the guy come to find out, I got set up. The inmate figured what my reaction would be, that I might stick up for this dude, so he played on it. And I took the bait. And I went to bat for the guy and I got burned. I got shit from both ends of the deal. And it's hard, because you want to do your job, yet you still don't want to look like a pansy-ass asskisser.

The correctional officer's frustrations also have another source. While the officer faces resistances from traditionalists, "progressive" elements may refuse to accept him. They may question his judgment, challenge his right to act, relegate him to ancillary roles, doubt his integrity, and stereotype him.

When the officer discovers he is isolated and friendless, he may question his own judgment, contribution and efficacy. He may dwell on his lack of credentials, his academic unpreparedness. He may see himself as having transcended his appropriate function.

GH 1: I went to the parole board personally and I spoke to one of the parole officers who was responsible for Timothy, and he in turn got in touch with his superior. He made his superior available to me and I discussed the possible stopping of Timothy's conditional release. Now normally this is unusual. But Frank and myself and Herbie discussed this, and we felt that it was the wrong move . . . the input that we have is respected to the point where if we say "look, we really feel this," they'll consider it. They'll look into the possibility. Number one, we found out that he was going out to a YMCA. On his own program, in other words a reasonable assurance type thing. Timothy was in no condition to go out to a YMCA unsupervised. Number two, he didn't have a job. Nobody was going to hire Timothy, not in the condition he was in. So we figured he would go out there, somebody would take advantage of him or he would get himself in a position where he'd get locked up again, or shot, and we couldn't see this happening. We just felt that after six months or so, even though we knew it was wrong what we were doing, keeping him locked up like this, it was existence, you know? And it beat being shot. So I intervened and they canceled his conditional release as a result of my going up there. Then about a month later I noticed that two ladies came, one from the Department of Social Services in New York City and one from the Civil Liberties Union. Both very very well-read, very professional people. One was a lawyer, one was a lady, I think she had a psychologist's degree, something like this, but she was from a Department of Social Services. And they were working on a program for Timothy. Now where they became interested in Timothy I don't know. They had like a bulldog determination to get this kid out of Green Haven and into the street. I told them, I explained to them what the past had been like. They didn't feel that we had observed him properly and they felt that him going out there on the street he was going to be O.K. . . . even though I was keeping him incarcerated, which is really a rotten thing, I hate it myself, being here incarcerated eight hours a day, I still think that had he gone out there Frank and I and Herbie would have been the ones that pulled the trigger on him had he gotten hurt. We really felt that way, and that's why we did it. Even though I tangibly went upstairs and said "look, do this," we had discussed it. I don't know if I was trying to spread the guilt a little bit, but anyway we had discussed it and I said "look, let me be the spokesman," and I went ahead and did it . . . and I think a big factor involved in Timothy's not relating that well with us — although we felt that he did, he obviously didn't do that well with us, because he left in worse condition than he came — was the idea that we had to wear two hats with Timothy. I think if we would have shook the uniform, and it had been a lot more informal. Even though we would have lost the security, and we would have lost the respect that the security gave us, I think we would have gained somebody that was worthwhile and we could have helped. I really do believe that.

I: You think you could have reached him if you could have gotten away from the role of guard?

GH 1: I think, naturally I really don't know. But I'm sure it would have helped. I felt very insecure inasmuch as I didn't have the education or the knowledge to be able to say to him "listen, I want to help you," and know what I was going to do, know where to start and in which direction to go in. I don't know what work I'm looking for but I just didn't feel, I wished that I would have had an education or a degree in psychiatry at the time because Timothy wanted to be helped and it was something that we experienced on a daily basis, and it was almost like a waste, you know, that we just sat there and watched him regress to the point where there was nothing else we could do after his maximum term expired, we went ahead and got in touch with the psychiatrist, we had a 3PC civil commitment put on him. Even at the end, it seemed so cruel what we were doing, but we just felt that after so many months as Timothy had been with us, and by that I mean on the tier, we just couldn't see throwing him to the dogs. So we got him a commitment in a civil hospital. Which isn't the best thing in the world, but at least it was a structured environment where if he wanted the help it would have been available to him.

"Corrections officer" is not a sterile label. Men fit under the label, in ways that make sense. We admit that there are few such men. Some day there may be more. On the other hand, there may not be. The corrections officer role is tender, the soil is arid, and it is infested by the custody ethic. New life needs nurturance. It needs strong support from its setting.

Men at the top of prisons often talk corrections and act custodially. Their formula is "humane custody." But humane custody is a myth, because it is a paradox. Where custody thrives, humaneness does not. Security defines a staff-inmate gap which widens, and makes men obdurate and difficult. A man usually bites the hand that reluctantly feeds him.

Our new "keeper" (if he survives) will be a "brother's keeper." He will be a man who cares and relates and helps. If we want such a man, we must care in turn. Officers must be appreciated, rewarded, assisted and their work disseminated. We must build our own ethic of support. Such an ethic builds bridges across human gaps — such as those between institutional staff and their clients.

Note

1. The interviews were conducted as part of a research program entitled "Interventions for Inmate Survival." This project was funded as Grant No. 77N-99-0030 by the National Institute of Law Enforcement and Criminal Justice (LEAA). Officers were interviewed in five maximum security institutions operated by the New York State Department of Correctional Services. We are grateful to the officers and their supervisors for making these interviews possible.

Chapter 7

Informal Helping Networks in Prison: The Shape of Grass-Roots Correctional Intervention*

Robert Johnson

Prisons address multiple, often contradictory goals. The conflicting goals of custody and treatment are perhaps the most significant examples of this phenomenon. However, neither of these goals takes account of the central fact that imprisonment is a disruptive, stressful, and often crisis-engendering experience. The failure of correctional systems to define as a principal task the identification and amelioration of inmate adjustment problems and crises may partially explain the prevalence of custodial problems and the dismal showing of many rehabilitation efforts. An exploration of the sources of this failure to address basic concerns of prisoners may indicate key challenges for correctional administrators who seek to run humane institutions and to use prisons as vehicles for treatment and planned personal change.

Inmate adjustment problems are a relevant consideration for both treatment and custodial staff. Broadly speaking, both groups are responsible for the living environments they help create and maintain. More concretely, the tasks of both groups are directly affected by the problems in living that inmates experience in prison. Thus, treatment staff, whether we are speaking of psychiatrists, psychologists, or counselors, must assist inmates with problems or crises of adjustment if they are to get down to their primary task, which is that of fostering insight and personal change among their clients. Custodial workers must also be responsive to stress among their inmates, even if this amounts to nothing more than a timely referral, if they are to maintain a stable prison environment. While it may be possible to isolate formal treatment programs (like psychotherapy or group counseling) from formal custodial tasks (like lock-ups and counts), responsibility for helping people with problems is not so readily parceled out. Inmates who are lonely, fearful, or simmering with resentment require an immediate and tangible response to their problems. They may need little more than elementary assistance: a word of friendly advice,

---

* Copyright 1976, Pergamon Press, Ltd. Reprinted with permission from *Journal of Criminal Justice*, Vol. 4.

contact with someone to whom they can safely ventilate their concerns, or minor technical assistance, as when a guard bends a rule to better fit an inmate's situation. These are examples of "basic human services," in the sense that virtually any concerned person can and should provide the needed help. Recognition of shared obligations to inmates in terms of providing such human services may form the basis for ongoing cooperation between treatment and custodial staff. Such cooperation, in turn, may lay the groundwork for relations with inmates that encourage trust, personal commitment, and the willingness to change.

Comparatively little thought has been devoted to promoting staff cooperation in the delivery of human services to prisoners.[1] This partly reflects the unwillingness to look closely at the kinds of living environments our prisons create, other than to note the troublesome presence of inmate subcultures and roles that somehow anesthetize inmates against the "pains of imprisonment" and otherwise operate to disrupt treatment programs (Sykes, 1966; Toch, 1975). There is also the tendency to focus change efforts on the treatment-custody divide, a chasm that may prove unbridgeable, or at least inordinately difficult to close. The overriding problem may be that we lock both inmates and staff into restrictive roles, and then we set about to undo what we have done by changing names (Weber, 1969) or by creating intermediary or linking roles (Glaser, 1969; Briggs and Dowling, 1964). By taking a more functional view of the problem — by looking in detail at what various staff and inmates actually do in their day-to-day prison lives — we may uncover creative possibilities for evolving cooperative solutions to shared problems.

We know, for example, that a significant minority of prison guards — one survey reports one in five — combine custodial and human service obligations in carrying out their jobs (Johnson, 1977). These individuals are a largely untapped correctional resource. They are neither identified on organizational charts nor supported in their efforts. They must operate cautiously, aware of stereotypes and resistances shared by both inmates and staff. Many of them, untutored and unassisted, yield to pressures to assume a purely custodial role. Others persist in their helping efforts, sometimes accomplishing minor miracles for the inmates in crisis overlooked or shunned by the prison's formal treatment system. A few such guards establish unannounced working links with treatment staff. These guards, and the treatment staff with whom they work, operate as allies and constitute "informal helping networks." That is, they informally expand their roles to include more or less binding responsibilities shared with other staff in the identification, referral, and provision of a range of basic human services to susceptible inmates. Analysis of the factors that influence the operation and effect of such informal helping networks may indicate more efficient ways to deploy existing correctional resources in the amelioration of inmate adjustment problems.

METHOD

Data

The data for this paper consist of interviews conducted with a sample of custodial and treatment workers (N = 48) in two New York State prisons for men. This is the second part of a two-part research project. Part I of the study entailed a preliminary delineation of the nature and extent of helping roles played by prison guards (see Johnson, 1977). Samples were subsequently drawn from the staffs of the two prisons to provide information on patterns of cooperation and noncooperation between treatment staff and guards who viewed themselves as helping persons. The aim in this phase of the study was to reconstruct through interviews the parameters of informal helping networks, to identify factors that encouraged or inhibited their development, and to obtain some indication of their utility in the helping process.

In identifying candidates for this phase of the study, we assumed that cooperation (or lack of it) often begins at the top, in this case with members of the treatment staff. We therefore began our interviews with the treatment staff (counselors and psychologists, N = 10). The interviews were used to explore the helping roles (if any) allocated to prison guards. We solicited the names of guards who were viewed as resources by treatment personnel, and subsequently interviewed them (N = 20). We also sought peer nominations from members of the custodial staff to obtain access to guards who displayed a helping orientation but who might not have a working relationship with the treatment staff (N = 18).

The interviews centred on interactions between staff members and inmates with adjustment problems. No attempt was made to specify the range of inmate adjustment problems, though it was apparent that loneliness, fear, and resentment were prevalent concerns.[2] The focus of the research was on mapping the broad outlines of the human service delivery process. Thus, the interview format called for a step-by-step reconstruction of the process by which inmates with adjustment problems were identified and handled by staff. The nature of the services delivered, the roles ascribed to the various personnel, and the perceived impact of interventions were explored in depth.

All but two (4.2 percent) of the interviews were tape-recorded with the consent of the interviewee. Unrecorded interviews were summarized on tape immediately after the session. The verbatim interviews and interview summaries were subsequently transcribed and will be used to illustrate important points.

Findings

Interviews revealed that most of the treatment staff did not establish systematic working links with custodial personnel. In fact, three of the ten treatment staff interviewed indicated no involvement whatsoever with custodial staff in the delivery of helping services, other than the elementary expectation that guards would observe clients and record unusual symptoms. The remaining treatment staff in our sample indicated cooperative relations with one or two on-line custodial personnel who were viewed as resources for problem management and crisis intervention. However, these resources were, for the most part, sparingly deployed; the guards made comparatively few referrals to treatment staff, and in turn were rarely called on to provide assistance to clients.

Interviews with guards designated as helping persons by other members of the custodial staff produced equivalent findings. Ten of these eighteen men indicated limited involvement with members of the treatment staff. And fully half of this group perceived treatment staff as unresponsive to input from guards and as largely unable to assist inmates with problems.

In only two instances were informal helping networks involving four or more persons identified. One such network proved quite extensive. Here, a corrections counselor established ongoing cooperative links with ten members of the custodial staff. These men, in turn, were able to influence some of their peers to play constructive roles in the helping process. The guards viewed themselves as part of a "team" led by the counselor and provided illustrations of an informal helping network in action.

The sources of cooperation and noncooperation revealed in interviews with treatment and custodial staff provided a context for exploring the obstacles to human service delivery in prison and the conditions under which informal problem-solving teams or networks emerge.

DISCUSSION

Obstacles to Human Service Delivery

The delivery of human services in prison may be impeded by the conflict and antagonism that often characterize the relationships between custodial and treatment staff. While both groups can be conceptualized as agents of change (Hall, Williams, and Tomaino, 1969) — a task that requires a human relations perspective in dealing with inmates — the immediate requirements of custody and treatment often differ substantially, making it difficult for understanding, empathy, and trust to develop among these groups. Routine interactions, in which the business of custody interrupts or sidetracks treatment (and vice versa), can highlight such role conflicts and lead to nonproductive interactions.

One of our respondents, an officer turned counselor, described conflict between custodial and treatment personnel as a matter of mutual exclusion and mistrust. While he could circumvent such problems —

because he has played both roles and has modified his behavior accordingly — most staff members cannot:

> Treatment Staff A: The dynamics of the prison is security versus civilian. Neither one trusts the other. For example, many counselors have trouble getting through doors and the guard will just look at them and eventually open the door, you know, or [say] "I haven't got time right now." And then again the counselors don't understand the functions of the officers. Like especially if the counselor goes into the block and wants to see a man. Well, if you go into a block at a special time, that officer is awfully busy and he has certain things that he has to do — and having been an officer I can understand this and I know when I can get to the man and when I can't get to the man. And in many cases, he'll give me the key, and I take it and go.

Lower level prison guards, like their police counterparts, form a kind of subculture that stands as a shield against threats from outsiders. Such defensiveness is reinforced by the hierarchical, authoritarian organization of the prison, in which the guard is comparatively powerless and vulnerable. Problems are compounded when treatment staff, who may be insensitive to the guard's position, act in ways that produce fear and resentment. And, independent of their actions, prison professionals must contend with guards who are prone to view them as probable enemies rather than as potential allies:

> Treatment Staff A: The guards stick together. You see, we are in a military-type of structure here in a prison and they become paranoid, should we say, of a civilian. Because if he gets a write-up — okay, if the sergeant comes down here and says, "What did you do to this guy? The counselor said you did this." And right away the guard hates the counselor and out goes the word about the counselor. And so this is what they are fighting. They don't want the openers. They . . . have nothing to hide, though. They have nothing to hide, . . . it is just the structure of society among the officers. They are all sticking together and you are a civilian and you are on the outside.

Treatment staff, for their part, may also see themselves as an embattled minority in the prison. They are likely to be aware that many guards don't take them seriously, often characterizing them as at best impractical, and sometimes as wishy-washy, effeminate, or snobby. Since the tempo and climate of day-to-day prison life on the tiers and yards is influenced heavily by the custodial staff, treatment staff who venture forth from their offices in search of clients may come to feel vulnerable and out of place. Interactions with guards, in which respect for titles and degrees is sometimes conspicuously absent, may add to problems of alienation and leave treatment staff feeling unappreciated and abused:

> Treatment Staff A: His skin has got to be as thick as this table. He has got to be able to take harrassment and handle it. And if he can't

take harrassment then he shouldn't be a counselor. . . . Now I kid with the men — the officers — and I kid hard and they kid hard; but it is surface. But a lot of guys take this too seriously. They don't know how to handle it.

Treatment staff may become defensive under such pressures and respond by ruling guards out of the helping process. In describing their lack of involvement with guards, they stipulate that inmates don't share their problems with guards, or routinely dupe guards into invoking the prison's treatment staff unnecessarily. A similar move entails scheduling clients in a mechanical fashion, without regard to input (in the form of perceived emergencies) from on-line staff or inmates:

> Treatment Staff B: Well, as a rule, [an] inmate won't confide a problem to the custodial. He just says, "I have a problem and I want to see my counselor." And of course we have a lot of people that will feign a problem to get the guard to call. So these are things we have to watch for.
> Treatment Staff C: I run a very rigid list. If a man puts in a note [to see me] I schedule him and I go right down the list, name after name. Because the inmates have a tendency to break in any way they can if they feel they have an immediate problem, and this creates conflict for me.

Excluding guards from human service work unnecessarily restricts the ameliorative resources available to inmates with problems. Such a posture on the part of treatment staff also places guards who want to play combined custodial and helping roles in a bind. Some prison guards feel their job requires sensitivity to the human dimension of the prison experience. Their proximity to inmates and the relationships this can create makes them ideal candidates for helping roles. Yet when they are unable to get help for men in trouble — because their input is not taken seriously by treatment staff — the aggrieved inmate will blame them:

> Custodial Staff A: If something happened like an emergency, . . . (of course, you have to realize that the inmate thinks it is an emergency), in his mind it is an emergency.
> I: Yeah.
> A: And you go to the service unit and you tell them that it is an emergency — that a man has an emergency and you try to put yourself in the man's shoes.
> I: Yeah.
> A: See, they look up to us and you have to stand by them. But you try to talk to the service unit and they say, "Write me a note and I will see him the next time I have a meeting." And that really gets a man mad.
> I: And you have got to go back and tell the man?
> A: I have to go back and tell the man. And then you have got to go back and tell him that's the way it is: "The service unit says this

is not an emergency." All right, you tell the man and he gets mad at you.
I: That leaves you stuck?
A: It puts me in the middle. And you try to talk to him, and in a case like that, it's hard. In fact, there was one man there (he put in for a furlough), he blew up at me and I just listened. It was nothing personal, I understand that. I knew where it was directed . . . and he [came] back to me later and he apologized. He said, "I didn't mean to," and I said, "Don't worry about it. I understand. I have been through this before."

Such scenarios may breed demoralization. This appears to be particularly true when failure to obtain or provide assistance for susceptible inmates culminates in personal crises. In the face of such setbacks, the guard may begin to doubt his skills as a helper, or question his competence in the absence of technical training. He may conclude that he is cast in the role of second-class citizen by prison professionals, who will ignore his input as a matter of course. Whatever the response, we find a residue of bitterness and self-doubt that will contaminate future interactions with inmates in crisis and those formally designated to help them:

Custodial Staff B: I felt that I wanted to help him, and I felt very insecure inasmuch as I didn't have the education or the knowledge to be able to say to him, "Listen, I want to help you," and know what I was going to do, know where to start and in which direction to go. . . . I don't know what word I'm looking for but I just didn't feel . . . I wished that I . . . had an education or a degree in psychiatry at the time because Timothy wanted to be helped and it was something that we experienced on a daily basis; and it was almost like a waste, you know, that we just sat there and watched him regress to the point where there was nothing else we could do.
Custodial Staff C: The biggest complaint is the civilians complain because they don't have . . . cooperation with the officers. "We can't get no cooperation with the officers." *We* can't get no cooperation with them either. I mean like I said before, you get educated people up there and you tell them, and they don't listen to you because they feel that you're one step ahead of the inmate — you're just a dummy. So consequently this is the way these things end up.

A potentially more serious problem is that interactions with unresponsive treatment staff may spawn a kind of guerilla warfare in which the natives (concerned guards) attempt to exclude the foreigners (treatment staff) from the human service delivery process. At best, the preserve of treatment personnel may be limited by guards to last-ditch interventions with out-and-out psychotics. For the substantial remainder of inmates with less disabling adjustment problems, the guard may designate himself as the sole source of assistance or support:

> Custodial Staff D: What I usually do is I watch them. I don't throw in a psychiatric report on them. I try to find out what is their problem, just by general view of how they are acting. . . . Because there [are] very few people that you can talk to that will do anything about it, and you might as well do it yourself. . . . I don't bother to write psychiatric reports any more. If the guy is ready to go nuts, I try to talk to him and find out what is the matter. And God bless him if I can't help him.

Many guards describe the prison's formal treatment system as unresponsive, cumbersome, unpredictable, and, for the most part, impotent. Neither they (unassisted) nor the treatment staff (without their aid) appear able to effectively address inmate adjustment problems. The inmate with problems, as the guards see it, is apt to be ignored, routinely medicated, or otherwise unhelped:

> Custodial Staff E: I don't think that either [I] or the individual himself can get the proper satisfaction from the service unit if it is a pressure problem or the conditions that he is trying to exist under. I could not. I don't think that the service unit could help him cope with it. By the same token, in my opinion, I know that there is a lot of medication that is being used [by psychiatrists] to help these people cope with the problems, but I don't think that it is actually helping them cope with their problems. I just think that it is just helping them exist with the problem and not cope with the problems.
> Custodial Staff F: If he is ready to go off the deep end, you know, you should get him up to the hospital or something. But then, to take a guy out of his cell and put him in the hospital, personally, to me, I think that there is still more pressure up there. And you have to go through so much procedure to have a guy stay up there, committed up there. And I think that the delay and the breakdown is not doing the individual any good that needs attention.
> I: So you don't feel too good about that existing resolution of problems?
> F: No. No. No. I think that when they come back a lot of times they are on a lot of medication. . . . [The psychiatrists] give it by the officers in the blocks. And the medication that is given is prescribed. However, you see, that is not the solution. Most of the cases that come back here, they go off the deep end anyway.

Given such perceptions, guards may develop a cautious approach to inmates with problems. Intervention, they know, is a risky, strenuous, thankless job. Treatment staff, ironically, may take a similar stance. Having marked off human service work as their exclusive province, they may find themselves unable to meet the overwhelming demand for their services. A compromise may thus emerge in the form of quasi-helping roles in which surface relationships substitute for genuine involvement. The inmate, somehow, is presumed the beneficiary in this arrangement:

Treatment Staff D: I don't find a lack of opportunity to work with men. It is just that there are so many men and we have so little help that you don't find time to really do the things that you would like to do. And you have to be a little cautious, because you can't really build someone up for a tumble; you can't suddenly immerse yourself in their problems and attempt to work with them toward achievement and solutions and then suddenly cut this person off because you are limited timewise. Consequently, you have to place a lot of control on yourself — just to what point are you going to commit yourself to this person? — because going too far could be even more frustrating than if you had just not bothered with the man in the first place.

Conflicts centering on the nature and ownership of helping roles thus may produce a system that is often unable to intervene and assist inmates in trouble. The result is that all involved parties, and particularly the inmates, come out losers.

Grass-Roots Intervention

Not all staff are stymied in their efforts to play helping roles. Some, for example, develop innovative means of mobilizing otherwise unresponsive human service resources. A guard, denied direct access to the psychiatrist, may invoke the disciplinary process to highlight an inmate's need and place the weight of custodial officialdom behind his request:

Custodial Staff G: A disciplinary report was the only way that I felt that I could get him to the psychiatrist.
I: Because the man didn't want to go or the psychiatrist didn't have time?
G: Because the psychiatrist didn't have the time. In other words, when you lock a man in his cell, he has . . . to see the adjustment committee, which consists of a lieutenant, the guy that is counseling him, and a correction officer. . . . Now I attach a psychiatric report. The lieutenant, who then was the head man on the adjustment committee, would not handle this end of the man's case. So naturally he would refer him to the psychiatrist. So the lieutenant refers them and then there is going to be action.
I: So this was your way of getting help for this guy?
G: Right.

Other guards are willing to bend prison rules and depart from informal norms to secure assistance for inmates. Where necessary, they may involve inmates in the helping process and make moves that open them to problems with their superiors. For example:

Custodial Staff H: And the other inmate came to me and said, "Let's put everything aside, you're an officer and I'm an inmate, but let's think of him as a man." And he had a very good point. But the only solution that I could come up with was the fact that I had already put in an observation report and it came back with the man, there wasn't that much involved in it. The main thing was they didn't have an interpreter with them at the time, I don't believe. So what I did, I went around the system a little bit and I told this inmate, "Explain to him that he has to go on sick call in the morning to see the psychiatrist, and what you do, you put a slip in for a sick call in the morning with the man. This way you'll both go to the psychiatrist together, you'll be there to interpret." I said, "You may have a little bit of problems with the sergeant, but explain to the sergeant why you're there. If he has any questions, tell him to come to me." The next day he thanked me because they had moved the man out.

Treatment staff may engage in more direct advocacy for the troubled inmate. They may give special attention to nonroutine cases, even encouraging inmates to write to officials in their own behalf and to involve their families in the campaign. Where fellow professionals are unresponsive, it may prove helpful to play staff off against one another, and to carefully document the handling (or mishandling) of a case. If all else fails, the advocate can approach the superintendent, memos in hand, to force a response.

The following excerpt, depicting a counselor's efforts to secure psychiatric transfers for prisoners, illustrates these points:

> Treatment Staff A: You see, there are many ways to write a transfer. You can just open the file and give all the data or you can really get into the man and put your feelings on the paper, that you feel that this man should go. And I also advise the man to write the commissioner himself. You see, I feel that a prisoner should have all avenues to go after for his mental health, because then he knows, "Well, geesh, this guy told me to write to this man who is the head of the department," and then he regains faith. Look, I am not going to hide anything from him; "So you go your way and you get to your family and I will go to mine; and then maybe the two of us, we can pull it off."
> I: And what do you do if the guy can't be transferred. What other resources do you have available to you?
> A: The resource that I have is the psychistrist, and I use him quite a bit. I refer men to him and then, if I don't like the diagnosis, I confront him on it. And I also use Dr. C., who is the resident doctor, to back me up. Now if we have a man — I had one man in this case: a young fellow, a young white lad who was deathly afraid of [the prison] population — [who] had been in homosexual swindles before and was mentally ill, (not the homosexual ill part — but mentally ill besides that). He was generally distracted and this was his makeup. Well, the man kept living in special housing and I kept writing and writing and the man was rotting. And they gave him medicine so that would calm him down, but the man was still rotting

in that cell. And so finally I just came right out with it, told the psychiatrist exactly what was happening, and went right to the superintendent. I had three cases and I forced the psychiatrist to see him to make up his mind, "What are we going to do with this man?" And I won the ball game in two of the cases and I lost one.
I: And you say that you went to the superintendent also?
A: Yes. I went to the superintendent. You see, I find in our department that if you put it in writing, you will get answers.

Such single-handed confrontations with an obdurate treatment system are not the most common means of securing help for inmates whose adjustment difficulties go unattended. More often, a process of selective involvement among similarly motivated staff provides a vehicle for intervention. Through friendship, trial and error, or simple persistence, some custodial and treatment staff develop working links with others who share a human service orientation. Acting as members of informal helping networks or teams, these individuals work cooperatively to extend or supplement the range of services available to inmates.

One of our officers, for example, noted that the rapport he had with officers who had become counselors formed the basis for cooperation across staff lines when problems arose. For other men, assignment of a responsive treatment person to their work area provided a context for shared problem-solving efforts:

Custodial Staff I: You usually go to the person that you know best. Any officer would. Like some of the personnel that work in the service unit used to be officers, and you can relate to them better than a person from outside.
I: So you feel that you can work a little better with the counselors that had been officers formerly?
Custodial Staff I: Definitely. There is no problem with them. Definitely. I found out that you get better results because they have come across the same [types of situations] when they were officers and they know what the officer has to put up with and the problems that they have and they really try to help out — more so I think, than the civilians.
Custodial Staff J: See, no mail is censored anymore. And the first man they usually see is the officer. So what I will do (I've got a good service unit man, he's assigned to the shop area), I call automatically when they come to me with a problem, about correspondence, home problems, I call him right away. And he says to me that he'll try to get down as soon as possible, I think he's real good. He's one of the men that understands inmate problems. All of them that work in the service unit, I don't think they understand them all, or they don't try to understand them all, I don't know.
I: So this is one man that you have confidence in, that if you say something to him it's going to get done.
J: I have confidence in this service unit man, yeah.

There are two sides to this coin. Treatment staff, through exposure, may develop tremendous respect for mental health oriented officers. Two of the ten men interviewed could hardly contain their admiration for guards who made astute clinical observations during custodial rounds or who maintained a benevolent, human relations stance toward their inmates. For example:

> Treatment Staff E: This was an officer that was quite sensitive, and I find that . . . unique because he is in a very demanding situation — he is in reception, and the whole situation there is a great deal of traffic and transient type of movement.
> I: Yeah. So he almost picked this guy out of a crowd then?
> E: Right. He knew that the guy was in need of . . . care.
> I: Are there other officers of this type that refer people to you?
> E: Oh yes, yes. There is certainly a percentage of intelligent, competent officers who are sensitive to human needs and look at the inmates as other human beings, and not merely as inmates, and feel that needs for them are heightened because of their status as inmates.

Another professional was moved by the willingness of some guards to assist him in the care and treatment of susceptible inmates, noting that the prevalence of adjustment problems and crises in prison might plausibly make any guard callous and unconcerned:

> Treatment Staff F: On a number of occasions I have received a concerned response on behalf of the block officer or shop officer or perhaps civilian employee that would be in the immediate area and could help the situation. It has been surprising that it hasn't been a cold response, just because of the mere number of individuals involved in everyday talk of homosexuality, or aggressive inmates preying on weak inmates, or family problems. They have been quite receptive.

Two members of the treatment staff expressly solicited the assistance of officers and others who worked in close proximity to the inmates. These men operated at the hub of informal helping networks. Their resources included a wide range of on-line prison staff who support, monitor, and refer crisis-prone inmates for them. Such cooperation, these treatment staff members noted, could provide the critical edge in service delivery. For example:

> Treatment Staff G: It was a depression situation. The foundry man, Mr. K., was paying special attention to him and helping him, and if he would see that he was getting a little withdrawn, he would call me and I would then have him up. And we saved this problem a couple times by just getting him up here to just shoot the breeze with me. And he would get a whole lot of things out of his system and it seemed to soften him. But then while Mr. K. was out sick, nobody

paid any attention to him and he went out on one of these binges and I guess he was really almost out cold.
I: So in other words, when you have this man in the foundry who is paying attention to him and is rapidly referring him, you can control him?
G: That's right. It seems as though he was the key.
I: And without that referral he went off the deep end?
G: That's right. Plus I think that he found support from Mr. K., which he needed.

Allies outside the formal treatment system can substantially increase the resources available to the professional when problems arise. The same holds true for the custodial staff, who can rely on the treatment person to intervene on request. Members of these "teams" see themselves as part of a reciprocal helping system. Their shared goal, as they see it, is to provide assistance to inmates with adjustment problems.

The following interview excerpts illustrate these observations from the vantage point of a treatment person and an on-line staff member (a shop foreman), who class themselves as members of a helping team:

Treatment Staff G: I have quite a lot of resources to depend on. One of the reasons is they know that they can come back to me for . . . help when they have a problem. One of the things I find is that we become a team. I even get called about other counselors' people that won't, about the people that won't cooperate up there. And I am saying this to you very honestly and I am not saying it boastfully, just gratefully; my concern is for the men that are here. I am employed because I am to help with correction. And these people know that by the same token that they have problems, they can call me and, even if it is not my case, I will go and give them information or try and help the situation.

Custodial Staff K: Mr. G. and I, we have a working relationship and understanding. It is not an official understanding, but when he does have a man that is assigned to him with a problem — they might have a hard time adjusting or need a little supervision in some areas, such as adjusting to the institution, or perhaps because he is in this particular setting and is away from home and is lonely, or maybe is subject to pressure from his peers within the institution — he sends him to my shop. . . . And up here I take and give the inmates their choice of what they would like to do and I work with them in whatever they choose to do. And in working with him [the man with the problem], I try to keep an eye on his personal [relationships] with each one as I can. . . . And I also tell them that any problems that they have and I can help them with or give advice on, I will help them. And if I don't know the answer, I will find out the answer from them or refer them to the person who has the answer. And it has worked out very well.

The benefits of participation in informal helping networks appear enormous. In addition to rapid referral of inmates in crisis and cooperation in the implementation of treatment plans, the professional obtains access to the resources of team members. Guards who view themselves as allies in human service work, for example, may be able to induce their peers to play constructive roles and may otherwise open doors that might remain shut to treatment staff. We summarized an interview with a guard who performed just such a service for a man committed to his care:

> Custodial Staff L: Mr. G. on occasion asks him to watch some men or to support them and he will do this. And he gave us an example of a guy who the counselor told him had a problem and had to get into a good program. And this officer went out of his way to recommend to the man that he try to go into the auto maintenance shop. (Apparently he had noted that the man had hot rod magazines in his cell.) He also knew the auto maintenance man, knew that the shop was small, wouldn't have pressure, and would be a good setting for the man to work in. So the officer personally went to bat for the man. Now apparently the auto maintenance man goes out of his way to respond to recommendations from this officer because they are friends and also because this officer gets his car repaired in that shop, so the shop foreman has the feeling that he would only get serious recommendations from him. As it turned out the man did beautifully in that shop and seemed to be adjusting very well.

Additionally, guards may be more capable of securing follow-up for inmates with adjustment problems once they are out of the hands of treatment staff. They are more familiar with the workings of the prison system and may be more able to share information with relevant staff. It is also possible that their requests for supervision of susceptible inmates may be taken more seriously since they are likely to note the custodial connotations of the inmate's condition:

> Custodial Staff M: A great many times we have had different things come up where an inmate needs help. For example, he has lost his mother or his father and it was impossible for him to get home for the funeral. In cases like this, I also call the minister, whichever faith he is, and have him talk to him. And I also call the block officer where he locks in at night and make the block officer aware of the particular problem. And I let the cage door man and floor sergeant know so they can warn the watch commander at night so that if there is a slipup during the night, or the officer who would normally be on would not get the message and there is a relief man, that there is an awareness of the problem and they can check the cell a little more frequently in case a guy tries to commit suicide or do something violent. So when I find out something like this I try to find a way to follow it through, just for the protection of the individual and the institution.

On-line staff can also provide direct support and intervention for inmates in crisis. This may allow them to help inmates who are unresponsive to treatment personnel or who need on-the-spot assistance as their crisis unfolds. Here, the staff members can modulate the inmate's immediate environment to shield him from pressure and reduce suffering. As the following excerpt reveals, a shop officer who cares can literally shepherd the inmate through periods of serious and potentially disabling stress:

> Custodial Staff N: When his grandmother died, he wasn't able to go to the funeral. Now I knew that he couldn't go and he was quite sure that he couldn't, yet he wanted someone to check. So I got ahold of his counselor and we discussed it and I kept the inmate in the office when I did this so that he would at least know that someone was trying to do something. Then when it was over and he discovered that he couldn't go, the man goes and broke down into tears. And he sat right there and he was crying. And of course the other inmates were going by the office and some of them, you know, had the tendency to snicker a little bit. And just in general conversation with the inmates, I made it plain to them that in my eyes it required some degree of a man to care that much about his family. And I made sure that this particular inmate was there when I said it to kind of reassure him that at least someone in authority didn't consider that crying and concern over a member of the family was childish, was babyish. It was the type of action that one would expect from a sensitive man. . . .
>
> I had to keep him busy. I had to keep his mind occupied. But you can't drive a person like that. You have . . . to keep him busy enough to keep his problems off of his mind and at the same time try to communicate to him that . . . you haven't just disregarded him, that you care and you are interested in his problems and what is going on with his family, even though in most cases there is absolutely nothing that I can do about it. All I can do is give him some degree of understanding and try to help him if necessary, try to almost shield him from those individuals inside who might take a dim view of his actions, who might not care, because these people would only aggravate the situation. . . . There may be a block officer that, well, he just doesn't care. He doesn't care what goes on. So if you are working that night, if you have to bring out a crew for some type of work, you try and include this individual in it to get him away from this other influence. To give him every hour that you can give him to where he can try to readjust himself with a minimum of pressure.
>
> This is very difficult for me to put into words, because it all stems . . . , at least to me, from not pampering an inmate, because I don't feel that you can pamper these men, they don't want to be pampered, but from showing a legitimate concern. And you cannot hide this. If you are concerned about an inmate, he knows it. He might shoot his mouth off and he might raise a great deal of fuss,

but he knows that you care and when they realize this, the majority of inmates will respond. . . . How do you put concern into words? It is very difficult for me. It is just caring. It is being interested in that man's welfare and trying to use some degree of common sense in dealing with the problem right at that instant.

Familiarity with the inmates under their supervision, and with the culture of the prison community in which they operate, makes it possible for guards to tailor general intervention strategies to fit specific individuals and circumstances. This service may prove critical when the local wisdom of staff or inmates indicates singularly inappropriate conduct for an inmate with problems. For example, the advice given to inmates pressured by their peers is to fight back against their opponents thereby establishing their right to be left alone. Whatever the general value of this suggestion may be, the formula is selective in that it fails to account for inmates devoured by gangs they have unwisely challenged, or crushed at the hands of prisonwise inmates who gleefully respond to hollow threats. Fortunately, the self-destructive connotations of such gestures may be obvious to sensitive guards, who may be in a position to intervene and prevent a catastrophe:

> Custodial Staff O: He was a little guy who was afraid of everything and everybody and then all of a sudden in a day's time he started standing up, which he knew was foolish, but he started standing up to some of the roughest guys in the division. And it just wasn't him. And I was afraid that he was going to get hurt because these guys don't take that kind of stuff. It was a complete reversal.
> I: So it just stood out to you—here's a meek guy acting like a tiger.
> O: And plus it was all in a day's time. One day he was a meek guy and the next day he was on the move and he had just changed like that. . . . The kid was actually serious. He wasn't putting it on. It was actually a serious thing. He actually, if it came right down to it, would have taken these guys on. Regardless of . . . the consequences. This is what I feel anyway, and I knew he would get hurt. . . . So, you know, I had to step in and stop this.

Some officers develop great pride in their ability to play helping roles. They may come to view themselves as problem-solving specialists possessing techniques or perspectives that make them indispensible resources with certain types of inmates. Some men, for example, noted that the treatment staff routinely turned to them for assistance in the management of inmates with problems relating to authority figures. They attributed their success in such cases to a flexible, human relations approach to their job that set them apart from their more custodially oriented (and less effective) peers. For example:

> I: So you seem to have real success with these problem cases?
> Custodial Staff P: Yeah, I have done very well with them. And like

I don't, every time a guy steps out of line, I don't give him a ticket [disciplinary report]. I find out I can talk to them pretty good unless they back me in a corner. In other words, if they don't listen and they don't stop with their mouth, then I will give them a ticket. But ordinarily I can talk to them. And I usually like to get them alone so I can talk to them. And usually it works out pretty good. . . . So we talk over the problem that he is involved in and I find that in nine out of ten times I solve it right there on the spot, without a lock up and without a ticket. . . . Now others want to go by the book. Fine. That is the way they want to operate. I don't. I don't believe today in this place that you can go strictly by the book.

Informal helping networks, once established, may snowball. Thus, the counselor who cultivates resources among the custodial staff finds he has access (through a team member) to others among the guard ranks. A similar spread of influence may occur in reverse, with guards who are heavily involved in human service work obtaining the cooperation of treatment staff. The cooperation these guards received from treatment staff may reflect their credibility as helping persons. Treatment persons outside the guard's team may prove responsive to requests for assistance because they learn that a referral signals an inmate in real trouble:

Custodial Staff N: I find there are several counselors that are genuinely interested in the welfare of the inmates. And if a serious problem arises, then usually I can get them right up to see their counselors, because the counselors realize that if I call them and say, "Such-and-such has a serious problem," all right, here it is. [T]hey will immediately call that inmate up to discuss it if I feel that it is something that I can't simply handle.

Cooperative links between and among custodial and treatment staff may substantially expand the pool of services available to inmates with adjustment problems. The result, as we have seen, can entail more rapid referral, more reliable implementation of treatment plans, more comprehensive follow-up, and the prospect of timely crisis intervention. In such informal helping networks, we see a range of human service resources targeted on inmates with adjustment problems.

IMPLICATIONS

Correctional policy is currently undergoing what may amount to a radical change of focus. Incapacitation, hailed as the manifestation of a "justice model" (Fogel, 1975), or described as simply an accurate and honest statement of what corrections can accomplish (Wilson, 1975), is fast becoming a dominant feature of correctional policy. This may mean that correctional managers who wish to pursue rehabilitation, or at least to avoid or reduce the debilitating effects of human warehousing, can no longer rely on an infusion of programs to accomplish their objectives. Instead, they may need to look to the existing resources within the prison if they are to develop and maintain penal institutions in which effective adaptation and, ideally, constructive change can occur. One such resource — the deployment of staff in what we have called informal helping networks — has been described in this article. Staff networks can be identified and deployed as components of stress management and crisis intervention efforts. As we have seen, they may reduce unnecessary suffering among prisoners and promote more effective adjustment to prison. These networks may also contribute more directly to the correctional process. Effective human service delivery systems offer inmates constructive problem-solving options. Such options may compete with subcultural solutions to prison problems, which often feature denial of suffering and exploitation of peers as routes to self-esteem. Perhaps more importantly, the operation of staff teams in delivering human services may form the basis for the kinds of relationships through which planned change is presumed to occur (cf., Bennis, Benne, and Chin, 1969). In responding to the here and now problems of our captives, we may thus help create a context in which more long-term concerns can surface and be addressed.

The challenge for correctional managers of the future may increasingly entail the delineation of new roles for correctional clients, staff, and environments. Inmates, no longer the passive (if unwilling) beneficiaries of services, may need to play more active roles in the correctional process. There is, of course, no doubt that inmates occasionally play such roles, but little thought has been given to capitalizing on this resource in a systematic fashion. Staff can and sometimes do play broader roles than they are traditionally ascribed, though again, this well-recognized fact has not produced significant policy initiatives. Institutional settings, typically classified in terms of custody level or program focus, may need to be viewed as living environments, as indeed they are (cf., Toch 1977c), and be classified and used accordingly. The goal must be the development of a helping community within the penal institution, where resources are focused on the delivery of a broad range of human services that aid adaptation and provide a context for growth and change.

Organizational incentives for shared staff involvement in human service work may be essential if helping communities are to evolve in correctional settings. Broadening the scope of correctional accountability to include objectives and goals in the area of human service work that are applicable to all personnel may be one source of incentive. It is, of course, quite difficult to evaluate helping efforts. By contrast, rates of rule violation and attendance at counseling or therapy sessions provide readily usable (if imperfect) indices of traditional prison activities. Nevertheless, there are social science instruments for measuring attributes relevant to determining the outcomes of human service activities, such as perceived quality of life, social climate, and morale. Some of these instruments might be adapted and systematically deployed to describe the living environments of prisons (cf., Macht, Seidl, and Greene, 1977). Such measures, at a minimum, would provide feedback to staff on important environmental qualities of their prisons. And the information such instruments would yield over time might eventually form one component of staff training and evaluation programs.

In conjunction with experimental attempts to develop and implement measures of human service work, changes in staffing patterns and in inmate roles might also communicate a concern for correctional accountability. A flexible approach to staffing — one that would provide the latitude required for innovative, task-oriented teaming across formal staff lines — would underscore the aim of deploying human resources where and when they are needed. The serious willingness to integrate inmates on staff teams, admittedly a procedure that may be difficult to work out in practice, would highlight a commitment to extending the reach of helping services. Taken together, such strategies would substantially broaden the base of accountability for the well-being of correctional clients. These and other policy shifts aimed at enhancing the human service capacities of the prison might provide an organizational impetus for the kinds of grassroots change enterprises we have reviewed and contribute to the evolution of correctional roles within the prison community.

Acknowledgement

The study reported in this paper was part of a larger project designed to explore untapped human service resources within prisons. This study was in part made possible by Law Enforcement Assistant Administration grant 75N1-99—0030. The author is indebted to Hans Toch for his guidance in the research process and to Richard Myren, Ronald Weiner, and Madeline Aultman for their comments and suggestions on the report.

Notes

1. A number of attempts have been made to create more cooperative relations between custody and treatment staffs with an eye to more effective provision of treatment. There have been organizational changes (the creation of treatment teams) and the delineation of new or expanded roles (the correctional casework aide or "consultant") (Glaser, 1969; Briggs and Dowling, 1964). Such staffing innovations have reflected the notion that some of the tasks, skills, and concerns of custodial and treatment workers transcend their organizational roles. Specifically, the aim has been to capitalize on the treatment-relevant experiences and expertise of custodial staff, the persons closest to the correctional client (Wicks, 1974).

Such work has limited applicability to the typical maximum security prison. Most change strategies have been implemented in minimum custody settings or in treatment facilities (Weber, 1969; Grusky, 1969; Cressey, 1969a); have related to special populations, such as the mentally ill or the young (Ohlin, 1969; Toch, 1975); and have been made up of isolated, situation-specific programs (or what have been colorfully termed "innovation ghettoes"), that do not alter the roles and activities of regular staff (Toch, 1977a). Even formal redefinition of roles throughout a setting may prove ineffective. Rebaptizing training school house parents as treatment staff, for example, may do nothing more than shift the context of conflict from the cottage (or tier) to the conference table. The move can lead to an increase in alienation and distrust among staff when shared participation is promised but fails to materialize (Weber, 1969).

The few systematic attempts that have been made to use maximum security prison guards more directly in treatment efforts typically have involved formal changes in the roles and responsibilities of participants. Such changes have often produced unexpected negative side effects, however, contributing to morale problems among staff who fear they may become marginal members of the prison community (Grosser, 1969; Wicks, 1974). Some staff members apparently link such programs to career advancement and evidence limited commitment to treatment goals (Toch, 1977b). Others may use treatment rhetoric and discretion as a guise for punishment (Cressey, 1969b). There is, finally, an outer limit to the number of men who can be assigned formal treatment roles in traditional prisons, leaving the work (and expectations) of most custodial personnel unchanged.

2. This finding, in broad terms, parallels those of an in-depth study of adjustment problems and crises among confined men (Toch, 1975).

References

Bennis, W. G., Benne, K. D., and Chin, R. (1969). *The planning of change.* 2d ed. New York: Holt, Rinehart and Winston.

Briggs, D., and Dowling, J. (1964). "The correctional officer as a consultant: An emerging role in penology." *American journal of correction*, May-June: 28-31.

Cressey, D. R. (1969a). "Contradictory directives in complex organizations: The case of prison." In *Prison within society*, ed. L. Hazelrigg, 477-96. New York: Doubleday and Company.

———(1969b). "Achievement of an unstated organizational goal." In *Prison within society*, ed. L. Hazelrigg, 50-67. New York: Doubleday and Company.

Fogel, D. (1975). *We are the living proof . . . The justice model for corrections.* Cincinnati, OH: W. H. Anderson Co.

Glaser, D. (1969). *The effectiveness of a prison and parole system.* Indianapolis: Bobbs-Merrill Company, 130-45.

Grosser, G. (1969). "External setting and internal relations of the prison." In *Prison within society*, ed. L. Hazelrigg, 9-26. New York: Doubleday and Company.

Grusky, O. (1969). "Role conflict in organization: A study of prison camp officials." In *Prison within society*, ed. L. Hazelrigg, 455-76. New York: Doubleday and Company.

Hall, J., Williams, M., and Tomaino, L. (1969). "The challenge of correctional change: The interface of conformity and commitment." In *Prison within society*, ed. L. Hazelrigg, 308-28. New York: Doubleday and Company.

Johnson, R. (1977). "Ameliorating prison stress: Some helping roles for custodial personnel." *International journal of criminology and penology*, 5 (3): 263-73.

Macht, M. W., Seidl, F. W., and Greene, D. R. (1977). "Measuring inmate morale." *Social work*, July: 284-89.

Ohlin, L. E. (1969). "The reduction of role conflict in institutional staff." In *Prison within society*, ed. L. Hazelrigg, 497-508. New York: Doubleday and Company.

Sykes, G. (1966). *The society of captives*. New York: Atheneum.

Toch, H. (1975). *Men in crisis: Human breakdowns in prison*. Chicago: Adline Publishing Company, pp. 307-09.

────── (1977*a*). "Is a correctional officer, by any other name, a 'screw.'" See Chapter 6, *supra*.

────── (1977*b*). *Police, prisons and the problem of violence*. Crime and Delinquency issues monograph. National Institute of Mental Health.

────── (1977*c*). *Living in prison: The ecology of survival*. New York: The Free Press.

Weber, G. I. (1969). "Conflicts between professional and nonprofessional personnel in institutional delinquency treatment." In *Prisons within society*, ed. L. Hazelrigg, pp. 426-54. New York: Doubleday and Company.

Wicks, R. (1974). *Correctional psychology: Themes and problems in correcting the offender*. San Francisco: Canfield Press.

Wilson, J. Q. (1975). *Thinking about crime*. New York: Basic Books, Inc.

Chapter 8
Correctional Officers With Case Loads*

Richard J. Ward and
David Vandergoot

Since March 1974, an innovative program has been conducted by the Maryland Division of Correction. The division has assigned counseling and casework management to line correctional officers along with their custody responsibilities. Each officer carries a case load of 7 to 10 inmates and has primary responsibility for counseling, program planning, and custody.

A follow-up of 70 inmates who have been paroled from this program for 2 years or longer revealed that 7% have been returned to the division after being convicted of new crimes, 3% have had their paroles revoked, and 90% are still functioning in society.

At present, 24 officers and 3 supervisors are actively participating in the project. Plans are under way to expand the project to double the personnel. Conclusions are being drawn cautiously, but it appears that a number of correctional officers, with training and proper supervision, are capable of contributing more significantly to the rehabilitation of inmates than had been previously expected.

BACKGROUND

The correctional system is, and always will be, a social institution intended to control people who are a threat to the life or property of local citizens (Leeke & Clements, 1973). In this respect, Maryland's system has a 96% success rate for containing inmates and a 4% escape rate. However, if the correctional system is expected to change peoples' lives while it detains them, then it must also be evaluated on the percentages of releases who are convicted of new crimes and returned to custody. A 1974 random sample of 452 of 4,000 inmates released for 2 years indicated that 25.1% had been returned to Maryland's correctional system. In 1972 a task force was established to review and adjust the Maryland correctional system so that it would more effectively bring about a change in the lives of the people it was guarding without losing the effectiveness of its ability to maintain custody.

---

* Copyright 1977, the Haworth Press, Inc. Reprinted with permission from *Offender Rehabilitation*, Vol. 2, No. 1.

The task force, after reviewing correctional systems in all the states and seven foreign countries, concluded that the ability of the correctional institution to achieve its goals, both custodial and social, should involve a central concern with increasing the authority and professional scope of the correctional officer. (For a similar adjustment in education, consult the aggregation model as described by Janowitz, 1971.) It was found that correctional officers' responsibilities were limited almost solely to custody. These limitations were imposed as a result of the dilemmas facing correctional managers and administrators to implement the latest "correctional" technique within limited budget and staff resources.

Correctional systems were reacting to demands for increased rehabilitation by adapting in a superficial manner many new rehabilitation approaches that happened to be popular at the time and that would hopefully reduce recidivism (Dean, 1973). Sometimes the new solutions were not understood, much less implemented, but a title was borrowed so that a new name was given to an old, inefficient technique. For example, the function of a minimum security barracks remained the same, but it was called the "behavior modification center." In the push to produce programs, a correctional system designated its one lone psychologist as the "Department of Psychological Services."

Rather than maintain this patchwork approach, the task force focused its attention on the correctional officer. Although seemingly a contradiction, this concentration on the correctional officer was actually focusing on the totality of the system. The correctional officers' responsibilities were limited almost solely to custody as the "correctional" process was broken up into more and more specialized roles. This was justified by pointing to the number of correctional officers without college diplomas, the increased level of substantive knowledge in the field of human behavior, and the importance of specialists for such problems as alcoholism, narcotics addiction, and personality disorders. Therefore, the correctional officer was relegated to being a guard. The complexities of deviant behavior were given as the reason for the officers' subordination to experts in psychology, counseling, group work, and other fields (Dean, 1973).

This problem was compounded by the fact that correctional budgets did not have the funds to hire enough experts to work adequately with large numbers of inmates. Correctional salary scales had been traditionally inadequate and had not attracted the skilled professional. Professionals could only be attracted as occasional consultants. Hence, the specialist positions required by the new program were filled on paper, but the delivery of services was not adequate to meet the growing number of inmates.

The situation became more difficult as even these superficial approaches were severely curtailed and sometimes eliminated by budgetary slashes. In many instances the system could supply only the basics of food, clothing, and custody for the increasing number of persons being incarcerated. Constant tension grew as the expectations of the new rehabilitation approaches went unfulfilled. In addition, correctional officers originally encouraged by the new approaches became dissatisfied and functioned below their level of competency because they were told to enforce custody, and not to become "involved" with the inmates. There were correctional officers who felt they could help some of the inmates, but these officers were under orders solely to guard. Involvement could have cost them their jobs. In practice, however, some did get involved, because they realized that overburdened institutional counselors and psychologists could not possibly offer comprehensive services to all of the inmates. It was often the officer who became the person to whom the inmates turned for support (Glaser, 1964). Because of these occasional therapeutic relationships, it was time to take another look at the correctional system to evaluate whether there might not already be sufficient on-line personnel to meet the crisis in corrections if this personnel could be used to its maximum capacity.

DESCRIPTION OF THE PROGRAM

Maryland's small experimental program has established the correctional officer as the central manager of the inmates' correctional program. The correctional officer has been given the primary responsibility for organizing the conditions that can teach inmates how to live responsibly in society. In this process, teaching is accomplished through personal involvement with the inmate. This implies that the officer has the ability to function adequately in society, and also has technical proficiency in the social skills to be taught. The correctional officer makes use of specialists, but manages their introduction into the inmate's life. This is similar to the teacher who imparts the basics of reading, writing, and arithmetic and then refers a student to a specialist for an unusually complex educational or personal problem. The percentage of referrals is small and selective because the officer has been well equipped and is expected to deal with all but the most unique problems. Thus, the specialists in psychology, medicine, education, and testing assist in their areas of expertise, but they do not take over the primary role occupied by the correctional officer in the life of the inmate. Neither can there be any delay in access to these services. The officers are also professionals and are not made to wait a month or two before the specialists who work for them give the services requested.

The process Maryland is using recognizes that officer-inmate interaction is the primary catalyst for inmate growth. The officers are intelligently involved human beings who facilitate the personal and educational progress of the inmates on their case loads. The officers involve a variety of persons, both within and outside of the correctional institution, to ensure that the inmate has access to society's values and resources. In fact, the officer is trained and encouraged to expand the scope of such human resources for the inmate. There is no way of knowing in advance to whom an inmate will relate appropriately, or who will offer satisfactory and stable interpersonal contacts. One of the functions of the officer is to monitor the introduction of such contacts.

Correctional officers and the correctional materials used must indicate to inmates that someone is concerned about their basic needs. It was no accident that "old-time" guards testified to the fact that maximum security inmates responded positively when the guards ignored their superiors' directives of "noninvolvement" and began to try to help the inmates. The inmate who has serious personal needs wants to command the attention of a single person. Even assistance in group counseling, valuable as it is, hardly suffices to reach the core of an inmate's internal pressures. This need requires an administrative reliance on intensive human effort rather than on impersonal procedures. Concern with supplying a variety of educational, vocational, and counseling resources is important, but not as important as motivating the inmate to use these resources. A central question centers around the rewards and patterns of motivation that lead the inmate to undertake the necessary personal struggle and effort. These rewards are most effective if they are immediate and mediated through personal relations. Fellow humans, not abstractions, are the most effective carriers of meaning. In short, corrections must identify the needs of the inmates and must set up a system capable of meeting these needs.

The effective correctional officer in this system is one who is able to maintain custody/control while personalizing the management of rehabilitation resources. This is manifested by means as diverse as calling inmates by their proper name rather than a nickname, by the careful preparation of a contractual program, and by firmly and consistently holding inmates responsible for the completion of their programs.

It is a recognized fact that inmate attitude toward the correctional system and the correctional officers in general is an attitude of hostility and mistrust (Tyler, 1973). These tensions contribute to the creation of a group of inmate leaders who maintain their position by exploitation and even coercion. While these leaders personify opposition to authority, they themselves establish their own authoritarian system (Lawson, 1973). Within the confines of this culture there are those who survive the peer pressures and personally develop a new way of life. They are expressing either the consequences of confinement, the influence of gifted personnel or other inmates, or a maturing process resulting from long years of incarceration and a "growing up." This phenomenon may also be the result of sheer personal willpower.

The process now being implemented on a small scale in Maryland by which the line officer has been given personal responsibility for a small number of inmates appears to have established a milieu of rehabilitation practices that have transposed the normative and moral order of the traditional correctional institution. Correctional officers apparently have neutralized the power position of inmate leaders by helping all inmates establish a position of self-internal control. A commitment to individual inmate programming has become a dominant element in this correctional process. An insistence upon structure and discipline in implementing the individualized programs supplies immediate gratification to the inmates at the same time that it strengthens their individual dignity and self-respect in the immediate setting. From this base is developed a value system that looks to future achievement and future skills. This system is turned over completely to the correctional officers. It succeeds or fails depending upon this involvement. Thus, the officers' total professional involvement in the lives of the inmates attempts to meet the rehabilitative needs of the inmates and, hopefully, the vocational needs of the officers.

Correctional administrators provide the officers with support and adequate conditions to carry out their total job. Adequate preservice and in-service training were and are provided. The actual extent of training was quite comprehensive, and this brief reference to it should in no way minimize its importance. It is doubtful if the program would work without fully prepared correctional officers. Existing resources were examined and in some cases realigned to offer maximum utilization by the officers. Additional standard operating procedures were written to delineate how the administration wanted the officers to carry out these added duties. These procedures encompassed the following elements.

Casework Management

The major concern of this system is the assignment of a small number of inmates (7-10) to an individual correctional officer who is responsible for the overall management of the inmates' programs. This is seen as the crucial variable of change. The correctional officer is trained as a professional in the management of program resources and in basic counseling techniques. Because 24-hour coverage of the correctional institution is required, correctional officers work as a group of 8 with a team leader who supervises and coordinates.

The correctional officers accept the responsibility for helping inmates manage all aspects of their lives such as coordinating relations with the family or making arrangements for the inmates' participation in institutional programs as well as community programs. The correctional officer seeks to become involved in the inmates' lives to prevent them from becoming detached and isolated from stable human contacts and from the community to which they will return.

Emphasis is on organizational flexibility. Institutional management is designed to allow individualized programs. Mutual goals are identified in contractual programs between the inmates and the authorities. The correctional officer manages the inmates' involvement in the implementation of their individualized programs. Specialists such as psychologists or educators are not part of an external hierarchy under this system, but are resources that are utilized at the request of the officer.

Correctional officers receive extensive in-service training that assists them in becoming more and more proficient in the delivery of services. Wardens soon find themselves directing a group of involved, vocationally satisfied officers who are working together as a team. The team seeks to face the reality of inmates who have limited training and a general feeling of personal inadequacy in legitimate society.

The contractual program supplies a continuous development format that can deal with inmate transfers, can face the realities of differing achievement levels, and can seek to overcome potential failures. Inmates are permitted to proceed through the curriculum at a speed compatible with their capacity. Hence the inmates' rehabilitation now is placed in their own hands. The correction system supplies the structure of disciplined security and also offers the inmates freedom to move at their own rates of speed.

Staff meetings give the correctional officers the opportunity to see themselves through the eyes of their fellow team members. Excessively rigid or permissive attitudes can be brought to the attention of the officer and adjusted in a nonthreatening atmosphere. Under such a system fellow staff members, as well as consultants, serve to supply some in-service training.

Administration

This new system calls for greater centralization and uniformity in quality resources and general program goals while requiring decentralization of operations on an individual inmate basis. The administrative goal is to create the smallest possible operational unit, to give each unit the maximum amount of autonomy, and thus to expand drastically the use of resources for individualized programs.

Centralized administration of the correctional system will require that individual institutions meet standards for quality, individualized rehabilitation programs. It will also supply services to assist individual institutions in obtaining these resources. Wardens and superintendents of institutions have a major role in recruitment and selection of personnel, and authority to reallocate the resources at their disposal and to increase the number of resources needed to meet the demands of the individualized rehabilitation programs. They have the authority to allow inmates to leave the institution for rehabilitative programs and for community organizations or individuals to enter the institution for the same purpose.

Teams of 8 correctional officers are responsible for 36 to 40 inmates (2 of the officers on the team perform custody solely and work the night shift) and are under the supervision of a team leader. It is to be remembered that the individual correctional officers are the control persons in this organizational structure. They have the authority and autonomy to assist in developing and implementing an individualized treatment plan. The officer is held accountable for producing quality service and for meeting the overall rehabilitative goals of the correctional system. However, the officer is to participate intimately in the inmates' planning and is only monitored and guided by the team leader. This same policy of maximum personal responsibility and autonomy within a structured unit is to be followed all the way up the chain of command. Authorities will supply resources, monitor for quality service, and discharge incompetent staff, but must allow the officers the power to carry out their job as prescribed in the job description.

Although not described here, the system uses management tools that monitor the officer's work and the inmate's progress. These provide minimum but proper controls for the program. Thus, administrators maintain accountability without jeopardizing productivity. The system will be carefully researched in the next few years as it continues to expand throughout Maryland's Division of Correction.

References

Dean, C. W. "Contemporary trends in correctional rehabilitation." In R. E. Hardy & J. G. Cull (eds.), *Introduction to correctional rehabilitation.* Springfield, Ill.: Charles C. Thomas, 1973.

Glaser, D. *The effectiveness of a prison and parole system.* Indianapolis: Bobbs-Merrill, 1964.

Janowitz, M. *Institution building in urban education* (1st Phoenix ed.). Chicago: University of Chicago Press, 1971.

Lawson, R. G. "Effects of incarceration." In J. G. Cull & R. E. Hardy (eds.), *Fundamentals of criminal behavior and correctional systems.* Springfield, Ill.: Charles C Thomas, 1973.

Leeke, W. D., & Clements, H. M. "Correctional systems and programs — An overview." In J. G. Cull & R. E. Hardy (eds.), *Fundamentals of criminal behavior and correctional systems.* Springfield, Ill.: Charles C. Thomas, 1973.

Tyler, S. T. "Conflicts." In E. M. Scott & K. L. Scott (eds.), *Criminal rehabilitation . . . within and without the walls.* Springfield, Ill.: Charles C. Thomas, 1973.

Part IV
PSEUDO-GUARDS

We shape our buildings, then our buildings shape us.
                                                            Churchill

The two studies in this section were included primarily because they are likely to engender intensive discussion about guarding in prisons. They do *not* provide definitive conclusions about the issues they raise. Both address the general question of what might happen if the duties of guards were performed not by *actual* guards but by laymen-civilians with no previous exposure to prisons.

The first selection is the now classic simulation study by Craig Haney, Curtis Banks, and Philip Zimbardo: the Stanford Prison Experiment, in which college student volunteers role-played prisoners or guards in a mock prison. This was not a real prison, nor were these real guards or prisoners, yet

> . . . in less than a week the experience of imprisonment undid (temporarily) a lifetime of learning; human values were suspended, self-concepts were challenged and the ugliest, most base, pathological side of human nature surfaced. We were horrified because we saw some boys (guards) treat others as if they were despicable animals, taking pleasure in cruelty, while other boys (prisoners) became servile, dehumanized robots who thought only of escape, of their own individual survival and of their mounting hatred for the guards. (Zimbardo, 1973: 163).

The reader, it is hoped, will wish to think about the degree to which one can generalize from a mock prison to an actual correctional institution, from college student pseudo-guards to real guards, from play-acting in a laboratory to actual guarding in a real prison. The reader might wonder whether the students were only reacting to what they thought were the expectations and requirements of the experiment or were deliberately trying to emulate the behavior of guards about which they had learned only through the Hollywood depiction of prisons. Such questions should be asked. They should not lead the reader to dismiss the important implications of the study, particularly the suggestion (though not the proof) that the occurrence of abusive behavior by some guards in prisons may not be a reflection of some character defect or personal pathology that might predispose them to abusive behavior (and to seek employment which allows its expression), but may be determined by the *situation* in which they work. Zimbardo concluded, "Many people, perhaps the majority, can be made to do almost anything when put into psychologically-compelling situations — regardless of their morals, ethics, values, attitudes, beliefs, or personal convictions" (Zimbardo, 1973: 164).

The second selection is also a study of prisons which are guarded not by actual correctional officers but by inexperienced pseudo-guards. In this case the prisoners were real prisoners and the prisons real prisons. The guards were "citizen-soldiers" — National Guard personnel who replaced the correctional officers in Wisconsin's prisons during a strike of state employees. As we shall discuss in Part VI of this book, strikes by prison guards constitute an increasing problem in corrections. This study is important not only because it investigated the impact of such a strike on the functioning of a number of prisons but also because it took advantage of a unique opportunity to study the interpersonal dynamics of the prison, to examine some of the factors which influence guard-prisoner interactions, and to study the perceptions, attitudes and behavior of more than a thousand men who experienced the work of the prison guard for the first time. The article clearly notes the limitations of the study. These should be kept firmly in mind as the reader considers the implications of this innovative study, which is included because it is thought-provoking, if not entirely persuasive.

Reference

Zimbardo, P. "The psychological power and pathology of imprisonment." In E. Aronson & R. Helmreich (eds.) *Social Psychology*. New York: Van Nostrand, 1973.

Chapter 9
Interpersonal Dynamics in a Simulated Prison*

Craig Haney, Curtis Banks and Philip Zimbardo

INTRODUCTION

After he had spent four years in a Siberian prison the great Russian novelist Dostoevsky commented, surprisingly, that his time in prison had created in him a deep optimism about the ultimate future of mankind because, as he put it, if man could survive the horrors of prison life he must surely be a "creature who could withstanding anything." The cruel irony which Dostoevsky overlooked is that the reality of prison bears witness not only to the resilience and adaptiveness of the men who tolerate life within its walls, but as well to the "ingenuity" and tenacity of those who devised and still maintain our correctional and reformatory systems.

Nevertheless, in the century which has passed since Dostoevsky's imprisonment, little has changed to render the main thrust of his statement less relevant. Although we have passed through periods of enlightened humanitarian reform, in which physical conditions within prisons have improved somewhat and the rhetoric of rehabilitation has replaced the language of punitive incarceration, the social institution of prison has continued to fail. On purely pragmatic grounds, there is substantial evidence that prisons in fact neither "rehabilitate" nor act as a deterrent to future crime — in America, recidivism rates upwards of 75% speak quite decisively to these criteria. And, to perpetuate what is additionally an economic failure, American taxpayers alone must provide an expenditure for "corrections" of 1.5 billion dollars annually. On humanitarian grounds as well, prisons have failed: our mass media are increasingly filled with accounts of atrocities committed daily, man against man, in reaction to the penal system or in the name of it. The experience of prison undeniably creates, almost to the point of cliché, an intense hatred and disrespect in most inmates for the authority and the established order of society into which they will eventually return. And the toll which it takes on the deterioration of human spirit for those who must administer it, as well as for those upon whom it is inflicted, is incalculable.

---

* Copyright 1973, Academic Press Inc. (London). Reprinted with permission from *International Journal of Criminology and Penology*, Vol. 1.

Attempts to provide an explanation of the deplorable condition of our penal system and its dehumanising effects upon prisoners and guards, often focus upon what might be called the *dispositional hypothesis*. While this explanation is rarely expressed explicitly, it is central to a prevalent non-conscious ideology: that the state of the social institution of prison is due to the "nature" of the people who administer it, or the "nature" of the people who populate it, or both. That is, a major contributing cause to despicable conditions, violence, brutality, dehumanization and degradation existing within any prison can be traced to some innate or acquired characteristic of the correctional and inmate population. Thus on the one hand, there is the contention that violence and brutality exist within prison because guards are sadistic, uneducated, and insensitive people. It is the "guard mentality," a unique syndrome of negative traits which they bring into the situation, that engenders the inhumane treatment of prisoners. Or, from other quarters comes the argument that violence and brutality in prison are the logical and predictable result of the involuntary confinement of a collective of individuals whose life histories are, by definition, characterised by disregard for law, order and social convention and a concurrent propensity for impulsiveness and aggression. Logically, it follows that these individuals, having proved themselves incapable of functioning satisfactorily within the "normal" structure of society, cannot do so either inside the structure provided by prisons. To control such men as these, the argument continues, whose basic orientation to any conflict situation is to react with physical power or deception, force must be met with force, and a certain number of violent encounters must be expected and tolerated by the public.

The dispositional hypothesis has been embraced by the proponents of the prison *status quo* (blaming conditions on the evil in the prisoners), as well as by its critics (attributing the evil to guards and staff with their evil motives and deficient personality structures). The appealing simplicity of this proposition localises the source of prison riots, recidivism and corruption in these "bad seeds" and not in the conditions of the "prison soil." Such an analysis directs attention away from the complex matrix of social, economic and political forces which combine to make prisons what they are — and which would require complex, expensive, revolutionary solutions to bring about any meaningful change. Instead, rioting prisoners are identified, punished, transferred to maximum security institutions or shot, outside agitators sought and corrupt officials suspended — while the system itself goes on essentially unchanged, its basic structure unexamined and unchallenged.

However, a critical evaluation of the dispositional hypothesis cannot be made directly through observation in existing prison settings, since such naturalistic observation necessarily confounds the acute effects of the environment with the chronic characteristics of the inmate and guard populations. To separate the effects of the prison environment *per se* from those attributable to *à priori* dispositions of its inhabitants requires a research strategy in which a "new" prison is constructed, comparable in its fundamental social-psychological milieu to existing prison systems, but entirely populated by individuals who are undifferentiated in all essential dimensions from the rest of society.

Such was the approach taken in the present empirical study, namely, to create a prison-like situation in which the guards and inmates were initially comparable and characterised as being "normal-average," and then to observe the patterns of behaviour which resulted, as well as the cognitive, emotional and attitudinal reactions which emerged. Thus, we began our experiment with a sample of individuals who did not deviate from the normal range of the general population on a variety of dimensions we were able to measure. Half were randomly assigned to the role of "prisoner", the others to that of "guard," neither group having any history of crime, emotional disability, physical handicap nor even intellectual or social disadvantage.

The environment created was that of a "mock" prison which physically constrained the prisoners in barred cells and psychologically conveyed the sense of imprisonment to all participants. Our intention was not to create a *literal* simulation of an American prison, but rather a functional representation of one. For ethical, moral and pragmatic reasons we could not detain our subjects for extended or indefinite periods of time, we could not exercise the threat and promise of severe physical punishment, we could not allow homosexual or racist practices to flourish, nor could we duplicate certain other specific aspects of prison life. Nevertheless, we believed that we could create a situation with sufficient mundane realism to allow the role-playing participants to go beyond the superficial demands of their assignment into the deep structure of the characters they represented. To do so, we established functional equivalents for the activities and experiences of actual prison life which were expected to produce qualitatively similar psychological reactions in our subjects — feelings of power and powerlessness, of control and oppression, of satisfaction and frustration, of arbitrary rule and resistance to authority, of status and anonymity, of machismo and emasculation. In the conventional terminology of experimental social psychology, we first identified a number of relevant conceptual variables through analysis of existing prison situations, then designed a setting in which these variables were made operational. No specific hypotheses were advanced other than the general one that assignment to the treatment of "guard" or "prisoner" would result in significantly different reactions on behavioural measures of interaction, emotional measures of mood state and pathology, attitudes toward self, as well as other indices of coping and adaptation to this novel situation. What follows is the mechanics of how we created and peopled our prison, what we observed, what our subjects reported, and finally, what we can conclude about the nature of the prison environment and the experience of imprisonment which can account for the failure of our prisons.

METHOD

Overview

The effects of playing the role of "guard" or "prisoner" were studied in the context of an experimental simulation of a prison environment. The research design was a relatively simple one, involving as it did only a single treatment variable, the random assignment to either a "guard" or "prisoner" condition. These roles were enacted over an extended period of time (nearly one week) within an environment which was physically constructed to resemble a prison. Central to the methodology of creating and maintaining a psychological state of imprisonment was the functional simulation of significant properties of "real prison life" (established through information from former inmates, correctional personnel and texts).

The "guards" were free with certain limits to implement the procedures of induction into the prison setting and maintenance of custodial retention of the "prisoners". These inmates, having voluntarily submitted to the conditions of this total institution in which they now lived, coped in various ways with its stresses and its challenges. The behaviour of both groups of subjects was observed, recorded and analysed. The dependent measures were of two general types: transactions between and within each group of subjects, recorded on video and audio tape as well as directly observed; individual reactions on questionnaires, mood inventories, personality tests, daily guard shift reports, and post experimental interviews.

Subjects

The 21 subjects who participated in the experiment were selected from an initial pool of 75 respondents, who answered a newspaper advertisement asking for male volunteers to participate in a psychological study of "prison life" in return for payment of $15 per day. Those who responded to the notice completed an extensive questionnaire concerning their family background, physical and mental health history, prior experience and attitudinal propensities with respect to sources of psychopathology (including their involvement in crime). Each respondent who completed the background questionnaire was interviewed by one of two experimenters. Finally, the 24 subjects who were judged to be most stable (physically and mentally), most mature, and least involved in anti-social behaviour were selected to participate in the study. On a random basis, half of the subjects were assigned the role of "guard", half to the role of "prisoner".

The subjects were normal, healthy males attending colleges throughout the United States who were in the Stanford area during the summer. They were largely of middle class socio-economic status, Caucasians (with the exception of the Oriental subject). Initially they were strangers to each other, a selection precaution taken to avoid the disruption of any pre-existing friendship patterns and to mitigate against any transfer into the experimental situation of previously established relationships or patterns of behaviour.

This final sample of subjects was administered a battery of psychological tests on the day prior to the start of the simulation, but to avoid any selective bias on the part of the experimenter-observers, scores were not tabulated until the study was completed.

Two subjects who were assigned to be "stand-bys" in case an additional "prisoner" was needed were not called, and one subject assigned to be a "stand-by" guard decided against participating just before the simulation phase began — thus, our data analysis is based upon ten prisoners and eleven guards in our experimental conditions.

Procedure

Physical Aspects of the Prison
The prison was built in a 35-ft. section of a basement corridor in the psychology building at Stanford University. It was partitioned by two fabricated walls, one of which was fitted with the only entrance door to the cell block, the other contained a small observation screen. Three small cells (6 x 9 ft.) were made from converted laboratory rooms by replacing the usual doors with steel barred, black painted ones, and removing all furniture.

A cot (with mattress, sheet and pillow) for each prisoner was the only furniture in the cells. A small closet across from the cells served as a solitary confinement facility; its dimensions were extremely small (2 x 2 x 7 ft.) and it was unlit.

In addition, several rooms in an adjacent wing of the building were used as guards' quarters (to change in and out of uniform or for rest and relaxation), a bedroom for the "warden" and "superintendent", and an interview-testing room. Behind the observation screen at one end of the "yard" was video recording equipment and sufficient space for several observers.

Operational Details
The "prisoner" subjects remained in the mock-prison 24 hours per day for the duration of the study. Three were arbitrarily assigned to each of the three cells; the others were on stand-by call at their homes. The "guard" subjects worked on three-man, eight-hour shifts; remaining in the prison environment only during their work shift, going about their usual lives at other times.

Role Instruction

All subjects had been told that they would be assigned either the guard or the prisoner role on a completely random basis and all had voluntarily agreed to play either role for $15.00 per day for up to two weeks. They signed a contract guaranteeing a minimally adequate diet, clothing, housing and medical care as well as the financial remuneration in return for their stated "intention" of serving in the assigned role for the duration of the study.

It was made explicit in the contract that those assigned to be prisoners should expect to be under surveillance (have little or no privacy) and to have some of their basic civil rights suspended during their imprisonment, excluding physical abuse. They were given no other information about what to expect nor instructions about behaviour appropriate for a prisoner role. Those actually assigned to this treatment were informed by phone to be available at their place of residence on a given Sunday when we would start the experiment.

The subjects assigned to be guards attended an orientation meeting on the day prior to the induction of the prisoners. At this time they were introduced to the principal investigators, the "Superintendent" of the prison (P.G.Z.) and an undergraduate research assistant who assumed the administrative role of "Warden". They were told that we wanted to try to simulate a prison environment within the limits imposed by pragmatic and ethical considerations. Their assigned task was to "maintain the reasonable degree of order within the prison necessary for its effective functioning", although the specifics of how this duty might be implemented were not explicitly detailed. They were made aware of the fact that while many of the contingencies with which they might be confronted were essentially unpredictable (e.g., prisoner escape attempts), part of their task was to be prepared for such eventualities and to be able to deal appropriately with the variety of situations that might arise. The "Warden" instructed the guards in the administrative details, including: the work-shifts, the mandatory daily completion of shift reports concerning the activity of guards and prisoners, the completion of "critical incident" reports which detailed unusual occurrences and the administration of meals, work and recreation programmes for the prisoners. In order to begin to involve these subjects in their roles even before the first prisoner was incarcerated, the guards assisted in the final phases of completing the prison complex — putting the cots in the cells, signs on the walls, setting up the guards' quarters, moving furniture, water coolers, refrigerators, etc.

The guards generally believed that we were primarily interested in studying the behaviour of the prisoners. Of course, we were equally interested in the effect which enacting the role of guard in this environment would have on their behaviour and subjective states.

CHAPTER 9 INTERPERSONAL DYNAMICS — SIMULATED PRISON 143

To optimise the extent to which their behaviour would reflect their genuine reactions to the experimental prison situation and not simply their ability to follow instructions, they were intentionally given only minimal guidelines for what it meant to be a guard. An explicit and categorical prohibition against the use of physical punishment or physical aggression was, however, emphasized by the experimenters. Thus, with this single notable exception, their roles were relatively unstructured initially, requiring each "guard" to carry out activities necessary for interacting with a group of "prisoners" as well as with other "guards" and the "correctional staff."

Uniform

In order to promote feelings of anonymity in the subjects each group was issued identical uniforms. For the guards, the uniform consisted of: plain khaki shirts and trousers, a whistle, a police night stick (wooden batons) and reflecting sunglasses which made eye contact impossible. The prisoners' uniforms consisted of loosely fitted muslin smocks with an identification number on front and back. No underclothes were worn beneath these "dresses." A chain and lock were placed around one ankle. On their feet they wore rubber sandals and their hair was covered with a nylon stocking made into a cap. Each prisoner was also issued a toothbrush, soap, soapdish, towel and bed linen. No personal belongings were allowed in the cells.

The outfitting of both prisoners and guards in this manner served to enhance group identity and reduce individual uniqueness within the two groups. The khaki uniforms were intended to convey a military attitude, while the whistle and night-stick were carried as symbols of control and power. The prisoners' uniforms were designed not only to deindividuate the prisoners but to be humiliating and serve as symbols of their dependence and subservience. The ankle chain was a constant reminder (even during their sleep when it hit the other ankle) of the oppressiveness of the environment. The stocking cap removed any distinctiveness associated with hair length, colour or style (as does shaving of heads in some "real" prisons and the military). The ill-fitting uniforms made the prisoners feel awkward in their movements, since these dresses were worn without undergarments, the uniforms forced them to assume unfamiliar postures, more like those of a woman than a man — another part of the emasculating process of becoming a prisoner.

Induction Procedure

With the cooperation of Palo Alto City Police Department all of the subjects assigned to the prisoner treatment were unexpectedly "arrested" at their residences. A police officer charged them with suspicion of burglary or armed robbery, advised them of their legal rights, handcuffed them, thoroughly searched them (often as curious neighbours looked on) and carried them off to the police station in the rear of the police car. At the station they went through the standard routines of being fingerprinted, having an identification file prepared and then being placed in a detention cell. Each prisoner was blindfolded and subsequently driven by one of the experimenters and a subject-guard to our mock prison. Throughout the entire arrest procedure, the police officers involved maintained a formal, serious attitude, avoiding answering any questions of clarification as to the relation of this "arrest" to the mock prison study.

Upon arrival at our experimental prison, each prisoner was stripped, sprayed with a delousing preparation (a deodorant spray) and made to stand alone naked for a while in the cell yard. After being given the uniform described previously and having an I.D. picture taken ("mug shot"), the prisoner was put in his cell and ordered to remain silent.

Administrative Routine
When all the cells were occupied, the warden greeted the prisoners and read them the rules of the institution (developed by the guards and the warden). They were to be memorised and to be followed. Prisoners were to be referred to only by the number on their uniforms, also in an effort to depersonalise them.

The prisoners were to be served three bland meals per day, were allowed three supervised toilet visits, and given two hours daily for the privilege of reading or letterwriting. Work assignments were issued for which the prisoners were to receive an hourly wage to constitute their $15 daily payment. Two visiting periods per week were scheduled, as were movie rights and exercise periods. Three times a day all prisoners were lined up for a "count" (one on each guard work-shift). The initial purpose of the "count" was to ascertain that all prisoners were present, and to test them on their knowledge of the rules and their I.D. numbers. The first perfunctory counts lasted only about 10 minutes, but on each successive day (or night) they were spontaneously increased in duration until some lasted several hours. Many of the pre-established features of administrative routine were modified or abandoned by the guards, and some were forgotten by the staff over the course of the study.

Data Collection (Dependent Measures)
The exploratory nature of this investigation and the absence of specific hypotheses led us to adopt the strategy of surveying as many as possible behavioural and psychological manifestations of the prison experience on the guards and the prisoners. In fact, one major methodological problem in a study of this kind is defining the limits of the "data", since relevant data emerged from virtually every interaction between any of the participants, as well as from subjective and behavioural reactions of individual prisoners, guards, the warden, superintendent, research assistants and

visitors to the prison. It will also be clear when the results are presented that causal direction cannot always be established in the patterns of interaction where any given behaviour might be the consequence of a current or prior instigation by another subject and, in turn, might serve as impetus for eliciting reactions from others.

Data collection was organised around the following sources:

(1) *Videotaping*. About 12 hours of recordings were made of daily, regularly occurring events, such as the counts and meals, as well as unusual interactions, such as a prisoner rebellion, visits from a priest, a lawyer and parents, Parole Board meetings and others. Concealed video equipment recorded these events through a screen in the partition at one end of the cell-block yard or in a conference room (for parole meetings).

(2) *Audio recording*. Over 30 hours of recordings were made of verbal interactions between guards and prisoners on the prison yard. Concealed microphones picked up all conversation taking place in the yard as well as some within the cells. Other concealed recordings were made in the testing-interview room on selected occasions — interactions between the warden, superintendent and the prisoners' Grievance Committee, parents, other visitors and prisoners released early. In addition, each subject was interviewed by one of the experimenters (or by other research associates) during the study, and most just prior to its termination.

(3) *Rating scales*. Mood adjective checklists and sociometric measures were administered on several occasions to assess emotional changes in affective state and interpersonal dynamics among the guard and prisoner groups.

(4) *Individual difference scales*. One day prior to the start of the simulation all subjects completed a series of paper and pencil personality tests. These tests were selected to provide dispositional indicators of interpersonal behaviour styles — the F scale of Authoritarian Personality[1] and the Machiavellianism Scale[2] — as well as areas of possible personality pathology through the newly developed Comrey Personality Scale.[3] The subscales of this latter test consist of:

(a) trustworthiness
(b) orderliness
(c) conformity
(d) activity
(e) stability
(f) extroversion
(g) masculinity
(h) empathy

(5) *Personal observations*. The guards made daily reports of their observations after each shift, the experimenters kept informal diaries and all subjects completed post-experimental questionnaires of their reactions to the experience about a month after the study was over.

Data analyses presented problems of several kinds. First, some of the data was subject to possible errors due to selective sampling. The video and audio recordings tended to be focussed upon the more interesting, dramatic events which occurred. Over time, the experimenters became more personally involved in the transaction and were not as distant and objective as they should have been. Second, there are not complete data on all subjects for each measure because of prisoners being released at different times and because of unexpected disruptions, conflicts and administrative problems. Finally, we have a relatively small sample on which to make cross-tabulations by possible independent and individual difference variables.

However, despite these shortcomings some of the overall effects in the data are powerful enough to reveal clear, reliable results. Also some of the more subtle analyses were able to yield statistically significant results even with the small sample size. Most crucial for the conclusions generated by this exploratory study is the consistency in the pattern of relationships which emerge across a wide range of measuring instruments and different observers. Special analyses were required only of the video and audio material, the other data sources were analysed following established scoring procedures.

Video Analysis

There were 25 relatively discrete incidents identifiable on the tapes of prisoner-guard interactions. Each incident or scene was scored for the presence of nine behavioural (and verbal) categories. Two judges who had not been involved with the simulation study scored these tapes. These categories were defined as follows:

Question. All questions asked, requests for information or assistance (excluding rhetorical questions).

Command. An order to commence or abstain from a specific behaviour, directed either to individuals or groups. Also generalised orders, e.g. "Settle down."

Information. A specific piece of information proffered by anyone whether requested or not, dealing with any contingency of the simulation.

Individuating reference. Positive: use of a person's real name, nickname or allusion to special positive physical characteristics. Negative: use of prison number, title, generalised "you" or reference to derogatory characteristic.

Threat. Verbal statement of contingent negative consequences of a wide variety, e.g. no meal, long count, pushups, lock-up in hole, no visitors, etc.

Deprecation insult. Use of obscenity, slander, malicious statement directed toward individual or group, e.g. "You lead a life of mendacity" or "You guys are really stupid."

Resistance. Any physical resistance, usually prisoners to guards, such as holding on to beds, blocking doors, shoving guard or prisoner, taking off stocking caps, refusing to carry out orders.

Help. Person physically assisting another (i.e. excludes verbal statements of support), e.g. guard helping another to open door, prisoner helping another prisoner in cleanup duties.

Use of instruments. Use of any physical instrument to either intimidate, threaten, or achieve specific end, e.g. fire extinguisher, batons, whistles.

Audio Analysis

For purposes of classifying the verbal behaviour recorded from interviews with guards and prisoners, eleven categories were devised. Each statement made by the interviewee was assigned to the appropriate category by judges. At the end of this process for any given interview analysis, a list had been compiled of the nature and frequencies of the interviewee's discourse. The eleven categories for assignment of verbal expressions were:

Questions. All questions asked, requests for information or assistance (excluding rhetorical questions).

Informative statements. A specific piece of information proffered by anyone whether requested or not, dealing with any contingency of the simulation.

Demands. Declarative statements of need or imperative requests.

Requests. Deferential statements for material or personal consideration.

Commands. Orders to commence or abstain from a specific behaviour, directed either to individuals or groups.

Outlook, positive/negative. Expressions of expectancies for future experiences or future events; either negative or positive in tone, e.g. "I don't think I can make it" *v.* "I believe I will feel better."

Criticism. Expressions of critical evaluation concerning other subjects, the experimenters or the experiment itself.

Statements of identifying reference, deindividuating/individuating. Statements wherein a subject makes some reference to another subject specifically by allusion to given name or distinctive characteristics (individuating reference), or by allusion to non-specific identity or institutional number (deindividuating reference).

Desire to continue. Any expression of a subject's wish to continue or to curtail participation in the experiment.

Self-evaluation, positive/negative. Statements of self-esteem or self-degradation, e.g. "I feel pretty good about the way I've adjusted" *v.* "I hate myself for being so oppressive."

Action intentions, positive/negative including "intent to aggress". Statements concerning interviewees' intentions to do something in the future, either of a positive, constructive nature or a negative, destructive nature, e.g. "I'm not going to be so mean from now on" *v.* "I'll break the door down."

RESULTS

Overview

Although it is difficult to anticipate exactly what the influence of incarceration will be upon the individuals who are subjected to it and those charged with its maintenance (especially in a simulated reproduction), the results of the present experiment support many commonly held conceptions of prison life and validate anecdotal evidence supplied by articulate ex-convicts. The environment of arbitrary custody had great impact upon the affective states of both guards and prisoners as well as upon the interpersonal processes taking place between and within those role-groups.

In general, guards and prisoners showed a marked tendency toward increased negativity of affect and their overall outlook became increasingly negative. As the experiment progressed, prisoners expressed intentions to do harm to others more frequently. For both prisoners and guards, self-evaluations were more deprecating as the experience of the prison environment became internalised.

Overt behaviour was generally consistent with the subjective self-reports and affective expressions of the subjects. Despite the fact that guards and prisoners were essentially free to engage in any form of interaction (positive or negative, supportive or affrontive, etc.), the characteristic nature of their encounters tended to be negative, hostile, affrontive and dehumanising. Prisoners immediately adopted a generally passive response mode while guards assumed a very active initiating role in all interactions. Throughout the experiment, commands were the most frequent form of verbal behaviour and, generally, verbal exchanges were strikingly impersonal, with few references to individual identity. Although it was clear to all subjects that the experimenters would not permit physical violence to take place, varieties of less direct aggressive behaviour were observed frequently (especially on the part of guards). In lieu of physical violence, verbal affronts were used as one of the most frequent forms of interpersonal contact between guards and prisoners.

The most dramatic evidence of the impact of this situation upon the participants was seen in the gross reactions of five prisoners who had to be released because of extreme emotional depression, crying, rage and acute anxiety. The pattern of symptoms was quite similar in four of the subjects and began as early as the second day of imprisonment. The fifth subject was released after being treated for a psychosomatic rash which covered portions of his body. Of the remaining prisoners, only two said they were not willing to forfeit the money they had earned in return for being "paroled." When the experiment was terminated prematurely after only six days, all the remaining prisoners were delighted by their unexpected good fortune. In contrast, most of the guards seemed to be distressed by the decision to stop the experiment and it appeared to us that they had become sufficiently involved in their roles so that they now enjoyed the extreme control and power which they exercised and were reluctant to give it up. One guard did report being personally upset at the suffering of the prisoners and claimed to have considered asking to change his role to become one of them — but never did so. None of the guards ever failed to come to work on time for their shift, and indeed, on several occasions guards remained on duty voluntarily and uncomplaining for extra hours — without additional pay.

The extremely pathological reactions which emerged in both groups of subjects testify to the power of the social forces operating, but still there were individual differences seen in styles of coping with this novel experience and in degrees of successful adaptation to it. Half the prisoners did endure the oppressive atmosphere, and not all the guards resorted to hostility. Some guards were tough but fair ("played by the rules"), some went far beyond their roles to engage in creative cruelty and harassment, while a few were passive and rarely instigated any coercive control over the prisoners.

These differential reactions to the experiment of imprisonment were not suggested by or predictable from the self-report measures of personality and attitude or the reviews taken before the experiment began. The standardised tests employed indicated that a perfectly normal emotionally stable sample of subjects had been selected. In those few instances where differential test scores do discriminate between subjects, there is an opportunity to, partially at least, discern some of the personality variables which may be critical in the adaptation to and tolerance of prison confinement.

Initial Personality and Attitude Measures

Overall, it is apparent that initial personality-attitude dispositions account for an extremely small part of the variation in reactions to this mock prison experience. However, in a few select instances, such dispositions do seem to be correlated with the prisoners' abilities to adjust to the experimental prison environment.

Comrey Scale

The Comrey Personality Inventory[3] was the primary personality scale administered to both guards and prisoners. The mean scores for prisoners and guards on the eight sub-scales of the test are shown in Table 1. No differences between prisoner and guard mean scores on any scale even approach statistical significance. Furthermore, in no case does any group

Table 1

MEAN SCORES FOR PRISONERS AND GUARDS ON EIGHT COMREY SUBSCALES

Scale	Prisoners	Guards
Trustworthiness — high score indicates belief in the basic honesty and good intentions of others	$\bar{X} = 92.56$	$\bar{X} = 89.64$
Orderliness — extent to which person is meticulous and concerned with neatness and orderliness	$\bar{X} = 75.67$	$\bar{X} = 73.82$
Conformity — indicates belief in law enforcement, acceptance of society as it is, resentment of non-conformity in others	$\bar{X} = 65.67$	$\bar{X} = 63.18$
Activity — liking for physical activity, hard work, and exercise	$\bar{X} = 89.78$	$\bar{X} = 91.73$
Stability — high score indicates calm, optimistic, stable, confident individual	$\bar{X} = 98.33$	$\bar{X} = 101.45$
Extroversion — suggests outgoing, easy to meet person	$\bar{X} = 83.22$	$\bar{X} = 81.91$
Masculinity — "people who are not bothered by crawling creatures, the sight of blood, vulgarity, who do not cry easily and are not interested in love stories"	$\bar{X} = 88.44$	$\bar{X} = 87.00$
Empathy — high score indicates individuals who are sympathetic, helpful, generous and interested in devoting their lives to the service of others	$\bar{X} = 91.78$	$\bar{X} = 95.36$

mean fall outside of the 40 to 60 percentile range of the normative male population reported by Comrey.

Table 2 shows the mean scores on the Comrey sub-scales for prisoners who remained compared with prisoners who were released early due to severe emotional reactions to the environment. Although none of the comparisons achieved statistical significance, three seemed at least suggestive as possible discriminators of those who were able to tolerate this type of confinement and those who were not. Compared with those who had to be released, prisoners who remained in prison until the termination of the study: scored higher on conformity ("acceptance of society as it is"), showed substantially higher average scores on Comrey's measure of extroversion and also scored higher on a scale of empathy (helpfulness, sympathy and generosity).

F-Scale

The *F*-scale is designed to measure rigid adherence to conventional values and a submissive, uncritical attitude towards authority. There was no

Table 2

MEAN SCORES FOR "REMAINING" V. "EARLY RELEASED" PRISONERS ON COMREY SUBSCALES

Scale	Remaining prisoners	Early Released prisoners	Mean difference
Trustworthiness	93.4	90.8	+2.6
Orderliness	76.6	78.0	−1.4
Conformity	67.2	59.4	+7.8
Activity	91.4	86.8	+4.6
Stability	99.2	99.6	−0.4
Extroversion	98.4	76.2	+22.2
Masculinity	91.6	86.0	+5.6
Empathy	103.8	85.6	+17.2

difference between the mean score for prisoners (4.78) and the mean score for guards (4.36) on this scale.

Again, comparing those prisoners who remained with those who were released early, we notice an interesting trend. This intra-group comparison shows remaining prisoners scoring more than twice as high on conventionality and authoritarianism ($\bar{X} = 7.78$) than those prisoners released early ($\bar{X} = 3.20$). While the difference between these means fails to reach acceptable levels of significance, it is striking to note that a rank-ordering of prisoners on the F-scale correlates highly with the duration of their stay in the experiment ($r_s = 0.898$, $P < 0.005$). To the extent that a prisoner was high in rigidity, in adherence to conventional values, and in the acceptance of authority, he was likely to remain longer and adjust more effectively to this authoritarian prison environment.

Machiavellianism

There were no significant mean differences found between guards ($\bar{X} = 7.73$) and prisoners ($\bar{X} = 8.77$) on this measure of effective interpersonal manipulation. In addition, the Mach Scale was of no help in predicting the likelihood that a prisoner would tolerate the prison situation and remain in the study until its termination.

This latter finding, the lack of any mean differences between prisoners who remained v. those who were released from the study, is somewhat surprising since one might expect the Hi Mach's skill at manipulating social interaction and mediating favourable outcomes for himself might be acutely relevant to the simulated prison environment. Indeed, the two prisoners who scored highest on the Machiavellianism scale were also among those adjudged by the experimenters to have made unusually effective adaptations to their confinement. Yet, paradoxically (and this may give the reader some feeling for the anomalies we encountered in attempting to predict in-prison behaviour from personality measures), the other two prisoners whom we categorised as having effectively adjusted to confinement actually obtained the lowest Mach scores of any prisoners.

Video Recordings

An analysis of the video recordings indicates a preponderance of genuinely negative interactions, i.e., physical aggression, threats, deprecations, etc. It is also clear that any assertive activity was largely the prerogative of the guards, while prisoners generally assumed a relatively passive demeanour. Guards more often aggressed, more often insulted, more often threatened. Prisoners, when they reacted at all, engaged primarily in resistance to these guard behaviours.

For guards, the most frequent verbal behaviour was the giving of commands and their most frequent form of physical behaviour was aggression. The most frequent form of prisoners' verbal behaviour was question-asking, their most frequent form of physical behaviour was resistance. On the other hand, the most infrequent behaviour engaged in overall throughout the experiment was "helping" — only one such incident was noted from all the video recording collected. That solitary sign of human concern for a fellow occurred between two prisoners.

Although question-asking was the most frequent form of verbal behaviour for the prisoners, guards actually asked questions more frequently overall than did prisoners (but not significantly so). This is reflective of the fact that the overall level of behaviour emitted was much higher for the guards than for the prisoners. All of those verbal acts categorised as commands were engaged in by guards. Obviously, prisoners had no opportunity to give commands at all, that behaviour becoming the exclusive "right" of guards.

Of a total 61 incidents of direct interpersonal reference observed (incidents in which one subject spoke directly to another with the use of some identifying reference, i.e., "Hey, Peter"; "you there", etc.), 58 involved the use of some deindividuating rather than some individuating form of reference. (Recall that we characterised this distinction as follows: an individuating reference involved the use of a person's actual name, nickname or allusion to special physical characteristics, whereas a deindividuating reference involved the use of a prison number, or a generalised "you" — thus being a very depersonalising form of reference.) Since all subjects were at liberty to refer to one another in either mode, it is significant that such a large proportion of the references noted involved were in the deindividuating mode ($Z = 6.9$, $P < 0.01$). Deindividuating references were made more often by guards in speaking to prisoners than the reverse ($Z = 3.67$, $P < 0.01$). (This finding, as all prisoner-guard comparisons for specific categories, may be somewhat confounded by the fact that guards apparently enjoyed a greater freedom to initiate verbal as well as other forms of behaviour. Note, however, that the existence of this greater "freedom" on the part of the guards is itself an empirical finding since it was not prescribed *à priori*.) It is of additional interest to point out that in the only three cases in which verbal exchange involved some individuating reference, it was prisoners who personalised guards.

A total of 32 incidents were observed which involved a verbal threat spoken by one subject to another. Of these, 27 such incidents involved a guard threatening a prisoner. Again, the indulgence of guards in this form of behaviour was significantly greater than the indulgence of prisoners, the observed frequencies deviating significantly from an equal distribution of threats across both groups ($Z = 3.88$, $P < 0.01$).

Guards more often deprecated and insulted prisoners than prisoners did of guards. Of a total of 67 observed incidents, the deprecation-insult was expressed disproportionately by guards to prisoners 61 times; ($Z = 6.72$, $P < 0.01$).

Physical resistance was observed 34 different times. Of these, 32 incidents involved resistance by a prisoner. Thus, as we might expect, at least in this reactive behaviour domain, prisoner responses far exceeded those of the guards ($Z = 5.14$, $P < 0.01$).

The use of some object or instrument in the achievement of an intended purpose or in some interpersonal interaction was observed 29 times. Twenty-three such incidents involved the use of an instrument by a guard rather than a prisoner. This disproportionate frequency is significantly variant from an equal random use by both prisoners and guards ($Z = 316$, $P < 0.01$).

Over time, from day to day, guards were observed to generally escalate their harassment of the prisoners. In particular, a comparison of two of the first prison-guard interactions (during the counts) with two of the last counts in the experiment yielded significant differences in: the use of deindividuating references per unit time ($\overline{X}t_1 = 0.0$ and $\overline{X}t_2 = 5.40$, respectively; $t = 3.65$, $P < 0.10$); the incidence of deprecation-insult per unit time ($\overline{X}t_1 = 0.3$ and $\overline{X}t_2 = 5.70$, respectively; $t = 3.16$, $P < 0.10$). On the other hand, a temporal analysis of the prisoner video data indicated a general decrease across all categories over time: prisoners came to initiate acts far less frequently and responded (if at all) more passively to the acts of others — they simply *behaved less*.

Although the harassment by the guards escalated overall as the experiment wore on, there was some variation in the extent to which the three different guard shifts contributed to the harassment in general. With the exception of the 2.30 a.m. count, prisoners enjoyed some respite during the late night guard shift (10.00 p.m. to 6.00 a.m.). But they really were "under the gun" during the evening shift. This was obvious in our observations and in subsequent interviews with the prisoners and was also confirmed in analysis of the video taped interactions. Comparing the three different guard shifts, the evening shift was significantly different from the other two in resorting to commands; the means being 9.30 and 4.04, respectively, for standardised units of time ($t = 2.50$, $P < 0.05$). In addition, the guards on this "tough and cruel" shift showed more than twice as many deprecation-insults towards the prisoners (means of 5.17 and 2.29, respectively, $P < 0.20$). They also tended to use instruments more often than other shifts to keep the prisoners in line.

Audio Recordings

The audio recordings made throughout the prison simulation afforded one opportunity to systematically collect self-report data from prisoners and guards regarding (among other things) their emotional reactions, their outlook, and their interpersonal evaluations and activities within the experimental setting. Recorded interviews with both prisoners and guards offered evidence that: guards tended to express nearly as much negative outlook and negative self-regard as most prisoners (one concerned guard, in fact, expressed more negative self-regard than any prisoner and more general negative affect than all but one of the prisoners); prisoner interviews were marked by negativity in expressions of affect, self-regard and action intentions (including intent to aggress and negative outlook).

Analysis of the prisoner interviews also gave *post hoc* support to our informal impressions and subjective decisions concerning the differential emotional effects of the experiment upon those prisoners who remained and those who were released early from the study. A comparison of the mean number of expressions of negative outlook, negative affect, negative self-regard and intentions to aggress made by remaining v. released prisoners (per interview) yielded the following results: prisoners released early expressed more negative expectations during interviews than those who remained ($t = 2.32$, $P < 0.10$) and also more negative affect ($t = 2.17$, $P < 0.10$); prisoners released early expressed more negative self-regard, and four times as many "intentions to aggress" as prisoners who remained (although those comparisons fail to reach an acceptable level of significance).

Since we could video-record only public interactions on the "yard", it was of special interest to discover what was occurring among prisoners in private. What were they talking about in the cells — their college life, their vocation, girl friends, what they would do for the remainder of the summer once the experiment was over. We were surprised to discover that fully 90% of all conversations among prisoners were related to prison topics, while only 10% to non-prison topics such as the above. They were most concerned about food, guard harassment, setting up a grievance committee, escape plans, visitors, reactions of prisoners in the other cells and in solitary. Thus, in their private conversations when they might escape the roles they were playing in public, they did not. There was no discontinuity between their presentation of self when under survillance and when alone.

Even more remarkable was the discovery that the prisoners had begun to adopt and accept the guards' negative attitude toward them. Half of all reported private interactions between prisoners could be classified as non-supportive and non-cooperative. Moreover, when prisoners made evaluation statements of or expressed regard for, their fellow prisoners, 85% of the time they were uncomplimentary and deprecating. This set of observed frequencies departs significantly from chance expectations based on a conservative binominal probability frequency ($P < 0.01$ for prison $v.$ non-prison topics; $P < 0.05$ for negative $v.$ positive or neutral regard).

Mood Adjective Self-reports

Twice during the progress of the experiment each subject was asked to complete a mood adjective checklist and indicate his current affective state. The data gleaned from these self-reports did not lend themselves readily to statistical analysis. However, the trends suggested by simple enumeration are important enough to be included without reference to statistical significance. In these written self-reports, prisoners expressed nearly three times as much negative as positive affect. Prisoners roughly expressed three times as much negative affect as guards. Guards expressed slightly more negative than positive affect. While prisoners expressed about twice as much emotionality as did guards, a comparison of mood self-reports over time reveals that the prisoners showed two to three times as much mood fluctuation as did the relatively stable guards. On the dimension of activity-passivity, prisoners tended to score twice as high, indicating twice as much internal "agitation" as guards (although, as stated above, prisoners were seen to be markedly less active than guards in terms of overt behaviour).

It would seem from these results that while the experience had a categorically negative emotional impact upon both guards and prisoners, the effects upon prisoners were more profound and unstable.

When the mood scales were administered for a third time, just after the subjects were told the study had been terminated (and the early released subjects returned for the debriefing encounter session), marked changes in mood were evident. All of the now "ex-convicts" selected self-descriptive adjectives which characterised their mood as less negative and much more positive. In addition, they now felt less passive than before. There were no longer any differences on the sub-scales of this test between prisoners released early and those who remained throughout. Both groups of subjects had returned to their pre-experimental baselines of emotional responding. This seems to reflect the situational specificity of the depression and stress reactions experienced while in the role of prisoner.

Representative Personal Statements

Much of the flavour and impact of this prison experience is unavoidably lost in the relatively formal, objective analyses outlined in this paper. The following quotations taken from interviews, conversations and questionnaires provide a more personal view of what it was like to be a prisoner or guard in the "Stanford County Prison" experiment.

Guards

"They [the prisoners] seemed to lose touch with the reality of the experiment — they took me so seriously."

". . . I didn't interfere with any of the guards' actions. Usually if what they were doing bothered me, I would walk out and take another duty."

". . . looking back, I am impressed by how little I felt for them . . ."

". . . They [the prisoners] didn't see it as an experiment. It was real and they were fighting to keep their identity. But we were always there to show them just who was boss."

". . . I was tired of seeing the prisoners in their rags and smelling the strong odours of their bodies that filled the cells. I watched them tear at each other, on orders given by us."

". . . Acting authoritatively can be fun. Power can be a great pleasure."

". . . During the inspection, I went to cell 2 to mess up a bed which the prisoner had made and he grabbed me, screaming that he had just made it, and he wasn't going to let me mess it up. He grabbed my throat, and although he was laughing I was pretty scared. I lashed out with my stick and hit him in the chin (although not very hard) and when I freed myself I became angry."

Prisoners

". . . The way we were made to degrade ourselves really brought us down and that's why we all sat docile towards the end of the experiment."

". . . I realized now (after it's over) that no matter how together I thought I was inside my head, my prison behaviour was often less under my control than I realised. No matter how open, friendly and helpful I was with other prisoners I was still operating as an isolated, self-centred person, being rational rather than compassionate."

". . . I began to feel I was losing my identity, that the person I call ——————————, the person who volunteered to get me into this prison (because it was a prison to me, it *still* is a prison to me, I don't regard it as an experiment or a simulation . . .) was distant from me, was remote until finally I wasn't *that* person, I was 416. I was really my number and 416 was really going to have to decide what to do."

"I learned that people can easily forget that others are human."

Debriefing Encounter Sessions

Because of the unexpectedly intense reactions (such as the above) generated by this mock-prison experience, we decided to terminate the study at the end of six days rather than continue for the second week. Three separate encounter sessions were held, first, for the prisoners, then for the guards and finally for all participants together. Subjects and staff openly discussed their reactions and strong feelings were expressed and shared. We analysed the moral conflicts posed by this experience and used the debriefing sessions to make explicit alternative courses of action that would lead to more moral behaviour in future comparable situations.

Follow-ups on each subject over the year following termination of the study revealed the negative effects of participation had been temporary, while the personal gain to the subjects endured.

CONCLUSIONS AND DISCUSSION

It should be apparent that the elaborate procedures (and staging) employed by the experimenters to insure a high degree of mundane realism in this mock prison contributed to its effective functional simulation of the psychological dynamics operating in "real" prisons. We observed empirical relationships in the simulated prison environment which were strikingly isomorphic to the internal relations of real prisons, corroborating many of the documented reports of what occurs behind prison walls.

The conferring of differential power on the status of "guard" and "prisoner" constituted, in effect, the institutional validation of those roles. But further, many of the subjects ceased distinguishing between prison role and their prior self-identities. When this occurred, within what was a surprisingly short period of time, we witnessed a sample of normal, healthy American college students fractionate into a group of prison guards who seemed to derive pleasure from insulting, threatening, humiliating and dehumanising their peers — those who by chance selection had been assigned to the "prisoner" role. The typical prisoner syndrome was one of passivity, dependency, depression, helplessness and self-deprecation. Prisoner participation in the social reality which the guards had structured for them lent increasing validity to it and, as the prisoners became resigned to their treatment over time, many acted in ways to justify their fate at the hands of the guards, adopting attitudes and behaviour which helped to sanction their victimisation. Most dramatic and distressing to us was the observation of the ease with which sadistic behaviour could be elicited in individuals who were not "sadistic types" and the frequency with which acute emotional breakdowns could occur in men selected precisely for their emotional stability.

Situational v. Dispositional Attribution

To what can we attribute these deviant behaviour patterns? If these reactions had been observed within the confines of an existing penal institution, it is probable that a dispositional hypothesis would be invoked as an explanation. Some cruel guards might be singled out as sadistic or passive-aggressive personality types who chose to work in a correctional institution because of the outlets provided for sanctioned aggression. Aberrant reactions on the part of the inmate population would likewise be viewed as an extrapolation from the prior social histories of these men as violent, anti-social, psychopathic, unstable character types.

Existing penal institutions may be viewed as *natural experiments* in social control in which any attempts at providing a casual attribution for observed behaviour hopelessly confound dispositional and situational causes. In contrast, the design of our study minimised the utility of trait or prior social history explanations by means of judicious subject selection and random assignment to roles. Considerable effort and care went into determining the composition of the final subject population from which our guards and prisoners were drawn. Through case histories, personal interviews and a battery of personality tests, the subjects chosen to participate manifested no apparent abnormalities, anti-social tendencies or social backgrounds which were other than exemplary. On every one of the scores of the diagnostic tests each subject scored within the normal-average range. Our subjects then, were highly representative of middle-class, Caucasian American society (17 to 30 years of age), although above average in both intelligence and emotional stability.

Nevertheless, in less than one week their *behaviour* in this simulated prison could be characterised as pathological and anti-social. The negative, anti-social reactions observed were not the product of an environment created by combining a collection of deviant personalities, but rather, the result of an intrinsically pathological situation which could distort and rechannel the behaviour of essentially normal individuals. The abnormality here resided in the psychological nature of the situation and not in those who passed through it. Thus, we offer another instance in support of Mischel's[4] social-learning analysis of the power of situational variables to shape complex social behaviour. Our results are also congruent with those of Milgram[5] who most convincingly demonstrated the proposition that evil acts are not necessarily the deeds of evil men, but may be attributable to the operation of powerful social forces. Our findings go one step further, however, in removing the immediate presence of the dominant experimenter-authority figure, giving the subjects-as-guards a freer range of behavioural alternatives, and involving the participants for a much more extended period of time.

Despite the evidence favouring a situational causal analysis in this experiment, it should be clear that the research design actually *minimised* the effects of individual differences by use of a homogenous middle-range subject population. It did not allow the strongest possible test of the relative utility of the two types of explanation. We cannot say that personality differences do not have an important effect on behaviour in situations such as the one reported here. Rather, we may assert that the variance in behaviour observed could be reliably attributed to variations in situational rather than personality variables. The inherently pathological characteristics of the prison situation itself, at least as functionally simulated in our study, were a *sufficient* condition to produce aberrant, anti-social behaviour. (An alternative design which would maximise the potential operation of personality or dispositional variables would assign subjects who were extreme on pre-selected personality dimensions to each of the two experimental treatments. Such a design would, however, require a larger subject population and more resources than we had available.)

The failure of personality assessment variables to reliably discriminate the various patterns of prison behaviour, guard reactions as well as prisoner coping styles is reminiscent of the inability of personality tests to contribute to an understanding of the psychological differences between American P.O.W.s in Korea who succumbed to alleged Chinese Communist brain-washing by "collaborating with the enemy" and those who resisted.[6] It seems to us that there is little reason to expect paper-and-pencil behavioural reactions on personality tests taken under "normal" conditions to generalise into coping behaviours under novel, stressful or abnormal environmental conditions. It may be that the best predictor of behaviour in situations of stress and power, as occurs in prisons, is overt behaviour in functionally comparable simulated environments.

In the situation of imprisonment faced by our subjects, despite the potent situational control, individual differences were nevertheless manifested both in coping styles among the prisoners and in the extent and type of aggression and exercise of power among the guards. Personality variables, conceived as learned behaviour styles can act as moderator variables in allaying or intensifying the impact of social situational variables. Their predictive utility depends upon acknowledging the inter-active relationship of such learned dispositional tendencies with the eliciting force of the situational variables.

Reality of the Simulation

At this point it seems necessary to confront the critical question of "reality" in the simulated prison environment: were the behaviours observed more than the mere acting out of assigned roles convincingly? To be sure, ethical, legal and practical considerations set limits upon the degree to which this situation could approach the conditions existing in actual prisons and penitentiaries. Necessarily absent were some of the most salient aspects of prison life reported by criminologists and documented in the writing of prisoners.[7,8] There was no involuntary homosexuality, no racism, no physical beatings, no threat to life by prisoners against each other or the guards. Moreover, the maximum anticipated "sentence" was only two weeks and, unlike some prison systems, could not be extended indefinitely for infractions of the internal operating rules of the prison.

In one sense, the profound psychological effects we observed under the relatively minimal prison-like conditions which existed in our mock prison make the results even more significant and force us to wonder about the devastating impact of chronic incarceration in real prisons. Nevertheless, we must contend with the criticism that the conditions which prevailed in the mock prison were too minimal to provide a meaningful analogue to existing prisons. It is necessary to demonstrate that the participants in this experiment transcended the conscious limits of their preconceived stereotyped roles and their awareness of the artificiality and limited duration of imprisonment. We feel there is abundant evidence that virtually all of the subjects at one time or another experienced reactions which went well beyond the surface demands of role-playing and penetrated the deep structure of the psychology of imprisonment.

Although instructions about how to behave in the roles of guard or prisoner were not explicitly defined, demand characteristics in the experiment obviously exerted some directing influence. Therefore, it is enlightening to look to circumstances where role demands were minimal, where the subjects believed they were not being observed, or where they should not have been behaving under the constraints imposed by their roles (as in "private" situations), in order to assess whether the role behaviours reflected anything more than public conformity or good acting.

When the private conversations of the prisoners were monitored, we learned that almost all (a full 90%) of what they talked about was directly related to immediate prison conditions, that is, food, privileges, punishment, guard harassment, etc. Only one-tenth of the time did their conversations deal with their life outside the prison. Consequently, although they had lived together under such intense conditions, the prisoners knew surprisingly little about each other's past history or future plans. This excessive concentration on the vicissitudes of their current situation helped to make the prison experience more oppressive for the prisoners because, instead of escaping from it when they had a chance to do so in the privacy of their cells, the prisoners continued to allow it to dominate their thoughts and social relations. The guards too, rarely exchanged personal information during their relaxation breaks. They either talked about "problem prisoners", or other prison topics, or did not talk at all. There were few instances of any personal communication across the two role groups. Moreover, when prisoners referred to other prisoners during interviews, they typically deprecated each other, seemingly adopting the guards' negative attitude.

From post-experimental data, we discovered that when individual guards were alone with solitary prisoners and out of range of any recording equipment, as on the way to or in the toilet, harassment often was greater than it was in the "Yard." Similarly, video-taped analyses of total guard aggression showed a daily escalation even after most prisoners had ceased resisting and prisoner deterioration had become visibly obvious to them. Thus guard aggression was no longer elicited as it was initially in response to perceived threats, but was emitted simply as a "natural" consequence of being in the uniform of a "guard" and asserting the power inherent in that role. In specific instances we noted cases of a guard (who did not know he was being observed) in the early morning hours pacing the "Yard" as the prisoners slept — vigorously pounding his night stick into his hand while he "kept watch" over his captives. Or another guard who detained an "incorrigible" prisoner in solitary confinement beyond the duration set by the guards' own rules and then he conspired to keep him in the hole all night while attempting to conceal this information from the experimenters who were thought to be too soft on the prisoners.

In passing, we may note an additional point about the nature of role-playing and the extent to which actual behaviour is "explained away" by reference to it. It will be recalled that many guards continued to intensify their harassment and aggressive behaviour even after the second day of the study, when prisoner deterioration became marked and visible and emotional breakdowns began to occur (in the presence of the guards). When questioned after the study about their persistent affrontive and harrassing behaviour in the face of prisoner emotional trauma, most guards replied that they were "just playing the role" of a tough guard, although none ever doubted the magnitude or validity of the prisoners' emotional response. The reader may wish to consider to what extremes an individual may go, how great must be the consequences of his behaviour for others, before he can no longer rightfully attribute his actions to "playing a role" and thereby abdicate responsibility.

When introduced to a Catholic priest, many of the role-playing prisoners referred to themselves by their prison number rather than their Christian names. Some even asked him to get a lawyer to help them get out. When a public defender was summoned to interview those prisoners who had not yet been released, almost all of them strenuously demanded that he "bail" them out immediately.

One of the most remarkable incidents of the study occurred during a parole board hearing when each of five prisoners eligible for parole was asked by the senior authority whether he would be willing to forfeit all the money earned as a prisoner if he were to be paroled (released from the study). Three of the five prisoners said, "yes", they would be willing to do this. Notice that the original incentive for participating in the study had been the promise of money, and they were, after only four days, prepared to give this up completely. And, more surprisingly, when told that this possibility would have to be discussed with the members of the staff before a decision could be made, each prisoner got up quietly and was escorted by a guard back to his cell. If they regarded themselves simply as "subjects" participating in an experiment for money, there was no longer any incentive to remain in the study and they could have easily escaped this situation which had so clearly become aversive for them by quitting. Yet, so powerful was the control which the situation had come to have over them, so much a reality had this simulated environment become, that they were unable to see that their original and singular motive for remaining no longer obtained, and they returned to their cells to await a "parole" decision by their captors.

The reality of the prison was also attested to by our prison consultant who had spent over 16 years in prison, as well as the priest who had been a prison chaplain and the public defender who were all brought into direct contact with our simulated prison environment. Further, the depressed affect of the prisoners, the guards' willingness to work overtime for no additional pay, the spontaneous use of prison titles and I.D. numbers in non role-related situations all point to a level of reality as real as any other in the lives of all those who shared this experience.

To understand how an illusion of imprisonment could have become so real, we need now to consider the uses of power by the guards as well as the effects of such power in shaping the prisoner mentality.

Pathology of Power

Being a guard carried with it social status within the prison, a group identity (when wearing the uniform), and above all, the freedom to exercise an unprecedented degree of control over the lives of other human beings. This control was invariably expressed in terms of sanctions, punishment, demands and with the threat of manifest physical power. There was no need for the guards to rationally justify a request, as they do in their ordinary lives and merely to make a demand was sufficient to have it carried out. Many of the guards showed in their behaviour and revealed in post-experimental statements that this sense of power was exhilarating.

The use of power was self-aggrandising and self-perpetuating. The guard power, derived initially from an arbitrary label, was intensified whenever there was any perceived threat by the prisoners and this new level subsequently became the baseline from which further hostility and harassment would begin. The most hostile guards on each shift moved spontaneously into the leadership roles of giving orders and deciding on punishments. They became role models whose behaviour was emulated by other members of the shift. Despite minimal contact between the three separate guard shifts and nearly 16 hours a day spent away from the prison, the absolute level of aggression as well as more subtle and "creative" forms of aggression manifested, increased in a spiralling function. Not to be tough and arrogant was to be seen as a sign of weakness by the guards and even those "good" guards who did not get as drawn into the power syndrome as the others respected the implicit norm of *never* contradicting or even interfering with an action of a more hostile guard on their shift.

After the first day of the study, practically all prisoner's rights (even such things as the time and conditions of sleeping and eating) came to be redefined by the guards as "privileges" which were to be earned for obedient behaviour. Constructive activities such as watching movies or reading (previously planned and suggested by the experimenters) were arbitrarily cancelled until further notice by the guards — and were subsequently never allowed. "Reward", then became granting approval for prisoners to eat, sleep, go to the toilet, talk, smoke a cigarette, wear glasses or the temporary diminution of harassment. One wonders about the conceptual nature of "positive" reinforcement when subjects are in such conditions of deprivation, and the extent to which even minimally acceptable conditions become rewarding when experienced in the context of such an impoverished environment.

We might also question whether there are meaningful non-violent alternatives as models for behaviour modification in real prisons. In a world where men are either powerful or powerless, everyone learns to despise the lack of power in others and in oneself. It seems to us, that prisoners learn to admire power for its own sake — power becoming the ultimate reward. Real prisoners soon learn the means to gain power whether through ingratiation, informing, sexual control of other prisoners or development of powerful cliques. When they are released from prison, it is unlikely they will ever want to feel so powerless again and will take action to establish and assert a sense of power.

The Pathological Prisoner Syndrome

Various coping strategies were employed by our prisoners as they began to react to their perceived loss of personal identity and the arbitrary control of their lives. At first they exhibited disbelief at the total invasion of their privacy, constant surveillance and atmosphere of oppression in which they were living. Their next response was rebellion, first by the use of direct force, and later with subtle divisive tactics designed to foster distrust among the prisoners. They then tried to work within the system by setting up an elected grievance committee. When that collective action failed to produce meaningful changes in their existence, individual self-interests emerged. The breakdown in prisoner cohesion was the start of social disintegration which gave rise not only to feelings of isolation but deprecation of other prisoners as well. As noted before, half the prisoners coped with the prison situation by becoming extremely disturbed emotionally — as a passive way of demanding attention and help. Others became excessively obedient in trying to be "good" prisoners. They sided with the guards against a solitary fellow prisoner who coped with his situation by refusing to eat. Instead of supporting this final and major act of rebellion, the prisoners treated him as a trouble-maker who deserved to be punished for his disobedience. It is likely that the negative self-regard among the prisoners noted by the end of the study was the product of their coming to believe that the continued hostility toward all of them was justified because they "deserved it".[9] As the days wore on, the model prisoner reaction was one of passivity, dependence and flattened affect.

Let us briefly consider some of the relevant processes involved in bringing about these reactions.

Loss of personal identity. Identity is, for most people, conferred by social recognition of one's uniqueness, and established through one's name, dress, appearance, behaviour style and history. Living among strangers who do not know your name or history (who refer to you only by number), dressed in a uniform exactly like all other prisoners, not wanting to call attention to one's self because of the unpredictable consequences it might provoke — all led to a weakening of self identity among the prisoners. As they began to lose initiative and emotional responsivity, while acting ever more compliantly, indeed, the prisoners became de-individuated not only to the guards and the observers, but also to themselves.

Arbitrary control. On post-experimental questionnaires, the most frequently mentioned aversive aspect of the prison experience was that of being subjugated to the apparently arbitrary, capricious decisions and rules of the guards. A question by a prisoner as often elicited derogation and aggression as it did a rational answer. Smiling at a joke could be punished in the same way that failing to smile might be. An individual acting in defiance of the rules could bring punishment to innocent cell partners (who became, in effect, "mutually yoked controls"), to himself, or to all.

As the environment became more unpredictable, and previously learned assumptions about a just and orderly world were no longer functional, prisoners ceased to initiate any action. They moved about on orders and when in their cells rarely engaged in any purposeful activity. Their zombie-like reaction was the functional equivalent of the learned helplessness phenomenon reported by Seligman and Groves.[10] Since their behaviour did not seem to have any contingent relationship to environmental consequences, the prisoners essentially gave up and stopped behaving. Thus the subjective magnitude of aversiveness was manipulated by the guards not in terms of physical punishment but rather by controlling the psychological dimension of environmental predictability.[11]

Dependency and emasculation. The network of dependency relations established by the guards not only promoted helplessness in the prisoners but served to emasculate them as well. The arbitrary control by the guards put the prisoners at their mercy for even the daily, commonplace functions like going to the toilet. To do so, required publicly obtained permission (not always granted) and then a personal escort to the toilet while blindfolded and handcuffed. The same was true for many other activities ordinarily practised spontaneously without thought, such as lighting up a cigarette, reading a novel, writing a letter, drinking a glass of water or brushing one's teeth. These were all privileged activities requiring permission and necessitating a prior show of good behaviour. These low level dependencies engendered a regressive orientation in the prisoners. Their dependency was defined in terms of the extent of the domain of control over all aspects of their lives which they allowed other individuals (the guards and prison staff) to exercise.

As in real prisons, the assertive, independent, aggressive nature of male prisoners posed a threat which was overcome by a variety of tactics. The prisoner uniforms resembled smocks or dresses, which made them look silly and enabled the guards to refer to them as "sissies" or "girls." Wearing these uniforms without any underclothes forced the prisoners to move and sit in unfamiliar, feminine postures. Any sign of individual rebellion was labelled as indicative of "incorrigibility" and resulted in loss of privileges, solitary confinement, humiliation or punishment of cell mates. Physically smaller guards were able to induce stronger prisoners to act foolishly and obediently. Prisoners were encouraged to belittle each other publicly during the counts. These and other tactics all served to engender in the prisoners a lessened sense of their masculinity (as defined by their external culture). It follows then, that although the prisoners usually outnumbered the guards during line-ups and counts (nine *v.* three) there never was an attempt to directly overpower them. (Interestingly, after the study was terminated, the prisoners expressed the belief that the basis for assignment to guard and prisoner groups was physical size. They perceived the guards were "bigger," when, in fact, there was no difference in average height or weight between these randomly determined groups.)

In conclusion, we believe this demonstration reveals new dimensions in the social psychology of imprisonment worth pursuing in future research. In addition, this research provides a paradigm and information base for studying alternatives to existing guard training, as well as for questioning the basic operating principles on which penal institutions rest.

If our mock prison could generate the extent of pathology it did in such a short time, then the punishment of being imprisoned in a real prison does not "fit the crime" for most prisoners — indeed, it far exceeds it! Moreover, since prisoners and guards are locked into a dynamic, symbiotic relationship which is destructive to their human nature, guards are also society's prisoners.

Shortly after our study was terminated, the indiscriminate killings at San Quentin and Attica occurred, emphasising the urgency for prison reforms that recognise the dignity and humanity of both prisoners and guards who are constantly forced into one of the most intimate and potentially deadly encounters known to man.

Acknowledgements

This research was funded by an ONR grant: N00014-67-A-0112-0041 to Professor Philip G. Zimbardo.

The ideas expressed in this paper are those of the authors and do not imply endorsement of ONR or any sponsoring agency. We wish to extend our thanks and appreciation for the contributions to this research by David Jaffe who served as "warden" and pre-tested some of the variables in the mock prison situation. In addition, Greg White provided invaluable assistance during the data reduction phase of this study. Many others (most notably Carolyn Burkhart, Susie Phillips and Kathy Rosenfeld), helped at various stages of the experiment, with the construction of the prison, prisoner arrest, interviewing, testing, and data analysis — we extend our sincere thanks to each of these collaborators. Finally, we wish especially to thank Carlo Prescott, our prison consultant, whose personal experience gave us invaluable insights into the nature of imprisonment.

References

1. T. W. Adorno, E. Frenkel-Brunswick, D. J. Levinson & R. N. Sanford. *The Authoritatian Personality.* New York, Harper, 1950.
2. R. Christie & F. L. Geis (eds.). *Studies in Machiavellianism.* New York, Academic Press. 1970.
3. A. L. Comrey. *Comrey Personality Scales.* San Diego, Educational and Industrial Testing Service. 1970.
4. W. Mischel. *Personality and Assessment.* New York, Wiley. 1968.
5. S. Milgram. "Some conditions of obedience and disobedience to authority," *Human Relations* 1965, 18(1), 57-76.
6. G. Jackson. *Soledad Brother: the Prison Letters of George Jackson.* New York, Bantam Books. 1970.
7. E. Schein. *Coercive Persuasion.* New York, Norton. 1961.
8. H. Charrière. *Papillion.* Paris, Robert Laffont. 1969.

9. E. Walster. "Assignment of responsibility for an accident," *Journal of Personality and Social Psychology* 1966, 3(1), 73-79.
10. M. E. Seligman & D. P. Groves. "Nontransient learned helplessness," *Psychonomic Science* 1970, 19(3), 191-192.
11. D. C. Glass & J. E. Singer. "Behavioural after effects of unpredictable and uncontrollable aversive events," *American Scientist* 1972, 6(4), 457-465.

Chapter 10
Changing of the Guard: Citizen Soldiers in Wisconsin Correctional Institutions*

The League of Women Voters of Wisconsin

I. INTRODUCTION

The Strike — A Unique Experience

Shortly after midnight on the damp summer night of July 2, 1977, a red alert went out to National Guard units around the state. Members of the Wisconsin State Employees Union had voted to strike. During the next twelve hours striking employees at Wisconsin correctional institutions were systematically replaced by National Guard personnel, implementing a pre-set emergency plan. In the cell blocks, dining halls, recreation areas, workshops and kitchens, and on the guard towers, the transition took place. None of the participants knew just what to expect in the hours and days to follow.

Never before, it is believed, has so large or diverse a group of citizens experienced the environment of the correctional institution. During the 16 days (July 2-18) of this strike several thousand citizen-soldiers became a part of the life of those sentenced to confinement by the justice system, and with the guidance of the regular supervisory and other personnel at each institution who did not strike, carried out the required duties. The National Guard members' orders charged them "to provide minimum essential services."

A Chance to Learn

Following the strike, Acting Governor Martin J. Schreiber wrote a letter thanking Adjutant General Hugh Simonson and his National Guard members. The letter included the following:

> It occurs to me that there is another major benefit yet to be derived from your troops' presence at our correctional institutions. . . . I believe that the citizens of Wisconsin, their elected representatives and the Department of Health and Social Services would be better

---

* Copyright, The League of Women Voters of Wisconsin, Inc. Editor's revision of the original pamphlet prepared by Beth Ross. Barbara Burkholder was Project-Director and Nicholas G. Retson, Research Analyst. Funding was provided by the Wisconsin Council on Criminal Justice and the Department of Health and Social Services, State of Wisconsin.

informed if the National Guard personnel who served in those institutions would be willing to share their perspectives and observations . . . in some systematic way.

Some press reports during the strike presented the view that relations between the National Guard and residents were amazingly good. Other people expressed the view that these reports were overly rosy and not a true indication of the conditions that existed. This study was an attempt to see what could be learned from the unique opportunity presented during the "changing of the guard." A survey of those present at five Wisconsin correctional institutions during the strike period is the basis for this study.

The Institutions Studied

The study was limited to Wisconsin's two maximum and three medium security correctional institutions:
Maximum security
　Wisconsin State Prison at *Waupun*
　Wisconsin State Reformatory at *Green Bay*
Medium security
　Fox Lake Correctional Institution
　Kettle Moraine Correctional Institution
　Taycheedah Correctional Institution

Each institution is unique. Facilities, services, rules and composition of populations vary. The amount and type of contact between National Guard members and residents during the strike also varied from institution to institution. One reason for this was the type of housing provided for National Guard members. At Kettle Moraine, the National Guard command room and quarters were in the administration building. Other rooms in this building were used by residents during the day, which brought the residents and National Guard into close contact. At Green Bay, the National Guard stayed in the National Guard Armory. At Taycheedah, Guard members were housed in unoccupied facilities at the institution. At Fox Lake, Guard members lived in a "tent city" just outside the institution fence. At Waupun, troops were quartered in city school buildings. In some cases the National Guard shared recreation areas with residents. Such differences in contact between the National Guard and residents may have influenced relationships in a way that was reflected in the results of the survey.

The Groups Studied

The study that evolved concerned the perceptions, observations and reactions of four groups of people most affected by the strike. They are: (1) correctional officers, (2) National Guard members, (3) residents of the correctional institutions, and (4) supervisory personnel. To be eligible for inclusion in the study an individual must have been present at one of the five institutions or on an employee list for at least one day during the strike. All individuals in these groups who were eligible for the study were given questionnaires. A description of each group follows.

1. *Correctional officers.* This group was limited to those correctional officers who went on strike and who were still employed at one of the five institutions on February 1, 1978. The correctional officers are the security guards and the employees who have the most contact with residents. These correctional officers are members of the Security and Public Safety Unit of the Wisconsin State Employees Union. This union was formed 46 years ago with the goal of seeking improved working conditions for State of Wisconsin employees. Not all union members observed the strike, nor are all correctional officers dues-paying members of the union.

2. *National Guard.* This includes Guard members who served during the strike at one of the five institutions studied. These men and women come from towns and cities all over Wisconsin. They include persons of diverse occupational background. Guard members devote one weekend per month and fifteen additional days each year to National Guard duty. They may be called to active duty by the President of the United States in a national emergency, or, as in this case, they may be called for emergency duty in Wisconsin by the Governor. During the strike of state employees about 6,000 National Guardsmen served in a total of 25 institutions, including 18 correctional institutions, mental health institutes, the three colonies for developmentally disabled, and the King home for veterans.

3. *Residents.* This includes men and women who were confined to one of the five correctional institutions at the time of the strike and at the time of the survey in March 1978. Most of the residents had served a rather short time on their current sentence at the time of the strike. Statistics from the DHSS show that 41% of residents had been in an institution less than one year from current admission, 54% had been in one to five years, and only 5% had been in the institution more than five years. Residents are sometimes moved from one institution to another which means that some residents may have been in one institution during the strike, and in another institution at the time of the survey.

4. *Supervisory personnel.* This includes personnel on duty during the strike, and who were still employed on February 1, 1978. Supervisory staff are not members of a union. They include superintendents, associate superintendents (directors of treatment or security), security captains and lieutenants, supervisors (including food service and maintenance), medical professionals (including doctors and dentists), and accountants.

The questionnaires administered for this survey included demographic questions on age, education, race, length of employment or incarceration of respondents, and location during the strike. The responses to these questions show that the majority of the residents and National Guard members were under 30 years old. The majority of correctional officers and supervisory personnel were over 40 years old. Minority group members (including black, Native American, Latino and "others") comprised 47% of the resident population, while they represented only one to three percent of the other three groups studied.

A total of 6,220 questionnaires were sent to members of the four groups described above in March 1978. An overall response rate of 44.9% was achieved by the cut-off date of April 28, 1978.

Some questionnaires returned were not suitable for inclusion in the study. The most frequent reason was that the questionnaire was returned not answered. In some cases the respondent was not present at the time of the strike. A few questionnaires were destroyed and returned in pieces.

Methodology

An advisory group composed of members of the League of Women Voters and technical advisers from the involved groups planned and reviewed each step of the survey process. In addition, advice from specialists was sought as the study progressed.

In order to develop the questionnaires used, trained personnel interviewed members of each of the four groups to determine areas of concern. Information from these interviews was used as the basis for developing the final set of questionnaires.

II. CAUTIONS ON INTERPRETATION

In evaluating the results of this study it is important to keep several relevant facts in mind concerning the background and conditions of the strike period.

Negotiations between the Wisconsin State Employees Union and the State of Wisconsin, Division of Employee Relations, Department of Administration, had been under way since proposals had been exchanged on February 25, 1977, and it was rumored that a strike might occur. The National Guard was alerted in late June to the possibility of a strike, and existing plans were updated to staff the correctional institutions in case of such an emergency. Personnel from the correctional institutions and the Division of Corrections held briefing meetings at the institutions with representatives of the National Guard. Because of the planning, National Guard units were in the institutions within a few hours after they were called to duty.

The residents in the institution also had some knowledge that the strike might occur. During preliminary interviews for the study, several residents reported that their leaders passed the word to "keep things cool" in the event of a strike. These residents told interviewers that residents didn't want to make the striking correctional officers look good by causing trouble while they were off duty.

Where significant differences were found in the residents' attitudes toward their regular correctional officers and the National Guard who replaced them, the figures must be carefully interpreted. The position of the National Guard members, who assumed correctional officers' duties was different in many ways from that of the regular correctional officers. The National Guard knew their duty was temporary. They had two to three times as many people on duty compared to the normal staffing by the regular correctional officers. This is reflected in the fact that only 614 questionnaires were sent to the striking correctional officers, whereas 1,368 National Guard members were on duty July 10th, midway through the strike.[1] The number of National Guard members on duty fluctuated during the course of the strike. Although the strike lasted 16 days, many Guard members were there for a shorter length of time — the normal tour of duty in the National Guard was seven days. As many as 25% of the Guard volunteered for longer duty.

The National Guard members were ordered to keep things under control but were much freer than the regular correctional officers to exercise individual discretion in relaxing rules and initiating off-duty activities. The Guard members were free to interact with residents in ways prohibited to the regular staff. For example, the Guard organized such activities as baseball games with the residents. The National Guard spent more time just talking with the residents.

These observations are not meant to detract in any way from the job the National Guard did in managing an unfamiliar, complex and difficult assignment. They are meant to emphasize that it is neither possible nor desirable to read this study as a comparison of the competence of the two groups of personnel most centrally involved.

III. WHAT HAPPENED DURING THE STRIKE

Residents Responded Well

The sixty preliminary interviews conducted by League of Women Voters personnel and the results of the final survey clearly indicate that the manner in which the National Guard carried out its duties during the strike elicited a positive response from most of the residents of the institutions. There was no apparent increase in problems with or among the residents. As the strike went on, most of the residents reported feeling more cooperative, relaxed, useful and able to take responsibility. These reports tend to be supported by the fact that 90% of the National Guard members and almost 80% of the supervisory personnel agreed that residents helped the Guard. A large majority of residents reported resident morale to be higher during the strike than before it.

This Was Unexpected

It is interesting to note that when the residents learned that the Guard was coming, they did not expect things to work out as well as they did. While about half did not expect that there would be conflict between the residents and Guard or that the residents would cause trouble, a large majority (69%) expected a "lock-down" (confinement to individual cells or other living quarters). In fact, the greater degree of freedom and relaxed enforcement of rules that occurred were not expected *either* by most of the residents *or* most of the Guard. Over 80% in both groups reported that things were better than they had expected them to be during the strike. The Guard members' report of their expectations reflected a great deal of uncertainty and concern. Most expressed some concern about their personal safety, and over 40% expected that the residents would cause trouble and that there would be conflicts between residents and the Guard.

As the strike went on, a majority of the National Guard members became less worried about their safety, typified by the remark of one Guard member. "On the first day, walking through a large group of residents, I'll admit I was a bit apprehensive. After that I was not concerned about my safety." A large majority of the supervisory personnel said that they were never worried about their safety during the strike. In fact, more said they are worried now about their personal safety than were worried during the strike.

Some Things to Consider

Acknowledging the special circumstances of the strike period, there is useful information to be obtained from the observations of those involved. The report now turns to a discussion of some of the factors which may have contributed to the positive response of the residents and the atmosphere which prevailed at the institutions while the National Guard was there.

"Treated Like Men"

In a draft from Adjutant General Simonson, June 30, 1977, the Guard was told, "Your mission is to assist the superintendent in maintaining essential services at the institution to include security, food service, and medical service." At least one commander further instructed his men to "treat the residents like human beings."[2] Acknowledgment of this kind of treatment was a prevailing theme in the interviews and questionnaires for the period when the National Guard was in the institutions. When the residents were asked to respond to the question, "For you, what was the most important thing that happened during the strike," the highest number answered that it was "being treated like a man." This was supported by the fact that a majority of residents and supervisory staff said the National Guard treated residents as equals.

Sample remarks from residents included:

> (I) was treated like a real human being and a man! Treated warmly and with sincerity.
> I got treated like I was a man fair and equal, and my family got treated good and fair when they came to visit me.
> The National Guard came inside and treated us like men and human beings — and we reciprocated.

Relaxed Rules

Relaxation in general discipline and in enforcement of rules (such as talking and dress rules) seemed to be of key importance in the improved morale during the strike. In at least one institution an abbreviated set of rules was prepared by the supervisory staff for National Guard use. Almost all of the Guard members on duty said they had some or a lot of discretion in enforcing the rules. It was usually their supervisors in the Guard and supervisory staff who told the Guard members what rules to enforce, but about one in four of the Guard members said that residents told them also. Over half of the residents said that rules for dress, talking, movement, recreation, and visiting other residents were less strictly enforced during the strike. In general the supervisory staff agreed with the residents' assessment in these areas. The majority of National Guard members thought the enforcement of these rules was appropriate during the strike. One example of relaxed rules occurred at Waupun where residents were no longer required to march in silence to the dining hall. Other examples reflected the hot weather that occurred during the strike. One resident said he liked being able to wear shorts and go without a shirt. Another said that in his institution residents could go for ice anytime instead of three times a day. Exchanging things and talking between cells were relaxed in some instances.

A majority of residents and supervisory staff also said discipline was less strict during the strike. This is reflected in remarks on the questionnaires indicating that fewer tickets or conduct reports were given during the strike for such things as being late to roll call, or not making the bed.

No Increase in Illegal or Prohibited Behavior

Despite relaxed rules and greater freedom given residents during the strike, there was apparently no increase in reported illegal or prohibited behavior by residents. A majority of the residents and supervisory personnel on duty reported that illegal or prohibited behavior either remained at usual levels or was reduced during the strike. Many of the supervisory personnel and residents said they did not know about sexual assaults, alcohol and weapons in the institution during the strike. Residents who said they *did* know said they saw less than usual. Residents also reported less stealing, drugs and fights. Most supervisors said they noticed about the same number of these violations as usual. A large majority of the National Guard members did not see rule violations in any of the areas, but each violation was seen by a few of the Guard members.

Services — Good but Limited

Some services were shut down during the strike, mainly in areas of classes, industry, social services and psychological services. Where services were provided, they were reported to be adequately staffed with National Guard personnel. Residents liked the less strict way rules were applied, including the fact that the Guard took part in games. "They played pool with us," one resident said. Residents also liked it when the Guard helped with work, like mopping, or sat down and worshiped with them at religious services. These activities may have been possible because of the number of National Guard on duty, or the Guard members' proximity to institutions during free hours. Much of this informal interaction is prohibited to regular correctional officers, partially because of insufficient staff coverage.

How It Looked Inside the Walls

The scene during the 16 days of the strike, as sketched by responses to the survey, shows supervisory staff working long hours to facilitate the smooth operation of the institutions. The largest number of supervisors said that the most important thing during the strike was that a crisis was averted. They briefed the Guard, carried out their regular duties and filled in wherever their skills were needed. "I got burned out from overwork and long hours," one supervisor said.

The picture shows a large staff of National Guard personnel cooperating with supervisors, enforcing rules differently, with the time and authorization to develop friendly relations with the residents by talking with them, and entering into their activities. One Guardsman said, "I was able to communicate on a sincere and honest basis putting all trouble aside. I was able to treat residents a bit more humanly and receive same."

The residents' reactions to the novel situation included higher morale, increased feelings of responsibility and helpfulness, and a positive feeling toward the Guard personnel. Some residents were eager to express their feelings, and wrote long paragraphs on the margins of their questionnaires. Here are some excerpts from their remarks:

> I developed a close working relationship with most of the National Guard that I had dealings with.
> We were able to show that, for the first time, we can function better under less stricter rules.
> The atmosphere became one of adults acting rationally, increased sense of responsibility on the part of inmates.

The National Guard treated me as a person, not like a criminal, but as a person who had feeling and responsibility that should of been expected of me!

Some Exceptions to This View

There was a question in the survey asking all respondents if they felt the media were accurate in their coverage during the strike. The correctional officers were more critical of press coverage than the other goups. A majority of correctional officers said newspapers, TV and radio were inaccurate in their coverage of the behavior of the National Guard and of residents. Two of the correctional officers' comments included the following, "They (the Guard) really only kept the lid on," and "They (the residents) had the run of the place."

In Section IV of the report, which is concerned with the time period after the strike, survey participants further temper the observations of the strike period. Answers to a speculative question about what survey participants thought might have happened had the National Guard stayed in the institutions for three months or longer are shown in Figure E in that section. There are interesting differences of opinion among groups on these surmises, as well as on conditions after the strike.

IV. FOUR GROUPS LOOK AT EACH OTHER

Describing the Residents

One of the most striking findings of this study lies in the very different way the residents were described by each of the other three groups. The same 30-word adjective (trait) list was presented to correctional officers, National Guard and supervisory personnel with the instruction: "If you believe the word describes the *majority* of the residents, check 'yes.' If not, check 'no.' " Traits receiving the highest percent of "yes" answers are presented in Figure A.

Figure A

TRAITS OF RESIDENTS AS PERCEIVED BY THE NATIONAL GUARD AND STAFF GROUPS

Highest percent of "yes" replies by:

National Guard		Supervisory Personnel		Correctional Officers	
Cooperative	91%	Ordinary	79%	Demanding	88%
Friendly	84	Impulsive	78	Impulsive	81
Good-humored	79	Relaxed	74	Restless	81
Relaxed	79	Demanding	72	Unreliable	80
Respectful	79	Cooperative	70	Sneaky	72

The National Guard and the correctional officers appear to be describing two very different groups. Either the Guard members were very naive, the behavior of the residents remarkably improved during the strike, or the regular correctional officers have become cynical about the residents they work with on a daily basis. The best guess is that all three observations are probably true to some degree. Whether or not the Guard members' evaluation of the residents was realistic, it obviously contrasted sharply with that of the correctional officers and partially accounts for the fact that the Guard was able to interact with the residents in different ways from the correctional officers. Some of those different ways have already been discussed; others will be taken up in the next section of the report. One conclusion is obvious. The Guard's assessment of the residents during the strike was significantly more positive than the assessment of residents by either the regular correctional officers or the supervisory personnel. The assessments by supervisors were between the other two almost-polar assessments (Figure D).

Another significant difference in perception of the residents apparently exists within the regular staff, namely, between the supervisors and the correctional officers. While both groups tended to agree that the majority of residents are demanding, impulsive and bored, significantly more correctional officers viewed them as tense, sneaky, uncooperative, uncommunicative, disrespectful, irritable, hostile, unpleasant and dangerous than did supervisory personnel. This sharp difference of opinion between the group primarily responsible for *establishing* policy and rules, and the group primarily responsible for *enforcing* them appears to have the potential for creating serious problems. Evidence concerning some of the problems which may exist between these two groups will appear in Section V in the analysis of questions concerning communication and job satisfaction.

In Tables 30 and 31, the adjective list has been arranged into desirable and undesirable traits. In Figure B the percent "yes" replies have been averaged.

The Residents Rate the Other Three Groups

The residents were asked to react to a series of questions about the National Guard, the correctional officers and supervisory personnel. Their responses are shown in Figure C. The percents indicate "yes" answers by residents.

On the factors measured, the attitude of the residents emerges as strongly positive toward the Guard and strongly negative toward both groups of regular staff. There are no significant differences in the residents' evaluation of the two regular staff groups, although, as shown in the trait ratings, the two staff groups appear to have quite different views of the residents.

Figure B

SUMMARY OF AVERAGE PERCENTS OF DESIRABLE AND UNDESIRABLE TRAITS OF RESIDENTS AS PERCEIVED BY NATIONAL GUARD AND STAFF GROUPS

Traits of Residents[a]	National Guard	Supervisory Personnel	Correctional Officers
Desirable traits	72%	52%	31%
Undesirable traits	19	34	60

[a] The percents of *yes* replies for 11 desirable traits were averaged as were percents for 14 undesirable traits.

No judgment is implied concerning treatment of residents as equals in a correctional institution, other than that it is considered highly desirable by the residents. Over 70% of the residents said the correctional officers and supervisors treat them as children, but only 2% said the National Guard members treated them as children. These answers give further indication of the importance the residents place on being treated as equals.

Figure C

RESIDENTS' RATINGS OF BEHAVIORS OF THE OTHER THREE GROUPS REGARDING TREATMENT OF RESIDENTS

	Groups rated by residents		
Behaviors rated by residents[a]	Correctional Officers	National Guard	Supervisory Personnel
Fair with residents	19%	93%	15%
Strict	72	8	76
Treat residents as equals	7	89	6
Seem relaxed	24	85	27
Care about residents	7	85	7
Talk easily with residents	17	92	14
Try to help residents	7	85	9
Are friendly	19	93	16
Treat residents as children	75	2	72

[a] Percent *yes* replies. (Other possible responses were "no" and "don't know.")

Correctional Officers, National Guard, and Supervisors Rate Each Other

On the same factors given the residents, other groups were asked to evaluate each other. As before, Figure D deals with percent of "yes" replies.

The supervisory personnel clearly do not share the residents' view of the correctional officers. They gave the correctional officers somewhat higher ratings than they gave the National Guard on all factors except friendliness and treating residents as equals. The ratings of the supervisory personnel by the National Guard and correctional officers were, with one exception, remarkably similar.

It is important to emphasize that the data from Figures A, B, C, and D represent perceptions, not established facts. In this study there was no objective measure of the behavior of any of the four groups. However, people's perceptions of each other tend to influence the way in which they interact. In summary, residents perceived that they received better treatment from the Guard than from the regular staff. The Guard members had more positive attitudes toward residents than the staff did. These combined observations give further evidence of the positive relationship between the National Guard and the residents during the strike.

Figure D

RATINGS OF CORRECTIONAL OFFICERS, NATIONAL GUARD AND SUPERVISORY PERSONNEL TOWARD EACH OTHER REGARDING TREATMENT OF RESIDENTS

Behaviors rated[a]	Correctional Officers as rated by Supervisors	National Guard as rated by Supervisors	Supervisory Personnel as rated by Correctional Officers	Supervisory Personnel as rated by National Guard
Fair with residents	87%	86%	77%	71%
Strict	27	11	22	58
Treat residents as equals	40	66	47	37
Seem relaxed	69	60	41	50
Care about residents	75	50	61	56
Talk easily with residents	78	68	62	64
Try to help residents	75	48	59	55
Are friendly	86	90	68	73
Treat residents as children	6	4	27	13

[a] Percent *yes* replies. (Other possible responses were "no" and "don't know.")

What If the Strike Had Continued

Because of the short duration of the National Guard stay in the institutions a speculative question was included in the survey. All four groups were asked what might have happened if the Guard had stayed on duty three months or more.

Figure E shows that over 80% of the two staff groups (correctional officers and supervisory personnel) thought tension would have increased along with fights and violence, and that more security would have been needed. Over 90% of both staff groups felt that the Guard would have needed more training. A majority of the Guard members agreed with the staff about the need for more training. Almost all of the staff thought things would *not* have improved.

In sharp contrast, almost all of the residents and National Guard members thought things would have improved if the National Guard had stayed three months or more. The two groups strongly agreed that they

Figure E

POSSIBLE EFFECTS OF A THREE MONTH STAY BY THE NATIONAL GUARD

If the National Guard had stayed on duty for 3 months or more, do you think...[a]	Correctional Officers	National Guard	Residents	Supervisory Personnel
More security would have been needed	89%	37%	8%	80%
Petty rules would have been permanently dropped	60	60	84	29
Tension would have increased	86	39	9	86
There would have been more fights and violence	92	34	6	82
The National Guard would have become less friendly toward the residents	92	42	12	88
There would have been a riot	62	8	4	28
The National Guard would have kept things cool	10	90	89	38
The National Guard would have needed more training	94	55	25	90
Residents would have kept things cool	18	73	86	28
Things would have improved	3	71	88	5

[a] Percent *yes* replies. (Other possible answer was "no.")

would have kept things cool, that some rules perceived as petty would have been permanently dropped, and that tension would not have increased. A majority of Guard members and residents did not believe more security would have been needed.

V. AFTER THE STRIKE

Correctional Officers Return to the Job

When the correctional officers returned to their jobs after the strike, a sizable majority said working conditions were worse than before. Their major complaints concerned the residents' behavior and the condition of the facility. One correctional officer said, "They (residents) were used to not following rules — hard to get residents to return to normal procedures." The majority of the correctional officers said relations with their supervisors were about the same, but the majority believed relations with the non-striking staff were worse.

Resident Morale After the Strike

A large majority of residents said the morale of the residents was lower after the strike than during the strike. Very few residents think they are treated fairly, in spite of almost unanimous agreement by both staff groups that residents are treated fairly. A majority of the residents are sometimes or always worried about their personal safety. About half said the correctional officers treated them more strictly after the strike than before.

Job Attitudes: Comparison of Groups

A majority of the correctional officers said that union members' morale was worse after the strike than before it. They made some other complaints about working conditions which may well influence morale. For one thing, 83% of the correctional officers reported that they are always or sometimes worried about their personal safety. By contrast, half of the supervisors said they are never worried and most of the others said they are sometimes worried (Table 36). Both the correctional officers and supervisors agreed that correctional officers need more backing from administration. Another area of strong agreement between the correctional officers and supervisors concerns training. It was almost unanimous among them that more staff training is needed.

A comparison of job attitudes of the correctional officers, the National Guard, and supervisory personnel is made in Figure F below. The comparison shows that both supervisors and National Guard have more positive views of their jobs in the correctional institutions — of their influence, their enjoyment of their job, and the appreciation given to them — than do the correctional officers. Almost all members of all three groups said they have responsible jobs. Attitudes toward the job affect

Figure F
ATTITUDES OF EMPLOYEES AND NATIONAL GUARD TOWARD THEIR JOBS IN THE CORRECTIONAL INSTITUTION

	Respondents		
Attitudes toward jobs[a]	Correctional Officers	National Guard	Supervisory Personnel
Proud to serve at correctional institution	—[b]	91%	—
Proud to work at correctional institution	71%	—	82%
A lot of good people in the National Guard	—	96	—
Best people available are hired	5	—	24
Have a responsible job	94	96	99
Well trained for my job	66	65	92
Residents appreciate the job I do	56	91	69
Supervisors appreciate the job I do	69	95	86
Supervisors listen to my suggestions	52	81	86
Supervisors act on my suggestions	36	71	72
Can use own judgment in any situation	38	71	59
Supervisors back up my decisions	47	85	79
Pay is reasonable	34	—	67
Enjoyed the experience	—	85	—
Enjoy my work	73	—	83
Able to influence rule and policy changes	26	44	64

[a] Percent *agree/strongly agree* replies combined. (Other possible replies were "disagree" and "strongly disagree.")
[b] "—" means that this question was not asked of this group. This symbol will have the same meaning in all remaining Figures.

morale. The fact that about 25% of the correctional officers reported that they do not enjoy their jobs and are not proud to be correctional officers is important.

About half of the correctional officers reported that their supervisors listen to their suggestions, but a majority said the supervisors don't act on the suggestions. Seventy-four percent of correctional officers reported that they are not able to influence rule and policy change. On the other hand, a majority of supervisors reported that they can influence change, and that their superiors do listen to their suggestions.

Correctional Officers Job: Would National Guard Want It?

The National Guard members were asked if they would consider working at a correctional institution if they were looking for a job. Twenty-eight percent said that they would. Some of the reasons they gave were that they would like to help the residents, that they liked the type of work, and that they could earn a decent living. A typical answer from a Guard member who would consider working at a correctional institution was, "I like to work with people who need help." A frequent reason Guard members gave for not seeking work at a correctional institution was that they are trained for and prefer other careers.

What About Rule Changes?

There was agreement by 97% of both correctional officers and supervisory personnel that more uniform interpretation of the rules is needed. This might be seen as a conflict with the statement by a majority of correctional officers that they would like more discretion in enforcing rules. However, this is not necessarily true. It may be that they would like clear definition as to which rules are absolute and which are subject to individual discretion, with the knowledge that their decisions would be backed up by supervisors. A majority of correctional officers and supervisors would like stricter rules for residents and uniform dress for correctional officers. Correctional officers would also like stricter dress codes for residents. They said the residents have too much freedom.

Neither the correctional offices nor the supervisors believed there were any important changes in rules resulting from the strike experience. About half the residents said the rules are stricter today than they were before the strike.

What Are the Rules Used For?

Everyone was asked what they think the rules are used for now. Most reported that rules keep residents under control and keep things running smoothly. It is interesting that a majority of all but the *residents* said rules are used to protect residents, and all but the *correctional officers* said rules are used to protect staff. Only the residents thought that rules and procedures are used to carry out personal grudges.

Needed: More Staff Communication

Over 90% of the correctional officers and supervisory personnel agreed that more communication is needed among staff members. This clear need for better communication is illustrated by the differences correctional officers and supervisors have in their perception of the residents, discussed in Part IV. Possibly better communication could give correctional officers more influence in policy changes, which they desire. Better communication might also contribute to better operation where both staff groups are shown to agree, as in the desire for uniform interpretation of rules, and in the need for more backing from supervisors for correctional officers.

Needed: More Resident-Staff Communication

The National Guard, the correctional officers, and most strongly, the residents themselves, believed the institutions need more communication among residents and staff. However, only a minority of the supervisors agreed with this. The Offender Participation Advisory Committees (OPAC) are one avenue of resident-staff communication.

VI. DISCUSSION ABOUT CORRECTIONAL INSTITUTIONS

The Outsiders' View

Over a thousand citizens from outside the world of the correctional institutions have looked at that world and given their opinions. These citizens are, of course, the National Guard members who served during the strike. Increased knowledge of the institutions was one of the two most frequent answers given by the Guard to the question, "For you what was the most important thing that happened during the strike?" (The other was, "It ended!") As one National Guardsman put it, "I learned what really goes on behind the walls." Another comment was, "I was very much impressed by the facility and by the confidence that the non-striking staff demonstrated during the early days of the emergency." Still another, "I saw something every young person should see and experience. Then such facilities would surely be less populated in future years."

Are Facilities Adequate?

Questions concerning facilities were asked of all four groups. Over 65% of the correctional officers and residents strongly disagreed with the statement that the institutions are well-planned for rehabilitation. A sizable minority of the Guard members agreed with them. Half of the Guard and over three-fourths of the other three groups said the institutions are too crowded. The answers also show that both staff groups would like more security features. Slightly fewer than half of the National Guard members said that the buildings need improvements. The Guard members' answers indicate that a majority found the physical plants satisfactory. In every section of the question, the residents were the group most critical of the facilities.

Other Suggestions for Change

A strikingly large number of respondents from all groups said that there are not enough jobs for residents. A majority of all the groups also thought residents should be given more responsibility. As with the question about facilities, it is the residents who are most critical of various aspects of their life such as food, recreation, degree of privacy and the way the institutions are run. Over seventy percent of both residents and correctional officers disagreed with the statement that the institution is well-run, as compared with the opposite perceptions by the National Guard and supervisors. These and other replies on institutional life are in Figure G.

Hiring: A Trouble Spot

At the time of the survey, a very large majority of the correctional officers and supervisors were not satisfied with procedures for hiring correctional officers and did not believe that the best applicants were hired. These two staff groups were almost unanimous in believing that higher qualifications should be required, and that vacancies should be filled faster. A majority said that newly hired staff are too young, especially at the maximum security institutions. This degree of dissatisfaction with hiring procedures may well have a negative effect on employee morale. Some of the problems of hiring may have been alleviated since the questionnaires were answered. The extremely unpopular system of random selection of new correctional officers from among qualified applicants was changed during the month of the survey.

Staffing: Is It Adequate?

The three groups who were in a position to know (correctional officers, residents and supervisory personnel) were asked about adequacy of number of staff in different services. A majority of all three groups thought there was enough staff in most areas. Both staff groups strongly indicated a need for more security staff. Not surprisingly, the residents said there are already

Figure G

ATTITUDES TOWARD INSTITUTIONAL LIFE

Today how do you feel about each of the following statements?[a]	Correctional Officers	National Guard	Residents	Supervisory Personnel
The food is good	88%	71%	30%	98%
There are not enough jobs for residents	83	60	81	82
More recreation is needed	26	45	86	31
Residents have enough privacy	89	71	18	71
Residents should be given more responsibility	60	59	89	57
The institution is well run	28	74	11	75
Residents have too much freedom	75	19	4	50

[a] Percentage *agree* and *strongly agree* replies combined. (Other possible replies were "disagree" and "strongly disagree.")

too many people in security. About half of the residents and correctional officers said there is not enough medical staff.

VII. SUMMARY

Following the strike of public employees in July 1977, the League of Women Voters of Wisconsin accepted the responsibility to survey the opinions of National Guard members, correctional officers, supervisory personnel and residents of five correctional institutions. Some of the more interesting findings shown by the data gathered are summarized below. It is important to keep in mind when reading these brief statements, that the strike period was unique. It lasted for a short time, during which many of the institutional programs were curtailed. The large number of National Guard members on duty plus their special instructions contributed to the Guard's ability to interact with the residents in ways the regular correctional officers could not. *The study is in no way meant to be a comparison of the competence of the two groups, for such comparison is not possible.* The purpose of the study is to identify problems and opportunities for constructive change in the correctional institutions. Although a potentially volatile situation existed, a crisis was averted as a result of pre-planning and cooperation among the supervisory personnel, the National Guard and the residents of the institutions.

During the Strike

. . . Over three-fourths of the National Guard members and supervisory personnel agreed that residents helped the Guard during the strike.

. . . Seventy-nine percent of the residents reported resident morale to be higher during the strike than before.

. . . Neither National Guard members nor residents expected that there would be relaxed enforcement of rules or greater freedom during the strike. Both apparently did occur. More than 80% of residents and Guard members said that during the strike things were better than they expected.

. . . The most frequent response any group gave to the question, "For you what was the most important thing that happened during the strike?" was the residents' reply, "I was treated like a man," or some paraphrase of that statement.

. . . Residents and supervisors reported that during the strike there was no appreciable increase in a variety of kinds of illegal behavior, although both groups reported that the rules were relatively less strict during the strike.

. . . Residents demonstrated that in this emergency situation they were able to take some responsibility.

. . . Almost all of the two staff groups believed that the National Guard would have needed more training if they had stayed on duty three months or more.

A Look at Each Other

. . . The National Guard used more positive adjectives in describing residents than did the correctional officers. In fact they appeared to be describing two different groups of people.

. . . There was also a striking difference in the way correctional officers and supervisors described the residents. For example, more correctional officers than supervisors saw residents as dangerous and hostile.

. . . Residents described the National Guard positively and the correctional officers negatively when asked to respond to a series of seven statements on such qualities as friendliness, fairness and helpfulness. This perception may have influenced their behavior.

. . . Supervisory staff described the correctional officers slightly more favorably than they described the Guard members when asked to respond to the seven statements described above.

. . . A majority of all four groups involved in the study said that the residents should be given more responsibility.

After the Strike

. . . A majority of correctional officers reported that their morale was lower after the strike than before it. A majority of residents reported that their morale was lower after the strike than during it.

. . . Ninety-seven percent of both staff groups said more uniform interpretation of the rules is needed.

. . . Correctional officers said that they are not able to influence rule and policy changes, and that their supervisors do not act on their suggestions. Morale and job dissatisfaction appear to be real problems for correctional officers.

. . . Both staff groups emphasize the need for more staff training.

. . . Over 90% of the correctional officers and supervisory personnel said more communication is needed among staff members.

. . . There was support from the National Guard, correctional officers and residents for more staff-resident communication.

. . . A majority of correctional officers and residents did not agree with the statement that the institutions are well-planned for rehabilitation.

. . . Both staff groups were very dissatisfied with hiring procedures for correctional officers that were used at the time. (These procedures have since been changed. Over 90% said that the best people available are not hired.

. . . A strong majority of all four groups agreed that more jobs are needed for residents.

There was a brief "changing of the guard" in Wisconsin correctional institutions. The reports of the experiences of the National Guard members who took over for the striking correctional officers prompted this study. The data show that the National Guard responded well to the challenge of staffing the correctional institutions during a difficult and far-from-normal period. The residents' morale rose, and they responded well to the way the Guard members related to them. Supervisory personnel worked long hours to help avert a crisis, and their importance during the strike period should not be overlooked. The frustration expressed by the correctional officers about their job, viewed as a long-term occupation, contrasts with the National Guard members' satisfaction with their limited duty in the correctional institutions as part-time soldiers. This contrast may account for some of the differences which were observed in the study.

It is important that these findings be carefully studied. The strike situation provided a unique opportunity to view life at five Wisconsin correctional institutions through the eyes of four different groups. The data presented provide compelling evidence which should be carefully considered by those responsible for determining policies and procedures of correctional institutions.

Notes

1. Figure from the State of Wisconsin, Department of Military Affairs After Action Report — State Employee Strike, Inclusion 9.

2. Memo from Col. Wulgaert to General Simonson after the strike, April 1978.

Part V
FEMALE CORRECTIONAL OFFICERS

Working out the practical problems of having women in the prisons may necessitate looking at things we should have dealt with long before.
Loretta McCarthy, 1979

Women have long been employed as correctional officers in prisons for women but social scientists have ignored them at least as much as they have ignored the female offenders they guard. The introduction of women as correctional officers in prisons for *men* is a relatively recent phenomenon and one which has attracted much more attention primarily because of controversy about potential violation of male inmates' privacy, doubts about a female's ability to perform duties requiring physical strength, concern about the women's safety, and apprehension that their presence may adversely affect prison discipline. These anxieties are thoroughly analyzed in the following chapters.

In Chapter 11, James Jacobs critically reviews the available evidence on such issues in the context of his discussion of a U.S. Supreme Court ruling on a case which represented an important test of the legal problems associated with employing women as guards in men's prisons. His article provides a comprehensive review of the literature on this topic and raises and suggests some thoughtful solutions to the important policy issues which have risen as a result of womens' participation as guards.

Chapter 12 provides a report on the current status of the employment of women as prison guards. It is based on information collected and extensive surveys conducted through the resources of Contact Inc.*, an international information clearinghouse in the criminal justice field. Many of the issues raised in Jacob's article are discussed in Chapter 12 from the point of view of women who have had experience as guards in men's prisons. Sandra Nicolai's cooperation in preparing the report for this book is appreciated.

---

* Contact, Inc., P.O. Box 81826 Lincoln, Nebraska.

Reference

McCarthy, L. Quoted in "You've come a long way baby." *Corrections Compendium*, 1979, July, *3*, No. 12, 1.

Chapter 11

The Sexual Integration of the Prison's Guard Force: A Few Comments on Dothard v. Rawlinson*

James B. Jacobs

Some state correctional systems, as well as the Federal Bureau of Prisons, have begun hiring women to fill guard positions in men's prisons. This departure from previous policy descends from the social and political power of the women's movement, federal equal employment opportunity law,[1] the public employee union movement,[2] and the penological theory that women guards will contribute to prisoner rehabilitation by "normalizing"[3] the penal environment. Opponents of this change, including rank-and-file male guards, dispute the capacity of women to maintain order and discipline. It has also been argued that stationing women guards in cell houses invades male inmates' rights of privacy.[4] Furthermore, some critics resist the idea of women guards in men's prisons because they fear it will require broadening the role of male guards in women's prisons.

Like many other contemporary issues of penal policy, the opposite-sex guard question is now being thrashed out in the courts. Women have attacked explicit employment restrictions in all-male prisons[5] as well as facially neutral height and weight requirements that disproportionately disqualify them.[6] In a few cases, prisoners themselves have sought to reverse on privacy grounds a state correctional department's decision to hire opposite-sex guards.[7]

The issue facing corrections is whether prisons will continue as single sex institutions or whether women employees will have a major role in their administration and day-to-day functioning. The thesis of this article is that concerns for a stable penal environment and prisoners' privacy complaints are not insurmountable obstacles to equal employment opportunities. In those jurisdictions that employ women guards in men's facilities, the experience so far indicates no break-down of order.[8] Structural changes in the cell houses and selectivity in assignments can greatly mitigate, and possibly resolve, the privacy problem.

The time is now ripe to cast off traditional stereotypes about both women and prisons.[9] The notion that men's prisons must inevitably be

---

* Reprinted by permission of the University of Toledo Law Review, Vol. 10 (1979).

powder kegs of violence may prove to be more a consequence of societal expectations than an immutable feature of penal institutions.[10] It may be that institutions perpetually braced for violence do indeed experience it, or at least perceive that they are experiencing it. Perhaps if women were more fully integrated into the prison staff, expectations of conduct would change and violence would decrease. In any case, despite the dangerousness of prisons, Title VII[11] requires that women be allowed to compete individually for all positions in corrections.

I. DOTHARD V. RAWLINSON

Dothard v. Rawlinson[12] provides a starting point for analyzing the policy issues and legal problems associated with the sexual integration of the prison guard force. Prior to graduating from the University of Alabama with a degree in correctional psychology, Dianne Rawlinson applied to the Alabama Board of Corrections for a job as a correctional counselor, commonly known as a prison guard. Despite her superior educational qualifications, she was rejected because she failed by five pounds to meet the minimum statutory weight requirement for the position.[13] Rawlinson filed a sex discrimination charge with the Equal Employment Opportunity Commission. After receiving a right-to-sue letter, she brought a federal class action charging that Alabama's height and weight qualifications for law enforcement positions violated Title VII.[14] She also challenged an administrative regulation, adopted during the pendency of the lawsuit, barring women from "contact positions" (posts requiring "continual close proximity to inmates") in men's maximum security prisons.[15]

The three-judge district court held that height and weight qualifications that disproportionately disqualify women constitute prima facie violations of Title VII.[16] Since the Alabama Board of Corrections failed to show how height and weight requirements are job related, the court enjoined their use. The court also struck down the state's no contact rule because the state failed to produce evidence showing that women could not serve successfully in men's prisons. Indeed, plaintiff's witnesses testified that females were *successfully* serving in several Alabama male youth facilities and that women guards in other correctional systems had contributed to the "normalization" of the penal environment.[17] The court rejected arguments that maximum security prisons are too dangerous for women and that the presence of women guards would infringe upon the privacy of male prisoners.[18]

The Supreme Court, in an opinion of Justice Stewart,[19] affirmed the elimination of the height and weight requirements, but reversed the invalidation of the "no contact" rule, holding that the guard position falls within the bona fide occupational qualification (bfoq) exception to Title VII.[20] Justice Rehnquist, in a concurring opinion joined by Chief Justice Burger and Justice Blackmun, suggested that height and weight requirements might well be upheld in other contexts.[21] Justice Marshall, joined by Justice Brennan, agreed that the height and weight requirements could not pass Title VII muster, but disagreed about the legality of the no contact rule.[22] Justice White dissented because he did not think there had been a prima facie showing of sex discrimination.[23]

Rawlinson is the first decision by the Supreme Court, or any federal appellate court, upholding an employer's claim that a job should be limited to members of one sex. The case is all the more remarkable because the Supreme Court chose to broaden the reach of Title VII's bfoq exception in spite of a three-judge lower court finding that there was no evidence to support the employer's claim. In effect, the Supreme Court held that the lower court was clearly erroneous, without being able to point to any evidence on the record showing that women could not serve successfully in Alabama's men's prisons. Unfortunately, the opinion reflects a "gut reaction" rather than a careful consideration of women's statutory rights to equal employment opportunity and the realities of prison life.

Since *Rawlinson* is the Supreme Court's first pronouncement on the scope of Title VII's bfoq exception, the full implications of the decision for women's employment opportunities are not yet clear. It was in the context of Alabama's very dangerous and poorly managed maximum security prisons[24] that Justice Stewart's opinion upheld the exclusion of women from the guard force on the ground that they would be vulnerable to assault by predatory sex offenders. Perhaps the opinion will not warrant finding a bfoq exception in less deplorable prisons in other states.[25] However, such a narrow interpretation of *Rawlinson* is unlikely. The deference paid to the claims of prison officials by the *Rawlinson* majority strongly suggests that women will be held legally excludable from all maximum security prisons, and perhaps from medium and minimum security institutions as well. Prisons, by definition, are populated by individuals who pose serious threats to the community, and all maximum security prisons hold at least some "predatory sex offenders." Unless prospective women guards are able to prove the negative — that they will not be more vulnerable to attack and will not destabilize the prison regime — the momentum of the *Rawlinson* decision will probably lead other courts to conclude that the role of women in men's penal facilities should be limited. The effects of the decision may also radiate to juvenile institutions, other male dominated law enforcement agencies like the police, and even to the armed forces where women have made important strides in the last few years.[26]

A. Height and Weight Standards

Despite the *Rawlinson* holding that facially neutral height and weight standards cannot be used to bar applicants from guard positions, this ruling may actually open the way for law enforcement departments to limit job opportunities for women. We will consider this issue — as did the *Rawlinson* Court — before examining Title VII's bfoq exception.

The *Rawlinson* majority held that national statistics on the sex distribution of height and weight showed that the minima imposed by Alabama disproportionately disqualified women from law enforcement positions and thus constituted a prima facie violation of Title VII.[27] According to Justice Stewart, the Board of Corrections had not carried its burden of proving how height and weight minima are job related. This much of the opinion would be a victory for women's efforts to achieve equality of employment opportunity were it not for the Court's suggestion that strength might be upheld as job related. Law enforcement agencies might now be tempted to establish strength tests, or to justify height and weight requirements on the ground that they are correlated with strength.

Justice Rehnquist's opinion, in which Chief Justice Burger and Justice Blackmun joined, supports this reading of *Rawlinson* as a retreat from Title VII's mandate for equal employment opportunity. Justice Rehnquist concurred in that part of Justice Stewart's opinion that invalidated the height and weight requirements because he did not think that the district court's conclusion — that there was no evidence on the record to demonstrate a relationship between height and weight and strength — was clearly erroneous. Justice Rehnquist emphasized, however, that the district court's conclusion was "by no means *required* by the proffered evidence."[28] If the lower court had decided that there was sufficient evidence to demonstrate such a relationship, Justice Rehnquist certainly would have permitted the height and weight criteria to stand. Thus, he stated, "In other cases there could be different evidence which could lead a District Court to conclude that height and weight *are* in fact an accurate enough predictor of strength to justify, under all the circumstances, such minima."[29] Justice Rehnquist's warning that the Court's decision should not be taken as a repudiation of height and weight qualifications for law enforcement jobs opened a door that most lower courts had assumed was closed.[30] He also pointed out that a corrections department could justify height and weight qualifications due to their relation to the *appearance of strength*, which contributes to the effective exercise of authority.[31] Police departments and other agencies, which have revised their height and weight requirements in response to a slough of recent federal court decisions, may now interpret *Rawlinson* as a signal to resurrect old standards, or to construct new ones. Future litigation may focus on whether women, who tend to be smaller and lighter than men, demonstrate the appearance of strength.

1. The Importance of Strength

In *Rawlinson*, the Alabama Board of Corrections failed to introduce evidence on the relationship between height and weight and strength. It is possible that in future litigation law enforcement agencies will be able to prove that these variables are correlated, especially if strength is defined in terms of capacity to lift heavy weights. Mere correlation, however, does not contradict the fact that height and weight criteria would bar from employment many small and light individuals of both sexes who could lift as much weight, or more, than taller, heavier persons. Therefore, if the ability to lift weight is job related, a department of corrections should still be required to test applicants individually rather than relying on height and weight as a crude surrogate for strength. This is especially true because height and weight criteria discriminate against women and hispanics[32] — two groups protected by Title VII.

It is unlikely that law enforcement agencies, particularly departments of correction, are really trying to screen out poor weight lifters. These agencies are probably looking for employees who can handle physical confrontations competently. While research has disclosed no data on the relationship between height and weight and the ability and willingness to use physical force, these variables do not intuitively seem to be strongly correlated. Common experience reinforces the notion that self-defense skills are easily learned and displayed by individuals of all sizes and shapes. Aggressiveness and courage may be even more randomly distributed. Prisoners themselves, a group highly skewed in the direction of physical combativeness, do not appear to vary from the rest of the population (of similar aged persons) in height and weight. And even if smaller persons generally test lower on physical combat skills, those who apply for law enforcement positions are a self selected sample. Short, light individuals who seek careers in law enforcement may be unusual in the degree to which they have developed highly effective combat skills.

Studies in various police departments lend no support to the contention that the appearance of strength is an important qualification of law enforcement work. A Portland study found no significant relationship between a police officer's height and the probability of being assaulted.[33] Swanson and Hale found little difference between the heights of assaulted and nonassaulted police officers in thirteen southwestern cities.[34] Bloch and Anderson's careful analysis of the District of Columbia Police Department concluded that taller officers perform *more poorly* than smaller ones.[35] While the San Diego Police Department reported contrary findings,[36] methodological flaws and the self-interest of the department cast considerable doubt on the conclusions.[37] Most important, the final report of a year long study on patrolwomen in Washington exploded many of the myths about women's reactions to violence.[38] Observers noted that neither sex had a general advantage during threatening situations encountered on patrol.[39] Additionally, the majority of citizens rated men and women about the same in handling aggressive behavior. A similar study done in New York City concluded that women had greater success than men in cooling violent situations.[40]

There is simply no compelling, or even strong, evidence to justify excluding smaller and lighter individuals from law enforcement jobs. At the very least, Title VII should put the burden on employers to demonstrate that height and weight are strongly correlated with a specific operational definition of strength that can be shown to be job related. Even when this burden is met, law enforcement agencies should be compelled to test applicants individually rather than exclude them categorically. This is especially true where, as here, characteristics like height and weight disproportionately exclude members of groups explicitly protected by Title VII.

2. *Qualifications for Prison Guards*

Unfortunately the prison guard has not been the subject of much scholarly study;[41] little is known about the extent to which guards must rely on force and coercion. There is a body of research, however, that does suggest that skillful interpersonal relations are more important than physical force.[42] Of course, guards must effectively exercise authority. An officer must be able to tell prisoners what to do and what not to do and must stop a fight if one breaks out. But on a day to day basis, a guard's authority and effectiveness depend more upon negotiation and accommodation than coercion.

The prison guard is expected to carry out a wide range of activities, from reporting prison rule violations to counseling prisoners about personal problems.[43] Duties such as supervising and keeping order among prisoners, taking required action in emergencies to prevent escapes or suppress disorders, and enforcing rules[44] require the ability to exercise authority confidently. But each guard is far outnumbered by prisoners, and the need to coexist for months and years with prisoners places a premium on maturity, leadership, self-confidence, judgment, and effective interpersonal relations. It is simply not necessary (and probably not possible) for a guard to rely on force or threat of force to carry out job responsibilities.[45] Numerous women employees who successfully function in tough juvenile institutions,[46] as well as physically unfit and aging male guards who work in maximum security prisons,[47] attest to this fact as does the absence of any requirements for guards to remain physically fit after they join the force. It should also be recalled that women teachers, secretaries, nurses, and administrators have been regularly functioning members of the prison staff, for at least the last decade. While their duties differ from those of prison guards, they still experience much sustained contact with prisoners, and the degree to which they are now accepted is instructive — earlier in the century it would not have been thought possible to employ women in these roles either.

Corrections departments might do well to require good health and physical fitness and then evaluate candidates on a variety of measures. Some candidates, deficient in combat skills, may compensate by their experience, motivation, and skill in interpersonal relations. A well-balanced guard force might be composed of several different types of guards who might even be following divergent career paths. Some athletic types might seek to move up the custody ranks to lieutenant and captain, while other guards, oriented toward interpersonal relations, might aspire to become counselors, trainers and the like. Whatever the job qualications, the important point is to break away from stereotyped thinking about both prisons and sex roles.

B. The No Contact Rule

The second and more far-reaching issued in *Rawlinson* was whether Alabama could justify its refusal to hire women for contact positions in men's maximum security prisons under the bona fide occupational qualification (bfoq) exception to Title VII.[48] Prior to *Rawlinson*, courts had construed the bfoq exception very narrowly. In *Weeks v. Southern Bell Telephone Co.*,[49] the employer sought to exclude women from jobs that required lifting more than thirty pounds. The Fifth Circuit found that Congress intended to allow women to decide for themselves what jobs are too physically demanding or dangerous.[50] The court held that to establish a bfoq, "the employer has the burden of proving that he had reasonable cause to believe . . . that all, or substantially all women would be unable to perform safely and efficiently the duties of the job involved."[51] The Court of Appeals for the Fifth Circuit reaffirmed this holding in *Diaz v. Pan American World Airlines*,[52] where it rejected the district court's finding that customer preference for female stewardesses justified the exclusion of males from the occupation. The Ninth Circuit in *Rosenfeld v. Southern Pacific Co.*[53] rejected a railroad's argument that certain jobs should be certified as "male only" with an even narrower interpretation of the bfoq exception: "Equality of footing is established only if employees otherwise entitled to the position, whether male or female, are excluded *only on a showing of individual incapacity.*"[54]

With this background of judicial disinclination to accept the bfoq defense, it is not surprising that the three-judge district court in *Rawlinson* rejected the (state) employer's contention that being male should constitute a bfoq for the position of prison guard. It concluded that "labelling a job as 'strenuous' and then relying on stereotyped characterization of women will not meet the burden of demonstrating a bfoq. There must be some objective, demonstrable evidence that women cannot perform the duties associated with the job."[55]

Although Justice Stewart acknowledged that Congress intended the bfoq exception to be very narrow, he found that the deplorable conditions of the Alabama prisons, fueled by the presence of "predatory male sex offenders," justified the exclusion of women. He reasoned that a woman could not successfully serve as a prison guard in the Alabama prisons because womanhood itself made female officers uniquely vulnerable to sexual assault, thereby increasing the instability of the total prison environment.[56]

The validity of Justice Stewart's opinion is questionable in light of the facts. The only evidence on the record of a woman's special vulnerability was testimony of one attack on a female clerical worker in an Alabama prison and "an incident" involving a woman student who was taken hostage during a visit to one of the maximum security prisons. The record did not provide comparative data on the percentage of male guards involved in similar conflicts with prisoners during the same period. Thus, there was no basis for concluding that women are more susceptible to assault than men.[57] The Supreme Court's handling of the issue is even less satisfactory because it treated the lower court's findings as clearly erroneous.

Even if evidence had been offered to show that women were more frequently assaulted than men, it would still have been arguable that Title VII prohibits excluding *all women* from the job.[58] Proof that more women than men are assaulted is not incompatible with the possibility that *some (and possibly many) women* either are not victimized or are victimized less frequently than most men. To justify a blanket exclusion of all women, a state should be required to prove that the cause of assaults on women officers is necessarily connected with "womanhood" and does not vary among individual women. Justice Stewart made exactly this point by asserting that by being a woman, a female guard was more likely to be assaulted by "predatory sex offenders."[59] This "conclusion," however, was not based on the record. One could not determine from the record whether predatory sex offenders are more likely to assault female guards than male guards.[60] Moreover, the record did not indicate whether the two "incidents" involving women were perpetrated by "sex offenders."[61] This unsupported premise in the majority opinion seems to reflect nothing more than a "gut reaction" that it is not appropriate for women to serve in male maximum security prisons.

Assuming the unproven assertion that female guards are more likely to be assaulted is true, it is still insufficient justification for denying women the opportunity to choose a dangerous occupation. Title VII promises to end employment discrimination based upon notions of "romantic paternalism," and allow women to work in dangerous occupations if they so desire.[62] Many courts have stated that employers must have reasons, other than the protection of women workers, to justify discriminating on the basis of sex.[63] In this regard, Justice Stewart stated, again without explanation, that the extra vulnerability of women to attack (by predatory sex offenders) would have a ripple effect on the whole prison environment, endangering the lives and safety of other guards and employees.[64] At best, this is an unproven hypothesis; there simply are no data to support it. Even if valid, it should not have ended the analysis. One still needs to consider whether any increase in overall dangerousness would suffice to exclude all women or whether increased instability in the penal environment, unless substantial, is a cost which must be borne in order to vindicate other societal goals and individual rights. After all, the extension of all constitutional rights to prisoners arguably increases danger to some degree — at least this could be said of decisions limiting censorship and arbitrary discipline. A few attacks, more or less, in the "jungle atmosphere" of the Alabama prison should not justify a categorical denial of employment opportunities for women.[65] To hold the contrary would mean that women could legally be barred from all administrative, medical, educational, and clerical positions on the ground that their presence marginally increases overall instability.

Finally, if a woman's vulnerability to sexual assault does significantly increase the instability of the penal environment, the special advantages that women staff members could bring to the job might outweigh the disadvantages associated with increased dangerousness. Justice Stewart did not discuss the advantages women guards might bring to the prison. This point, however, should not be overlooked.[66] As Justice Marshall said in his dissent:

> Presumably, one of the goals of the Alabama prison system is the eradication of inmates' antisocial behavior patterns so that prisoners will be able to live one day in free society. Sex offenders can begin this process by learning to relate to women guards in a socially acceptable manner.[67]

The same point was made at the trial in *Dothard* by Ray Nelson, an expert witness for the plaintiffs and at the time was warden of the Federal Bureau of Prisons' Metropolitan Correctional Center in Chicago. He stated that it was the policy of the Federal Bureau of Prisons to move toward "normalization" of the prison environment by integrating women into the guard force at men's institutions.[68] Theoretically, a prisoner will be better prepared to adjust to society by learning how to function in a realistic custodial environment.[69] Since prisoners, (especially) including "predatory sex offenders," will have to learn how to live in a world populated by both sexes, it is important to allow them to *interact* "normally" with women while in prison. Norval Morris and Gordon Hawkins, two prominent penologists, strenuously advocate the sexual integration of the guard force for this reason.[70] Additionally, they argue that "women bring a softening influence to the prison society, assisting men to strengthen their inner controls through a variety of deeply entrenched processes of psychological growth."[71]

II. PRISONERS' PRIVACY

The Supreme Court in *Rawlinson* did not address the issue of prisoners' privacy rights as an independent justification, under either Title VII's bfoq exception or the Constitution, for limiting women's employment opportunities in corrections. In light of recent decisions against prisoners,[72] one suspects that the Court was not anxious to resolve *Rawlinson* by recognizing a privacy right or interest, despite the fact that such a position might have been more defensible than the one the Court actually took. The courts will be required to deal with the privacy issue if prisoners attempt to use the Civil Rights Act[73] to challenge the presence of opposite sex guards, or if correctional departments claim that prisoners' privacy justifies a bfoq even when prison conditions do not justify a bfoq on *Rawlinson* grounds.

A. Privacy, Nudity, and Bodily Integrity

1. *Constitutional Rights*

The constitutional right of privacy propounded by the Supreme Court in *Griswold v. Connecticut*,[74] and relied upon by the Court in such cases as *Eisenstadt v. Baird*[75] and *Roe v. Wade*[76] continues to defy definitive explication. The very concept of privacy has so many meanings and connotations that one searching for either a philosophical or a legal point of departure is inevitably left disappointed and frustrated.[77] Any attempt to develop a unified theory of privacy, constitutional or otherwise, is clearly beyond the scope of this article. We can be certain, however, that no Supreme Court decision hints that an individual has a constitutional right not to be placed in a position where he or she risks observation or physical contact by persons of the opposite sex while undressed. For example, it seems highly unlikely, that a female public school student could succeed in a § 1983 action against a male gym teacher who improperly touched or spied on her, despite whatever tort remedies she might pursue in state court.

Of course, no one can safely predict that the Supreme Court will never articulate a right of privacy broad enough to include a right to same-sex gym teachers, police officers (at least those who conduct searches), locker room attendants, and prison guards. But despite the myriad privacy claims it has encountered, the Court has resisted the temptation to expand the Constitutional right of privacy beyond the area of contraception and child bearing.[78] Thus, it is difficult to see how a prisoner could successfully prosecute a § 1983 suit against a department that utilized a sexually integrated guard force.[79] It is quite another matter whether a department of corrections itself could refuse to hire women for guard positions in all men's facilities on the grounds that to do so would interfere with prisoners' legitimate interests (albeit not constitutional rights) in privacy.

2. Everyday Notions of Privacy

Despite the lack of any recognized constitutional right to have one's modesty respected by the state, one cannot ignore a strong societal consensus that supports certain obvious privacy norms. Separate toilet facilities and locker rooms are so standard a part of American society as to be taken for granted. The propriety of hiring same-sex persons to work in public restrooms and teach high school gym classes seems obvious.

In most public institutions respect for personal dignity and modesty is a matter of common decency and politeness, and the question of constitutional rights rarely arises. Only in public hospitals is it routine for orderlies, nurses, and doctors to have close contact with partially clad members of the opposite sex, and even in this setting every effort is made to avoid embarrassment. A prison, of course, is hardly a hospital. While the professionalism of the medical setting negates any sexual connotations to intimate physical contacts, the prison is a highly sexually charged setting, particularly because of the inmates' enforced heterosexual celibacy.

3. Privacy in the Prison

Assuming that these everyday norms of privacy, short of constitutional right, recognize the propriety of separating men and women in facilities where nudity or intimate contacts are likely to occur, these norms are not necessarily applicable in the unique world of the prison.[80] The prison is probably society's least private institution. Prisoners are never out of the sight and presence of guards and other inmates.[81] Close and continuous supervision is more than customary; it is an organizational imperative.[82] Thus one might rightly ask whether privacy is compatible with incarceration.

There is scattered support for an affirmative answer to this question of prisoners' privacy in federal case law.[83] Most interestingly, the Supreme Court's recent decision in *Houchins v. KQED*[84] stated that "[i]nmates in jails, prisons, or mental institutions retain certain fundamental rights of privacy; they are not like animals in a zoo to be filmed and photographed at will by the public or by media reporters, however 'educational' the process may be for others."[85] *Bonner v. Coughlin*,[86] Seventh Circuit opinion authored by Judge (now Justice) John Paul Stevens, also supports the proposition that some elements of privacy do survive imprisonment. In *Bonner*, a prisoner claimed that a retaliatory "shake-down" of his cell and seizure of legal papers violated his fourth amendment rights. Judge Stevens, while holding that a prisoner's fourth amendment rights are not coincident with those of free citizens, stated:

> Unquestionably, entry into a controlled environment entails a dramatic loss of privacy. Moreover, the justifiable reasons for invading an inmate's privacy are both obvious and well established. We are persuaded, however, that the surrender of privacy is not total and

that some residuum meriting the protection of the fourth amendment survives.[87]

A few cases[88] involving strip searches and examination of body cavities hold to the same effect. For instance, the district court in *Hodges v. Klein*,[89] held that the state had no interest in requiring anal examination before or after a segregation inmate is moved within the segregation area or anywhere in the prison while under escort or observation. While the court's constitutional analysis may be questionable its recognition that some privacy norms should prevail in prison seems sound. Although it is not possible to simply dismiss prisoners' privacy claims as nonexistent, these claims, like claims of privacy in other settings, must be closely scrutinized, especially when they seem to conflict with employment opportunities of other parties.

B. Privacy and Title VII's BFOQ Exception

Even if the constitutional right of privacy is not broad enough to encompass the individual's embarrassment at being touched or seen in some immodest state by members of the opposite sex, it is still possible that Title VII does not require or justify hiring persons of both sexes for a job which regularly requires intimate physical or visual contacts between the employee and third parties. On its face, Title VII forbids any employment discrimination on the basis of sex and provides no exemption for jobs in which the privacy interests of third parties might be infringed. Legislative history, consisting of only the most cursory comments by three legislators, barely hints that privacy norms might be considered relevant to the bfoq determination.[90] Equal Employment Opportunity Commission Guidelines, which clarify the bfoq exception, explicitly state:

> (1) The Commission will find that the following situations do not warrant the application of the bona fide occupational qualification exception.
> . . . .
> (iii) The refusal to hire an individual because of the preference of co-workers, the employer, clients, or customers except as covered explicitly in subparagraph (2) of this paragraph.
> (2) Where it is necessary for the purpose of authenticity or genuineness . . . *e.g.* an actor or actress.[91]

Obviously, these guidelines do not justify an employer's refusal to hire persons of both sexes as locker room and restroom attendants, gym teachers, or prison guards. If privacy interests do permit certain jobs to be classified as appropriate for one sex only, it will require an interpretation of Title VII found in neither the statutory language nor the clarifying regulations.

Given our strong societal consensus on the impropriety of mixed sex contacts in certain situations, it is tempting to read Title VII in light of what Congress would have done had lawmakers considered the possibility that this federal law would require male gym teachers to be hired for girls' gym classes or women locker room attendants to be hired for men's locker rooms. Surely, it is inconceivable, particularly in light of the symbolic importance of the "potty issue" for the Equal Rights Amendment debate, that Congress would have imposed such a unisex standard of employment on the entire country.

A few lower courts have considered the privacy interests of third parties as they effect the opportunities of opposite sex employees. Perhaps the best known case is *Ludtke v. Klein*,[92] in which a female news reporter demanded the same access as male reporters to a baseball team's locker room immediately following each ballgame. In this case the New York Yankees were following the Major League Baseball Commissioner's order to ban women from the locker room, despite a players' vote in favor of admitting women reporters. Although the Commission relied in part on the privacy rights of the ballplayers, the district court scarcely considered whether any privacy rights or privacy interests were at stake. Judge Motley spoke of the reporter's fundamental right to pursue her profession and pointed out that there were many alternatives available for protecting the modesty of the athletes. For example, they could avoid a woman reporter's line of vision by hanging a curtain over the cubicle that they used for dressing.

A similar issue arose in *Fesel v. Masonic Hospital*,[93] with regard to the refusal of a Retirement Home to hire a male nurse's aid because of the preference of the female residents. In that case the district court found that an employer was obliged to protect its customers' personal privacy interests, and therefore permitted a retirement home to use female sex as a bfoq in hiring nurses' aids who provided intimate personal "total care." The court held, however, that privacy interests could not be the basis of a bfoq unless the employer can pass a two-part test:

> The employer must prove not only that it had a factual basis for believing that hiring of any members of one sex would directly undermine the essence of the job involved or the employer's business, but also that it could not assign job responsibilities selectively in such a way that there would be minimal clash between privacy interests of the customers and the nondiscrimination principles of Title VII.[94]

Both the *Ludtke* and *Fesel* cases suggest that privacy interests of lower stature than rights are entitled to some consideration in determining Title VII's employment requirements, as well as limiting a third party's right to pursue a calling.

C. Reconciling Privacy and Equal Employment Opportunity in Prisons

Prior to *Rawlinson*, state courts rejected sex discrimination suits by women seeking employment in correctional facilities — with little attempt to explore possible ways of reconciling privacy with equal employment opportunity. The district court in *Rawlinson*[95] recognized that under some circumstances opposite sex guards might infringe upon inmates' privacy, but stated that a reasonable compromise could be found.[96] The district court referred to selective job assignments and shoulder high partitions in toilet areas as possible solutions. These suggestions seem eminently sensible.

Several departments of correction that have pressed forward to hire women guards have made substantial progress in defining workable rules to govern job responsibilities for guards of the opposite sex. California, for example, has promulgated the following guideline:

> Correctional personnel, other than qualified medical staff, will not conduct unclothed body inspections or searches of inmates of the opposite sex. This does not preclude routine inspections or searches of clothed inmates without regard for the sex of the inmate or of personnel making such inspections or searches.[97]

Likewise, in 1976, the New York Commissioner of Correctional Services issued *Guidelines for Assignments of Male and Female Correctional Officers:*

> 1. Security staff members of the opposite sex to the inmate population are not to be permanently assigned to shower areas where one has to work in open view of showering inmates.
> 2. Escort duty outside a facility should be performed only by officers of the same sex as the inmates to be escorted.
> 3. At least one officer of the same sex as the inmate population at a facility must be assigned to each housing block.
> 4. No assignment is to be made requiring an officer to conduct strip frisks of inmates of the opposite sex.
> 5. Security employees of opposite sex to the inmate population cannot exceed one-third of the total security staff at the facilities designated as maximum or medium security.
> 6. Superintendents, with the approval of the appropriate Deputy Commissioner, can make adjustments in particular assignments based upon specific institutional needs.
> 7. Unless emergency conditions dictate otherwise, correction officers of the opposite sex shall announce their presence in housing areas to avoid unnecessarily invading the privacy of the inmates of the opposite sex.[98]

Both California and New York have used their respective guidelines to go forward with the sexual integration of the guard force. These rules provide precisely the kind of reasonable accommodation between equality of employment opportunity and privacy that is required in the prison setting. The California and New York provisions demonstrate bona fide efforts to find successful solutions.

There is every reason to believe that women can be integrated into corrections, even into front line positions, without unduly infringing upon the privacy and dignity of male prisoners. My own experience and personal interviews suggest that male guards are more opposed to women correctional officers than are male prisoners.[99] Indeed, I suspect that, as in the case of the New York Yankees, a vote would show that male prisoners are generally in favor of women guards.

Not all prison guards must be assigned to cell houses, and even those who are so assigned will often work during periods when there is no excessive nudity. Guards of either sex can, as a matter of politeness, discreetly avoid eye contact with prisoners who are nude or engaged in bodily functions. Structural changes, such as shoulder-high partitions in front of toilets, would promote privacy, whatever the sex of the guards. Whenever possible, body searches should be carried out by same sex guards, although light "pat downs" would not seem to be overly intrusive, even when conducted by the opposite sex. When male guards are not available or when emergencies require, women may be required to carry out body searches and any other duties that are part of a guard's job, just as male or female police officers, at times, must carry out intrusive searches on members of the opposite sex. As Justice Marshall stated in *Rawlinson*, one may hope that the highest professional standards will be adhered to by prison staffs, especially when called upon to carry out tasks that are sensitive.[100] Disciplinary measures and even civil and criminal penalties remain available to punish guards who abuse their authority under whatever circumstances.

III. MALE GUARDS AND WOMEN'S PRISONS

The spectre of women guards in men's prisons leads inevitably to speculation and concern about male guards in women's prisons. If Title VII requires women to be hired for front-line positions in men's prisons, it presumably also requires broadening the role of male guards in women's prisons. This possibility is likely to stimulate emotional reactions from the public. A double standard of sexual propriety is deeply rooted in our society. While claims by men that women are humiliating them sexually or are invading their modesty, might be treated as quaint and even humorous by various segments of society, a claim that male jailers are humiliating and sexually abusing female prisoners will be seen by the public as a serious matter. Efforts to bring women into corrections however, should not be allowed to founder on this issue.

The propriety of male guards serving in women's prisons arose in New York State in 1976 when the Department of Correctional Services announced that it had acceded to the demands of the guard union for the elimination of sex certification for correction officers. Shortly after this announcement, ten female prisoners brought a class action[101] claiming, *inter alia*, that their constitutional privacy rights were being violated because male guards "look into women's rooms and toilets unannounced and often times when the inmates are nude or partially clad. They have, in this manner, without the women inmates' consent, observed women inmates on various occasions seated on the toilet performing excretory and female hygiene functions."[102]

The female prisoners also alleged privacy violations because male guards stationed themselves in shower areas, conducted searches and made sexual advances. Without a hearing on the merits or any analysis of the putative constitutional privacy right involved, and despite new state guidelines aimed at respecting prisoner privacy, Judge Owen granted the plaintiff's motion to enjoin the department from assigning male guards to housing units. He also ordered the department to remove male guards currently assigned.[103]

Judge Owen displayed the same kind of stereotyped thinking about relations between the sexes as did Justice Stewart in *Rawlinson*. He rhetorically asked why a woman inmate "must ask a corrections officer (who would often be a man) to come and close her door every time during every day she wished to use the toilet" or "should have to dry off in a damp shower stall instead of an anteroom made for that purpose" or "has to be awakened or observed during sleep by a male guard, her night clothes in possible disarray" or "must discuss personal female problems with hospital staff when male officers are in the room."[104] This case is yet another example of the courts' failure to adequately analyze the constitutional right of privacy in this sensitive area of evolving sex roles in public institutions.[105] In the absence of a Supreme Court decision greatly expanding the constitutional right of privacy, it seems doubtful that men or women prisoners should have a remedy in federal court to remove opposite sex guards. While women have no constitutional right to same sex guards, whether a department of corrections should respect women's privacy through selective assignments of male and female guards is another question. Throughout history women have been sexually abused by men. Furthermore, some of the worst cases of sexual abuse have been perpetrated by male jailers on women prisoners, as is demonstrated by the recent *Joan Little* case.[106] It is one thing to say that women should have the opportunity to work in dangerous occupations, even if there is a threat of sexual assault; it is another to say that women must be placed *involuntarily* in a situation where they may be sexually abused.

The problem of sexual abuse by male guards in women's prisons should not be lightly dismissed. The desire for consistency and the aspiration for an emerging society in which the sexes can function on an equal footing should not blind us to certain realities based upon long experience. There is little doubt that employing male guards to supervise female prisoners creates a higher risk of sexual abuse of prisoners than does employing women to guard men. Therefore, courts should be less reluctant to permit a bfoq classification for guard positions in women's prisons. Furthermore, much less is at stake for men as a class since men, unlike women, have never been denied equal employment opportunity in corrections and only a small fraction of all guard positions in a state prison system are found in women's facilities.[107] Nevertheless, the goal should be to adapt all prisons so that men and women can be employed on an equal basis while still protecting prisoners from sexual abuse and unnecessary invasion of privacy. Despite the need for caution, we should assume for purposes of policy analysis that male guards can and will function competently as front-line staff in women's prisons.

IV. CONCLUSION

Pressures to achieve equal employment opportunities have begun to bring about changes in American prisons. Some departments of corrections have responded to these demands by eliminating sex stereotypical hiring and assignment policies. In some states, as in New York, the union movement has generated pressure to end separate personnel policies for men and women. The most important factor, however, in the change of correctional policy in this area has been the threat of Title VII suits. Correctional officials, like other bureaucrats, are anxious to stay out of court and on the right side of the law.

Dothard v. Rawlinson may prove to be a significant setback for women wishing to serve in corrections. While the decision prohibits the use of arbitrary height and weight requirements to deny correctional jobs to women, similar requirements may yet survive if officials can show that height and weight standards are correlated with strength. Quite possibly, strength tests will be upheld. Standards requiring recruits to demonstrate competency in self-defense and effective use of physical force will undoubtedly be found to be job related. In addition, Justice Rehnquist's opinion in *Rawlinson* may encourage corrections departments to attempt to justify excluding women on the basis of the appearance of strength, a proposition that may appeal to judges who are reluctant to interfere with penal management.

Assuming that women can hurdle height, weight, and strength requirements, they may still be barred from most prison jobs because of "no contact" rules. It is conceivable, of course, that future decisions may limit the reach of *Rawlinson* to the worst prisons in the nation. But all maximum security prisons are dangerous, and none specially isolate sex offenders. Therefore, the argument that women's vulnerability to sexual assaults will increase the instability of the penal environment will be readily available in all such situations. This raises the real question of whether women will be permitted to continue serving as cottage parents and as front line staff in tough juvenile institutions. The future of women parole officers is also in doubt, since deprived sex offenders might be especially disposed to assault them, thereby jeopardizing the safety of fellow officers.

Rank-and-file male guards have often opposed, sometimes strongly, the introduction of women into the men's prisons. Departments may succumb to pressure, stop hiring women and remove those who are employed. This would be an unfortunate result. The expansion of Title VII's bfoq exception to limit employment opportunities for women, without any evidence to indicate that women cannot serve as effectively as men, threatens the inroads women have made not only in prison systems but also in other heretofore male-dominated social control organizations.

The privacy problems that inevitably arise as greater numbers of women are integrated in the prison's guard force cannot be ignored, either by courts or by departments of corrections. These problems are neither negligible nor insurmountable. Unfortunately, courts have hardly begun to engage in serious analysis of the tension between equality of employment opportunity and personal privacy. The record of some corrections departments is better, since they have attempted to anticipate privacy problems and draft regulations accordingly.

In my view, legal analysis has been inhibited because of the over emphasis upon constitutional rights. Needless to say, not every wrong finds a federal constitutional redress. To constitutionalize all of our privacy norms would go a long way toward merging constitutional law with the private law of torts. This would unduly burden the federal courts, and not necessarily achieve beneficial results. In any case, it is most unlikely that the Supreme Court will expand the constitutional law of privacy to provide a right of action for prisoners who complain of intimate visual and physical contact by guards of the opposite sex.

But simply because prisoners' concerns about privacy do not rise to the level of a constitutional right, does not mean that they should not count at all. Privacy is a value, and an important one, in American society and it should be accommodated both by law and public policy. Permitting a public or private employer to rely upon the bona fides privacy concerns of third parties as a justification for classifying some positions as bfoq's is a sensible approach. Of course, this is not to say that it should be used to discriminate. Before any job is classified as a bfoq on privacy grounds, every effort must be made to find practical, workable accommodations.

This is especially vital in prisons, where the potential contribution of women is so great.

Acknowledgement

I want to express my grateful appreciation to Kevin Clermont, Ron Goldstock, Michael Gold, Charles Morris, and Robert Sedler for helpful suggestions, and to Susan Forney and Edith Richardson for valuable research assistance.

Notes

1. 42 U.S.C. § 2000e-2 (1976).
2. This has been the case in New York, where union demands to merge seniority lists finally led the Department of Correctional Services to abolish sex qualifications for hiring. See text accompanying notes 96-100 *infra*. See also J. Jacobs & N. Crotty, *Guard Unions and the Future of the Prisons* (1978).
3. *See* text accompanying notes 65-68 *infra*.
4. *See* Brief of Appellants at 43-45, 49-53, *Dothard v. Rawlinson*, 433 U.S. 321 (1977).
5. *Dothard v. Rawlinson*, 433 U.S. 321 (1977); *Human Rights Comm'n v. Correctional Serv.*, 61 App. Div. 2d 25 (N.Y. 1978).
6. *Dothard v. Rawlinson*, 433 U.S. 321 (1977) (female applicant for position as correctional officer sued because state regulations prohibited her assignment at a men's maximum security prison); *Long v. California State Personnel Board*, 41 Cal. App. 3d 1000, 116 Cal. Rptr. 562 (1974) (female sued because she was denied a position as chaplain in a center for male youth offenders). *See also City of Philadelphia v. Pennsylvania Human Relations Comm'n.* 7 Pa. Commw. Ct. 500, 300 A. 2d 97 (1973). The Pennsylvania court dealt with a similar issue after the Commission refused to approve sex as a BFOQ for supervisors of Philadelphia's Youth Center. The city wished to limit female supervision to female wards but not male supervision to male wards.
7. *Forts v. Ward*, 434 F. Supp. 946 (S.D.N.Y.), *rev'd*, 566 F. 2d 849 (2d Cir. 1977) (male guards assigned to women's living units in a state prison); *Reynolds v. Wise*, 375 F. Supp. 145 (N.D. Tex. 1974) (female guard assigned to male prisoners in a federal penitentiary); *Hand v. Briggs*, 360 F. Supp. 484 (N.D. Cal. 1973 (female guards supervising bathroom areas in men's federal penitentiary); *In re Long*, 55 Cal. App. 3d 788 (opinion omitted), 127 Cal. Rptr. 732 (1976) (male wards of a state youth facility complained about presence of female employees in dormitories).
8. There are no published studies on the performance of women guards. I draw this conclusion from informal interviews with prison officials in New York, Illinois, Minnesota, California and the Federal Bureau of Prisons.
9. Those who "instinctively" feel that women cannot function in the front lines of law enforcement should recall the fate of a similar stereotype about

the capacity of blacks to serve in military combat. The myth that black soldiers could not fight was not dispelled until the Korean War. *See* Moskos, "The American Dilemma in Uniform: Race in the Armed Forces," 406 *Annals* 94 (1973).

10. I know of no sound research that documents crime rates in prisons. In a previous publication I pointed out that the number of very serious crimes at Stateville Penitentiary, Illinois' largest maximum security prison, was quite small. This was despite much rhetoric from guards and inmates to the contrary. Jacobs, "Prison Violence and Formal Organization" in *Prison Violence* (A. Cohen et al., eds. 1976). None of the other articles in the volume in which my article appeared shows that prisons are any more dangerous than core areas in our big cities. I believe that the data would show most prisons to be less dangerous. No one has yet proposed banning women from dangerous inner city areas. It seems strange to assume that many women who have grown up in high crime rate areas have not developed the savvy and street sense to deal effectively with male prisoners.

11. 42 U.S.C. § 2000e-2 (1976).
12. 433 U.S. 321 (1977).
13. *Ala. Code Tit.* 55, § 373 (109) (1973 Supp.) requires, *inter alia*, that prison guard applicants weigh at least 120 pounds.
14. In the suit below, another plaintiff, Brenda Mieth, challenged the 5'9" and 160 pound qualification for a position as state trooper, as a violation of the equal protection clause. The claim was brought under 42 U.S.C. § 1983 (1976). The court invalidated the standards because they were not rationally related to a valid state interest. The state did not appeal. *Mieth v. Dothard*, 418 F. Supp. 1169 (N.D. Ala. 1976).
15. Administrative Regulation 204 provides that positions with the Alabama Board of Corrections will be open to members of both sexes, except where a process of "selective certification" designates a position as only appropriate for members of one sex. The grounds for obtaining a selective certification are the following:

    A. That the presence of the opposite sex would cause disruption of the orderly running and security of the institution.
    B. That the position would require contact with the inmates of the opposite sex without the presence of others.
    C. That the position would require patrolling dormitories, restrooms, or showers while in use, frequently, during the day or night.
    D. That the position would require search of inmates of the opposite sex on a regular basis.
    E. That the position would require that the Correctional Counselor Trainee not be armed with a firearm.

Id. at 1175-76.
16. *Id.* at 1180.
17. *Id.* at 1184.
18. *Id.* at 1185.
19. *Dothard v. Rawlinson*, 433 U.S. 321 (1977).
20. § 703(e) of Title VII, 42 U.S.C. § 2000e-2(e) (1976).
21. 433 U.S. at 337.

22. *Id.* at 340-41.

23. *Id.* at 348. In Justice White's view, proof that height and weight requirements automatically disqualified the majority of American women from consideration for corrections jobs does not constitute prima facie sex discrimination. Instead, he would require proof of the requirements' impact on the applicant pool. *Id.* at 347-48. This position does not seem compatible with the Court's opinion in *Griggs v. Duke Power Co.*, 401 U.S. 424 (1971), which was cited by the majority for the proposition that a statistical analysis to show the disproportionate impact of a standard need not be based on the actual applicant pool. *See Dothard v. Rawlinson*, 433 U.S. at 330.

Lower courts have also followed Griggs in sex discrimination suits. *See Peltier v. City of Fargo*, 396 F. Supp. 710 (D.N.D. 1975); and, *Meadows v. Ford Motor Co.*, 62 F.R.D. 98 (W.D.Ky. 1973).

24. In *Pugh v. Locke*, 406 F. Supp. 318 (M.D. Ala. 1976), *aff'd sub nom. Newman v. Alabama*, 559 F. 2d 283 (5th Cir. 1977), prisoners brought a consolidated class action suit against state officials and the Board of Corrections to seek relief of conditions allegedly depriving them of their eighth and fourteenth amendment rights. The district court found that "the rampant violence and jungle atmosphere existing throughout Alabama's penal institutions . . . ," 406 F. Supp. at 325, justified the prisoner's claims. Specifically the court determined that:

> inmates are housed in virtually unguarded, overcrowded dormitories, with no realistic attempt by officials to separate violent, aggressive inmates from those who are passive or weak. The tension generated by idleness and deplorable living conditions contributes further to the everpresent threat of violence from which inmates have no refuge.

Id. at 329-30.

25. *See Human Rights Comm'n v. Correctional Serv.*, 61 App. Div 2d 25 (N.Y. 1978) (New York appellate court reversing holding that sexual identity is a bona fide occupational qualification for the position of cook in a minimum security prison for males).

26. For an overview of litigation on the military, see Beans, "Sex Discrimination in the Military," 67 *Mil. L. Rev.* 19 (1975); for sex discrimination suits against police, see *Smith v. Troyan*, 520 F. 2d 492 (6th Cir.), *cert. denied*, 426 U.S. 934 (1975); *Officers for Justice v. Civil Serv. Comm'n of San Francisco*, 395 F. Supp. 378 (N.D. Cal. 1975); *Peltier v. City of Fargo*, 396 F. Supp. 710 (D.N.D. 1975); *Hardy v. Stumpf*, 37 Cal. App. 3d 958, 112 Cal. Rptr. 739 (1974).

27. 433 U.S. at 331.

28. *Id.* at 339.

29. *Id.*

30. In *Officers for Justice v. Civil Serv. Comm'n of San Francisco*, 395 F. Supp. 378 (N.D. Cal. 1975), the San Francisco Police Department attempted to justify its 5'6" height requirement for Q-2 patrol positions on the basis of a relationship between a police officer's height and the frequency of assaults against him. Despite a weak positive correlation, the court refused to permit

the Department to maintain the test. On the other hand, in *Smith v. Troyan,* 520 F. 2d 492 (6th Cir. 1975), the Sixth Circuit accepted the 5'8" height requirement for East Cleveland police officers on the ground that (1) taller officers have a psychological advantage and (2) there is an advantage of height in effecting arrests and emergency aid. The court rejected the 150 pound weight requirement as having no correlation to physical strength or to psychological advantage.

In response to the many questions raised by these suits, a study was undertaken to consider whether height is related to police performance. T. White and P. Bloch, *Police Officer Height and Selected Aspects of Performance* (1975). Police departments from Dallas, Oakland, Nassau County, New York, and Dade County, Florida submitted data. Since the participating departments used different formats for recording personnel information the authors could not make performance comparisons among the various groups. Nonetheless, within several of the groups studied, seniority and duty assignment significantly affected officer performance, while height did not. *Id.* at 10, 13. Furthermore, in two departments (Nassau County and Dallas) where the experience variable was controlled, height differences had negligible effect on performance. *Id.* at 6. Unfortunately, the study is almost exclusively confined to data on officers 5'7" and taller. *Id.* It is possible that under that threshold, performance would be affected.

31. Justice Rehnquist provides no support for the argument. He merely flags the issue for future litigation:

> [T]he primary job of [a] correctional counselor in Alabama prisons "is to maintain security and control of the inmates . . . ," a function that I at least would imagine is aided by the psychological impact on prisoners of the presence of tall and heavy guards.

433 U.S. at 339-40. The validity of this hypothesis is not supported by evidence in the *Rawlinson* case nor by research data. Social psychological data suggest that the impact of size on the successful exercise of authority is probably not great. Research on the relationship between height and status or authority, tends to show the reverse of the relationship suggested by advocates of height standards. Several recent studies show that perception of height is affected by the status attributed to the one perceived. The results were the same when status was conferred either by social standing, academic achievement or employment position. *See* Kaulack & Luthill, "Height Perception: Function of Social Distance," 4 *Canadian J. of Behavioral Sci.* 50-53 (1972); Wilson, "Perceptual Distortion of Height as a Function of Ascribed Status," 74 *J. of Soc. Psych.*, 97-102 (1968); Dannenmaier and Thumin, "Authority Status as a Factor in Perceptual Distortion of Size," 63 *J. of Soc. Psych.* 361-65 (1964).

A few articles in popular magazines indicate that American employers are biased in favor of hiring tall applicants. The trend may reflect social conditioning that encourages respect for tall people, but because no serious research on this trend has been complete this conclusion is purely speculative. *See U.S. News and World Report,* March 28, 1977, at 68-69; *Time,* Oct. 4, 1971, at 64; *Psychology Today,* Aug. 1971, at 102.

32. See, e.g., *Castro v. Beecher*, 334 F. Supp. 930 (D. Mass. 1971), aff'd in part, rev'd in part, 459 F. 2d 725 (1st Cir. 1972); on remand 365 F. Supp. 655 (D. Mass. 1973).

33. McNamara, "Analysts of Assaulted and Non-Assaulted Officers by Height, Weight, Tenure and Assignment" (February, 1973).

34. Swanson & Hale, "A Question of Height Revisited: Assaults on Police," 3 *J. Police Sci. & Ad.* 183-188 (1975).

35. P. Bloch & D. Anderson, *Police Women on Patrol: Final Report* (1974). Taller officers were given lower overall performance ratings by the department and lower ratings on the Chief's Survey on their general ability to patrol. They were less likely than shorter officers to have received favorable comments from the public, and they were observed to evoke comparatively poor reactions from victims. The only favorable relationship found between height and performance was that tall men were observed to receive more favorable reactions when they handled arguments inside residences. *Id.* at 60.

36. Hoobler and McQuenny, "A Question of Height," *The Police Chief*, 42-48 (Nov. 1973).

37. A telling criticism of all these studies is that they can only provide data on the likelihood of assault for officers currently on the force, all of whom are at least five-foot-six. It is arguable that even if no significant correlation is found, the results would be different for officers below the five-foot-six threshold.

38. Bloch and Anderson studied the performance of 95 patrolwomen for one year from 1972-73. The majority of the women were completely new to the force while a few were reassigned from other duties in the department. A group of patrolmen with comparable experience on the job, provided additional data for comparison, P. Bloch, D. Anderson & P. Gervais, *Police Women on Patrol* (Major Findings: First Report, Vol. I) 2-4 (1973).

The data were collected in several ways. Some performance statistics (i.e., arrests, injuries, driving incidents, etc.) came from records regularly kept by the department. Information about police interactions while on patrol was solicited via a survey of citizens who came into contact with the patrolmen. The two groups were also compared according to the individual evaluations given by their superior officers and other officials within the department. Finally, twenty-three trained observers went on patrol with the officers to record information about their performance, as well as to gauge the attitudes of citizens toward them. P. Bloch & D. Anderson, *supra* note 35, at 8.

39. *Id.* at 18.

40. J. Greenwald, H. Connolly & P. Bloch, *New York City Policewomen on Patrol* (1974).

41. Most of the existing scholarship on prison guards is discussed in D. Fogel, *We are the Living Proof: The Justice Model for Corrections*, ch. 2 (1975); G. Hawkins, *The Prison: Policy and Practice*, ch. 4 (1976). My own research on the subject includes J. Jacobs, *Stateville: The Penitentiary in Mass Society*, ch. 7 (1977); J. Jacobs & N. Crotty, *Guard Unions and the Future of the Prisons* (1978); Jacobs and Grear, "Dropouts and Rejects: An Analysis of the Prison Guard's Revolving Door," 2 *Crim. Just. Rev.* 57-70 (1977);

Jacobs & Kraft, "Integrating the Keepers: A Comparison of Black and White Prison Guards in Illinois," 25 *Soc. Prob.* 304-18 (1978); Jacobs & Retsky, "Prison Guard," 4 *Urb. Life* 5-29 (1975); Jacobs, "What Prison Guards Think: A Profile of the Illinois Force, 24 *Crime and Delinquency* 185-96 (1978).

42. See D. Glaser, *The Effectiveness of a Prison and Parole System* (1964); Jacobs & Retsky, *supra* note 41; Sykes, "The Corruption of Authority and Rehabilitation," 34 *Soc. Forces* 257-62 (1956).

Guards must live with the knowledge that they could be attacked or taken hostage at almost any time. While the prisoners often arm themselves with "shivs" (knives), pipes or other makeshift weapons, the guards (except for those in the towers) do not carry weapons. A guard working in the cellhouse, on the yard, in the shops or in the dining room can be outnumbered by as many as 100 to 1. Under such circumstances, an officer does not maintain his authority through combat skill but through effective leadership.

43. The Alabama Board of Corrections provides the following job description:

Patrols prisons and prison yards; stands watch in halls, at gates, or in wall towers; makes regular reports to supervisors. Supervises and keeps order among prisoners assigned to work in prison kitchens, shops, mills, laundries, or on farms. Enforces regulations covering sanitation and personal care. Inspects all traffic into and out of prison proper. Maintains constant watch for and reports unusual conditions or disturbances; keeps firearms in readiness for use if necessary; takes required action in emergencies to prevent escapes or suppress disorder; assists in recapture of escaped prisoners. Explains to inmates rules, procedures and services available at correctional institutions; counsels individual inmates regarding personal problems, educational and vocational opportunities and work assignments. Evaluates inmate behavior and adjustment to a correctional environment; submits evaluation reports. Instructs inmates in personal hygiene, discipline and proper etiquette. Performs related work as required.

44. 418 F. Supp. at 1175.

45. My former co-author Harold Retsky (*see* Jacobs & Retsky, *supra* note 41), a man of slight stature became a prison guard at age 57. He achieved remarkable success in his three years on the job, relating to prisoners with wit, intelligence and compassion. He was highly respected. He would surely not have been able to rely on force and coercion.

46. A woman staff member at George Junior Republic, a juvenile institution for teenage offenders near Ithaca, New York, reports that she has never been assaulted in her four years at the institution. She claims that this is generally true of the other women counselors and that women have on several occasions interposed themselves between male youths and staff to prevent fisticuffs. At George Junior Republic the cottage living units are supervised by married couples. In at least one case a woman employee ran a cottage by herself for over a year. The feeling at the institution is that the women cottage parents have had no more problems, and perhaps less, in controlling their charges. Interview with Sue Smithson (Dec. 1977).

Ray Nelson reports that during his tenure as warden of the Federal Bureau of Prison's Metropolitan Correctional Center in Chicago, a female officer was called upon to break up a fight between two inmates. Despite her diminutive size (96 pounds), she stepped right in and performed her duty without any problem. Apparently her training in self-defense was a more important factor than her size. Interview with Ray Nelson, Warden, Federal Correction Institution, Danbury, Connecticut.

47. The median age of guards in Illinois is forty-five, while fifteen percent are beyond the age of sixty. By contrast, the median age of the prisoner population is typically about twenty-five or younger. While advanced age alone does not prove an individual physically unfit, it strongly suggests that a substantial segment of the prison work force operates at a severe physical disadvantage. During several years as a participant-observer, I noted with surprise the substantial number of prison guards who are overweight or otherwise out of shape.

48. The bfoq exception is provided in Title VII of the Civil Rights Act of 1964, § 703(e), 42 U.S.C. § 2000e-2(e) (1976) as follows:

> Notwithstanding any other provisions of this subchapter [42 USC §§ 2000e-1 to 2000e-17], (1) it shall not be unlawful employment practice for an employer to hire and employ employees, for an employment agency to classify, or refer for employment any individual, for a labor organization to classify its membership or to classify or refer for employment any individual, or for an employer, labor organization, or joint labor-management committee controlling apprenticeship or other training or retraining programs to admit or employ any individual in any such program, on the basis of his religion, sex, or national origin in those certain instances where religion, sex or national origin *is a bona fide occupational qualification reasonably necessary to the normal operation of that particular business or enterprise*. . . . (emphasis added).

49. 408 F. 2d 228 (5th Cir. 1969).

50. In part, the Court said:

> Moreover, Title VII rejects just this type of romantic paternalism as unduly Victorian and instead vests individual women with the power to decide whether or not to take on unromantic tasks. Men have always had the right to determine whether the incremental increase in remuneration for strenuous, dangerous, obnoxious, boring or unromantic tasks is worth the candle. The promise of Title VII is that women are now to be on equal footing. We cannot conclude that by including the bona fide occupational qualification exception Congress intended to renege on that promise.

Id. at 236.

51. *Id.* at 235.
52. 442 F.2d 385 (5th Cir.), *cert. denied*, 404 U.S. 950 (1971).
53. 444 F.2d 1219 (9th Cir. 1971).
54. *Id.* at 1225.
55. *Mieth v. Dothard*, 418 F. Supp. 1169, 1180 (M.D. Ala. 1976).
56. *Dothard v. Rawlinson*, 433 U.S. 321, 336 (1977).
57. There are no empirical studies on this subject to date. Personal inquiry indicates that no major problems have appeared in the states that have moved

to expand job opportunities for women in corrections. Illinois officials report that there have been no attacks on female officers by male prisoners since they have been introduced into male facilities. As of November, 1977, 39 women officers and 28 trainees are serving in medium or maximum male facilities. Despite a knife attack on one woman officer at Attica, New York's corrections officials feel that the sexual integration of the guards has been a success. Approximately 157 women are serving in male facilities throughout the state. (Subsequent to the attack at Attica a prisoner committee presented a formal apology.)

The California Attorney General filed an amicus brief which informed the Court that "The integration of women into the staffs of previously all male facilities has been going on for more than ten years." Motion of State of California for Leave to File Brief as Amicus Curiae and Amicus Curiae Brief at 3, *Dothard v. Rawlinson*, 433 U.S. 321 (1977) [hereinafter cited as *Amicus Brief*].

In a personal interview conducted with Warden Nelson, he reported that during the first two years of operation there were no sexual assaults to his knowledge on female staff at the MCC, despite the fact that they made up approximately one-fourth of the force and were assigned duties without regard to sex. While the MCC is a federal jail, not a state prison, it handles a wide range of state and federal prisoners, the former residing at the jail when they are in town on writs.

The situation in Illinois' state prisons is similar. According to the chief of program services, "The reaction of the line staff is mixed with some being totally supportive, some being amused, and some being outright hostile (sic)." Letter from Phillip G. Shayne, Chief of Program Services, State of Illinois Department of Corrections to James B. Jacobs (Nov. 10, 1977).

Commenting on his experience with female guards in Illinois' Joliet Correctional Center (an all-male maximum security prison), Warden Dennis J. Wolff said, "The presence of women is long overdue. We're glad to see women in our facility. It adds a new dimension to corrections. It's a little too soon to say, but I tend to think that women are more respected than male guards." Gleinman, "As Guards Women help Bring down Prison Walls," *Chi. Tribune*, Feb. 5, 1978.

58. Guidelines published by the EEOC specifically state that such wholesale exclusion undermines the basic thrust of Title VII: "The principle of nondiscrimination requires that individuals be considered on the basis of individual capacities and not on the basis of any characteristics generally attributed to the group." EEOC Guidelines on Sex Discrimination, 29 C.F.R. § 1604.2(a)(ii) (1976).

59. *Dothard v. Rawlinson*, 433 U.S. 321, 336 (1977).

60. Male guards also can be sexually assaulted by prisoners. This occurred when male hostages were seized at Illinois' Stateville Penitentiary. *See* J. Jacobs, *Stateville: The Penitentiary in Mass Society* 166 (1977).

61. The opinion indicates that Alabama had no method of classifying its prisoners. Nonetheless, the Court noticed that approximately 20 percent were sex offenders at the time the suit arose. 433 U.S. at 335.

62. *Id.*
63. *Id.*
64. *Id.* at 336.
65. Justice Marshall's dissent observed that running a state penal system in violation of the eighth amendment should not justify employment discrimination against women.

> The statute requires that a bfoq be "reasonably necessary to the normal operation of that particular business or enterprise." But no governmental "business" may operate "normally" in violation of the Constitution. . . . A prison system operating in blatant violation of the Eighth Amendment is an exception that should be remedied with all possible speed, as Judge Johnson's comprehensive order in *Pugh v. Locke,* . . ., is designed to do. In the meantime, the existence of such violations should not be legitimated by calling them "normal." Nor should the court accept them as justifying conduct that would otherwise violate a statute intended to remedy age-old discrimination.

433 U.S. at 342. Judge Marshall also warned that the notion that women are "seductive sex objects" is a traditional basis for treating them as second class citizens:

> with all respect, this rationale regrettably perpetuates one of the most insidious of the old myths about women — that women, wittingly or not, are seductive sexual objects. The effect of the decision, made I am sure with the best of intentions, is to punish women because their very presence might provoke sexual assaults. It is women who are to pay the price in lost job opportunities for the threat of depraved conduct by prison inmates. Once again, "[t]he pedestal upon which women have been placed has . . ., upon closer inspection been revealed as a cage." (citing *Sail'er Inn, Inc. v. Kirby,* 5 Cal. 3d 1, 20, 485 P.2d 529, 541 (1971).)

433 U.S. at 345.
66. *See* Ruback, "The Sexually Integrated Prison: A Legal and Policy Evaluation," 3 *Am. J. Crim. L.* 301 (1974-75).

According to Ruback, federal prisoners housed in sexually integrated facilities find that the presence of women brings "humanizing influence to the prison and reduces violence among male prisoners." He suggests that additional female staff members may help to reduce homosexuality in all male institutions. *Id.* at 315. Ruback does not go on to explore additional effects that female guards might have on all-male prisons, although he speculates that separating the sexes at the same prison would heighten sexual frustration. *Id.* at 327. Arguably, assignment of female guards to male living units would create a similar problem.
67. 433 U.S. at 346.
68. Compare the normalization theory articulated in the *Amicus Brief* of the State of California, at 3:

> The Department of Corrections and the Youth Authority have adopted as one of their primary responsibilities a policy of "normalization" within their respective institutions. Officials of these depart-

ments believe that rehabilitation will be enhanced by providing an environment which includes trained and competent professional staff of both sexes because that environment more closely approximates society than does a unisexual institution.

69. A characteristically shrewd and colorful observation by my late friend and teacher Hans Mattick pointed out that a prisoner could no more be trained within a prison for future life on the streets than could an aviator be readied for flying by service in a submarine.

70. N. Morris & G. Hawkins, *The Honest Politician's Guide to Crime Control* (1969). Morris and Hawkins anticipated four possible disadvantages to hiring women: loss of discipline, a barrage of obscenity, sexual assault and successful courtship. They either discounted the seriousness of each of these problems or felt that better staff training more than compensates for initial dislocations. *Id.* at 133.

Actual experience with women guards in men's prisons indicates that discipline has not deteriorated; obscenity more often comes from disgruntled male colleagues than from the inmates; and sexual assaults are not prevalent. While there have been a few reports of romance between male prisoners and female guards, this should not be viewed as a compelling reason for refusing to hire women guards. Homosexual liasons between staff and prisoners in male and female prisons have long plagued correctional managers. The possibility of heterosexual relations poses no greater threat. Staff training and good administration can address both problems.

71. *Id.* at 133. The proposition that women will invariably bring a softening influence to the prison is contradicted by the figure of the female concentration camp commandant in Lina Wertmuller's film, *Seven Beauties.*

72. *E.g., Jones v. North Carolina Prisoners' Labor Union, Inc.,* 433 U.S. 119 (1977); *Meacham v. Fano,* 427 U.S. 215 (1974).

73. 42 U.S.C. § 1983 (1976).

74. 381 U.S. 479 (1965).

75. 405 U.S. 438 (1972).

76. 410 U.S. 113 (1973).

77. For a review of the topic and an effort to clarify privacy, see *L. Tribe, American Constitutional Law* 886-990 (1978).

78. *See, e.g., Whalen v. Roe,* 429 U.S. 589 (1977); *Doe v. Commonwealth's Atty. for Richmond,* 425 U.S. 901 (1976), *aff'g,* 403 F. Supp. 1199 (E.D. Va. 1975); *Paul v. Davis,* 424 U.S. 693 (1976); *Village of Belle Terre v. Boraas,* 416 U.S. 1 (1974).

79. *See Hand v. Briggs,* 360 F. Supp. 484 (N.D. Cal. 1973), where a prisoner at San Quentin brought a civil rights action against two female guards, alleging that they were in a position to watch him bathe and to carry out several biological functions normally performed in private. He also claimed their presence constituted cruel and unusual punishment because one of the women resembled his wife with whom he had normal marital relations before he went to prison. The court dismissed the complaint because the prisoner did not allege that the defendants actually invaded his privacy. The court also dismissed the allegations based on cruel and unusual punishment as frivolous.

But see In re Long, 55 Cal. App. 3d 788 (opinion omitted), 127 Cal. Rptr. 732 (1976). A California appellate court ordered a youth correctional facility to remove female staff members from the dormitories and gymnasium on the grounds that inmates' privacy rights were violated.

The court relied on a state constitutional right of privacy, but gave no indication of how the state right was to be distinguished from privacy norms in general.

80. *See* Singer, "Privacy, Autonomy and Dignity in the Prison: A Preliminary Inquiry Concerning Constitutional Aspects of the Degradation Process in Our Prisons," 21 *Buffalo L. Rev.* 669 (1972).

81. *See* Schwartz, "Deprivation of Privacy as a 'Functional Prerequisite': The Case of the Prison," 63 *J. Crim. L. C. & P.S.* 229, 238 (1972).

82. *See generally* E. Goffman, *Asylums* (1961).

83. *See also* the recent prison law reform effort of the American Bar Association, Joint Committee on the Legal Status of Prisoners. "Tentative Draft of Standards Relating to the Legal Status of Prisoners," 14 *Am. Crim. L. Rev.* 377 (1977). Standard 6.6 recognizes prisoners' privacy rights and places limits on searches of inmates' cells and persons. *Id.* at 526.

84. 98 S.Ct. 2588 (1978).

85. *Id.* at 2592 n.2.

86. 517 F.2d 1311 (7th Cir. 1975).

87. *Id.* at 1316.

88. *Daughtery v. Harris,* 476 F.2d 292 (10th Cir.), *cert denied,* 414 U.S. 872 (1973); *Penn El v. Riddle,* 399 F. Supp. 1059 (E.D. Va. 1975).

89. 412 F. Supp. 896 (D.N.J. 1976).

90. *See* 110 CONG. REC. 2718 (1964) (remarks of Rep. Goodell); *Id.* at 7212-13 (interpretative memo introduced by Sens. Clark and Case).

91. 29 C.F.R. § 1604.2(a) (1976).

92. 461 F. Supp. 86, (S.D.N.Y. 1978).

93. 447 F. Supp. 1346 (D. Del. 1978).

94. *Id.* at 1351.

95. *Mieth v. Dothard,* 418 F. Supp. 1169 (M.D. Ala. 1976), *rev'd sub nom. Dothard v. Rawlinson,* 433 U.S. 321 (1977).

96. A few state courts, faced with similar problems, reached different results. In *City of Philadelphia v. Pennsylvania Human Relations Comm'n,* 7 Pa. Commonw. Ct. 500, 300 A.2d 97 (1973) the court held that female sex could be a bfoq for supervisor positions in youth centers because the job required supervision of children (ages 7-16) when they are unclothed and because such problem children related better to members of the same sex. The second proposition lacks both a theoretical and an empirical basis. Juvenile institutions were originally staffed by women in order to shield residents from the brutality usually associated with adult facilities. Women have for decades served effectively in institutions for male juveniles. In *Long v. California State Personnel Bd.,* 41 Cal. App. 2d 1000, 116 Cal. Rptr. 562 (1974), a California court rejected a clergy woman's claim that refusing to consider her application for a chaplain's position in a juvenile institution for males violated Title VII. The court justified its position on the ground that if she were raped, it could

have a devastating effect on the youth (ages 18-23) center's rehabilitation program!

97. Article 1 of the California Department of Corrections Administrative Manual entitled "Body Cavity Searches, Inmates." Article 1 — General Policy, Section 4851. California has already implemented these guidelines. Interview with Philip A. Guthrie, Assistant Director for Public Information, California Department of Corrections (Oct. 1977).

98. *New York State Department of Correctional Services Directive, Classification # 2230* (1976). *See also Federal Prison System Policy Statement, No. 200001.4* (May 9, 1977).

99. A female guard at Clinton Correctional Facility in upstate New York reports that some of her fellow officers are less cooperative than the inmates. They also persist in making off-court comments and obscene gestures while female officers are in the duty room waiting for assignments. Interview with female guards at Clinton Correctional Facility, Dannamora, New York (Oct. 3, 1977). Illinois officials also report that male correctional officers cause women employees far more problems than the prisoners.

100. 433 U.S. at 346 n.5 (Marshall, J., dissenting).

101. *Forts v. Ward*, 434 F. Supp. 946 (S.D.N.Y. 1977).

102. Plaintiff's Complaint at 8, *Forts v. Ward*, 434 F. Supp. 946 (S.D.N.Y. 1977). The complaint also alleged that the religious rights of Black Muslim women were denied inasmuch as their religion forbids them from exposing their bodies to any other men except their husbands, fathers and certain other relatives by blood and marriage. *Id.* at 10.

103. Order with Notice of Settlement, *Forts v. Ward*, 434 F. Supp. 946 (S.D.N.Y. 1977) (order dated June 22, 1977). *See Forts v. Ward*, 77 Civ. 1560 (S.D.N.Y. 1977).

104. Memorandum and Order, *Forts v. Ward*, 434 F. Supp. 946 (S.D.N.Y. 1977). *See Forts v. Ward*, 77 Civ. 1560 (S.D.N.Y. 1977).

105. On appeal, the Second Circuit reversed the preliminary injunction, holding that a factual hearing should have been held before judgment and remanded for that purpose. The case is now pending. *Forts v. Ward*, 566 F.2d 849 (2d Cir. 1977).

106. *See* J. Reston, *The Innocence of Joan Little* (1977).

107. Females comprise less than 5 percent of all state and federal prisoners. Since most states have no more than one women's facility (and some have none) there are very few jobs at stake in women's penal institutions.

Chapter 12
The Upward Mobility of Women in Corrections*

Sandra Nicolai

HISTORY

Although women have been involved in corrections for many years, they have historically been relegated to serving the offender/client only in institutions where the incarcerated are of the same sex. Although there have been exceptions, as in the case of Warden Clara Waters, who ran an adult male institution in Oklahoma in the 1930s, this same sex attitude has prevailed.

In 1969, the Joint Commission on Correctional Manpower and Training recommended that there be a maximum expansion of opportunities for women working in corrections.[1] The Civil Rights Act of 1964 was amended in part in 1972, when Title VII was expanded to prohibit against discrimination in state and local governments; this action was especially significant to corrections in light of the fact that 90% of state correctional systems did not initiate the hiring of women in their adult male institutions (wherein lay the majority of available positions) until after this mandate.[2]

Released in 1973, the National Advisory Commission on Criminal Justice Standards and Goals also spoke to this issue by encouraging recruitment and hiring of more women for *all types of positions in corrections.* The Commission encouraged policy changes, lateral entry of women to administrative positions, development of improved staff selection, removal of "unreasonable" barriers to employment of women in corrections, and encouragement of personnel systems towards taking a positive stance in the employment of women in full correctional roles.[3] In 1975, an LEAA Task Force produced a study of overall LEAA efforts related to women in criminal justice.[4] But, as late as 1977, when the Law Enforcement Assistance Administration published guidelines concerning the use of women in corrections, it only mandated that the level of women employed in corrections must be proportional to the relevant labor market, in this case the number of female offenders which at that time was only 5% of the incarcerated population.[5] Although at that time the number of women employed in corrections significantly exceeded the proportional number of incarcerated women[6], this attitude and the difficulties en-

---

* This article was prepared expressly for this volume.

countered in integrating the use of women correctional officers into male institutions has made progress slow and thus inhibited the job pool and promotions for women working in this field.

Even with the adoption of an affirmative action policy statement in 1976 by the American Correctional Association, the number of women currently employed in all types of positions in correctional institutions was approximately 26,771 in 1979, which is still quite low in consideration of the total offender population of approximately 274,100 during that same time period[7], and the 51% representation of women in the general population. According to projects made in *The National Manpower Survey of the Criminal Justice System*, by 1985, employment in adult correctional institutions will increase by 58%, if increasing social pressure to incarcerate offenders continues.[8]

Figures such as those touted by the National Manpower Survey would indicate that corrections will be a burgeoning field in the future, and also, that unless women are encouraged to work in, and are well utilized in full-role capacities in corrections (female offender populations in 1979 were only around 10,042)[9], there could be a critical labor shortage in the field. Currently, with inadequate salaries and poor working conditions there are already difficulties in recruiting desirable candidates for employment.

Two court cases have, within the past few years, played a significant role in the area of women working in correctional institutions and their major impact has not yet been felt. The first, *Dothard v. Rawlinson*, 433 U.S. 321 (1977) banned the use of female correctional officers in a prison where conditions were very poor and where a woman, by virtue of her sex could undermine the security of the institution if unable to provide adequate control of the population. This case, of course, has had a dampening effect on the hiring of women in corrections, although it is felt that it will not generally be followed, in light of a new decision in *Gunther v. Iowa*, 462 F. Supp. 952 (1979). *Gunther v. Iowa* brought to the forefront another issue that had been raised and unanswered in *Dothard*, i.e. an inmate's right to privacy. Both of these cases avoided making a definitive ruling on the privacy issue, however, the *Gunther* ruling stated that privacy shall not take precedence over a female correctional officer's right to promotion and that institutional administration *will* make the necessary scheduling adjustments for women within institutions without placing them in direct confrontation with an inmate's privacy. Translated into practical terms, this means that while women may not hold every post or pull every task within an institution (working in housing units), they will still be equally eligible to be promoted up the normal chain of command based on their seniority and capability.

It is fair to say, that the greatest area of potential numbers of jobs for correctional officers is the supervision of offenders in adult male institutions, and that the central issue surrounding the hiring and utilization of female correctional officers has now polarized, not so much anymore in the issue of security, but in the prisoner's rights issue of privacy.

USAGE

As reported by Joann B. Morton in "A Study of Employment of Women As Correctional Officers in State Level Adult Male Correctional Institutions", in 1978, women comprised 23% of the total correctional work force in comparison to the 12% found by the Joint Commission on Correctional Manpower and Training in 1969. This 11% difference occurring over the 9-year period represented a 91.7% increase in women employed by correctional agencies. Also, according to Morton's study, on a national average 6.6% of the correctional officer work force in state male correctional institutions were women.[10] In compiling her figures, Morton ranked states by percentages of employment of women, deriving her numbers by comparing the total number of officers in male facilities (as of December, 1978) with the total number of female officers in male facilities. Of those states responding (Alaska, Pennsylvania, Texas, and Utah reported that they do not hire; Hawaii provided incomplete data; Mississippi did not respond), the five states ranking highest were Louisiana, 18.23%; Wyoming 16.05%; Kentucky, 15.90%; Oklahoma, 13.88%; and South Carolina, 13.02%. Many states fell in a 4.5% category. The five states ranking lowest were: New Jersey 1.45%; Arizona, 1.39%; Montana, .62%; Rhode Island; and Maine although they reported they did hire women correctional officers in adult male institutions, reported that they currently had none on staff.[11]

Interestingly enough a geographic breakdown done by Ms. Morton, showed that states in the West South Central and East South Central portions of the country had the highest incidence of women as correctional officers in male institutions. The New England and Middle Atlantic regions were significant laggers.[12] Another interesting observation noted by Ms. Morton was that there appeared to be no correlation between the number of women correctional officers and the size (populations) of state systems.

When queried about the reasons for hiring women correctional officers, 65% of the states surveyed cited some aspect of an affirmative action program. Other reasons given for hiring women were:

1. meet some need of the system such as to search female visitors (7 systems)
2. receipt of qualified applicants (4 systems)
3. expansion of the work force making such an action more acceptable (2 systems)
4. shortage of male applicants (2 systems)[13]

The Morton study also found an inverse relationship between employing higher percentages of women and the level of the security of the institution. Taken as an average, 4% of female correctional officers were employed in maximum security, 5% in medium, and 9% in minimum. 17% of the systems surveyed reported over 10% women in maximum security; 25% of medium security institutions employed more than 10% female officers, as did 49% of minimum security institutions.[14]

In 1979, the Corrections Compendium staff of CONtact, Inc. conducted a survey of Departments of Corrections to determine not only which states were utilizing women correctional officers in male institutions, but also in what types of positions and with what limitations, if any, the women were working. At the time of this survey, Montana and Wyoming did not respond, and only Pennsylvania, Rhode Island and Texas indicated that they hired no female correctional officers in male institutions. Of the 45 states that responded that they did hire female correctional officers into positions in adult male institutions, 37 of these specifically stated that the women correctional officers were restricted from positions in housing areas, or any position that would require them to view inmate showers and toilets unless for specific counts, service delivery functions, or in the event of an emergency. In almost all states, women were assigned to positions in the tower, sally port, control room, front desk, front gate, dining room, or to escort visitors through the institutions, or frisk female visitors coming into the institutions. New Mexico, Nevada, New York, Tennessee, and Delaware were the only states that indicated no employment restrictions on positions held, and all seemingly allowed female correctional officers in male housing units. In regard to questions asked about women correctional officers performing strip searches on male inmates, with the exception of Delaware, and a few other states who cited it was allowed in emergency conditions, the vast majority of states responded with a unanimous "No".[15]

As a follow-up to the July 1979 survey, fourteen selected states were recontacted in May of 1980 to determine how they were faring with the usage of female correctional officers employed in male institutions. Those selected were states that appeared to have the most zealous and affirmative usage of female correctional officers. The questions asked were meant to be answered in a general fashion and asked for a discussion of any scheduling adjustments that these states were making to utilize female correctional officers without invading the privacy of inmates and also, what, if any, special training female correctional officers may be receiving for dealing with male inmates. Some of the replies were encouraging and others extremely discouraging, from the perspecitive of increased job opportunities for women correctional officers in male institutions.

New Mexico, which had previously indicated no restrictions (other than strip searchs) in 1979, were found in 1980 not to have any female correctional officers employed in their male institutions. Nevada, in 1980, had 13 female employees in male institutions (one employment counselor, three correctional classification counselors, two sergeants, and seven senior correctional officers), with no special problems. The only restrictions indicated were that a female could not patdown or search an inmate of the opposite sex. Nevada also reported that the male correctional officers were not opposed to the additional task thrust upon them, and that they felt that the presence of females had a calming effect in some instances within the institutions.

The state of New York gave the following report of activities within their system:

> The department does not make scheduling adjustments in promoting female correctional officers. Advancement is based on passing the promotional exam and the rank of the individual. This arrangement has been implemented several times recently with the establishment of a new promotional sergeant list, and there appears to be no problem with female sergeant appointees to male facilities or with male sergeant appointees to female facilities.
> Special consideration of invasion of privacy rights is not given in assigning female sergeants to male facilities, nor is it given in assigning male sergeants to female facilities.
> This department has had to respond to a court order regarding privacy rights of female inmates at a facility utilizing male correction officers and make changes in staffing and the physical structure of the facility to ensure privacy. However, this was not a class action and has not yet become an order for any facility other than the one directly involved.
> In general, departmental policy regarding inmates' right to privacy has not extended to the supervisory levels since direct inmate supervision is not an issue.
> Problems have arisen in some facilities when scheduling adjustments have had to be made for inmate privacy; safety of the officer; and security of the facility. At this time, existing written policy specifies no more than one-third females at male facilities and vice-versa. The actual rule of thumb used is about ten percent. The number which can be effectively used depends upon the individual facility.
> As bids are posted, female officers can bid any job. However, due to policy, the jobs cannot be awarded to them if the inmates privacy is violated, if the job involves the shower area or where strip frisking, i.e. must be done. In addition, in an area utilizing two officers, one can be a female, however, problems may arise when a team of two (one male officer, one female officer) working a housing unit must split up to respond to a request for help in another area. The question to be addressed in a situation such as this is whether to send the male officer and leave the female officer alone on the male housing unit or to send some female officer to respond to the emergency call. In some instances, the presence of a female officer may not be facilitative in handling the emergency.
> Because of the bidding system and the female officer's right to bid, it's not always possible to balance pass groups and there are times

when there is a large concentration of female officers on duty. It is difficult to effectively deploy the female officers according to policy. In order to do so, female officers must be assigned to posts such as the package room or the key room, posts which appeal to many officers and are heavily bid. This may create resentment on the part of male officers who would also like to be assigned to posts of this type.

Some female correction officers are assigned to facilities which are not their preferred location choice in order to distribute them more effectively among all facilities. This is not always according to labor-management agreements, but at times it has been necessary.

The department continues to address the issue of how many female correction officers each male facility can accommodate, and vice-versa. The department is drafting guidelines for assignment of the opposite sex correction officers which are based on job-relatedness. As such, each facility will have unique formal male/female numerical restrictions.[16]

Kansas also responded with information about specific action taken to find proper placements for female correctional officers:

To provide promotional opportunities for female officers, the Department of Corrections has identified certain positions to which females can be promoted. These positions are not in a part of the male institutions where the inmates' right to privacy would be abridged by the presence of a female officer. No scheduling assignments (special accommodations have been made for these positions — either by differentiating between the scope of the duties performed by male and female officers assigned to the same post or shift; or by restricting the assignment of females to certain shifts.

... some male officers assigned to the cellhouses have stated that it is unfair for female officers to receive the same pay as they do, but not work under the same conditions. For the most part, problems of this nature are usually resolved at the institutions.[17]

New Hampshire, which currently has eight full-time and one part-time female correctional officers has a policy that female officers will perform the same duties as male correctional officers with the exception of supervising showers and performing "strip" searches. New Hampshire feels that female officers have been accepted not more, or not less by the male inmates than other officers, and they have experienced no major friction between male and female correctional officers.[18]

Minnesota experienced a policy change between the 1979 and 1980 inquiries. This policy reads in part:

The Department of Corrections fully recognizes the importance of actively supporting and implementing its Affirmative Action Plan through its personnel policies. The department also recognizes its duty and responsibility to provide safe, orderly and secure correctional institutions while, at the same time, protecting to the extent possible the rights of its inmates and staff.[19]

Minnesota still indicates that they try to hire as many women as the policy will allow, however, the effect of the policy has had the effect of making hiring and promotional practices generally more restrictive. Women are encouraged to apply for promotion; cell house experience is waived. However, Minnesota is under a strict union contract with mandatory seniority provisions and cannot make schedule changes to accommodate the promotion of females. An example of Minnesota's policy is given in the following paragraph:

> This institution's (Stillwater, MN) Affirmative Action Committee reviewed all correctional counselor positions in order to determine those positions which are single sex according to this policy, and consequently to determine the areas where female officers could be assigned without restrictions. The investigation showed that the institution was able to assign, without violating the policy, 17 female officers. Using that figure, which equals 6% of the 253 correctional counselor positions, the committee recommended that 6% of the correctional counselor III positions (3) and 6% of the correctional counselors IV positions (1), be filled by female officers..
>
> It is not difficult for female correctional counselors I and II to bid into jobs that meet the policy. It becomes somewhat more difficult to provide upward mobility to correctional counselors III and IV positions, since there are a fixed number of positions of which a majority require duties that would violate the right of privacy. In order to be eligible for promotion, officers must complete specific college coursework and meet minimal tenure requirements. Currently employed here are three female correctional counselors III, and one female correctional counselor IV.
>
> Female correctional counselors who meet educational and tenure requirements also are eligible for promotion to institution security caseworker as vacancies exist. These positions do not violate the privacy rights and are equally available to female and male correctional counselors.[20]

Delaware, which has been a leader in the field, and has had one of the most progressive, permissive systems in this regard, reported that no special scheduling adjustments are made for female correctional officers in male institutions. Officers are assigned to posts regardless of sex. Currently, Delaware stated that they had one woman who had been promoted above the correctional officer level, to correctional lieutenant. Delaware, however, is experiencing severe discomfort, and the entire policy towards the hiring and utilization of female correctional officers is being reviewed, as the result of a report made by a Governor's Investigative Task Force. Delaware is also under fire in the form of two prisoner's rights law suits filed by inmates alleging that that female officers in their housing units are violating their right to privacy. A group of male correctional officers have also filed a grievance in Delaware, stating that female correctional officers constitute a security risk and that the women are shown favoritism by being assigned to easier posts by the institutional managers.[21]

Although it appears from these studies that women are making inroads and performing an increasing number of duties and filling increasing numbers of positions in correctional facilities, it is obvious by the experience of Delaware, and the action of the courts, that total integration into the correctional work force has not been, and may not be achieved. Should the time come that the courts of the nation rule that females may work in any and all correctional institutions and in any and all positions within those institutions without jeopardizing security or invading the inmate's rights to privacy then the administrative burden to accommodate equal employment opportunity for women in corrections will be eased.

EFFECT

In late 1975, the Boulder County Sheriff's Office hired 10 females to handle the same duties as male officers (with the exception of strip searches which are verboten in other correctional facilities also, except in the case of emergencies). In July of 1976 and June of 1977 a survey was conducted by questionnaires circulated to inmates and to male and female staff, to determine how each group felt about the effect that the addition of women to the staff had on the functioning of the institution.

The first issue that the Boulder study explored was the relationship of female staff to inmates and whether the inmates would act differently toward female staff because of their sex. This included abusive language, physical aggression and other forms of manipulation. Questions surrounding this issue also asked if inmates responded more positively rather than negatively (honesty, protective behaviors, etc.) toward the women personnel. When asked if they saw or heard other inmates trying to shock female staff, 52% of the inmates responded they never did. 54% of the inmates said they would be less likely to be physically aggressive toward female staff; only 41% responded they would be less likely to be verbally aggressive. Only 11% of the inmates surveyed indicated that female staff were easier to manipulate or intimidate than male staff and less than half, 43% said they take a protective role in regard to female staff. In regard to honesty, 10% indicated they would be more honest to females, and 67% said it did not matter.[22] The authors of the paper written on this study, Peter J. Kissel and Paul Katsampes, state that "to the extent (that the inmates surveyed show a reluctance to act physically aggressive toward females on staff), the presence of women could be said to exert a 'softening' influence on inmate behavior which could avert some potential crisis situations before they grow into physical confrontations."[23]

Inmates were also asked questions about some of the psychological effects of having women on staff. When asked about sexual frustration, 34.5% of the inmates felt that the presence of women increased sexual frustration a little, 38% felt that there was no effect and 21% felt that the women's presence decreased frustration. Many inmates, 53%, were in favor of being supervised by women, 37% expressed no difference and only 10% said they resented supervision by women. Resentment about taking orders from female staff as opposed to male staff was also studied. Of the Boulder inmates, 55% responded that the presence of women effected their sense of privacy not at all, 29% said not much and 16% felt that it did some or a lot.[24]

> The inmate response on the other issues of privacy and resentment toward female supervision do not seem to indicate that these issues are regarded as serious problems by the majority of inmates.
> In responding to whether the presence of female staff made special contributions to the institution, a majority of inmates (74%) felt they increased the livability of the institution. Responses which indicated that in certain situations inmates felt the presence of women staff might create some potential problems included the response that 64.5% of the inmates felt men controlled disturbances better than female staff and that men are more effective in dealing with crisis situations. A vast majority (82%) also felt men would be much more effective in breaking-up fights between inmates than would women. Thus, inmates felt women made a special contribution by making the institution a better place to live, but did pose problems in relation to violent or crisis situations where it was felt that the male personnel would be more effective, presumably because of the lack of physical size and strength of most women.[25]

The results of this study largely indicated that inmates felt that women on staff had little effect on them, 42% said they received few personal benefits from having the women on staff, 58% indicated none. Overall when asked about the benefits of having women correctional officers on staff, 48% felt it made no significant difference and 42% felt it was beneficial.[26]

Male correctional staff were also surveyed, 68% felt that women did a satisfactory job and 32% thought that the women were performing very effectively, *none* indicated that the women were doing an ineffective job. 92% of male staff felt that women made special contributions to the facility, 96% felt that women personnel increased "livability" within the facility, and 79% revealed that the presence of female officers increased their own enjoyment of the job.[27]

Problems were also studied. 56% of male staff felt that female staff brought special problems to the job; many male personnel felt the need to protect female staff occasionally, but thought that women were not more easily intimidated or manipulated by the inmates than other male staff. Complaints by inmates about invasion of privacy were recorded by half of the male staff.

The most crucial bone of contention seemed to be the issue of protection during crisis situations: 72% of male staff felt the need to protect female staff occasionally (12% responded never, 16% often). However, 54.5% of the male staff surveyed indicated that they thought that the inmates' behavior had improved since women began working in the institution.[28]

In general, when asked questions relating to their perceptions of the effect of female staff on inmates, male correctional officers felt that the presence of women was favorable (68%) and that in most types of situations, sex did not matter as much as the qualities of the individual officer.[29] This sense of individualism lapped over into the answers of male correctional officers when asked about with whom they would rather work, males or females.

> The vast majority reacted favorably to women performing similar duties to men, and felt that female staff provided a compliment to the male personnel. Gender was not a factor for the vast majority of males when responding to whom they would like to work most closely with, indicating that females in general were not considered to be a great liability or hazard to work alongside. The main determining factor of who male staff would prefer to work with was the particular qualities of the person involved, and not the sex of that person.
> In summarizing how male personnel felt about female employees, it can be said that in general it was felt women performed satisfactorily and made a special contribution by increasing the livability of the institution.
> . . . The one problem area identified which ran counter to this general acceptance was potentially violent crisis situations which were already in progress, where women were perceived as not as effective as male staff due to their lack of physical strength. While women might be somewhat beneficial in preventing such crisis situations from arising due to the softening effect which seems to accompany their presence, once a violent situation occurred, female staff were regarded as a liability by the men on the staff.[30]

WOMEN'S INPUT

Kissel and Katsampes also surveyed female correctional personnel to ascertain how they perceived their own performance as compared to male officers, if their effectiveness was inhibited by prejudice, if they felt restricted by their sex, if they thought equal responsibility was given them, and whether they felt their sex made some of their duties in adult male institutions uncomfortable. Most of the women surveyed (92%) were satisfied with their performance and 100% felt they performed equal to their male counterparts. An equal number (46%) said they experienced occasional difficulty performing duties due to others' prejudice as those that said they never encountered prejudice. 85% felt that being a woman did not restrict performance of duty and 91% felt they were given equal responsibility, however, 85% did express some discomfort in performing particular duties because of their sex.[31]

Lack of physical size seemed to be the greatest sex linked disability. Women were split on the issue of gender affecting security duties; 31% felt it had an adverse effect, 23% a favorable effect, and 46% no effect. 77% of the women surveyed expressed greater feelings of vulnerability because of their sex.

> Comments on the 1st issue of handling crisis situations explained that in extremely dangerous situations any staff member, regardless of sex, would ask for assistance from any other staff member regardless of sex, who was available and in a position to be of help. The responses indicated sometimes women feel their gender may affect their performance of security duties in a positive way, presumably because of the tension reducing influence the presence of women appears to have on certain inmates.[32]

Perceptions of inmates' reactions were also sought from the female correctional staff surveyed. 92% of the female staff felt that inmates responded favorably as compared to males and 83% felt that their presence had improved inmates' behavior, even though only 45% of those polled said that their sex favorably affected counseling effectiveness (46% said it was not affected). Most women expressed concern over the inmate's right to privacy and their presence as an invasion, but only 42% indicated that they had actually heard inmates complain about the lack of privacy. The other 58% said they never heard a complaint on this issue.

As the result of this research the opinion seems to be that women are quite capable of performing and functioning as correctional officers in adult male institutions, with two possible problematic areas: inmate invasion of privacy and crisis situations that have already progressed to violence.[33]

Of course, adult male institutions are not the only penal facilities where female correctional employees are making a valuable contribution. Many women are working in other institutions and in the criminal justice field and encountering typical sets of problems and prejudices. Under the auspices of the American Correctional Association Affirmation Action Committee, a special Task Force on Women was created to address itself to the unique position of women in the field of corrections. Towards this goal, a survey was conducted in 1979 to assess the needs, desires and problems of women working in departments of correction, jails, courts, federal prisons, community correction centers, and human service agencies involved in corrections. Constructed and disseminated through the Task

Force network, the results of the 1979 survey were compiled, evaluated and codified by the author.

Respondents were divided into groups by state and then subcategorized by job classification as the individual job categories had a major impact on the women's perceptions and responses. The three specific areas of job classification were: Administration and Management Positions; Client Contact Positions; and Clerical and Support Positions. Although only 21 states, Canada and the District of Columbia were represented when the deadline for compilation was drawn, the results by their striking similarities indicate a validity of their own.

The survey confirmed several things that are already common knowledge, one being that women are still relatively new in the general field of corrections (i.e. when not exclusively used to work with female prisoners). In various states the majority of respondents grouped in clusters in terms of length of service. Often this length was quite short and many women responded that the short length of time in the field of corrections barred them from training and promotion opportunities. The majority of women were currently in their first position in corrections. For those not in their first job, a significant number of clerical people had been promoted into administrative positions and others, such as correctional officers, had been promoted generally within that chain.

Recruitment was found to be the most significant method of introducing women into the field of corrections. This was generally done by the passing of a merit exam and/or directly applying for the job. Often, as is typical in business, women were made aware and became interested in positions in corrections as a result of personal contacts. Many clerical people were transferred into corrections from other positions within state systems. A number of persons in internships and practicums were later moved into full-time paid positions. Again, as is evidenced by the clusters of persons with the same category of length of service, there is an indication during which years specific states may have maintained recruiting campaigns of women.

The overwhelming majority of women responding to this survey expressed a desire to remain in corrections. Most women desired to move up through client contact positions to positions as wardens and administrators. Not surprisingly, persons in health care positions considered themselves to be health care professionals first; clerical workers were split in terms of a desire to remain exclusively affiliated with the field of corrections and possibilities of advancement in other fields. A number of reasons were given why these women would consider leaving corrections. The primary four to come out of this Task Force study, were given in order: inability to promote, salaries, bureaucracy (includes inability to effect change), and burn-out (over-work, stress, etc.). Other reasons, also given in order of numbers of responses, were a desire for further education, a desire to join the private sector, family considerations, and a lack of interest (almost exclusively found among clerical and support personnel).[34]

Levels of education were generally high with most women expressing a desire for even further education, either formalized or through in-service or seminars. In response to the question of whether or not the women surveyed had received specialized training many women listed their academic education as their sole source of training. Others indicated that they received basic training, in-service training and on-the-job training. Internships and out-of-house seminars ranked last on the list as sources of training. Many respondents felt that they had *no* special training for their positions. One enthusiastic woman responded to this question with the answer: "I have five children."[35] Her response, while humorous, on its face indicates an acknowledgement of the kind of phenomena Katsampes and Kissel found in their study. While women correctional officers may be less able at quelling violence once it has erupted, they *appear* to be more able than male CO's in defusing initial conflicts. The ability to deal with five children may indeed be special training for a position as an effective correctional officer.

Very few of the respondents in the study felt that there were sufficient opportunities for training. Most were emphatic that opportunities were needed to improve their work-related skills and almost all were very eager to do so. The types of training cited as being perceived to be the most beneficial made up an extensive list. Heading all others, in the eyes of the women surveyed, however, was the express need for training in comprehensive administration and management skills (i.e. supervision, personnel, budgets, systems design, program planning, etc.). Following this chief concern, were improved client contact skills, continuing formal education, assertiveness training, training in policies and procedures, a comprehensive knowledge of law and the criminal justice system, and help in preparation for job exams. In spite of the perceived lack of training opportunities available to *all* those working in corrections, most women respondents felt that they were given an equal opportunity to participate in training. However, those that felt they were not given an equal opportunity to train, first criticized lack of funding, then lack of their own seniority. Only following those, was sex discrimination cited as a bar to opportunity to train.

The preceding statement would have us believe that sex discrimination is not a major concern to women that work in corrections. This, however, would not be an accurate picture. Although women indicate that they are not specifically discriminated against by rules, procedures or other forms of paperwork, the issue of most concern and the area that the majority of the women surveyed by the ACA Task Force felt is the one problem that needs the most improvement is sexism. Most felt that they had to deal on a daily basis with attitudes that viewed them as an incapable minority, and thus, they were forced into the roles of super-achievers just in order to maintain an equal stance. Many women acknowledged that this discrimination works both ways, but it is inequality based on sex nonetheless. Even though these women felt they were given an equal opportunity to promote on paper, they still felt excluded from the "executive washroom" network of subtle contacts that cause men to be promoted ahead of them.

Following close on the heels of sexism was another concern that is closely tied to that issue. Administration and management skills acquisition was another target area for the women surveyed. Many respondents felt that they, often by virtue of their sex and upbringing, lack the necessary leadership experience and expertise to make them effective managers. The respondents felt that training, and training in professional attitudes and stance, would also enhance their opportunities for advancement. Another major issue or area these women saw to need improvement was closely tied to the other two issues. Knowledge of career opportunities, (how to advance, what is available, etc.) ranked next with the other issues of lack of support by supervisors, more peer group support, knowledge of promotion guidelines within individual systems and knowledge of affirmative action mandates and efforts following. Again one respondent wryly summed up the entire issue of training and advancement by saying: "Training is equal, advancement is not, as the good old boys are by definition, men."[36]

In some of the states where women were surveyed by the Task Force, low wage scales and inadequate salaries were a major source of dissatisfaction and an impetus for women to seek to pursue their professional goals *outside* the field of corrections. Many women in other states, felt that although they were being paid well, the responsibility and stress created by their jobs outweighed their financial remuneration. Overall, the overwhelming number of respondents studied in this ACA Task Force on Women Report felt that they were, and would remain as career professionals in corrections. This appears to manifest an intense loyalty and love for the field that has managed to supersede emotional stress, discrimination, lack of training, and inadequate financial compensation. One bewildered respondent remarked: "It appears that someone wants you just where you are now, 5 years from now."[37]

Notes

1. "A Study of Employment of Women As Correctional Officers in State Level Adult Male Correctional Institutions" by Joann B. Morton, Dissertation, University of Georgia, Athens, Georgia, 1980, 2.
2. Morton, 72.
3. Morton, 4.
4. *The Report of the LEAA Task Force on Women* by Marlene Bechman,

Chairperson, Law Enforcement Assistance Administration, Washington, D.C., 1975, 14.
   5. "Nondiscrimination in Federally Assisted Crime Control and Juvenile Delinquency Programs", U.S. Department of Justice, Washington, D.C., 9495.
   6. Morton, 37.
   7. *Juvenile and Adult Correctional Departments, Institutions, Agencies and Paroling Authorities: 1980 Directory,* American Correctional Association, College Park, MD, vii and x.
   8. ACA 1980 Dictionary, x.
   9. *The National Manpower Survey of the Criminal Justice System,* Vol. 1, *Summary Report,* Law Enforcement Assistance Administration, U.S. Department of Justice, Washington, D.C., U.S. Government Printing Office, 1978, 1.
   10. Morton, 67.
   11. Morton, 61.
   12. Morton, 62.
   13. Morton, 67.
   14. Morton, 68.
   15. *Corrections Compendium,* Vol. III, No. 12, "You've Come A Long Way, Baby", CONtact, Inc., Lincoln, NE, July 1979, 2 & 3.
   16. Letter to Sandra Nicolai, Corrections Compendium, CONtact, Inc. from Lola Wesner, Personnel Administrator, Department of Correctional Services, Albany, NY, May 5, 1980.
   17. Letter to Sandra Nicolai, Corrections Compendium, CONtact, Inc. from Philip L. Ronnau, Chief, Personnel Services Section, Department of Corrections, Topeka, KS, April 17, 1980.
   18. Letter to Sandra Nicolai, Corrections Compendium, CONtact, Inc., from Everett I. Perrin, Jr., Warden, New Hampshire State Prison, Concord, NH, April 15, 1980.
   19. Letter to Sandra Nicolai, Corrections Compendium, CONtact, Inc. from Leanne Phinney, Personnel Officer, Minnesota Department of Corrections, St. Paul, MN, May 5, 1980, Enclosure: Management Memo, Vol. 4, No. 8, December 15, 1979, Subject: Correctional Counselor Duty Assignment Policy.
   20. Letter to Sandra Nicolai, Corrections Compendium, CONtact, Inc. from Linda Harder, Director, Staff Development, Stillwater Correctional Facility, Stillwater, MN, May 19, 1980.
   21. Letter to Sandra Nicolai, Corrections Compendium, CONtact, Inc. from C. Wayne Faircloth, Personnel Administrator, Department of Correction, Smyrna, DE, May 19, 1980.
   22. "The Impact of Women Corrections Officers on the Functioning of Institutions Housing Male Inmates" by Peter J. Kissel and Paul Katsampes, 1979, 10.
   23. Kissel and Katsampes, 11.
   24. Kissel and Katsampes, 13.
   25. Kissel and Katsampes, 15.
   26. Kissel and Katsampes, 15.
   27. Kissel and Katsampes, 17.
   28. Kissel and Katsampes, 19.

29. Kissel and Katsampes, 20.
30. Kissel and Katsampes, 21-23.
31. Kissel and Katsampes, 25.
32. Kissel and Katsampes, 26.
33. Kissel and Katsampes, 28.
34. "1979 Survey by the American Correctional Association Task Force on Women" by Sandra Nicolai, for Jacqueline Crawford, Chairperson, ACA Task Force on Women, presented at the 1979 American Correctional Association Congress, Philadelphia, PA, August 1979, 36.
35. 1979 ACA Task Force on Women Survey, 39.
36. 1979 ACA Task Force on Women Survey, 39.
37. 1979 ACA Task Force on Women Survey, 39.

Part VI
CORRECTIONAL OFFICER SELECTION

Most guards didn't become guards in order to satisfy some latent sadism or other perversion in their characters; they simply answered all the want-ads and Corrections gave them a job.

Schroeder, 1976: 153

The correctional officer has long been one of the many popular scapegoats for prison management problems which, it is argued, could be obviated by improving the quality of guard selection. In this section we present two chapters which examine this assumption.

Chapter 13, by Krug-McKay, McKay & Ross critically evaluates the literature on selection through the application of psychological tests and raises doubts both about the efficacy of selection through such procedures and about the fundamental assumption upon which they rest.

Chapter 14, by Ross and McKay, presents a model for correctional officer selection. It provides an alternative to traditional approaches to selection which have attempted (unsuccessfully) to weed out poor candidates, particularly those with a high potential for abusive behaviour. Recognizing the complexity of violence and the multitude of factors influencing the correctional officer's behaviour, the model allows for system and situational as well as personal determinants in selection. The Ross & McKay model incorporates a positive approach to correctional officer selection in which emphasis is no longer on assessment of personality, temperament and character defects but on assessment of the skills and abilities which enable the officer to perform his work effectively without resorting to abusive or violent behaviour.

Reference

Schroeder, A. *Shaking it Rough.* Garden City, N.Y.: Doubleday, 1976.

Chapter 13

Psychological Tests For Correctional Officer Selection: Research and Issues*

Barbara Krug-McKay, Bryan McKay and Robert R. Ross

I. INTRODUCTION

The use of psychological tests in the selection of correctional officers has frequently been touted as an effective means of improving the quality of the correctional staff and, more specifically, as an effective method of decreasing the frequency of acts of violence perpetrated by correctional officers. Exhortations that correctional management incorporate psychological tests in the recruiting process have been made in a variety of commission reports on corrections, in political speeches, in conferences, in the media, and in the criminological literature.

It appears to be a common assumption that psychological tests can readily and reliably identify those correctional officer candidates who are likely to become violent and can, therefore, be used to weed out such inappropriate candidates during the initial recruitment stages. It is further assumed that psychological tests can effectively identify those candidates who have the potential to become exceptionally good correctional officers.

In 1978, the Ontario Ministry of Correctional Services initiated a research project to explore the value of psychological screening of candidates for the position of correctional officer, and, specifically, their value in identifying those candidates who have a propensity towards violence. In this report we present the major results of the project. The literature describing the available research on psychological screening of correctional officers is presented and critically evaluated. Conclusions about the value of psychological screening are presented, and a number of theoretical, ethical, economic and practical issues are discussed which should significantly influence the decision to use psychological tests either as a basis of identifying and rejecting totally inappropriate candidates or as a means of identifying and selecting the best candidates for correctional officer positions.

---

* Research supported by the Ontario Ministry of Correctional Services, Project #172. The encouragement and advice of ministry officials is gratefully acknowledged. Dr. Andy Birkenmayer stimulated and guided this research. We appreciate his help. Dr. Donald Amoroso provided helpful comments on an earlier draft.

II. PSYCHOLOGICAL TESTS IN THE SELECTION OF CORRECTIONAL OFFICERS: A REVIEW OF THE LITERATURE

Selection Practices

There seems to be agreement across a variety of correctional jurisdictions that the screening procedures for the selection of correctional officers deserve attention. Such statements usually follow closely the observation and appraisal of existing selection practices.

D. F. Lundberg commenting on U.S. prison guard selection practices in 1947 stated:

> Methods of selection of the Prison Guard are generally loose and include little study of validity. Of the some 13,000 guards in this country (U.S.A.), it is safe to say that over three-fourths have been selected by unscientific methods. (Downey & Signori, 1958: 234)

In 1953, the warden of Jackson Prison, Michigan, described his desperation-based hiring criterion:

> We would hire them if they were warm and alive. (American Correctional Association, 1970: 67)

The situation appears to have altered little in the ensuing two decades of correctional practice. We have heard similar sentiments expressed anecdotally and frequently by correctional administrators. Some State officials responding to Goldstein's (1975: 11) survey of U.S. selection practices indicated that,

> Any "warm body" passing the test would likely be hired.

The "test", in this instance, was comprised of a routine civil service written test of general information and a 5 to 10 minute oral test of "human relations" skills.

In their 1977 report to Parliament, the Sub-Committee on Penitentiary Services in Canada observed:

> (Officers are hired) because CPS is desperate for persons to fill poorly paid and low status positions in dangerous and unrewarding conditions working with under-trained associates in a hostile and low-morale environment. (MacGuigan, 1977: 62)

Willett (1973: ix, x) had earlier reported on the rather haphazard screening procedures he observed in the federal penitentiary system:

> Selection was a rather casual, spontaneous process in which selection board members adopted their own procedures within a loose-fitting framework. . . . Basic information on candidates was lacking at the interviews; no references or objective tests of education or intelligence were used as there was a mistaken assumption that they were not

allowed. Interviewers were not trained in selection, and the profile reports did not relate with confidential assessments used while under training nor on subsequent operational service. There was no feedback to selectors about the effectiveness of their work.

It is not entirely clear that if such information and training were to be available that selection practices would be necessarily different. With rather distressing frequency during the course of our research, respondents *with* information and training repeatedly stated that they would base their judgments almost entirely on an interview. In all cases, they were unable to articulate decision-making variables, none indicated systematic follow-up of their judgments, and all were from fields other than corrections (law enforcement, private industry).

It is probably fair to say that this practice accurately reflects the selection and screening procedures employed in most correctional jurisdictions today.

It is not surprising that practitioners have been thrown on their own initiative in attempting to devise some form of selection procedure in the hiring of correctional officers. Goldstein (1975) has pointed out that to date, specific research programs have not been developed for the selection process as it affects correctional officers.

A Method of Choice

A surprising unanimity was found for the idea that psychological tests should be a method of choice for selecting individuals possessing desirable characteristics for correctional officer jobs as well as for identifying those who would be particularly inclined to engage in inappropriate acts of violence or sadism toward their charges. For example, Shapiro (1978: 80, 81) states:

> There is a school of thought supporting the belief that appropriate psychological, intelligence, and aptitude tests can screen out unsuitable [correctional officer] applicants. . . . Personality tests may reveal sadistic tendencies, fundamental inferiority feelings or latent hostility and aggressiveness.

The *Report of the Parliamentary Sub-Committee on Penitentiary Services in Canada* also advocates appropriate personality testing to ensure that correctional officers have the aptitude, maturity and self-discipline required for the work (MacGuigan, et al., 1977). This strong belief in the efficacy of psychological tests in screening procedures is further illustrated by the screening practices reported in a 1975 review sponsored by the American Bar Association (Goldstein, 1975). Sixteen of the forty-six jurisdictions responding to this survey were using some form of test, about half of that number routinely used personality tests, the others employed them only when indicated by data developed by some other means.

The "State of the Art"

It is not surprising that practitioners have been thrown on their own initiative in attempting to devise some form of selection procedure in the hiring of correctional officers. Downey and Signori (1958: 234) reporting on the "state of the art" of psychological testing in correctional officer selection observed:

> ... so far as one can discover, there are no reported attempts to investigate the problem of prison guard selection in terms of interest and personality objective testing procedures.

More than fifteen years later, Goldstein (1974: 5), following an exhaustive review of the literature and a survey of practices in the United States correctional agencies, concluded:

> In 1974, data in this area is still lacking.

There is no reason to be any more optimistic today. The "state of the art" remains extremely primitive. Only three studies were located and described in Goldstein's review. In these, psychological tests were used to differentiate between guards rated as "good" by their superiors and those who were rated as "poor." The results of these studies cannot be characterized as particularly promising. While it is reported that some tests did discriminate between the two performance groups, overall, there appear to be few commonalities in test results. For example, Downey and Signori (1958) report significant relationships between guards' rated performance and some scales of the Minnesota Multiphasic Personality Inventory (MMPI). Negative correlations were obtained with the F Scale, Depression, Psychasthenia, Social Introversion, Hostility and positive correlations with Dominance. In Hammer's (1968) study, MMPI subscales did not discriminate between performance groups. In this study, which also employed the Strong Vocational Interest Blank, only the Cattell 16 Personality Factors (16 PF) was found to yield significant relationships with guard performance ratings.

The third study reported by Goldstein (Perdue, 1964) involved the use of the Johnson Temperament Analysis which purports to measure nine basic behavioural characteristics: Nervous, Depressive, Active, Cordial, Sympathetic, Subjective, Aggressive, Critical and Self-Mastery. A series of studies was conducted over a three-year period in an attempt to assess the utility of this test in the selection process. Initial observation suggested that the job performance ratings of new guards after six months of service generally corresponded to tests results. Exit interviews with guards who resigned also appeared to be consistent with test findings. Based on these observations, the test was administered to the total guard force of the institution (n = 160). From this group, the 37 officers with "Superior" job performance ratings were selected and their test profiles compared to the averages for the guard force as a whole. Although no statistical tests of significance were conducted and all the subscale scores for both groups were within the average range of the published norms for the general population, the author concluded that the "good" correctional officer is distinguished by several traits:

> ... those employees with better stability in such things as nervousness and work habits, more self-control and self-mastery and perhaps more reserve and caution in dealing with others, make the better type of custodial worker. (Perdue, 1964: 18)

As a final analysis the profiles of applicants who were rejected for employment were reviewed. These individuals were described as:

> ... [of] an apprehensive, anxious and unstable temperament whose inferiority tendencies cause a seeking of faults in others as overcompensation for real or imagined inadequacies — a type of temperament that lacks the basic ability to deal with others and who is very unpredictable, unsettled, and with very limited self-control, ...

This interpretation is offered in spite of the fact that all but three subscales (Subjective, Critical and Self-Mastery) were within the normal range and no tests of significance were conducted. In addition, the rejection decision was based mainly on test results, precluding comparisons with other selection procedures.

As Goldstein has also pointed out, the design of these studies does not provide an adequate basis for drawing conclusions about the utility of the instruments for future selection purposes. Demonstrating discrimination between previously selected groups only serves to confirm past decisions. It does not necessarily indicate the potential of the test instrument for predicting future job performance of new candidates. At best, where a relationship to job performance ratings has been demonstrated, tests predict to correctional officers whose behaviour is rated favourably by their supervisors. This does not necessarily address the issue of whether these individuals engage in inappropriate violent or aggressive behaviour in the course of their duties.

Goldstein's (1975) survey indicated that sixteen States were employing some form of tests in their screening procedures. Five reported using the MMPI: two of these would administer it only after hiring, and one, only if indicated after a routine psychological interview. One jurisdiction reported the use of the Cattell 16 PF during training; ten used "general information tests"; and three used in-house "Correctional Officer Examinations." No data are presented which would allow an assessment of the efficacy of these methods in selection.

Summarizing current practices in screening the psychologically unfit candidate for work as a correctional officer, Goldstein states:

All but four of the forty-six responding state agencies claim to test or screen prospective employees to identify those emotionally or psychologically unfit for correctional officer work. However, only eight of these jurisdictions claimed to have written policy statements or regulations regarding psychological fitness. The methods most often mentioned to identify psychological fitness were medical examinations, written tests, background checks, screening committee interviews, and trial (or probationary) service. The written tests reportedly used by 16 agencies were for the most part of the general information type. We found 30 states felt that their procedures were "effective," 12 states felt that their procedures were "not very effective," and 4 states felt that their procedures were "very effective." However, *we could not discern any patterns to account for the differences in reported effectiveness.* The percentage of applicants rejected on grounds of psychological unsuitability ranged from 0% to 75% with approximately a fourth of the responses in the 1-15% range. (Goldstein, 1975: 13, emphasis added)

Overall, the literature specific to the selection of correctional personnel is not of sufficient quality or quantity to encourage drawing any conclusions about the efficacy of psychological testing in the selection process. While psychological tests have been utilized in research with correctional officers, these reports have focused on personality characteristics or traits without addressing the selection issue.

III. ANALYSIS OF ASSUMPTIONS

The contradiction between the strength of belief in the efficacy of testing and the strength of evidence for its efficacy, suggested that a re-examination of basic assumptions might be needed. Three basic issues seemed relevant: the determinants of violent behavior; test error, and test suitability.

The Issue of Violence

The most basic assumption underlying the advocacy of psychological test usage as a screening device is that such tests are capable of predicting subsequent violent behavior by the candidate. At the very least it is assumed that those with a propensity for engaging in inappropriate violent behavior can be identified by means of a test or battery of tests administered during the pre-employment stage of selection. However, on the basis of a rapidly accumulating body of social science literature, it would seem that the prediction of violence is a much more complex undertaking than this assumption allows. On closer examination it is doubtful whether any test or test battery should be expected to identify correctional officer candidates who are potentially violent because violence is *not* simply a function of personality characteristics. Social scientists have generated a considerable body of research in attempting to develop theories and explanatory concepts which can account for violent and aggressive behavior. Their research has led to the identification of multiple determinants of violent behavior.

The complexity of the phenomenon is illustrated by a recent review of the literature pertaining only to "present" variables identified in current research on violence. ("Past" factors, such as personality dispositions or reinforcement histories were excluded.) Chase and Krames (1978) enumerate nine major explanatory concepts currently under investigation. Of these, five (dehumanization/deindividuation; emotional arousal/anger/cognitive labelling; stress/time factors; alcohol; and observation of models) were categorized as internal processes occurring within the individual. Possible situational or external determinants of violent behavior included victim pain cues; threat of retaliation or punishment; type of provocation; and personal space. This is far from reassuring to the adherents of simple, "common-sense" notions of violent behaviour and its prediction.

Much of the research on predicting violence is found in a more specialized area of inquiry — the prediction of dangerousness. Subjects of these investigations have been, for the most part, convicted offenders, often those classified as criminally insane or mentally ill. Typically they have engaged in some form of violent crime, usually murder, rape or serious assaults. While the issue of screening correctional officer candidates for emotional fitness or a propensity for violence might seem at first glance far removed from the study of dangerousness in offender populations, the literature is based on a shared assumption: that later violence can be predicted by previously collected information.

Megargee (1976) provides further analysis of the complexity of the study of violence and the profusion of variables which must be taken into account. Personality variables which must be considered include: motivation; internal inhibitions (which may vary depending on target characteristics, the function of the act, or the distance from the target); and habit strength (the extent to which aggressive responses have been reinforced in the past). The latter, habit strength, is particularly relevant to correctional officer selection.

> An appraisal of habit strength is particularly important when attempting to determine whether an individual will attempt to satisfy his or her needs for sex, power, mastery, wealth and the like by means of instrumental aggression and in the analysis of socially approved dangerous behaviour by people such as policemen and military personnel. (Megargee, 1976: 9)

Additionally, angry aggression must be differentiated from the instrumental variety. Hostility as opposed to anger must be evaluated differently because hostility is a relatively enduring characteristic whereas anger and rage are transitory emotional states. As such they tend to be highly individualized and situation specific.

The situational factors enumerated by Megargee are comprehensive and include: availability of a weapon; presence of onlookers; behaviour of the potential victim; level of frustration in the environment; and social approval of violence in a particular subculture. Factors related to "pervasive environmental influences" may be particularly important in determining the subsequent behaviour of the correctional worker. This listing of factors merely represents the identification of variables that *may* come into play. The assessment of the operation of each of these, with an acceptable degree of accuracy is also required. Obvious difficulties are found in this regard, given the transitory nature of the emotional states involved; the specificity of both instigations and the difficulty of obtaining adequate data about situational determinants. Available psychological tests as assessment instruments are simply not adequate to the task. As Megargee notes:

> Psychological tests are neat, efficient, and quantifiable, but they are not always the best samples of behaviour for the prediction of violence. (Megargee, 1976: 10)

Violent behaviour is a low base rate phenomenon. Both Megargee (1976) and Shah (1978) have discussed the difficulties of accurate prediction of any infrequent occurrence. In this instance, an error at any point in a complicated prediction process (identifying the relevant variables; assessing these factors; determining the interaction of variables; and, estimating the relative response potential of dangerous and nondangerous acts) will be magnified by the base rate problem.

> Whenever we attempt to predict infrequent events, even a moderate false positive rate will result in large numbers of people being erroneously diagnosed. (Megargee, 1976: 13)

Jacoby (1975) describes the difficulty experienced by researchers in the area in overprediction: where a large proportion of errors are made in predicting another incident of violent behaviour for individuals who do not engage in further violent acts. This finding has been a major problem with chronically violent offenders. With the substantially lower base rate of applicant behaviour the problem becomes acute, if not insurmountable.

Shah (1978) delineates further the conceptual problems which have beset research in the area. Viewing dangerous behaviour as determined by the individual's personality leads, in turn, to the mistaken assumption that samples of dangerous behaviour are typical of the individual and that such behaviour is likely to occur in other situations as well. This line of thinking encourages the labelling of the *individual* as dangerous rather than the more accurate categorization of certain aspects or occurrences of *behaviour* as being dangerous. The importance of situational determinants of violent behaviour cannot be over-emphasized.

> ... violent and dangerous acts tend to be relatively infrequent, occur in rather specific interpersonal and situational contexts, may be state dependent (e.g., under the influence of alcohol or other drugs), and may not be representative of the individual's more typical behavior. (Shah, 1978: 227)

The interaction of personality and situational variables also poses considerable problems for prediction:

> Efforts to understand, assess, predict, prevent, and change dangerous behaviors must consider the effects of setting and situational factors as well as the interactions between these and the characteristics of the individual. (Shah, 1978: 227)

Jacoby (1975) in commenting on the "state of the art" concludes:

> This research is one more bit of evidence contributing to the conclusion that the accurate prediction of dangerousness, even among such high-risk populations as mentally ill offenders, is not within the existing abilities of social or behavioral scientists.

The investigator or clinician dealing with an inmate or confined population has several advantages not generally found in a selection context. Background and behavioural information is readily available through case histories, family interviews and observation of the individual over extended periods of time. As well, many of the most powerful and well researched psychological assessment tools (such as the MMPI) were developed for and with such groups. Violent behaviour of some type may have occurred in the past, providing an opportunity to gather data about the situation in which it took place, improving the likelihood of predicting to similar situations in the future. Even with these advantages, the clinician has not fared well predicting within an acceptable range or error. It seems quite improbable that an assessment process without these advantages, and based on far less information, (as is the typical state of affairs in correctional officer selection procedures) will fare any better.

The Issue of Error

In any attempt to predict behaviour by psychological testing, there will be error (Megargee, 1976). These errors will be of two types: false positives — selecting candidates who "pass" testing but who later will perform poorly and; false negatives — rejecting candidates who would have been suitable. As Cordingley (1978) has pointed out, police agencies (and it would be safe to say, correctional jurisdictions as well) are more concerned with the first type, the selection of an individual who will later prove unsuitable, whether through inappropriate violent behaviour, inability to cope with the stresses of the job or, making unwise decisions under pressure. This is understandable given the far-reaching consequences of these kinds of failure for the correctional agency itself, the individual and his co-workers, and his charges — the inmates. As we know, inappropriate behaviour by a correctional officer can have major consequences: property damage, physical injuries and public allegations against both employer and employee. Correctional officer behaviour has frequently been identified as a critical variable in prison disturbances (e.g., MacGuigan et al., 1977; Shapiro, 1978; Swackhammer, 1973).

Less has been said about the second type of error, rejecting the applicant who would have performed well. There are two consequences of this type of error which deserve further consideration. Since, at the present time, it appears that there is a large pool of manpower from which correctional workers may be selected, making errors of this kind may not seem costly to the organization. However, it is likely that this manpower pool contains few individuals with either the requisite skills or the motivation for acquiring them. Willett (1973: ix) has described the conventional applicant group for positions in corrections as follows:

> They appeared to be normal young Canadian men from the lower middle or working class, who had previously suffered somewhat from the capriciousness of the labour market for semi-skilled and unskilled workers. There was no apparent motivation among them towards work in prisons apart from a certain curiosity about crime and criminals. . . .

Some writers have noted that candidates for correctional work are often coming off a period of unemployment (e.g., MacGuigan et al., 1977). Shapiro (1978: 80) has observed that

> too often the correctional recruiting system has proved to be a negative process that attracts people by chance, not by choice; the applicant would have preferred another type of job. Some candidates have been attracted to corrections because it represents a secure civil service position, others have been drawn by this curiosity about crime and criminals, and still others have fallen into the work as a second, third, or even last choice.

In short, the existence of a large number of adequate candidates available to fill correctional positions is largely illusory. Skilled individuals are few in number.

The false negative error also leads to concerns about the human or civil rights of the individual being considered and finally rejected for employment. The hiring agency is on firm ground only insofar as it can demonstrate that the criteria used to select employees are related to later on-the-job performance. Employment legislation in the United States has crystallized this issue within a legal framework (Perlman, 1973). In essence, no test may be used as the basis for rejection for employment unless the user can demonstrate that the test bears a direct relation to the requirements of the job. It is safe to say that few tests, as they are currently applied, will meet this standard. As Cordingley (1978: 30) succinctly observed:

> Making unwarranted decisions based on data from inappropriate tests, with far-reaching implications for tested individuals, clearly injures the well-being of those tested.

Given the state of the art of test validation in the literature pertaining to correctional officer selection, this observation seems particularly relevant. In sum, selection errors, both positive and negative, can be particularly costly in corrections: 1. rejecting the applicant who would have performed well, because there are really few skilled individuals available; 2. accepting the candidate who later performs poorly, because of the material and human costs of inadequate functioning of correctional institutions.

The Issue of Test Suitability

Special characteristics of psychological tests (as samples of behaviour) qualify further the uses to which they may legitimately be put. Psychological tests are "standardized": the information they yield is limited by the assumption that any testing will be conducted under similar conditions and with individuals like those of the normative sample. Personality tests were developed for and with specific kinds of people in quite specific situations. The MMPI, for example, was developed as an aid to therapy for hospitalized psychiatric patients. The major interest tests (Strong Vocational Interest Blank, Kuder Personal Preference Record) were also intended for use in a voluntary counselling relationship — presuming that the individual wanted to discover something about himself/herself and had no particular stake in the direction of the outcome. Contrast this with the typical motivation of someone looking for work. They, quite naturally, want to present themselves in the best manner possible and to ensure that the characteristics they display are likely to be those desired by the people doing the hiring. The individual seeking employment has as a goal: obtaining a job — not self-discovery or an improved relationship with a therapist.

Most tests of this ilk are "fakable." They were developed on the assumption of open self-disclosure by the respondent, often an unreasonable expectation for the job-seeker. There is also reason to believe that lie scales on many of these instruments are inadequate to detect deliberate misrepresentation:

> A bright, well-educated applicant is sometimes capable of faking mental health to a very successful degree in a short-range testing situation. (Molden, 1972: 31)

Suitability of the norms for the population under consideration poses an additional problem. Research on police personality lends credence to this hypothesis. For example, Saccuzzo et al. (1974) using the MMPI for research on the "modal police personality" reports that police groups typically "fake good." Rhead et al. (1968: 1578) having reviewed MMPI and other data for over one-thousand police applicants concluded:

> What appears as excessive in the normal population may well be in the service of the ego in a cross-section of candidates and police officers.

Other samples of police candidates and officers yield similar results in support of the notion that this group will respond to the test situations in a different way than a cross-section of the general adult population (Lefkowitz, 1975; Saccuzzo et al., 1974; Sheppard et al., 1974). Even allowing that norms are developed for an occupational group, it may be that further specificity is required. Comparing samples of police MMPI profiles, Saxe and Reiser (1976) concluded that local revalidation of norms was required. Specific data on patterns of test response for correctional officers would be required to determine the validity of these observations for their occupational group.

IV. SELECTING CORRECTIONAL OFFICERS: A POSITIVE APPROACH

Implicit in any discussion of screening devices for selection purposes is an emphasis on *screening out*. In this view, screening serves the purpose of early identification of unsuitable candidates where "suitability" refers to a reasonable expectation that the person has the requisite capacity to perform the job within satisfactory limits. An underlying assumption is that adequate screening procedures will reject the "misfit" and accept the "best fit" of the available manpower resource pool. Whatever remains is the best.

This interpretation of the purpose of the selection process is no longer tenable. Reflecting the view of many critics of this position, Shapiro (1978: 80) observes that:

> More recently, government agencies in both Canada and the United States have realized that recruitment must be turned into a positive process.

In this view, the selection process would emphasize desirable qualities, and seek to identify the most suitable candidates — screening *in* the best.

However defined, the selection task has not been made easier by the apparent lack of any precise articulation of the qualities or attributes which are likely to make certain kinds of people better or worse correctional officers than others. At the extremes of course, we do have unanimity. We

CHAPTER 13 PSYCHOLOGICAL TESTS — OFFICER SELECTION

wish to exclude the excessively violent or overly passive individual; the person who lacks the ego strength required to cope with the stresses of correctional work or the capacity to appreciate the impact of incarceration on others. That much is clear.

There also seems to be some consensus that certain kinds of attributes are associated with the *ideal* correctional officer. S/he must have personal qualities of patience, sensitivity and understanding; an ability to get along with people, and communicate effectively; stable enough to cope maturely with stress and be able to handle the responsibilities and obligations of authority. S/he must also be able to carry out instructions, maintain security, supervise and deliver coherent and accurate reports (MacGuigan et al., 1977).

The Canadian Corrections Association (1968) proposed that the correctional officer should be able to understand human behaviour, establish good human relations and function as part of a team in light of their crucial role in the treatment of offenders.

The Council of Europe (1967) reports that its member nations attempt to select officers who have: sufficient intelligence and education to permit instruction; stability, equilibrium, psychological aptitude or talent; integrity, the capacity to lead men and to live in the artificial framework of an institution.

A reasonably complete list of desirable attributes illustrating the recommendations issued by a variety of investigative bodies is contained in the *Report of the Royal Commission on the Toronto Jail and Custodial Services:*

> Although the correctional officer should not be thought of as a particular type, there are some personality traits and attitudes that may be considered assets in correctional work:
> (a) *Empathy* — Candidates should manifest an understanding of and an interest in people, and they should be approachable and open-minded.
> (b) *Self-confidence* — Prospective correctional officers should give an impression of assurance and general practical competence, of strength of character without appearing to be excessively authoritarian.
> (c) *Positive, interested attitude* — Applicants should display a reasonable degree of concern about the rehabilitation of offenders.
> (d) *Common sense* — Candidates should have an acceptable level of practical intelligence and problem-solving ability, an openness to alternative approaches, and a capacity to think quickly in stressful situations.
> (e) *Communication skills* — Correctional officers must have a reasonable command of English, competence in second language spoken by inmates is also an asset.

(f) *Flexibility* — Applicants should be able to adapt to shift work, intermittent overtime, training programs, and a variety of work assignments. (Shapiro, 1978: 76)

The empirical evidence, although supportive of the common-sense wisdom of the growing list of recommendations, is sparse. The few researchers who have actually used psychometric instruments to differentiate between officers rated as either "good" or "poor" by their superiors have reported attributes which include: stability, freedom from undue apprehension, sincerity with reserve, maturity, persistence, understanding of self (Perdue, 1964); stability, spontaneity, flexibility, ability to get along with others (Hammer, 1968); verbal ability, self confidence, social interest and few nervous anxieties (Downey & Signori, 1958).

Shifting emphasis to the positive attributes of a good correctional officer and selecting on the basis of identifying such attributes in job candidates appears eminently sensible. Unfortunately, descriptions of desirable qualities at such a global level are of very little help at an operational level. Moreover, such general descriptions do not reflect very well the actual skills required in the day to day reality of the correctional officer's work.

It seems unrealistic to seek candidates with all the positive traits listed above when the job is not very attractive in the first place or, if individuals like this are hired, to expect them to stay unless one can somehow improve career development opportunities. Applicants with such admirable qualities are unlikely to be attracted and, if hired, retained unless the correctional officer's prestige can be improved by enhancing the status of the job in the eyes of the public. This is unlikely to occur unless it is clear that the skills required in correctional work are special.

> Correctional endeavours . . . tend to be viewed as the common-sense application . . . of techniques either possessed or readily available to most persons of reasonable ability. [But] it is probably the possession of skills that are not easy to duplicate . . . that gives any vocation a particularly high standing. (Geis & Cavanaugh, 1966: 141)

"Professionalizing" the work of correctional officers has, of course, been advocated by others (e.g., Bennet, 1952; Flynn, 1953; American Correctional Association, 1970; MacGuigan et al., 1977; Shapiro, 1978). Unfortunately, thus far, no one has articulated how this could be accomplished. What is needed is a clear idea of what the correctional officer *actually* does rather than recommendations for selection strategies based on statements of what it is assumed correctional officers are supposed to do.

This kind of examination of correctional work is not much in evidence in the literature. To a large extent, the correctional officer appears to be the "forgotten man" (or woman) in corrections.

... precious little is known about the guard himself ... We do not even have a very good composite picture of the guard. The President's Crime Commission (1967), the Joint Correctional Manpower Commission (1969), and the National Advisory Commission on Criminal Justice Standards and Goals (1973) all recommended ways to improve management styles and skills and recruit better personnel, but none really probed with enough depth to understand and thereby know what to improve. (Fogel, 1975: 70)

Willett (1973: 1) has expressed similar sentiments:

> One of the characteristics of the already extensive research on prisons ... is its concentration on prisoners, and the relative neglect of the staff. ... There is little or nothing on, or by, those in the basic ranks of the prison hierarchy, the custodial staff.

For whatever reason, recommendations about correctional manpower continue to be issued, urging the adoption of selection and training strategies without a clear explication of what it is that is to be selected and trained for. As Fogel (1975: 70) has observed:

> All [commissions] called for better-trained and higher paid guards, but none spoke to the basic question of how the guard sees himself, how he develops his view of the prison world in which he must contain and manage men against their will. There is a tacit assumption in this literature that guard improvement is a function of his infinite malleability, if only management could figure out the right mold.

V. CONCLUSION

There is a virtual plethora of claims for the value of psychological tests in correction officer selection and a virtual dearth of evidence which would support such claims. We found many reports which said testing *should* be done, a few which said it *is* being done or *had been* done and, distressingly, none which could demonstrate that it had been done *effectively*.

To a certain extent, any consideration of the relative merits of various selection procedures is premature, pending the articulation of precise, objective behavioural criteria which would define what the correctional officer actually does. A more comprehensive understanding of the institutional and occupational realities of the correctional officer's working world is needed.

References

American Correctional Association. *Causes, Preventative Measures and Methods of Controlling Riots and Disturbances in Correctional Institutions.* 1970.

Bennet, J. V. "Prisons in turmoil." *Federal Probation.* 1952, *16* (3).
Canadian Corrections Association. "Criteria for treatment and training programs in prisons." *Canadian Journal of Corrections.* 1968, *10*, 57-69.
Chase, M. M.; Krames, L. *Situational Determinants of Violence and Aggression.* Solicitor General of Canada. Ottawa, 1978.
Cordingley, P. *Psychological Testing in Canadian Police Forces.* Canadian Police College. Ottawa, 1978.
Council of Europe. *Status, Selection and Training of Basic Grade Custodial Prison Staff.* Strasbourg, 1967.
Downey, R. W.; Signori, E. L. "The selection of prison guards." *Journal of Criminal Law, Criminology and Police Science.* 1958, *49*, 234-236.
Fogel, D. ". . . We are the Living Proof . . ." *The Justice Model for Corrections.* Cincinnati: W. H. Anderson Co., 1975.
Flynn, F. T. "Behind the prison riots." *Social Service Review.* 1953, *27*.
Geis, G.; Cavanaugh, E. "Recruitment and retention of correctional personnel." In E. Eldefonso (ed.) *Issues in Corrections: A Book of Readings.* Beverly Hills: Glencoe Press, 1974.
Goldstein, B. *Screening for Emotional and Psychological Fitness in Correctional Officer Hiring.* American Bar Association, Resource Centre on Correctional Law and Legal Services. Washington, 1975.
Hammer, M. "Differentiating good and bad officers in a progressive women's reformatory." *Corrective Psychiatry.* 1968, *14*, 114-118.
Jacoby, J. E. *Prediction of Dangerousness among Mentally Ill Offenders.* Paper presented at the Annual Meeting of the American Society of Criminology, Toronto, 1975.
Lefkowitz, J. "Psychological attributes of policemen: A review of research and opinion." *Journal of Social Issues.* 1975, *31* (1), 3-26.
MacGuigan, M. (Chairman). *Report to Parliament by the Sub-Committee on the Penitentiary System in Canada.* Ministry of Supply and Services, Ottawa, 1977.
Megargee, W. "The prediction of dangerous behaviour." *Criminal Justice and Behaviour.* 1976, *3* (1), 3-22.
Molden, J. "The use of probation in the selection process." *Police.* 1972, *31* (1), 31-34.
Perdue, W. C. "The screening of applicants for custodial work by means of a temperament test." *American Journal of Corrections.* 1964, *26*, 14-19.
Perlman, H. S. *Legislating for Correctional Line Officer Education and Training.* "American Bar Association, Resource Centre on Correctional Law and Legal Services." Washington, 1973.
Rhead, C.; Abrams, A.; Trosman, H.; Margolis, P. "The psychological assessment of police candidates." *American Journal of Psychiatry.* 1968, *124*, 1575-1580.
Saccuzzo, D. P.; Higgins, G.; Lewandowski, D. "Program for psychological assessment of law enforcement officers: Initial evaluation." *Psychological Reports.* 1974, *35*, 651-654.
Saxe, S. J.; Reiser, M. "A comparison of three police applicant groups using the MMPI." *Journal of Police Science and Administration.* 1976, *12*, 419-425.

Secretariat, United Nations. *The Recruitment, Training and Status of Personnel for Adult Penal and Correctional Institutions.* 1955. Cited in Geis, C.; Cavanaugh, E. "Recruitment and retention of correctional personnel." In E. Eldefonso (ed.) *Issues in Corrections: A Book of Readings.* Beverly Hills: Glencoe Press, 1974.

Shah, S. A. "Dangerousness: A paradigm for exploring some issues in law and psychology." *American Psychologist.* 1978, *33* (3), 224-238.

Shapiro, B. (Chairman). *Report of the Royal Commission on the Toronto Jail and Custodial Services.* Queen's Printer for Ontario, Toronto, 1978.

Sheppard, C.; Bates, C.; Fracchia, J.; Merlis, S. "Psychological need structures of law enforcement officers." *Psychological Reports.* 1974, *35*, 583-586.

Swackhammer, J. W. (Chairman). *Report of the Commission of Inquiry into Certain Disturbances at Kingston Penitentiary during April 1971.* Information Canada, 1973.

Willett, T. *Becoming a Correctional Officer in the Canadian Penitentiary Service: An Account of the Induction Process.* Canadian Penitentiary Service, 1973.

Chapter 14

The Correctional Officer: Selection Through Training*

Robert R. Ross and H. Bryan McKay

Strong claims have been made in speeches, in conferences, and in the media that programs of institutional management and treatment of the inmate can be greatly improved by screening correctional officers by the use of psychological tests. The major conclusion of our recent review of psychological screening of correctional officer candidates is that there is *no* screening procedure, test or device currently available which has been demonstrated within minimal standards of reliability or validity to be acceptable in the selection of correctional officers (Krug-McKay, McKay, & Ross, 1979).

In this paper we present an alternative model for correctional officer selection. It incorporates a multi-stage, continuous, systematic selection process in keeping with common current procedures but with some important refinements and additions. It is based on some assumptions about the prediction of abusive behavior by correctional officers, an alternative view of the goals of correctional officer selection, and a reconsideration of the characteristics of candidates which selection procedures should seek to identify.

Prediction of Abusive, Destructive and Violent Behavior by Correctional Officers

It has long been assumed that a basic purpose of correctional officer selection procedures is to identify applicants with a high potential for anti-social behavior, particularly violence. In Chapter 13 we argued that attempting to prevent incidents of violence by correctional officers through identifying, in pre-employment testing, those applicants with a high potential for violence is likely to be a fruitless task because it is based on some naive assumptions about the causes of violence, an overestimation of the power of psychological tests and, more generally, an erroneous conception about the predictability of violence. It is highly questionable whether any selection procedure should be expected to identify correctional officer candidates who are likely to abuse their charges unless it had been

---

* An edited version of a report by the same title to the Ontario Ministry of Correctional Services which supported the research on which it was based. We appreciate the encouragement and advice of Andy Birkenmayer.

or could be demonstrated that such behavior is predominantly a function of the pre-employment personality characteristics of the correctional officer. Research on the prediction of violence clearly demonstrates that violence cannot be adequately predicted within acceptable limits of accuracy simply on the basis of presumed pre-dispositional personality factors.

An adequate approach to prevention must be cognizant of the fact that violent behavior is multi-determined. It is simply fallacious to assume that explanation, prediction, or prevention of abuse can be achieved by attending to one single factor such as individual personality characteristics. On the contrary, attempts to explain or predict anti-social behavior among correctional officers must be based on a clear understanding of the reality of the correctional officer's working environment.

(a) *Institutional Realities*

> Prison life is . . . a perpetual cold war which at times warms up . . . (Menninger, 1966)

A vast body of literature on violence makes it abundantly clear that violent behavior can only be understood in terms of an interaction between personality, situational, and system variables. Whereas there are undoubtedly individuals who will tend to be abusive to others regardless of their environment, it is not at all clear that such individuals can always be readily and reliably identified. Moreover, the nature of the correctional institution is such that it can stimulate anti-social behavior in even the most pacific or conciliatory individual. It is difficult to remain tranquil and peaceable in an environment in which tension continually looms, where the potential for physical injury and even death is omnipresent, and where verbal and physical abuse from one's charges is commonplace. The correctional institution is a unique social environment in which employees must work in close association with many individuals who have demonstrated a propensity to engage, often without scruple, in rebellious, destructive, belligerent, and assaultive behaviors. The correctional officer's workaday world is a hostile atmosphere — a truly peculiar environment in which continual stress can distort even the most integrated personality. The institution has often been described as degrading for the kept; it is also degrading for the keepers.

> But the days and months that a guard has to spend on the ground (sometimes locked in a wing or cell-block with no gun-guard) are what destroys anything at all that was good, healthy or social about him before. Fear begets fear. (Fogel, 1975: 105)

(b) *Occupational Realities*

It is not only the behavior of the inmates that can be distressing for the correctional officer. There are other less obvious factors which may lead to a deterioration in the correctional officer's behavior. For example, the officer's self-esteem is not likely to be enhanced by his knowledge that he is in an occupation which enjoys little respect, status or prestige. A feeling of helplessness is likely to develop from the realization that those he is assigned to "correct" seem impervious to or actively reject his efforts and frequently recidivate. He is constantly reminded of failure. Feelings of powerlessness and resentment are likely to be engendered as he perceives that policy decisions which directly affect his occupational life *and his safety* are frequently made at levels well beyond his influence. Anxiety is likely to arise from the conflict, ambiguity, and uncertainty inherent in a role whose dimensions reflect the ambivalence of society towards the treatment of offenders and the purpose of its correctional institutions. Hopelessness is often the consequence of the limited career development opportunities that are available to the correctional officer.

> Being a prison guard is a dead end. To date no career ladders have been built to reward those guards who have shown particular promise on the job. The skills necessary for guarding are particularly limited to this occupation. (Fogel, 1975: 95)

Without completing the litany of stressful and distasteful working conditions which face the correctional officer, we suggest that such conditions can lead to a state akin to anomie — a state characterized by a weakened respect for legitimate social norms, rejection of occupational ideals and values, and disinhibition of extreme behaviors including destruction and violence.

The difficulties are compounded by the fact that a prerequisite for the employment of a correctional officer is that he *must* be able and willing to apply physical force and will be expected to do so on frequent occasions.

It is ironic that the correctional officer is hired partly on the basis of his ability to apply physical force and may well be fired when he applies this skill. It is not always a simple task to distinguish between necessary and unnecessary force. It is expecting a great deal from psychological tests or other measures that they be able to make such sensitive discriminations and make accurate predictions of the future behavior of individuals who are likely to be profoundly affected by the institutional environment and the demands and expectations of the job.

Implications

Given the limited success of attempts to predict violence it is unrealistic to expect that a major reduction in violence can be achieved by trying to select out potentially violent correctional officer candidates by an overreliance on pre-recruitment interview or test data. It is problematic at best to predict with reasonable accuracy future violent behavior in offenders. It seems all the more unlikely that one can do so in correctional officers, particularly when we try to do so without a measure of the individual's reaction to the stress of the prison environment. We have become thoroughly disenchanted with the notion that a single small sample of an individual's behavior such as can be obtained through an interview or a psychological test might reliably predict to later performance in the complex milieu which comprises the correctional institution. In the selection process psychological tests may be helpful, even necessary for some aspects of selection, but they (or any other single measure) are not likely to be sufficient and may even be misleading if used as violence predictors.

In developing the following proposal we were cognizant of the fact that an adequate approach to the problems of correctional officer violence must include strategies designed to ameliorate the violence engendering environmental and system stresses of the correctional institution. Whereas we have not incorporated recommendations regarding environmental changes in the present report, we emphasize that our proposals deal with only some aspects of the problem of institutional violence. We recognize that although many improvements can and have been made in the climate of institutions through structural changes, program modification and the like, severe interpersonal stress will always be present because it is and will continue to be the reality of institutional life that men and women must contain and manage other men and women against their will. However, it would be oversimplistic to deal with correctional officer selection without consideration of related manpower system factors which can create stress for the correctional officer. Accordingly, we have included, where appropriate, some recommendations regarding system factors upon which our proposals impinge.

It is our assumption that even without fundamental change in the correctional environment, significant reduction in correctional officer violence can be achieved by means of some modifications in the correctional manpower system. The refinements we propose include a reconceptualization of selection objectives; identification and classification of correctional officer skills; integration of selection and training; development and incorporation of objective assessments of performance; and adoption of explicit contingencies between job performance, skill enhancement, and career development.

AN ALTERNATIVE SELECTION MODEL

1. *Alternatives to Violence*

The basic tenet of our proposal is that rather than attempting to identify the violence potential of correctional officer candidates (however inaccurately), selection and recruitment should aim to assess the candidates in terms of the extent to which they have those skills which will enable them to do the job *without resorting to violence*. We advocate selecting those candidates who have the *potential to cope* with the correctional environment and then training these recruits in behaviors which will enable them to effectively respond to the environmental and system stresses and manage the inmates with skills which are incompatible with violence. In effect, we propose that rather than seeking, in vain, for some formula for weeding out the misfits, we emphasize the recruitment and training of the "best fits." It is, in our view, absurd to assume that by weeding out the clearly unsuitable recruits one is left with the best candidates.

Our assumption is that the most potent method of mitigating against correctional officer violence is to develop a cadre of officers who do not need to be violent in order to carry out their responsibilities and who recognize that their acquisition of alternative skills are admired by their peers and rewarded by management.

2. *Selection as a Process*
In order to obtain an adequate measure of how an individual is likely to behave in the unique environment of a correctional institution one must assess him under circumstances and in situations which clearly approximate the realities of the institution. It is probably inevitable that the correctional officer's behaviors, beliefs, values and attitudes will be significantly modified by his experience in the institution and, therefore, selection decisions cannot be based only on pre-recruitment assessment. Selection must be a continuing rather than a static process and must include *and give at least equal weighting* to ongoing assessment of the candidate's actual behavior on the job *as defined by explicit and objective performance criteria.*

The Elusive Prototype

1. *Positive Selection*
To this point we are in essential agreement with the views often expressed in the correctional literature to the effect that we should professionalize the job of the correctional officer and, specifically, recruit not on the basis of screening out those who are clearly unsuitable but attempt to emphasize in recruitment the positive qualities which are to be found in good correctional officers. Such an approach seems eminently sensible. Unfortunately, it is far from easy to implement. One can find few suggestions as to *how* it could be done.

2. *What Is the Best*
It is highly unlikely that a correctional agency could successfully follow a policy of recruiting the best correctional officer candidates because no clear idea has yet materialized as to what constitutes the best correctional officer.

There is, of course, an abundance of descriptions of the *ideal* correctional officer, but these tend to describe the requisite qualities at the most global level: "educated, emotional stable people, capable of using mature judgment, who are socially adept, understanding, warm, empathic and well educated." These are probably the same traits that one would hope to find in a worker in any social service field. They do not differentiate the correctional officer from the social worker, the pastor, or the industrial executive, and they probably do not reflect very accurately the actual traits and skills required by the reality of the correctional officer's work:

> We generalize and say we want warm, empathic, understanding, intelligent college graduates who can function in an authoritarian role with hostile, aggressive delinquents . . . But the stated qualities and the job setting often appear to be mutually exclusive. The warm, responsive type of person may not be able to work effectively in an authoritarian, controlling setting . . . Is the practitioner supposed to be a junior-grade psychiatrist . . . or is he supposed to engage primarily in acts of surveillance to assure compliance . . . , or is he supposed to be something completely different? . . . We cannot really answer the question concerning the kind of person we need to do the job —*what* job? (Secretariat, U.N.)

3. Best for What?

There is no clear consensus as to the qualities which comprise the best type of correctional officer because there is no clear explication of the *purposes* of the job. In corrections, perhaps more than in any other social endeavor, programs, philosophies, practices and goals are determined not by clear knowledge of what *should* be done but by what *must* be done to satisfy the public, the politicians, the treasury, the academics, the professionals, the labor unions, the human rights activists and many other "experts" most of whom disagree with each other as to the purpose of the correctional institution and its programs. Institutional policies and practices become a hybrid which tries to incorporate too many discordant philosophies and principles. Goals must often be re-evaluated before they are even properly articulated. When the goals of the correctional institution have not been determined and precisely enunciated it is impossible to determine the traits needed in correctional officers to achieve these goals.

A Behavioral Approach

Many authorities issuing recommendations about correctional manpower have urged the adoption of selection and training strategies based on a conceptualization of the *ideal* correctional officer and assumptions about what they are *supposed* to do rather on an examination of what *real* correctional officers *actually* do. The result has been the development of conflicting and/or unrealistic models of the ideal correctional officer which provide no adequate guidelines for training and only vague criteria for selection.

In contrast, we suggest that selection criteria be developed through a behavioral approach to the definition of the good correctional officer. This entails identifying the *skills* which enable the correctional officer to perform his actual tasks in a proficient manner. This approach changes the emphasis of the selection process from a personalistic to a behavioral orientation: selection/rejection decisions would be based on assessment of ability or aptitudes rather than personality or temperament. Selection should be based on assessment of the applicant's *skills* and/or his potential to acquire such skills through training.

The selection of the best qualified candidates is by itself insufficient for the development of a competent correctional officer corps. Correctional institutions are unique and rather peculiar working environments. It is unlikely that very many correctional candidates can be found who can function well in this environment and continue to do so unless they are thoroughly *trained* in the behaviors required for the job.

In effect we are suggesting that it is not possible to pre-select candidates on the basis of their possession of all of the skills that they must have in order to function as good correctional officers because they are likely to have had few opportunities to acquire or refine such skills. Many of the skills, we suggest, can only be acquired in the correctional institution or in almost identical places. Certainly there are similarities and overlap in the work of correctional officers and police officers, between correctional institutions and psychiatric institutions, between corrections and the military. But there are major differences in the setting, in the clientele, in the tasks required, in the manpower support systems, in the role expectancies, in the career opportunities and in the status of the job in the eyes of the public. Many of the skills acquired through experience in police work or in the militia do not readily transfer to the correctional institution, and when they do, may transfer negatively.

Fundamental to our proposal is the recommendation that training and staff development be integrated with selection and recruitment; that the core curriculum of staff training programs become training in those *skills* which have been identified as those which are part of the repertoire of good correctional officers and incompatible with violence. Recruitment/ rejection decisions and/or career development decisions should be made *contingent, at least in part, on successful completion of such skills training courses.*

In our model, recruitment and rejection decisions would be based on objective behavioral criteria. We propose extending the behavioral model such that throughout the correctional officer's career development, promotional decisions become tied to a *skill-based* performance appraisal system. We also suggest that this will serve to provide an initial step toward the establishment of a clear demarcation between the different levels of correctional officers so that a meaningful career ladder can be instituted. Promotion should always be contingent on demonstration of increases in proficiency in required skills.

> Correctional endeavours . . . tend to be viewed as the common-sense application . . . of techniques either possessed by or readily available to most persons of reasonable ability. (But) it is probably the possession of skills that are not easy to duplicate . . . that gives any vocation a particularly high standing. (Geis & Cavanaugh, 1974)

Skill Identification and Differentiation

The operationalization of the proposed behavioral approach to the definition of the good correctional officer which would enable establishment of objective criteria for selection, would entail four preliminary steps:

1. *TASKS:* Identifying in concrete and objective manner what it is that the correctional officer *actually* does: the *task* requirements of the job. These are the discrete units of behavior actually performed.

   It is conceivable that a selection procedure could be developed based simply on assessing candidates on their performance of these specific tasks. For example, in the selection process a candidate could be required to perform in task-simulation exercises and be assessed on his performance. However, such a procedure would seem to be impractical because of the number of tasks and their specificity and diversity and the lack of any clear-cut objective criteria against which to judge a candidate's performance.

2. *SKILLS:* A necessary second step in a behavioral approach is to identify the skills which will enable the officer to perform those tasks. This would enable the clustering of related skills within a small number of categories and thereby allow a more practical and economic mode of selection. It is likely that some tasks require specific skills whereas other tasks have considerable overlap in the abilities required. Accordingly, we can assess a candidate's suitability for performing a large number of tasks by assessing him on a small number of relevant skills.

3. *MINIMAL ESSENTIAL SKILLS AND TRAINABLE SKILLS:* Having identified the skills required to perform the tasks, these would be differentiated into two categories:

   (a) Minimal essential skills are those skills which could not be acquired through in-service training or which would require training so extensive that it would not be feasible because of cost/benefit considerations. The possession of these skills at an acceptable level would represent the minimal essential requirements for candidacy. They might include fundamental communication skills (writing, reading, speaking), the ability to follow instructions, perceptual-motor dexterity, etc. The applicant's skills in these dimensions would be assessed by *objective* tests. In the process which we will propose the candidate would be assessed on these skills and rejected if he does not have these skills at an acceptable level.

   (b) Trainable skills are those skills which the candidate may or may not have acquired at the time of recruitment, but could be acquired through in-service training programs which are cost effective and logistically feasible.

4. *BASIC ENTRY AND ADVANCEMENT SKILLS:* Trainable skills would be further subdivided into Basic Entry skills and Advancement skills.

   (a) *Basic Entry Skills* would be those which are required by the correctional officer recruit if he is to function adequately during his first weeks on the job (when he should be working under the close supervision of qualified correctional officers). Basic Entry skills would be those required for performance of routine procedures primarily of a security nature. In the selection system which we shall propose, Basic Entry skills are skills which the candidate must acquire before he is appointed as a probationary correctional officer (Correctional Officer 1).

   (b) *Advancement Skills* are skills which are identified as those required by a competent correctional officer to perform those tasks required of a fully fledged correctional officer (Correctional Officer Level 2). Some of the skills may be new and specialized skills whereas others may reflect increased proficiency in skills required for Probationary Correctional Officer 1 work. Acquisition of such skills would be acquired through institutional experience *and* staff training, and competence would again be assessed by objective measures.

SELECTION PROCESS

We propose a multi-stage, continuous, systematic selection process incorporating the basic format of the procedures currently used in most jurisdictions, but with some important refinements and several additions. The model incorporates a sequential process in which selection/rejection decisions can be made either by the corrections agency of the candidate at a number of critical points. The model provides the foundation for development of a meaningful career ladder. Within the model the probationary period becomes an opportunity for a comprehensive and reliable assessment under actual or simulated institutional conditions of the correctional officer's behavior, his training needs, and his potential. Assessment of the candidate at each stage would be based on objective measures including aptitude tests, tests of specific interpersonal skills, perceptual-motor dexterity tests, achievement tests and measures of problem solving, leadership and organizational skills. In our model the choice and application of psychological tests would be determined not by some abstract notion of desirable or undesirable traits or characteristics, but by a knowledge of the skills necessary to function competently in the correctional environment.

We should note at this point that all of the elements in the proposed system need not be adopted either in total or simultaneously; each one has particular merits but each must be considered in terms of its specific cost/benefits. The general system can stand and be of value in the absence of some of the elements. We present the proposal in time-series format, but are sensitive to the fact that the times allotted to each segment will have to be determined by manpower considerations. In short we are presenting a working model, the operationalization of which will require consideration of factors other than those addressed herein.

Stage 1

The first stage of the proposed selection process would consist of selecting out during the initial inquiry procedures those applicants who are totally unacceptable for employment by the agency's standards of minimum eligibility (e.g., age, physical characteristics, education).

Stage 2

Stage 2 includes two procedures which might occur simultaneously:

(A) *Minimal Essential Skills*

The applicant having been found eligible for recruitment would then be assessed by *objective measures* to determine whether he possesses, at an acceptable level, the minimum essential skills required for candidacy. As noted earlier, these skills are those which cannot be acquired through in-service training *or* which would require training which is considered economically not feasible. The identification of the skill-level required would be determined by a correctional management policy decision.

(B) *Background Checks*

We suggest that a detailed employment, social and personal history of each applicant be acquired by 1. his completion of a comprehensive biographical questionnaire, and 2. initiating an independent and thorough investigation of the applicant's background.

The applicant would be considered as a *Correctional Officer Candidate* only when: 1. he has demonstrated competence in the Minimal Essential Skills, and 2. no contraindications are revealed in the preliminary phases of the background investigation. (The investigation should continue as long as necessary to provide a thorough check of the applicant's background. A management policy decision will be required to determine how much information is necessary before candidature is awarded.) As a Correctional Officer Candidate, he would be eligible for appointment as casual staff and for further consideration for a position as correctional officer.

Stage 3

In this stage we propose commencing the use of training not only as a means of orienting the candidate to his work and equipping him with the knowledge and behaviors required for functioning under supervision in a correctional institution, but also as a means of *assessing* his skills in the basic tasks of the correctional officer and *assessing* his potential for the more complex tasks which will be required of him if he is accepted for a career in corrections. This assessment would be conducted by objective tests (written and practical) of his achievement of the content of the course and by assessment of his skills through objective appraisal of his performance in tasks (simulated and in vivo) involving routine and problem-related work with inmates. The candidate would not be eligible to proceed in the selection process unless and until he has satisfied a selection board (working with objective criteria) that he has acquired the essential knowledge and skills to perform the tasks of the correctional officer under supervision *and* that he has demonstrated a potential to be able to acquire the more advanced skills which are required of the correctional officer to perform his tasks independently.

Having satisfied the board, his status would become that of a *Probationary Correctional Officer* (Correctional Officer 1).

Stage 4

In this stage, training is again integrated with selection. The curriculum in this selection/training stage, in addition to other subjects judged important for a correctional officer's general correctional education, would focus on *skills* training necessary for advancement. The skills in question would be those which have been identified as required for satisfactory performance of the tasks which are required of a fully-fledged correctional officer at the Correctional Officer 2 level who must frequently work with minimal supervision and back-up and must rely on his own resources for problem-solving. We propose that training for these skills be programmed in a modular fashion, each module including a measurement component which would enable objective assessment of the candidate's skill achievement. By employing modular training the agency could increase the possibility of having some training occur within the institution in order to minimize the time and costs of training elsewhere. It would also make it possible for some candidates, by demonstrating competence in certain skills, to be exempted from specific training modules. Again we would stress that the training program emphasize actual in vivo training, simulation, and assessment in order to increase the transferability of acquired skills to the institution environment and to increase the value of the assessment process. We also favor curriculum development in which only those courses are selected which are demonstrably and not just conceptually related to the *tasks* the officer must perform.

Stage 5

The officer would on successful completion of Stage 4 be *eligible* for promotion to *Correctional Officer 2 rank*. His promotion would represent an endorsement by the agency that it has appraised the applicant's ability to perform the tasks required of this position.

We suggest that a clear demarcation be made in practice as well as in principle between *eligibility for promotion* and *eligibility for appointment to permanent staff*. We suggest that the candidate's appointment to permanent staff be contingent on satisfactory performance of his work in the institution and *not* on the basis of his satisfactory completion of staff training courses. On the other hand, we suggest that his *promotion* to the rank of fully fledged Correctional Officer not be automatic on completion of a probationary work period but, rather, reflect that the individual has actually demonstrated that he has acquired the skills required for the job through satisfactory completion of the requisite courses. Thus we are suggesting that promotion in the service reflect not mere time and satisfactory work experience but the demonstrated acquisition of skills; that it represent not an automatic right but an earned and contingent reward. As noted earlier, we feel that such a policy is fundamental if the work is to be viewed as a specialized endeavor (as it must be if its social standing is to be improved) and if the correctional officer is to feel that his job is not a dead end. He must recognize career development opportunities and pathways.

Relative to the assessment that is made of the correctional officer's eligibility for appointment to permanent staff, we again emphasize that the performance appraisal techniques must be *relevant* and *objective*.

Stage 6

Selection must be an ongoing process which applies not only to incoming recruits but continues throughout the service. The propensity toward violence of line staff correctional officers can be exacerbated, actively or passively stimulated, and even encouraged by supervisory personnel. The line officer must be supervised by correctional staff who both actively discourage violence and just as actively encourage behaviors which serve to prevent violence. The supervisor must be a model of the best correctional officer. Accordingly, an adequate manpower system approach to violence prevention must include effective selection not only of correctional officer candidates but also of supervisory correctional staff at all ranks. We propose that our model of the selection process (i.e., selection by skills/training/assessment) be continued throughout all levels. Obviously required is the development of advanced training courses for each level of staff in which training is geared to the actual tasks required of the position. Promotion throughout the service should always be contingent on skill development.

With increasing emphasis on alternatives to incarceration any proposals for change must incorporate a realistic appraisal of the relationship between the skills required for competency as a correctional officer and those required by the correctional worker in community programs.

POSITIVE SELECTION: A FINAL COMMENT

> Despite the realization that the custodial staff are an important synapse between policy-making and its implementation, . . . they have become a forgotten army tainted with the pejorative labels that it has become fashionable to apply to agents of social control in uniform. (Willett, 1973: 1)

The literature on correctional officers is very sparse. What literature there is highlights the difficulties of the work, the poor qualifications of the officers, the inadequacy of their training and the like. Generally the literature and the resulting public image focuses on their shortcomings and their failures. In our search of this literature we found a dearth of material relating to the *positive* contributions of the correctional officer.

Violent officers obtain much attention; non-violent officers, virtually none. Yet it is clear that there are highly competent correctional officers who have acquired skills which enable them to perform their difficult work in exemplary fashion. Most of the corrections officials with whom we consulted personally knew of such individuals. However, there appears to be virtually no information available as to *how* these individuals work, what techniques they employ, what personal characteristics (behavioral, attitudinal) they share, how they acquire their skills; how they are viewed by their peers, etc.

Rather than adding to the public impression that correctional officers are unskilled, unthinking, otherwise unemployable individuals with a penchant for violence, correctional agencies instead of paying particular attention in research or manpower programs to the violent officers, should conduct research to identify such prototypical officers. Their coping strategies should be studied with a view to recruiting individuals with similar interpersonal skills and/or training correctional officer recruits in such skills.

References

Fogel, D. ". . . We are the Living Proof . . ." *The Justice Model for Corrections.* Cincinnati: W. H. Anderson Co., 1975.

Geis, G.; Cavanaugh, E. "Recruitment and retention of correctional personnel." In E. Eldefonso (ed.) *Issues in Corrections: A Book of Readings.* Beverly Hills: Glencoe Press, 1974.

Krug-McKay, B., McKay, H. B., & Ross, R. R. "Psychological tests for correctional officer selection: Research and issues." Toronto: Ministry of Correctional Services, 1979.

Menninger, K. *Man Against Himself.* New York: Harcourt Brace, 1938.

Willett, T. *Becoming a Correctional Officer in the Canadian Penitentiary Service: An Account of the Induction Process.* Canadian Penitentiary Service, 1973.

Part VII

ORGANIZATION, MANAGEMENT AND RIGHTS

"If only", he may well be imagined to say to himself, "if only I could get rid of these malcontents how smooth and comfortable all would be."
The Roseberry Committee Report, 1883

Prison managers have always had an exceedingly difficult and perplexing task. They must manage inmates who are reluctant to be managed and must do so in ways which please not only the politicians by whom they themselves are managed, but also the social activists, traditionalists, humanists, liberalists and other vociferous members of the public who think they can manage the politicians. The correctional manager, caught in the middle of a gaggle of self-anointed correctional experts, who argue as much with each other as they do with him, must serve too many masters. Complicating the prison manager's task in recent years has been an increasing activism not only among inmates but also among prison guards who are proclaiming, through a variety of means including strikes, their right not only for expanded career opportunities, improved salaries and other employee benefits but also their right to participate in policy making — their right to have some control over their working lives. The paramilitary approach which for decades has typified employee management practices in prison is being severely threatened. The articles in this section examine several organizational and management issues related to the work of the correctional officer and consider how corrections should respond to the growing "liberation" of prison guards which is likely to have a profound impact on prisons in the future.

Much has been written about the oppositional inmate culture which functions in most prisons. In Chapter 15 David Duffee describes a correctional officer subculture which also can be a powerful antagonist to institution policy and practices but which, like the inmate culture, can and must be neutralized or mobilized as a supportive force through effective management approaches.*

In Chapter 16 James Jacobs and Mary Grear discuss a problem which has plagued corrections for many years: the frequency with which guards respond to the frustrations of prison work by leaving soon after they are hired. On the basis of a survey correctional officer "drop outs", they analyze why guards leave. They identify several contributing factors, the most significant of which is race relations between white guards and minority group inmates and between black guards and white superior officers.

The article by Arthur Brief, Jim Munro, and Ramon Aldag in Chapter 17 is included because it demonstrates that correctional officer dissatisfactions and unrest should be attributed not as is commonly done to some personal shortcoming in the officers, but to characteristics of the job. Their research suggests that they are probably not very much different in their attitudes to their work than workers in an industrial setting who also must contend with drudgery, limited task identity, and minimal autonomy. Their suggestions for improving the guard's job satisfactions by job enlargement have been echoed throughout this book.

> If the institution is to succeed for prisoners it should also succeed for staff, which means that they should grow to positions of larger responsibility in the prison service or elsewhere. (Morris, 1974: 111)

In Chapter 18, Joan Potter discusses another factor which strongly affects the guard's attitude and response to his work and has significant implications for correctional management: the unionization of correctional officers. She describes the nature of the demands of the unionists, the increasing activism which, at least in some settings, characterizes their tactics for achieving their demands through political lobbying, lawsuits and strikes, and the consequences of their collective bargaining on prison employees and prison managers.

It is fitting that this book which started by lamenting the fact that social scientists in their study of prisons have neglected the prison guard should end with a chapter by a social scientist, Stanley Brodsky, which presents a "Bill of Rights for the Correctional Officer."

Reference

Morris, N. *The Future of Imprisonment.* Chicago: University of Chicago Press, 1974.

---

* Duffee has elaborated his proposals in his recent book, *Correctional Management: Change and Control in Correctional Organizations.* Englewood Cliffs, N.J.: Prentice-Hall, 1980.

Chapter 15

The Correction Officer Subculture and Organizational Change*

David Duffee

It is not a radical suggestion that correctional officers might have their own subculture. The police, who face many similar problems, have been called the "blue minority," and research has found police to be a very cohesive group, both on and off duty.[1] Other analogies might be made with foremen in industry,[2] noncommissioned officers in the military, and orderlies and nurses in hospitals.[3] The correctional officer, like these others, is a man caught in the middle. He is responsible for the control of those below him in accordance with the rules of the organization, but he is usually (1) not given the necessary tools to do that job and (2) caught in the dilemma that full employment of the tools at his disposal usually causes disorder rather than order. He is stuck eight hours a day among a much larger body of men whom he may not like and with whom he is not supposed to fraternize, but with whose objections to his own bosses he can very well identify. Like the inmate, one of his favorite pastimes is identifying dishonesty and hypocrisy in those above him, and like the inmate he feels alienated from middle-class society, which has asked him to do its dirty work and then ignores him completely or condemns him as brutal and inhuman. Like inmates, he feels relegated to the same position in the organization for his entire life stay and explains the selection for the infrequent promotions as owing to "pull" and "politics." Again, like inmates, he feels the rewards of his job are inconsequential and the punishments unavoidable. So why work? Much like inmates, officers have very little idea of the continuity of correction. What becomes of inmates in the end has only a passing connection with their job. Parole is seen in terms of the inmates who return from it, and "the street" is relevant because it is so far away.

Correctional officers, of course, are not inmates. They have a great deal of power over a large number of human beings and they can leave the prison every day. The fact that they spend a lot of time with inmates and have a similar perspective on many aspects of prison life is not in itself sufficient to generate a subculture. A subculture becomes likely when the officer's situation as described becomes problematic.

---

* Copyright 1974, National Council on Crime and Delinquency. Reprinted with permission from *Journal of Research in Crime and Delinquency* (July, 1974).

Because the formation of a subculture is generally a group response to commonly felt conflict, the officer subculture, if it exists, is probably rather recent. While guards may have had a tense, low-paying job fifty years ago, they also had a rather clear-cut role. Officers were in power and inmates were out. Officers told inmates what to do and the inmates obeyed or were punished. In a confrontation, the administration assumed a guard's story was true and an inmate's was a fabrication.

As the image of the inmate has changed considerably in the last fifty years, and he is treated in a considerably different manner by prison administrators, so, too, has the image and treatment of the correctional officer changed. While fifty years ago he guarded subhumans and misbehavior against them was excusable, whenever it was even recognized, today a correctional officer is responsible for the management of human beings, whose word clinically and legally may stand up against his own. More importantly, most correctional officers openly agree that the change in policy is for the better. There may be some regrets about losing the clear-cut rules of yesterday, and there are certainly many complaints about the lack of power and respect today, but most correctional officers do not and would not care to deny that inmates are fellow human beings who should be "getting a better shake." It is only after this fundamental shift in the generally perceived humanity of inmates that the officer subculture has come about. The correctional officer subculture, more than anything else, is born of the frustrating belief that inmates on the whole deserve better treatment than officers (or others) are capable of giving under present circumstances. Just what correctional officers expect of themselves or correctional organizations is not always clear, but in keeping with the new view of inmates, *they expect something more and different from mere order.* As one officer expressed it: "I'm not sure what I'm here for; I know it is not security. Let's face it — the joint's secure. No, I must be good for something different."[4]

In part, much of the officer value complex may be built on this flight from ambiguity: that officers have discarded the goal of punishment and find in its place only the competing claims of professors, researchers, politicians, managers, counselors, and inmates, none of which they are willing to accept. They are in the anomic position of working for a goal which is negatively defined as the absence of punishment and is manifested by no acceptably measured results and is mediated by no reliably correlated means.[5]

EMPIRICAL INVESTIGATIONS OF THE OFFICER SUBCULTURE

While there has been an increasing amount of research into correctional processes and correctional organization, we still know rather little about the men who make up the largest bulk of correctional staff.[6] Much more of the research effort has been expended on the study of the offender. If the behavior of the offender is perceived, reported, and responded to by staff, this research emphasis is fatally inadequate. If the treated are interacting with the treaters, we must also keep systematic information on the treaters.[7] This lack of information also makes difficult any inferences about one segment of that group. It will be difficult to say officers belong to a subculture unless we can see the divergence between the way they feel and the way their superiors feel. Hence, we must also have data about the values of correctional managers.

Several kinds of information about correctional personnel can be gathered. For example, we can seek to know age, educational level, father's social status, number of previous jobs, number of cars owned, kinds of magazines read. Differences between managers and correctional officers on these kinds of variables might point to differences in values, but they would not give us any direct information about the way staff at any level perform in the correctional institution. This kind of background data, of course, might help us to explain some of the differences between values, if we found some. However, the program of action reported here was based on the assumption that organizational variables would have more effect on organizational performance than other kinds of variables. We assumed, for example, that an inference about a warden's treatment of offenders is more safely built on a knowledge of his correctional goals than on a knowledge of the university attended. Likewise, to know how an officer behaves, it is more important to know his values and beliefs about correction than his father's social status or the level of his income. Also, in terms of alternatives of planned change, it seems more likely that interventions can be made to help clarify and influence his views of correction more easily than can interventions be aimed at changing his father's social status or income level.

The investigation of an officer subculture was designed to employ three major variables: correctional policy, managerial behavior, and social climate. By comparing the scores of various hierarchical levels on these variables on three different questionnaire scales, we can decide whether there is sufficient distance between groups to label the officer scores the manifestation of a subculture.

THE RESEARCH SITE

The research was conducted in the Department of Correction of a northeastern state. Research entrée was gained during a management training seminar. The top managers of the Central Office and of each of the major institutions in the department responded to questionnaires measuring their correctional policy and their managerial behavior before attending the seminar. During the course of the seminar, it was decided jointly by the managers and the consultants that additional data were desirable about the consequence of managerial strategies. Questionnaires measuring social climate and supervisory behavior were then administered to a random sample of 20 per cent of all staff and inmates in the department.

Additionally, one superintendent volunteered his institution for more in-depth study on the correctional officer and inmate levels. A battery of interviews was conducted at this minimum security prison in order to validate the questionnaire findings and to fill the gaps in our knowledge of the process of policy formulation and implementation. Unless otherwise noted, the data presented in this paper were gathered in the departmental survey of six institutions. Observational and interview data were collected at the minimum security prison.

A major field experiment and organizational change program, the first phases of which are reported at the end of this paper, are now under way at the minimum security prison.

CORRECTIONAL POLICY

The correctional goals or correctional policy of the various groups in the institution was measured through the administration of the *Correctional Policy Inventory*.[8] This questionnaire attempts to measure official's relative preferences for four correction models. These models are founded on Kelman's research on qualitative differences in change strategies.[9] Basically, Kelman states that there are three strategies of changing people:

(1) *Compliance*, in which the change agent manipulates the punishment-reward system to guide the changee's responses. Change lasts no longer than surveillance.

(2) *Identification*, in which the changee values the relationship with the change agent. New behavior lasts as long as the relationship is salient.

(3) *Internalization*, in which the change agent provides the changee with new information and opportunities. Change tends to be lasting because new behaviors are adopted and internalized as congruent with the changee's value system.

Kelman's typology was "correctionalized" by distributing his change strategies over a two dimensional grid of specifically correctional concerns: concerns for the individual inmate and concern for the community.[10] By assuming a high and low on both of these concerns, four correctional models emerge.[11] (See Diagram 1.) The inventory using these models was given to top and middle management in the northeastern state before their seminar training, and simpler, adapted forms were administered to officers and inmates at the one minimum security prison. The resulting scores represent the presence of considerable conflict among prison and department personnel. While managers report their policy preference as Reintegration or Rehabilitation (either of which implies high concern for inmates), officers report that they guard inmates in a Reform fashion (high concern for community) and inmates report that they perceive only

Diagram 1
MODELS OF CORRECTIONAL POLICY

		Rehabilitation	Reintegration
CONCERN FOR INDIVIDUAL	HIGH	Identification focus	Internalization focus
	LOW	Restraint Organizational focus (no change)	Reform Compliance focus

LOW   HIGH
CONCERN FOR COMMUNITY

Restraint in operation (that the prison is run only with administrative ease in mind). (See Table 1.)

These policy configurations are interesting in several respects. First, the policy most desired by administration is not reaching the officer and inmate levels. Second, the same kind of conflict was apparent in interviews conducted at other state institutions, and was apparently not a function of variables limited to one institution. Third, reports from various correctional settings suggest that this trend may be standard nationally.[12]

It appears that, at the demonstration prison, the major policy transformation occurs at the officer level. Top and middle managers merely reverse first and second choices, while officers have a completely different

Table 1
AVERAGE POLICY SCORE BY ORGANIZATIONAL LEVEL*

Level	Reintegration	Rehabilitation	Reform	Restraint
Top Administration (N = 30)	<u>80.0</u>	76.8	57.7	48.2
Middle Managers (N = 25)	69.8	<u>80.3</u>	66.0	56.2
Officers (N = 42)	55.2	68.4	<u>77.7</u>	61.5
Inmates (N = 88)	59.7	57.0	80.0	<u>90.0</u>

* Explanation of Table 1. First choice of Level is underscored. All possible t-test differences significant at .01. The correctional policy questionnaire is based on a 1-10 scale for 40 questions. Each policy total has a range from 10-100. Significance of second and third choices may be analyzed in terms of how close they are to first choices. Top administration would rather quickly revert to Rehabilitation (a difference of 3.2 from Reintegration), while officer first choice is much higher than their second choice.

set of values, preferring change through compliance to any other strategy and opting for the Restraint Model, which offers no change at all, to the Reintegration Model. Since the officers have more contact with inmates than any other organizational members, a significant step in modernizing correctional practice, or implementing policies that have more change potential, is changing correctional officers' values.[13]

THE SOCIAL CLIMATE SCALE

While there may be many different specific reasons for the formation of values, a generalized behavioristic interpretation would be that values help to solve an individual's problems. In this case, we should seek a measure of the way in which the organization affects the individual officer. One way in which the organization affects him is the way in which the social patterns of behavior impress upon the individual and support his acting in certain ways. One measure of the "environmental press" upon individuals was devised by Rudolph Moos. Dr. Moos began his investigations on the effects of mental hospital atmosphere on mental patients. He then altered his instrument for application in correctional institutions. The pretest was administered in juvenile institutions in California.[14] It has since then been utilized in several adult correctional institutions.[15]

Moos broke his social environment into twelve fairly independent dimension: Spontaneity, Support, Practicality, Affiliation, Order, Insight, Involvement, Aggression, Variety, Clarity, Submission, and Autonomy. These dimensions are relevant to the world of staff as well as the world of inmates. Of interest for the hypothesized existence of an officer subculture are the dimensions as scored by different staff levels, by managerial type, and as correlated with policy scores.

A random sample of correctional staff and inmates was chosen by selecting every fifth name from inmate and staff files. The total population was divided into five hierarchical levels: (1) warden through lieutenants, (2) counselors and teachers, (3) clerical, (4) officers, and (5) inmates. Since the data are used here to analyze the possibility of an officer subculture, the scores of groups 1, 4, and 5 have been chosen as most relevant. The two other groups are tangential to the chain-of-command and to the major set of interactions that we wish to consider here. The social climate dimension means for the three groups are given in Table 2.

Evident in the data of Table 2 is a steady downward decline from warden to officer to inmate on the positive dimensions of the social climate scale and a steady increase from warden to inmate on the negative dimensions. The significance of the difference in the variation from level to level was tested through an analysis of variance. In all cases but on the dimensions of aggression and submission, there was an among-level variation in the dimension scores significant at the .01 level. In other words, these three different levels of the organization felt considerably different environ-

Table 2

SOCIAL CLIMATE DIMENSION MEANS FOR THREE HIERARCHICAL LEVELS

DIMENSION	MANAGERS N = 32	OFFICERS 182	INMATES 430
Spontaneity	4.03	4.13	2.45
Support	5.84	5.41	2.79
Practicality	6.44	5.88	4.38
Affiliation	6.69	6.39	3.39
Order	6.94	6.51	3.33
Insight	5.09	4.65	3.36
Involvement	4.62	3.84	3.44
Aggression	6.13	6.62	7.24
Variety	5.97	5.59	4.13
Clarity	5.41	5.02	2.16
Submission	7.16	6.66	7.23
Autonomy	3.56	3.52	2.13

mental presses or the three groups felt considerably different social forces that might influence their behavior.

MANAGERIAL BEHAVIOR

So far we have seen a considerable variation in the perception of the correctional policy operating in the institution, and a considerable difference in the social climate perceived at three different levels of the organization. A question arises about the process that intervenes between policy formation and daily action. What variable or variables might connect these three levels in such a way that variations in policy and social climate might be explained?

O'Leary and Duffee have argued that the managerial style of a supervisor is the most important intervening variable between the statement of a correctional policy and its implementation.[16] Several different methods of measuring managerial behavior have been used. Two of the best known are the two-dimensional approach of Blake and Mouton[17] and the autocratic-democratic continuum of Likert.[18] In order to test the relationships of managerial behavior, policy, and social climate, an "organizational profile" questionnaire was devised and administered to staff along with the social climate scale. The questionnaire was originally designed as a "reversed managerial grid," by which subordinates would rate their supervisors on the two dimensions of concern for employees and concern for production. However, the fifteen questions for each dimension did not prove independent. Therefore, the Blake-Mouton grid-format was discarded and a simple continuum was substituted. While the questionnaire does not measure concern for personnel and concern for organizational needs separately, it does measure the perception by personnel of general managerial "openness" or democratic orientation, and "closure" or autocratic orientation.

The original questionnaire consisted of thirty items. When it was seen that two-dimensionality was not achievable, the decision was made to choose the ten items with the highest correlation to the total score. Each item consists of two statements about a specific organizational activity, separated by a five-space scale. The respondents were asked to check the space that they felt represented the behavior of their organization on that activity (see sample below). The items were scored from zero at the item extreme that represented the perception of insensitivity, inaccuracy, or closure in the organization to four at the item extreme that represented the perception of sensitivity, accuracy, and openness in the organization. The scores on the ten-item questionnaire ranged from 0 (or completely closed) to 40 (or completely open).

1. The records which are kept in the organization fail to reflect the real work that is being done.	The records which are kept in the organization really measure how well the job is getting done.
: __ : __ : __ : __ : __ :	

Table 3 shows that the organization is perceived as most open by the role incumbents on the managerial level, and the organization is perceived as most closed by the role incumbents on the officer level. The scores for the counselor and clerical groups have been retained in this analysis in order to demonstrate the relationship of officers to all employed staff, and because an inmate comparison is not possible here. Needless to say, comparison of managers and officers alone also yields a

Table 3

ORGANIZATIONAL PROFILE MEANS FOR FOUR PRISON HIERARCHICAL LEVELS

LEVEL	N	MEAN
1. Managers	31	22.29
2. Counselors, Etc.	45	20.07
3. Clerical	14	20.71
4. Officers	181	16.91

Table 4
ORGANIZATIONAL PROFILE AS REPORTED BY STAFF, CLASSIFIED BY HIERARCHICAL LEVEL

	d.f.	M.S.	
Variance Among Staff Levels	3	354.60	
Residual	267	105.43	
Variance Ratio		3.36	(p>.05)

significant difference. Table 4 shows that the differences in the organizational profile scores among hierarchical groups are significant at considerably better than .05. There is, then, some evidence of correlation between a relatively healthy environmental press upon the individual and his perception of the organization as open or democratic, and, *vice versa*, there is a relationship between an unhealthy environmental press and the perception of the organization as closed or autocratic.

SOCIAL CLIMATE DIMENSIONS BY ORGANIZATIONAL PROFILE

In order to test the hypothesis that the organizational profile may be used to delineate distinct social climates, employee groups were devised that were within or without two standard deviations from the organizational profile mean. Three employee groups were thereby distinguished: (1) a group perceiving the organization as very open (scores of 28.5+); (2) a middle group perceiving the organization as average (scores from 7.5-28); and (3) a group perceiving the organization as very closed (scores of less than 7.5).[19] The analysis of variance performed on the social climate dimensions for these profile groups yielded significant differences on all dimensions but aggression and submission. (See Table 5.)

In all cases where there is a difference of significance, the comparison of social climate means demonstrates the impact of the perception of an open or democratic organization. (See Table 6.) For example, personnel who feel that they are managed in an open manner have a mean Support score of 7.15, while the average group has a mean of 5.95 and the group that feels managed in a closed manner has a mean of 3.92. The open group has a Practicality mean of 7.60, as opposed to 4.18 for the closed group. In other words, persons who feel that they are managed openly also feel that the prison social climate includes a consideration for the accomplishment of specific practical goals. Personnel who feel that they are managed in a closed fashion feel that the prison has little practical value. In the same way, the group managed openly feels it is much easier

Table 5
SOCIAL CLIMATE DIMENSIONS AS REPORTED BY STAFF, CLASSIFIED BY RESPONSE, ON ORGANIZATIONAL PROFILE QUESTIONNAIRE

Dimension	Variation Among Profile Score Levels (open, avg., closed) degrees of freedom	mean square	Residual degrees of freedom	mean square	Variance Ratio	p.
Spontaneity	2	15.18	268	3.52	4.31	p<.05
Support	2	136.90	268	4.00	34.20	p<.01
Practicality	2	157.49	268	5.25	28.54	p<.01
Affiliation	2	107.70	268	4.13	26.06	p<.01
Order	2	53.77	268	6.45	8.34	p<.01
Insight	2	12.91	268	3.90	3.30	p<.05
Involvement	2	123.31	268	6.18	19.97	p<.01
Aggression	2	27.31	268	30.14	.91	p>.10
Variety	2	31.47	268	10.15	3.10	p<.05
Clarity	2	190.00	268	7.30	26.02	p<.01
Submission	2	4.10	268	3.36	1.22	p>.10
Autonomy	2	41.32	268	3.87	10.68	p<.01
Positive Halo	2	19.42	268	1.44	13.52	p<.01
Negative Halo	2	11.32	268	4.84	2.32	p<.10

to make friends on the job (Affiliation mean of 7.77) than the group managed in a closed fashion (Affiliation mean of 4.94). Likewise, the open group feels more Spontaneity, Order, Insight, Involvement, Variety, Clarity, and Autonomy in the prison climate.

It seems clear that the way in which men perceive themselves to be managed has considerable influence on the kind of social situation they find themselves in. In general terms, the open-managed group lives in a healthy atmosphere; the closed group, in an unhealthy and strained one. The effects, then, that management can have on the ability of personnel to interact in open and considerate ways with inmates would seem to be great. It would seem much more likely for example, for officers who feel great amounts of Spontaneity, Support, and Practicality about their work situation to extend the much greater effort that is needed in order to make inmates perceive and react to Reintegrative and Rehabilitative behavioral patterns rather than Reform and Restraint patterns.

Table 6

SOCIAL CLIMATE MEANS FOR THREE ORGANIZATIONAL PROFILE LEVELS FOR STAFF IN SIX PRISONS OF A NORTHEASTERN STATE

Social Climate Dimension	LOW (Closed) N = 51	MEDIUM N = 168	HIGH (Open) N = 52
Spontaneity	3.65	4.36	4.69
Support	3.92	5.95	7.15
Practicality	4.18	6.37	7.60
Affiliation	4.94	6.80	7.75
Order	5.73	6.76	7.77
Insight	4.27	4.91	5.25
Involvement	2.75	4.48	5.83
Aggression	6.90	5.94	6.83
Variety	4.75	5.57	6.31
Clarity	3.45	5.27	7.29
Submission	6.63	6.58	6.15
Autonomy	2.84	3.74	4.63

CORRELATION OF ORGANIZATIONAL PROFILE AND SOCIAL CLIMATE

In Table 7, the direct relationship between social climate dimensions of Support, Practicality, Affiliation, Order, Involvement, Clarity, and Autonomy and the organizational profile score is visible. The higher, or more open, the employee reports the organization to be in its treatment of him, the higher the social climate dimensions.

SOCIAL CLIMATE DIMENSIONS AND CORRECTIONAL POLICY

O'Leary and Duffee have demonstrated that there is a strong correlation between particular styles of management and certain correctional policy choices.[20] Although they used the self-reported *Inventory of Managerial Styles*[21] as a measure of managerial behavior rather than the subordinate-reported autocratic-democratic continuum used here, we might expect similar results. Officers who report that management is more open also report a more livable social climate. Since we know that managers who are the most open most frequently espouse Reintegration or Rehabilitation as correctional policy, we might expect the officers with the most healthy climate to behave most frequently in ways supportive of Reintegration or Rehabilitation. Although the data on this point are admittedly slim, this is decidedly not the case. The social climate dimensions that correlated

Table 7

PRODUCT-MOMENT CORRELATIONS OF SOCIAL CLIMATE DIMENSION SCORES AND ORGANIZATIONAL PROFILE SCORE FOR STAFF OF SIX PRISONS IN A NORTHEASTERN STATE

Spontaneity	.1942
Support	.5319*
Practicality	.4441*
Affiliation	.4293*
Order	.2859*
Insight	.1587
Involvement	.4523*
Aggression	—.0534
Variety	.1202
Clarity	.4280*
Submission	—.0662
Autonomy	.2817*

N = 271 Correctional Personnel
* P = .01 when r = .254

most strongly with open management also correlate, on the officer level, with Reform and Restraint oriented behavior. These relationships are visible in Table 8. Reform oriented officer behavior correlates with Support (.32), Practicality (.40), Affiliation (.36), Order (.34), and Clarity (.56). In other words, the common-sense conclusion that a democratic and open management would produce an officer group who were open with inmates is not upheld. The correlation between organizational profile and social climate would suggest that officers *like* democratic superiors, but the correlation between climate and policy suggests that officers feel very uncomfortable if they behave, or are asked to behave, in a democratic manner with their own subordinates, the inmates.

It is evident that changing officer values about correctional policy involves change in a whole set of organizational variables that at the present time reinforce the Reform preference of Officers. Regardless of what administrators desire or research can show to be more effective with (and more desired by) inmates, officers received no reward for changing their own behavior if Reintegration and Rehabilitation strategies make them less satisfied with the job, or less comfortable in the institutional environment.

Part of the policy formulation-implementation gap must be seen in terms of daily operations of an on-going prison with considerable history behind it. While most administrators favor policies that involved high

Table 8

PRODUCT-MOMENT CORRELATIONS OF CORRECTIONAL POLICY TOTALS AND SOCIAL CLIMATE DIMENSION TOTALS FOR CORRECTIONAL OFFICERS

POLICY

Climate Dimension	Reintegration	Rehabilitation	Reform	Restraint
Spontaneity	.14	.38	—.14	—.38
Support	—.11	—.02	.32	—.10
Practicality	.08	—.06	.40	.42
Affiliation	.24	.10	.36	—.09
Order	.11	—.27	.34	.50
Insight	.46	.26	—.07	—.09
Involvement	.08	—.03	.03	.06
Aggression	—.15	.21	—.07	—.57
Variety	.19	—.35	.12	.17
Clarity	.11	—.18	.56	.42
Submission	.21	—.18	—.17	.45
Autonomy	—.16	.26	—.01	—.39

N = 18 and the resultant matrix should be used only as an indicator of possible relationships. Research into the officer level was not possible under the training grant, except where Managerial Style was an issue. These 18 men filled out additional questionnaires on their own time. They were randomly selected from the officer group, but N is quite small.

concern for inmates,[22] these newer policies have not been implemented from the ground up. Officers who for years have guarded maximum security inmates in the traditional manner of Reform or Restraint have been asked to switch affiliations rather suddenly, but many of their rewards and most of their ideas of what makes a good guard are still based on the traditional system of the paramilitary virtues of aloofness to their subordinates, strict adherence to rules, and unquestioning loyalty to the warden.[23] Hence, the new policies have remained intangible goals on lower organizational levels, and the tangible goals used in the evaluation of daily activity are a poor translation of long-range departmental desires. In such situations, officers are unlikely to perform "above and beyond the call of duty."[24]

SUMMARY OF RESEARCH FINDINGS

The research in this project involved three questionnaires measuring staff and inmate scores on the three scales of Correctional Policy, Organizational Profile, and Social Climate. The data of Table 1 demonstrated a significant divergence between top- and middle-management reports of the policy they preferred and the officer and inmate reports of the policy being implemented in the institution. Table 2 demonstrates that the social climate or environmental press impinging upon managers, officers, and inmates was also different. Managers perceived a relatively healthy social climate; officers, a considerably more strained or unhealthy atmosphere; and inmates, the most unhealthy social climate.

It was hypothesized that, at least on the staff level, divergencies in policy and climate might be explained by the way in which staff perceive themselves to be managed. The organizational profile questionnaire was devised to test these differences along an autocratic-democratic continuum. Table 3 demonstrated that managers perceived the organization to be most democratic and officers perceived the organization to be most autocratic. Table 4 showed these differences to be statistically significant.

Since there was a differential perception of organization by hierarchical level, and also a differential social climate by hierarchical level, the relationship between organizational profile and social climate was tested by analyzing the social climate by level of democracy-autocracy perceived by the respondents. Table 5 demonstrates that this analysis significantly distinguishes different social climates on all but two subscales. In Table 6 the social climate dimension means for the three organizational profile groups demonstrated that staff perceiving the most democratic supervision also perceive the healthiest social climate, and the staff perceiving the most autocratic supervision also perceive the least healthy social climate. Table 7 underscores the relationship of organizational profile and social climate in a different way, by presenting correlations of the two scores. There is a direct relationship between a healthy social climate and more democratic organizational profile scores.

Finally, Table 8 presents correlations that were available between correctional policy scores and social climate for officers. The assumptions that underlie this data presentation are most important to our conclusions. First, we have seen that the goals of the correctional institution chosen by managers are not implemented. Second, we have seen that different managerial behavior patterns are clearly related to the degree of comfort or health that staff feel in their social climate. Third, we have seen that officers, like everyone else, feel more comfortable under democratic supervision. The essential question, then, is what kind of social climate, which might be interpreted as the kind of social reward, do officers feel to be associated with the four correctional goals. Although the number of officers tested is small, the present data suggest that officers are fairly uncomfortable with the social climates associated with Reintegration and Rehabilitation. They find much stronger social reward with Reform and Restraint policies.

This finding contrasts strongly with previous research that O'Leary and Duffee conducted with correctional managers. On the managerial level it was found that the most democratic managers also preferred Reintegration and Rehabilitation policies. The present data suggest that while democratic supervision does provide a healthy social climate for officers, officers do not perceive a healthy climate to be associated with the goals of that supervision: namely, Reintegration and Rehabilitation policy.

In toto, the data seem to support the hypothesis of an officer occupational subculture, the values of which are antagonistic to the successful implementation of managerially desired correctional policy. While officers will find rewarding the social consequences of democratic management, they do not find rewarding the social consequences of the correctional policy desired by their superiors. It becomes crucial, then, to devise ways of changing the correctional officers' perceptions of the social rewards that they perceive to be associated with modern correctional policy.

IMPLICATIONS FOR TRAINING

While we now seem aware that changing an inmate is a much more complex, time consuming, and interesting activity than a high-flown lecture on morality and civil duty, most training for correctional officers (where any is offered) amounts to little more than that. In the course of an orientation class or within the rubric of a training academy, correctional officers may be given several hours of lectures on such things as "Role of the Counselor," "Human Behavior," and "Leadership and Employee Attitudes."[25] While the goal of such training is admirable and its implementation is long overdue, the process used to convey the content is not always compatible with the kind of behavior desired in correctional officers as a result of the training. The most common format of these sessions is straight, stand-up lectures by selected governmental personnel who have some functional relation to the topic to be covered. Lectures may be broken by films and on-site visits, and there is generally some time for question-answer-discussion sessions[26] after the formal talk. In other words, the "courses" in the training academies often tend to be taught in the style of a several-period lecture on the freshman level in a university.

It is likely that an hour or two of lecture on a particular subject has a miniscule effect on even the best students listening to the best professor in a good university. Such lectures are only effective as they counterpoint carefully selected readings and occur within the peculiar university atmosphere where foreign ideas, even in the least interested students, enjoy some prestige. Such is not the case in a correctional training academy where many officers hold little respect for "book learning,"[27] or for the men whose learning is from books rather than the real life of the cell block.

In spite of such problems, the usual educational techniques may be of some value—*so long as the goal of the educator is to impart information.* While it is true that our schools and colleges do change the behavior of the students who attend, it seems likely that changes in behavior can be attributed to the forceful socialization processes that occur in the institutions of education, not to the content of lectures. A quantum of information itself *may* change a person's behavior but it is likely to change his tactics *within* a pre-set perspective and pattern of behavior.[28] The information itself is likely to be received and interpreted within that mental and emotional framework. Within somebody else's circumstances, that piece of information may bring quite a different response. In correctional training where courses have been devised in order to change correctional officer behavior, it is quite possible that the wrong design is being used. If the major goal is to change behavior (i.e., to increase cooperation between custodial and treatment staff), a more effective design would be one that could cut through the ideological differences between the people involved. An analogous problem occurs when a counselor tries to break through the values of the inmate caste in order to reach the individual inmate.

We would no longer plan to change an inmate subculture by lecturing to inmates on the advantages of "doing your own time," or the virtues of obeying the rules. On the contrary, we are aware that such a subculture breaks down when it ceases to have pay-off, as when new careerists take on para-professional roles and learn new ways of gaining status, prestige, and money.[29] Similarly, the typical training program conducted for correctional officers ignores the problem that information received by officers in the course of training will be interpreted in terms of the values that they hold important. If the goal of officer training is to change officer behavior (i.e., to make it compatible with a certain policy), then methods of training should be employed that can change the weight that officers place on certain kinds of information.

CHANGING THE OFFICER SUBCULTURE

There is no reason why the method most recently employed and most successful in breaking down the inmate culture might not also be used in undermining the officer value-set. This strategy involves "use of products of a social problem in coping with the social problem."[30] The basic notion in this mode of change is that people will accept as trainees information and behavior that they would not accept as changees. Toch has had success both with violent inmates and violent policemen when they were enlisted in a project to study and change violent behavior in others.[31]

The problem to be confronted by this kind of technique used with correctional officers is not to reduce violence, but to reduce the pressures on the officer that lead him to be more comfortable with Reform and Restraint behavior patterns. The published literature at this point is so devoid of any reliable reports of what officers think about, want to do, or want to see changed in corrections that it is difficult at this time even to guess what these pressures might be. The suggestions advanced here are a summary of conclusions from a project that followed the research reported in this paper.[32]

The project began as a weekly discussion session involving six correctional officers and the author. The charge to the group was rather vague, because it was thought that locking the officers into particular issues should be avoided. The relevant goal of the group, as far as this discussion of an occupational subculture is concerned, was simply to examine the goals and operations of the institution in order to determine what problems the officers perceived as most relevant to their own echelon. The assumptions upon which the project started were that, if officers were given the role of helping to analyze organizational conflict and contributing to the resolution of conflict, part of that resolution would include changes in their own attitudes and behaviors toward inmates and toward managers. The results of fifty-two weeks of discussion were fairly rewarding. Not only did the officers identify several short-range but crucial problems, but they took organized steps to solve them.

Perhaps the project of greatest risk that they undertook involved changing a departmental policy that required urinalysis of inmates returning from furlough. The departmental policy stated that inmates should be selected at random for this test, the assumption being that the furloughed inmates' knowledge of the impending random selection would reduce drug abuse on furloughs. The officers took the position, however, that it was highly unfair for a man returning from furlough to be subjected at random to 48-hour lockup, if the test results were negative. The fact that six officers with an average length of service of thirteen years should take this position was surprising in and of itself. More telling, perhaps, is that the officers at the beginning of the discussion group project would definitely not have taken the inmates' point of view. It seemed to be the process of the group dynamics approach that changed their reference point.

They became so interested in doing a proficient job of seeking out and solving organizational problems that they began to adopt a researcher's point of view about the value of valid information. Thus, the furlough problem was identified and the officers' strategy to solve it was based upon discussions with disgruntled inmates. It became so important to this group to find out the other side of the story that both an ex-offender and an inmate were invited to become permanent discussion group members.

Through the discussion of the furlough problem and several other tasks that were undertaken, it became evident that the trainee or cohort role was an effective one for changing an officer's perception about the "best way to run a prison." As the project began, the officers were preoccupied with how inmates or superiors impinged upon them, placing them in double-bind situations that could not be resolved. As the discussions progressed, however, their perspective shifted to how all the groups in the prison were, or could be, organized in order to achieve more satisfactory results for everybody.

The major stumbling block that the group encountered turned out to be not their relationships with inmates, but their relationships with superiors. They much more readily accepted the inmates' point of view as valid than they did the point of view of the superintendent. Regardless of the fact that the superintendent had approved the project and had sanctioned their investigation of problems that were traditionally handled by middle-managers, the officers viewed the superintendent's hypothetical veto power as the greatest potential threat to their work and to their new point of view. This attitude on their part underlines the importance of carefully designing such projects from an organizational standpoint. If such a group changes while the organizational environment does not, the potential for damage is great.[33]

The major point for this research, however, is not the development of specific strategies but the evidence that value-changing techniques were rather effective in changing the behavior of six correctional officers. Based upon these principles, many parallel groups with different tasks have sprung up in the same prison. It seems likely to this researcher that traditional manpower development techniques, such as those discussed at the beginning of this section, would have considerably less utility. The transfer of information about correctional policy and "modern correctional practices," in and of itself, is not sufficient to change the behavior of correctional officers. Attention must also be given to the process by which information is gathered and disseminated. Officers in the discussion group had a commitment to gathering and using information about new correctional policy and opposing points of view in the institution. A retroflexive consequence of that activity was change in their own behavior, because they began to perceive social rewards for that behavior that they had previously doubted.

Notes

1. See Jerome Skolnick, *Justice Without Trial*, New York: Wiley, 1966, 42-70.

2. See Bensman and Gerver, "Crime and Punishment in the Factory: A Functional Analysis," Rosenberg, Gerver, and Houton, eds., *Mass Society in Crisis*, New York: Macmillan, 1964, 141-152.

3. On the similarities in a variety of "total institutions," see Erving Goffman, *Asylums*, Garden City: Doubleday, 1961, 1-25.

4. The quotation is taken from interviews conducted in a minimum security prison, which will be described momentarily. The sentiment expressed was representative of the feeling of roughly half of the officers in the institution.

5. See Donald Cressey, "Nature and Effectiveness of Correctional Techniques," *Law and Contemporary Problems*, 23 (Autumn 1958), 754-771.
6. John J. Calvin and Loren Daracki, *Manpower and Training in Correctional Institutions*, Joint Commission on Correctional Manpower and Training, Staff Report, December 1969, 11.
7. Leslie Wilkins, *Social Deviance*, Englewood Cliffs, N. J.: Prentice-Hall, 1966, 230-231.
8. See Vincent O'Leary and David Duffee, "Correctional Policy: A Classification of Goals Designed for Change," *Crime and Delinquency*, Vol. 7 (October 1971), 373-386. The inventory itself is also available: Vincent O'Leary, *The Correctional Policy Inventory*, Hackensack, N.J.: NCCD, 1970.
9. Herbert Kelman, "Compliance, Identification and Internalization: Three Processes of Attitude Change," *Journal of Convict Resolution*, Vol. 2 (1958), 51-60.
10. See, for example, Daniel Glaser, *Effectiveness of a Prison and Parole System*, Indianapolis: Bobbs-Merrill, 1969, chapter on the parole officers' role (protection and service); Robert P. Schenrell, "Variation and Decision Making in Correctional Social Work," *Issues in Criminology*, Vol. 4, No. 2, Fall 1969, 101; and Don Gottfredson, *Measuring Attitudes toward Juvenile Delinquency*, New York: National Council on Crime and Delinquency, 1968.
11. Glaser and Schrag use several of the following terms in their description of correctional eras. Daniel Glaser, "The Prospect for Corrections," paper prepared for the Arden House Conference on Manpower Needs in Corrections, mimeographed, 1964; Glarence Schrag, "Contemporary Corrections: An Analytical Model," paper prepared for the President's Commission on Law Enforcement and Administration of Justice, mimeographed, 1966.
12. David Street, Robert Vinter, and Charles Perrow, *Organization for Treatment*, New York: Free Press, 1966; Kim Nelson and Catherine Lovell, *Developing Correctional Administrators*, research report to the Joint Commission on Correctional Manpower and Training, December 1969; Mayer Zald, "Power Balance and Staff Conflict in Correctional Institutions," *Administrative Science Quarterly*, Vol. 6 (June 1962), 22-49.
13. While the work of O'Leary and Duffee is the only material to date that treats "Reintegration" in a measurable and systematic way, many other studies have suggested that Reintegrative Policy is the most promising method of effectuating successful inmate return to the community. Other than studies already mentioned, the work of Harold Bradley seems most convincing. See "Community-Based Treatment for Young Adult Offenders," *Journal of Crime and Delinquency*, Vol. 15, No. 3 (July 1969), 359-370, and Bradley *et al.*, *Design for Change: A Program for Correctional Management*, final report, Model Treatment Program, Sacramento, Calif.: Institute for the Study of Crime and Delinquency, July 1968.
14. Rudolph Moos, "The Assessment of the Social Climates of Correctional Institutions," *Journal of Research in Crime and Delinquency*, Vol. 5 (July 1968), 74-88; Ernst Wenk and Rudolph Moos, "Social Climate in Prisons: An Attempt to Conceptualize and Measure Environmental Factors in Total Institutions," *Journal of Research in Crime and Delinquency*, Vol. 9, No. 2

(July 1972), 134-148; and "Prison Environments — The Social Ecology of Correctional Institutions," *Crime and Delinquency Literature*, Vol. 4, No. 4 (December 1972), 591-621.

15. In addition to the present study and the Wenk and Moos articles (*supra* note 14), see Colin Frank and Randy Michel, "Inmate Performance Pay Demonstration Project: Final Report," Federal Bureau of Prisons, Jan. 1, 1972 (mimeo.).

16. Vincent O'Leary and David Duffee, "Managerial Behavior and Correctional Policy," *Public Administration Review* (November/December 1971), 603-616.

17. Robert Blake and Jane Mouton, *The Managerial Grid*, Houston: Gulf, 1964.

18. Rensis Likert, *New Patterns of Management*, New York: McGraw-Hill, 1961; *The Human Organization*, New York: Wiley, 1967.

19. These three groups may be considered analogous to Likert's System III, II, and I management patterns, respectively, *The Human Organization, op. cit. supra* note 18, 3-12.

20. O'Leary and Duffee, *supra* note 34, 611.

21. Jay Hall, Herry Harvey, and Martha Williams, Austin: Teliometrics, 1964.

22. They may do so for many reasons. In the training conferences conducted during this research, Reintegration was most popular with top administrators. They work in a time when the culture demands of professional personnel a new, compassionate view of inmates. The Reintegration Policy "sounds" better when reported to outside community groups. It is also intellectually more satisfying to discover a policy strategy in which concern for inmates and concern for community are seen as compatible, mutually satisfying concerns. Furthermore, this group of managers is highly educated and relatively talented — as well as elevated and isolated from the kind of pressure felt by officers. Indeed, all organizational pressures at the top level press for Reintegration, which, as a systemic policy, is most easily comprehended from the top, where interrelation of the entire department is recognized.

23. See Donald Cressey, "Contradictory Directives in Complex Organizations: The Case of the Prison," *Administrative Science Quarterly*, 4 (June 1959), 1-19.

24. See W. Keith Warner and A. Eugene Havens, "Goal Displacement and the Intangibility of Organizational Goals," *Administrative Science Quarterly*, 12, 9 (March 1968), 539-555.

25. Lecture topics have been taken from the Basic Training School course catalogue from one Eastern State. Other training academies provide similar offerings.

26. Trainees at two academies that the author is acquainted with personally usually select the discussion periods as the most rewarding.

27. The lack of respect, of course, may be caused by a number of other factors such as envy and anger at those who are educated, threat to self-image for not being educated, anger at and resentment of economic demands that precluded education, or disenchantment with college or academy programs that

do not reflect the realities of custodial supervision. Also, the suggestion was made elsewhere that traditional university education is only effective in the context of the campus culture. When training or retraining is to provide trainees with information and the ability to use it in non-university settings, considerably more attention must be paid to the process (as opposed to the content) of training. See Roger Harrison and Richard Hopkins, "The Design of Cross-cultural Training: An Alternative to the University Model," *Journal of Applied Behavioral Science*, Vol. III, No. 4 (1967), 431-460.

28. Within the "ideology," as that term is used by John Griffiths, "Ideology in Criminal Procedure or a Third Model of the Criminal Process," 79 *Yale Law Journal* (1970) at 359, footnote 1.

29. See, for example, *Ex-offenders as a Correctional Manpower Resource*, proceedings of a seminar of the Joint Commission on Correctional Manpower and Training, Washington, D.C.: American Correctional Association, 1966.

30. U.S. Department of H.E.W., *Experimental in Culture Expansion*, Report of Proceedings of a Conference on "The Use of Products of a Social Problem in Coping with the Problem," held at the California Rehabilitation Center, Norco, Calif., July 10, 11, and 12, 1963; and see Donald Cressey, "Social Psychological Foundations for Using Criminals in the Rehabilitation of Criminals," *Journal of Research in Crime and Delinquency*, Vol. 2 (1965), 44-55.

31. Hans Toch, *Violent Men*, Chicago: Aldine, 1970; and Hans Toch, J. D. Grant, and R. Galvin, *Agents of Change: Study in Police Reform*, Cambridge: Schenkeman, 1974. This type of change strategy is generally traced to Kurt Lewin's war work in changing buying habits of civilians. See Lewin, *Resolving Social Conflicts*, New York: Harper and Row, 1948; and "Group Decision and Social Change," in T. Newcomb and E. Hartley (eds.), *Readings in Social Psychology*, New York: Holt, Rinehart, and Winston, 1947.

32. A full report of the activities conducted by the officer discussion groups are available in David Duffee, *Using Correctional Officers in Planned Change*, final research report, National Institute of Law Enforcement and the Administration of Justice, N1-71-115 PG, October 1972. The fact that the National Institute of Law Enforcement and Criminal Justice furnished financial support to the activity described in this publication does not indicate the concurrence of the Institute in the statements or conclusions contained therein.

33. For an example of administrative cooptation of a project that had not gained administrative policy approval, see Elliot Studt, Sheldon L. Messinger, and Thomas P. Wilson, *G-Unit: Search for Community in Prison*, New York: Russell Sage, 1968.

Chapter 16

Drop-Outs and Rejects: An Analysis of the Prison Guard's Revolving Door*

**James B. Jacobs
and
Mary P. Grear**

INTRODUCTION

High turnover among rank and file correction officers is frequently cited as a major problem facing corrections. But the causes of turnover have never been systematically examined. In order to ascertain why correction officers leave their jobs, we conducted interviews with a sample[1] of guards who terminated their employment at Stateville Correction Center, Illinois' largest maximum security prison, between 1 July 1973 and 30 June 1974 (exclusive of medical discharge).[2] The 55 respondents consist of 27 whites, 24 blacks and 4 latinos; blacks and latinos have been grouped together in our tabulations. Guards from both of these minority groups view themselves (and are viewed by others) as outsiders to a force which has traditionally been dominated by white Southern Illinoisians.

DISCUSSION

The imagery which forms the administration view of guard turnover pictures a typical recruit taking the job because nothing else is available and staying only as long as it takes to find a better job. It is believed both that most individuals are not suited to work inside a penitentiary and that alternative job possibilities are almost always more attractive. The widely held view that guard turnover is caused by the inability of the average individual to adjust to the peculiar demands of the job supports the position of some of the top guards and administrators that "the situation is impossible" and that demands for radical change in conditions within the prison are totally unrealistic.

The guard recruit's assumed inability to adjust to the prison is reinforced by the informal policy of allowing almost all guards the opportunity to resign, no matter what the real reason for the termination of their employment. Formal records indicate a resignation when, in fact, the guard has been fired. The formal records at Stateville show 24% of our

---

* Reprinted with permission from *Criminal Justice Review*, Vol. 2, No. 2, 1977.

respondents as having been discharged while, according to their own reports, 40% had been discharged (See Table I). Even this figure may be understated due to reluctance to admit having been fired from a previous employment.

The high percentage of involuntary terminations within the prison turns our attention to the prison organization itself and away from the personal inadequacies of the guards.[3] It may well be that a high proportion of those who enter prison work are unsuited by training and temperament for life behind the walls, but this determination of unsuitability is made as often by the prison elite as by the employee himself.

Why is it that so many guards do not remain on the job longer? Perhaps the high turnover within the first six months reflects the fact that these former guards never intended to remain on the job from the beginning, but merely saw the job as an interim employment? The plausibility of this hypothesis is strengthened by "fishnet" recruitment which requires only that the candidate pass a physical examination and not have any felony convictions.

Yet, although it may be true that very few individuals grow up aspiring to become prison guards,[4] and although four respondents admitted that they had only taken the job as a temporary employment, the former guards whom we interviewed report a surprisingly high commitment toward the guard career. A greater percentage of blacks reported having taken the job with a career in mind. While it may be questionable how accurately a former prison guard can recall how long he intended to remain when he took the job, it is still most interesting that 58% of the guards (N = 19) who left within the first six months reported that at the time they took the job they had seriously considered making a career of it (See Table II). Several of the black respondents volunteered that they

Table I

RESPONDENTS' REPORTED REASONS FOR TERMINATING EMPLOYMENT

	Whites (N = 27)	Non-Whites (N = 28)	Total (N = 55)
Resigned	59%	39%	49%
Retired	22%	0%	11%
Discharged	7%	39%	24%
Resigned/Discharged[a]	11%	22%	16%

[a] This category includes those respondents who indicated that they resigned while a threat of discharge was hanging over them.

Table II
HOW LONG DID YOU EXPECT TO REMAIN ON THE JOB WHEN YOU WERE HIRED?

	Whites (N = 27)			Non-Whites (N = 28)		
	Discharged (N = 5)	Resigned (N = 16)	Retired (N = 6)	Discharged (N = 18)	Resigned (N = 10)	Retired (N = 0)
5 years or more	11%	15%	11%	43%	14%	0%
At least 'till certified	4%	11%	0%	21%	11%	0%
6 Months	0%	4%	4%	0%	7%	0%
Didn't know	4%	29%	8%	0%	4%	0%

had prepared themselves for a career in corrections by taking college courses.

Not only was a very high percentage of our respondents discharged, but the majority of all terminations occurred within the first six months (coterminous with the Civil Service probationary period). Of those who resigned, 41% (N = 11) did so within the first six months. Twenty out of twenty-two discharges also occurred during the first six months. Thus, 60% of our respondents left Stateville for one reason or another before completing the probationary period.[5]

Our respondents describe the process of accommodating to the uncommon world of the prison as a disorienting and stressful experience similar to what the inmate "fish" encounters (Irwin, 1970). Many respondents noted that a major source of strain during this period was the ambiguity of their formal status in the prison hierarchy. Because of what is perceived by the top guards to be a chronic manpower shortage the guard fish are sometimes called upon to act as regular guards, but the scope of their authority is ambiguous. Clothed in a special uniform that dramatized their differentness, the recruits found themselves the butt of ridicule from inmates and fellow officers.

The most serious problem experienced by the new guard is not normalizing face-to-face relations with the convicted felons, but the need to accommodate himself to the strict demands of the paramilitary regime. Fifty-four percent of the former guards (73% of the non-whites) who terminated either by resignation or discharge within the first six months attributed their greatest difficulties to their relationships with superior officers (See Table III). If one counts difficulties with co-workers as a closely related phenomenon, a picture emerges of guard recruits, particularly blacks,[6] failing to meet the expectations of old time and top

Table III

WITH WHICH GROUP DID YOU HAVE *MOST* TROUBLE?

	Whites (N = 26)*	Non-Whites (N = 28)	Total (N = 54)
Co-workers	19.2%	21.3%	20.4%
Superior Officers	15.3%	57.1%	37.0%
Counsellors	3.8%	0%	1.8%
Inmates	34.6%	3.6%	18.5%
Administrators	3.8%	10.7%	7.4%
No Group	19.2%	7.1%	13.0%
All of them	3.9%	0%	1.9%

* Question not applicable in one case.

echelon guards or refusing to accept the definition of the situation held by the elite. Culture conflict could be expected to be especially sharp between white veteran guards from southern Illinois who dominate the higher ranks (8 of 9 captains and 17 of 23 lieutenants) and young Chicago blacks who account for approximately 50% of the recruits.[7] In Table IV one can see that the tension between probationary guards and supervisory officers is complicated by the racial dissimilarity between the two groups.

Many recruits, particularly Chicago blacks, indicated that they were attracted to the job at Stateville by a desire to "help" inmates whom they felt were likely being unfairly treated.[8] Their empathy for the inmate was reinforced by the training program which emphasized the socio-economic roots of crime and pictured the inmate as a victim of his environment (Griffith, Note 1; Jacobs & Cohen, Note 2; Liebentritt, Note 4). The

Table IV

RANKING OF SUPERIOR OFFICERS

Attitude toward superior officer with respect to:	Percentage of Positive Ratings	
	Whites	Non-Whites
Job orientation	73.9%	40.7%
Support in meeting job problems	78.3%	45.4%
Support in inmate-related problems	90.9%	47.4%
Fairness in imposing work sanctions	65.2%	40.7%
Praising work accomplishment	65.2%	42.3%
Number of respondents	— — —	— — —

trainee was urged to place himself in the inmate's position in order that he might better understand the significance of ameliorating the inmate's hardships wherever possible. Respondents reported with pride how they gained the trust and respect of the inmates "by treating them like men," and explained how they had made special efforts to satisfy requests for such items as tooth paste or toilet paper.

Because several of these former guards had defined their role as one of helping inmates, it was a source of bitterness that the characteristic response to their efforts was disapproval. Many reported that while they were taught to be "firm but fair" what superior officers actually expected was only formal contact with inmates which stopped short of kindness and concern. While it is important to remember that these are the perceptions of those who left their prison employment, sometimes within six months, nevertheless, it was the consistent opinion of many respondents that success in establishing rapport with inmates was inversely related to chances for certification and promotion. To the extent that new training programs fail to change the attitudes of veteran guards or to prepare idealistic recruits for the traditional attitudes of the veterans toward inmates these training academies may contribute to job frustration.[9]

For guards who terminated their training within six months, the majority of whites responded positively to each of five separate items tapping attitudes toward superior officers (see Table IV). The majority of non-whites responded negatively to every inquiry about superior officers. Non-whites showed most dissatisfaction with training and discipline. It is also interesting to note that the small number of non-white respondents who did not leave until after having been certified (N = 6) replied positively to the questions about relations with superiors, although not as positively as whites staying beyond six months.

The difference in minority and white attitudes emerges even more sharply if we look at the total number of positive responses for five questions tapping attitude toward superior officers. For all whites 75% of the total number of responses were positive, while for non-whites 42% were positive. A significant difference remains even when we control for length of service.

What is most arresting about the discharge rate is the significantly higher percentage of minority officers who report leaving Stateville by discharge than whites; 61% as compared with 18%. Assuming the validity of these self reports, it might be suggested that a differential recruiting process is operating, and that it imposes higher standards on white applicants. Although quite recently the Department of Corrections has sent recruitment trucks into minority areas of Chicago to recruit applicants for guard positions, none of the individuals in our sample was hired in this manner. For our respondents there is no evidence that would lead us to accept the hypothesis of differential recruitment. Both whites and non-whites are routinely hired upon referral from the Department of Labor and also on a "walk-in" basis.

Even if white and non-white guards are recruited by universal standards, perhaps the minority guards perform more poorly on the job, therefore, accounting for their higher rate of discharge? The data do not sustain this hypothesis (See Table V). Within the six-month probationary period the guard recruit can be terminated for any reason. The most common reasons for dismissal are failure to come to work, failure to carry out orders, and "trafficking" with inmates. The first reason is perceived by administrators and top guards to be by far the most important. They claim that Stateville functions with a chronic and critical manpower shortage.[10] If 120 men are scheduled to appear on the 7 a.m.-3 p.m. shift, sometimes only 85% show up. This means certain posts will not be covered, certain programs cannot be carried out, and the daily routine can-

Table V
ABSENTEEISM

I. OUR RESPONDENTS (N = 55)

	Discharged Whites	Discharged Non-Whites	Resigned Whites	Resigned Non-Whites	Total Whites	Total Non-Whites
Median Days DOCKED per month	4.00	.95	.13	1.50	.25	1.17
Median Days ABSENT per month	.67	.46	.82	1.00	.80	.62

II. CONTROL GROUP: Employees who started working at Stateville between January 1 and May 1, 1974 and who are still employed as of February 25, 1975
N = 24

	N = 9 Whites	N = 15 Non-Whites	Total
Median Days DOCKED per month	.12	.20	.16
Median Days ABSENT per month	.90	.30	.61

not run on schedule. Supervisors suggest that the reason men do not come to work is because they do not want to work or because they have a commuting problem or because "they are not suited to prison."

Table V shows the attendance records for white and non-white dischargees and resignees in our sample and comparable figures for white and non-white guards who began employment in the first six months of 1974 (as did many of our respondents who were discharged) and who are still employed at Stateville. The surprising result is that, contrary to the opinion of the administrators and top guards, overall absenteeism of minority officers, both who have terminated their employment and who are still employed, is *lower* than for whites. On the other hand, minority officers are more often docked (not paid) for their absences. This can only be explained if they less often call the prison to explain their absences or fail to cover themselves in some other way, or if superior officers are more strict in evaluating the validity of the minority guard's excuse for his absence.

Table V also suggests that the absence record of whites who are discharged is worse than that of non-whites. Perhaps superior officers are more reluctant to discharge whites? Another explanation might be that a greater percentage of minority guards are discharged for reasons other than absenteeism. Stateville lieutenants and captains in private are not sanguine about the performance of recent minority guard recruits. They suspect that the higher rate of trafficking in contraband with inmates is attributable to the influx of minority employees hired out of the same Chicago neighborhoods from which inmates are drawn. They also object to what they describe as the "shuckin' " and "jivin' " that sometimes goes on between black guards and black inmates. An outside evaluation of the prison observed:

> The new breed who make up the second strata [of guards] are younger, more often black, and come from Chicago. These younger guards have been pouring into the system because it is one job that has opened up to blacks and other minorities. . . . The old guards mistrust and resent the new breed intensely. They feel that the new guards lack discipline, a respect for authority, a sense of the importance of maintaining vigilance against the violent and escape prone convict population. Moreover, and this may be more serious, the old guards feel that the new breed, since they are urban and perhaps from the same neighborhood as many of the convicts, may even identify more, in fact, secretly cooperate with the convicts. (Irwin, 1974, Appendix B, B2)

Records of the Employee Review Board, the three-man committee that adjudicates infractions of the rules by guards, also indicate a disproportionate number of black guards being disciplined and a disproportionate number being *severely* disciplined (by suspension). A survey of cases which the Board heard between January 20, 1975, to April 14, 1975, (N = 137) reveals that 65 percent of the findings (N = 83) involved black guards, while only 35 percent (N = 44) of the guards who were disciplined by the Board were white. Of the eighty-three black guards processed by the Board, 55 percent (N = 46) received suspensions, the most severe penalty. Of the forty-four whites who were disciplined, only 27 percent (N = 12) were suspended. The only lieutenant to be suspended was black.

The kind of extreme racism that has been described in some other prisons has not been evident at Stateville (Jacobs & Retsky, 1975; New York State, 1972; Wright, 1973). When we asked our respondents whether they had experienced "racial problems" on the job, 41% of the whites and 57% of the minority officers answered affirmatively. For those discharged the percentages of affirmative responses were 60% and 59% respectively. Non-whites who were discharged felt they had experienced racial discrimination no more frequently than non-whites who resigned.

The striking difference between the white and non-white respondents is the group to which they attributed their racial problems (See Table VI). Of the sixteen minority officers who reported experiencing racial problems, eleven named superior officers as a group responsible. Ten of the eleven whites experiencing racial problems named inmates as a group responsible, illuminating the familiar picture of racial and cultural conflict between a guard force dominated by whites and an 80% minority inmate population.

Black recruits expressed an awareness that they departed from the stereotype of a "good prison guard" (Goffman, 1961, 87). A few guards, including some young white guards, reported consciously presenting themselves to the inmates in ways that would distinguish them from the traditional guard stereotype. They wore mod clothes, fancy shoes, and

Table VI

WITH WHICH GROUPS DID YOU HAVE RACIAL TROUBLE?
(ONLY THOSE RESPONDENTS REPORTING RACIAL PROBLEMS N = 27)

	Whites (N = 11)	Non-Whites (N = 16)	Total (N = 27)
Co-workers	45%	44%	45%
Superior Officers	18%	70%	48%
Counsellors	0%	0%	0%
Inmates	91%	19%	48%
Administrators	0%	0%	0%

long hair, acted in an open and friendly way — chatting informally with inmates while on duty. This adaptation to the prison brought guards into conflict with superiors which, several respondents believed, was "the real reason" why they were forced to leave.

Institutional reaction to the new young black recruits was also felt at a more subtle level, especially by those who lived on the prison grounds. Officers are given the opportunity to live in the dorm for a nominal rent. To avoid the fifty-mile commute, this arrangement is attractive to many single officers who live in Chicago, most of them black. The rules prescribing dorm life are exceedingly stringent. No visitors are allowed in the rooms except other dorm residents. A man's room, (like an inmate's cell) can be "shaken down" at any time by other officers, whose identity and purpose need not be revealed. The fact that the guard himself may have his privacy arbitrarily invaded was viewed by many respondents as a device for maintaining control over non-conformity, especially by black guards. The result of these unexpected shakedowns, usually occurring while the resident was out of his room, was to create fear, distrust, and suspicion among the line officers. One respondent noted that "a guard is just an inmate with a few more privileges." There was a belief that some officers were spying on others in order to gain promotions.

Even those recruits who did not live in the dorm were amazed to find that as correctional officers, they could be discharged for misbehavior off-duty. Reports of traffic accidents and tickets get back, mysteriously, to supervisors. Upon reporting to work, one respondent was told by the shift commander to return home, "because a man who just had a fight with his wife is in no condition to work." The tower guard sitting above in the gatehouse had observed the argument in the parking lot and passed the information on to the commanding officer.

For old-time guards accustomed to working with a majority black inmate population, acceptance of blacks as co-workers of equal status to themselves might be a slow process. This recalcitrance is reinforced by the unwillingness of many new recruits to look upon inmates as different from themselves. Instead, they insist that it is merely fortuitous that the guard is on one side of the bars while the inmate is on the other. Perhaps this failure of the new recruit to profess moral superiority over the inmates in his charge is ultimately most threatening to the prison elite?

RESIGNATION

Why do guards resign? There are two general sets of variables that can be examined. The traditional thinking is that prison guards resign for exogenous reasons like pay, stigma, commuting distance and family problems. On the other hand, some students of the prison have stressed role strain, working conditions, and relationships with superiors and inmates (Jacobs & Retsky, 1975).

Salary dissatisfaction accounts for only a negligible part of the turnover. When respondents were confronted with a list of factors and were asked whether each factor "influenced you to leave," only 26% chose "amount of pay" (See Table VII). Related to the hypothesis that most resignations have to do with salary dissatisfactions is the suggestion that guards resign in order to take better jobs. Twenty-two percent of the resignees in our sample have been unemployed since terminating their employment at Stateville. Fifty-seven percent of the resignees reported working at a job that paid *less* than what they were making at Stateville, and nine percent reported making the same salary. Only 26% reported being employed at a better paying job.

Our data indicates that the effect of stigma attached to the guard role may be exaggerated. Indeed, several respondents pointed out that one advantage of being a prison guard was that it frequently made them the focus of conversation among friends and acquaintances (see Table VIII). There is a significant difference in which minorities and whites experienced some stigma effect. All but one of the former guards who reported being "embarrassed" about his job was non-white (although this still represented only 37% of all non-whites).

Other exogenous variables seem no more helpful in explaining the decision to drop out. Despite the widespread impression that commuting is a major cause of resignation, we found that only 22% of the resignees

Table VII

DID THE FOLLOWING INFLUENCE YOU TO RESIGN? N = 27

	Yes	No
Amount of Pay	26%	74%
Superior Officers	44%	56%
Co-workers	22%	78%
Administration	7%	93%
Inmates	22%	78%
Lack of Safety	52%	48%
Hours	33%	67%
Commuting Problems	22%	78%
Working Conditions	37%	63%
Your Assignment	22%	78%
Lack of job security	11%	89%
Lack of opportunity for promotion	44%	56%
Desire to return to school	15%	85%
Family responsibilities	37%	63%
Health	7%	93%

Table VIII

HOW DID YOU FEEL ABOUT YOUR JOB AS A GUARD?

	Whites (N = 26)*	Non-Whites (N = 28)	Total (N = 54)
Proud	34.6%	28.6%	31.5%
Just like any other job	61.5%	35.7%	48.1%
Embarrassed	3.9%	35.7%	20.4%

* Question not applicable in one case.

reported that commuting even contributed to their decision to resign. The percentage was only slightly higher for minority resignees (27%).

The only exogenous variable with any explanatory power was "family problems" and there is reason to believe that this reason is quite ambiguous. In many cases former guards characterized their wives' fears for their safety as a family responsibility which led them to quit their job. The peculiar problems of physical safety attached to guard work could arguably be considered an endogenous variable. Our respondents may have projected their own apprehensiveness onto family members. This hypothesis is strengthened by the fact that the single factor relating to resignation that received the most attention was "lack of safety." There is a prevailing belief that a guard can be attacked at any time. Fear was intensified by the January 1973 murder of a veteran white guard and by the seizure of 11 hostages on September 6, 1973.

Whites are more likely to express fear than blacks. For many of the rural whites with little exposure to urban blacks and particularly to the street gang culture prevailing among the inmates (Jacobs, 1974), the Stateville experience was frightening. Several of these guards left within the first two weeks.

Of the endogenous variables, unsatisfactory relations with superior officers is a frequently cited factor leading to the decision to quit. If we combine the 12 resignees who reported problems with superior officers with the 13 dischargees who expressed a similar difficulty, then 44% of the entire respondent group indicated this item as a job strain.

Part of the tension between subordinates and superordinates surrounds the question of promotions. There is a strong belief among the line personnel that "you can't get stripes unless you know somebody." Blacks consistently complained that they lacked entree to the top white ruling clique which determined promotions. Frequently the case of the meteoric rise of a young white guard to sergeant before the rest of his class was even certified was offered as a prime example of favoritism.

On the other hand, many white respondents, especially those with several years of experience, complained that "the only way to get anywhere these days is to be black."[11] They reported that one black had been promoted to lieutenant even though he had less seniority than many whites because the prison is under pressure to show that they are not discriminating.

CONCLUSION

We have attempted to displace some of the simplified imagery which informs the attrition among correctional officers at Stateville Penitentiary and suggest that the same racial and cultural conflicts that divide the inmates affect the guards. We are not arguing that turnover can be explained in the same way in all American maximum security prisons or that it has remained constant over time. To the contrary, our data suggest that like inmates, guards import into the prison the culture of the surrounding society.

We have sampled guard drop outs and rejects rather than guards who are currently employed in order to investigate the strains of the job. We believe that studying drop outs and rejects will have important payoffs in explaining the revolving door syndrome which characterizes the prison's lower participants.

Our results lead us to reject almost every one of the traditional assumptions of prison administrators. It is simply not true that guards are taking the state for a ride until they find a better job. Nor is it true that the turnover situation is explained by "mass resignation" over the issues of low pay and unsatisfactory relationships with inmates.

Turnover is the result of a complex process of interaction between a highly heterogenous and unskilled guard force and a highly in-grown, somewhat inflexible and very demanding prison regime. Race is the most critical variable in accounting for difficulties in adapting to the guard role. If turnover is to be attenuated, then the prison administration will have to discover a more accurate method of identifying and attracting guard recruits who can adjust to the peculiarities of prison or it will have to modify the peculiarities of the prison organization to accommodate the type of guards being recruited.

Finally, this study suggests that the integration of a previously homogeneous prison work force may lead to a break-down of the solidarity of the staff. If racial loyalties are carried from the street onto the job then one can expect the same type of developments among black correction officers that has occurred in some cities among black police who have organized their own professional organizations to protest discriminatory hiring and promotion policies as well as discriminatory policies in the enforcement of the law.[12]

Reference Notes

1. Griffith, S. *A training experience as a pseudo guard.* Unpublished manuscript, 1974. (Available from S. Griffith, Illinois Department of Corrections).
2. Jacobs, J. B., & Cohen, J. *The corrections academy: The emergence of a new criminal justice system institution.* Unpublished manuscript, 1977. (Available from J. B. Jacobs and J. Cohen, Cornell University Law School).
3. Jacobs, J. B., & Kraft, L. *Integrating the keepers: A comparison of black and white prison guards in Illinois.* Unpublished manuscript, 1977. (Available from J. B. Jacobs and L. Kraft, Cornell University Law School).
4. Liebentritt, D. *The making of a correctional officer, 1974.* Unpublished manuscript, 1975. (Available from D. Liebentritt, University of Chicago Law School).

References

Alex, N. *New York Cops Talk Back.* New York: John Wiley and Sons, 1976.
Clemmer, D. *The Prison Community.* New York: Rhinehart and Company, 1958.
Goffman, E. *Asylums.* New York: Anchor Books, 1961.
Hunt, I. C., & Cohen, B. *Minority Recruitment in the New York City police department.* New York: Rand Corporation, 1969.
Irwin, J. Memorandum of convict and staff relationships at Stateville. In *Program Evaluation Design of the Illinois Correctional Training Academy.* Washington, D.C.: Meta Metric, Inc., 1974.
Irwin, J. *The Felon.* Englewood Cliffs, N.J.: Prentice-Hall, 1970.
Jacobs, J. B. "Street gangs behind bars." *Social Problems,* 1974, *21,* 395-409.
Jacobs, J. B., & Retsky, H. "Prison guard." *Urban Life,* 1975, *4,* 5-29.
Joint Commission on Correctional Manpower and Training. *A Time To Act: Final Report.* Washington, D.C.: U.S. Government Printing Office, 1969.
New York State Special Commission on Attica. *Attica: The official report of the New York state special commission on Attica.* New York: Praeger, 1972.
Wright, E. O. *The politics of punishment.* New York: Harper and Row, 1973.

Notes

1. Due to time and financial constraints, we conducted telephone interviews with a 50% subsample. Because we anticipated difficulty in contacting respondents, we sent out letters explaining the purposes of the research and asked that the former guards call us if the telephone number we listed for them was inaccurate. Because these letters were mailed before our subsample of 135 was drawn, four individuals outside the subsample contacted us, and we included their interviews with our results, after preliminary inspection revealed nothing unique about their responses.

Eleven letters were returned with the notation that the addressee had moved, leaving no forwarding address. We were unable to obtain phone numbers from prison records for 19 former guards. Of those individuals in the subsample for whom we had phone numbers, we found that 34 phones had been disconnected. Another 11 phone numbers led us to families of former officers who could not (or would not) tell us the whereabouts of the men themselves. In addition, one member of our subsample had died and two refused to be interviewed. Ultimately, we were successful in completing 51 interviews (38%). Respondents do not differ from the entire subsample by age, length of service, residence or race.

2. The total number of terminations during this period was 269. In a companion study (Liebentritt, Note 4), we followed a cohort (N = 88) of guard recruits who were hired in the summer of 1975. By the end of the six-month probationary period, 63.5% had terminated their employment at Stateville.

3. Clemmer (1958, 182) several decades ago urged students of the prison community to view guards empathetically:

> It is unreasonable and illogical to expect guards to be more social in their thinking than the communities and interest-groups which produce them. . . . The occasional atavism is matched, no doubt, in other prisons and in the free world as well. Guards do not possess the reformer's zeal. They have their own lives to live; they have their own little frustrations, sorrows, and tragedies, and few people, guards included, have a sense of state. The personality problems of employees in prison may be quite as serious as those of the inmates with whose care they are charged. The student of social science does not hate a stupid, brutal guard, just as he does not hate the feebleminded rapist. For the betterment of society both need to be controlled, but the point of view must be kept objective. Perspective is everything.

4. A Lou Harris poll (Joint Commission, 1969) found that only 1% of high school students had ever given any consideration to a career as a guard.

5. Of 440 individuals hired in 1973, 53% did not last beyond six months. For 1974, there were 435 appointments and 267 guards separated before having completed six months of service.

6. While blacks constituted 42.3% of the officers appointed in 1974, they constituted 63.7% of the short-term (less than 6 months) terminations.

7. The increase in the proportion of black recruits in recent years, due to affirmative action pressures, is shown in the following table:

8. In their study of minority recruitment in the New York City Police Department, Hunt and Cohen (1969) found that "Black and Puerto Rican youths, unlike their white counterparts, find the service aspects of police work more attractive than the pay, fringe benefits or job security" (viii).

9. Apparently the organization is successful in screening out the minority guards who are most sympathetic to the prisoners. A survey of incumbent officers at Stateville (in process) shows no significant differences in the attitudes of black and white officers toward the prisoners (Jacobs & Kraft, Note 3).

10. There is reason to believe that the claims about staggering absenteeism are somewhat exaggerated. Many of the daily "absences" under closer exam-

ination turn out to be rescheduled days off or reassignment to training or escort duty. This, of course, does not alter the fact that the shift commander typically finds himself with insufficient officers to cover all posts.

11. Precisely the same resentment by whites of the new opportunities opening up for minority employees is documented in the case of the New York City Police Department (Alex, 1976).

12. In April 1976, a letter was sent to Governor Walker by an organization calling itself the Afro-American Correctional Officers Movement, complaining of racist oppression of minority employees as well as inmates at Stateville and other Illinois prisons and enclosing a list of seventeen demands. The demands called, among other things, for the resignation of the warden and several other senior white officials, for the removal of "Ku Klux Klan organizers" from Stateville, and for a review of all guard dismissals that had taken place within the last twelve months.

APPOINTMENTS OF WHITE AND BLACK EMPLOYEES, AND BLACK APPOINTMENTS AS A PERCENTAGE OF TOTAL APPOINTMENTS, 1967-1974

Year	White Appointments	Black Appointments	Total Appointments	Black Appointments As a Percentage of Total Appointments
1967	532	25	557	4.5%
1968	491	20	511	3.9%
1969	573	35	608	5.8%
1970	382	34	416	8.2%
1971	295	46	341	13.5%
1972	274	140	414	33.8%
1973	251	193	444	43.5%
1974	251	184	435	42.3%

Chapter 17

Correctional Employees' Reactions to Job Characteristics: A Data Based Argument for Job Enlargement*

Arthur P. Brief
Jim Munro
and
Ramon J. Aldag

There are probably few areas of criminal justice as over-researched and under-implemented as that of institutional corrections. The volume of applied psychological and social psychological research, much of which contains specific programmatic recommendations, is staggering; yet, the number of experimental or innovative programs seems to be quite small. While a variety of arguments might be advanced to explain the disparity between program recommendations flowing from research and the number of innovations implemented in institutions, an underlying theme in every argument would be the style and quality of correctional management. For several reasons, political, legal, and bureaucratic, the management of corrections, and especially the management of correctional institutions, has not been particularly creative.

The task force on corrections of the National Advisory Commission on Criminal Justice Standards and Goals (1973:444) noted that in corrections, "managerial thinking has tended to become constricted and reactive to the emergence of problems, rather than innovative and anticipatory."

Such a condition is particularly unfortunate in corrections for it means that not only programmatic innovations are resisted, but that internal administrative styles are such that innovation in personnel management also goes untried. This article is concerned with one type of personnel innovation in corrections — job enlargement.

Job enlargement is generally discussed in the context of industrial organization, and the standard definitions reflect this.

. . . job enlargement has been considered as the process of allowing individual workers to determine their own working pace (within limits), to serve as their own inspectors by giving them responsibility

---

* Copyright 1979, Pergamon Press, Ltd. Reprinted with permission from *Journal of Criminal Justice*, Vol. 7.

for quality control, to repair their own mistakes, to be responsible for their own machine set up and repair, and to attain choice of method. . . . It can also be seen that the process of job enlargement produces jobs at a higher level of skill, with varied work content and relative autonomy for the workers. (Hulin and Blood, 1968)

That some form of job enlargement seems necessary in corrections is attested to by a 1969 national personnel survey conducted for the Joint Commission on Correctional Manpower and Training. The survey reported that while "fifty-five percent of persons who have left the field had done so for economic reasons", thirty-eight percent left for reasons directly job related. (The remaining seven percent retired.) Among the factors most often mentioned by those who left for job related reasons were lack of advancement, pressures of the field and too much bureaucracy (presumably meaning too much red tape) (Joint Commission on Correctional Manpower and Training, 1969:17). While directly comparable data is not available from other fields, it is clear that on an absolute basis the area of corrections could benefit from improvement of task dimensions.

While part of the difficulty revealed by the survey certainly flows from the fractionalization of jobs usually associated with industrial employment, the problem in corrections is compounded by "a philosophic and operational separation of staff members whose duties are principally custodial from those whose responsibilities concern offender programs" (Joint Commission on Correctional Manpower and Training, 1969:445). This tends to mean that, in addition to the factors of repetitiveness and low skill level that flow from excessive work simplification, there is added the alienation-producing factors of status differential and goal displacement in the corrections setting. Almost twenty years ago, Cressey, in a discussion of limitations of treatment in prisons, summarized the guard's role.

> Most guards have nothing to do but guard; they do not "use" inmates productively any more than they themselves are used productively by prison managers. Guards manage and are managed in organizations where management is an end, not a means. (Cressey, 1960:79)

Given such a role, it is not surprising that fifty percent of all presently employed correctional employees (the majority of whom are guards) feel that "they do not have much freedom in doing their job" (Joint Commission on Correctional Manpower and Training, 1969:15).

Evidence from diverse sources generally supports the position that repetitive tasks involving a relatively low skill level are closely related to job dissatisfaction, labor turnover, absenteeism, and low productivity.[1] Research results also tend to show that intrinsic rewards satisfy higher-order employee needs, and that the satisfaction of such needs is closely related to performance (Lawler and Porter, 1969). Job enlargement, with its greater variety of tasks, demands more skill and aids in the creation of a less rigid organizational structure. Ideally, the management climate is also affected by job enlargement, resulting in less direct supervision and more employee participation.[2] This, in turn, should reduce employee dissatisfaction and the organizational negative consequences that flow from such dissatisfaction.

Little empirical work has been done in the corrections field to test the assumptions of job enlargement. The balance of this paper explores corrections employee reactions to selected job characteristics and discusses the implications of the findings for the management of correctional institutions.

METHOD

Research Setting and Subjects

The research was carried out in the Division of Corrections of a Midwestern state. The subjects were 104 participants in a division-sponsored training program and occupied a variety of jobs such as prison guard, youth counselor, and correctional officer. Data was collected prior to the beginning of the program with the explanation that responses were anonymous and that the research was unrelated to the remainder of the program. Seventy-eight percent of the subjects were males. The average age of the subjects was 41.1 years. The average length of employment with the division was 7.1 years.

Instruments and Measures

An enlarged job has been operationally defined as a set of tasks exhibiting the following four characteristics: skill variety — the job provides the opportunity to utilize a variety of skills; autonomy — the job provides the worker with a feeling of personal responsibility for his work; task identity — the job involves performing a sufficiently whole piece of work so that the worker feels that he has accomplished something of consequence; and feedback — the job provides meaningful feedback to the worker about what he has or has not accomplished. (Turner and Lawrence, 1965; Hackman and Lawler, 1971). Included in the questionnaire completed by the subjects were four scales aimed at measuring the degree to which the subject's job was seen by him to exhibit these salient task characteristics. The development, scoring, reliability, and validity of these scales are reported elsewhere (Hackman and Lawler, 1971; Brief and Aldag, 1974; Hackman, 1974). A few sample items and the dimensions they were instrumental in measuring were as follows:

> How much variety is there in the job? That is, to what extent does a person have to do many things on the job, using a variety of skills and talents? (Skill variety)

In general, how significant or important is the job? That is, are the results of work on the job likely to significantly affect the lives or well-being of other people? (Task significance)

How much autonomy is there in the job? That is, to what extent does a person decide on his own how to go about doing the job? (Autonomy)

Contained within the questionnaire was a scale designed to tap the subject's desire for the fulfillment of higher order needs. The scale was drawn from the Yale Job Inventory (Hackman, 1974). Higher order needs as used in this study include such needs as self-actualization and achievement. Previous investigations have shown that individuals with strong higher-order need strength respond more positively to enlarged jobs than do those individuals with weak higher-order need strength (Hackman and Lawler, 1971; Aldag and Brief, 1974; Wanous, 1974). Higher-order need strength was measured by asking respondents to indicate the extent to which they preferred one or the other of a pair of jobs. In each case, one of the jobs was relevant to fulfillment of needs for achievement, recognition, or growth, while the other job had as key elements such factors as pay, security, supervision, or working conditions. For example, a few job pairs for which respondents indicated relative preferences were:

A job where the pay is good.

A job where there is considerable opportunity to be creative and innovative.

A job where you are often required to make important decisions.

A job with many pleasant people to work with.

A job which provides constant opportunities for you to learn new and interesting things.

A job with a supervisor who respects you and treats you fairly.

The extent to which respondents showed preference for jobs offering opportunity to satisfy needs for factors such as achievement or growth was used to attain a measure of higher-order need strength.

Also drawn from the Yale Job Inventory were three measures of a worker's affective reactions to his job: level of internal work motivation, degree of job involvement, and general job satisfaction. Typical items from these scales, each with a seven-point response format, include:

Generally speaking, I am very satisfied with this job. (General satisfaction)

The most important things that happen to me involve my work on this job. (Job involvement)

I feel bad and unhappy when I discover I have not done well on this job. (Internal work motivation)

One additional dependent variable, satisfaction with work itself, was tapped. That measure was taken from the Job Descriptive Index and is composed of eighteen items concerning work itself (Smith, Kendall, and Hulin, 1969). For each item, the respondent indicates that he agrees, disagrees, or cannot decide if the item describes the type of work he does. Typical items are:

_____ Frustrating
_____ Satisfying
_____ Boring
_____ Challenging

RESULTS

Relationships between the Task Characteristics and Employee Affective Reactions

As indicated in Table 1, each of the salient task characteristics is significantly (p<.05) related to each of the affective reactions measured, with the exception of task identity to level of internal work motivation. Thus, it is clearly demonstrated that the degree to which the subject's jobs are enlarged is positively associated with higher levels of motivation, involvement, and satisfaction.

Higher Order Need Strength

Table 2 depicts the differences in reactions between those subjects whose higher-order need strength scores fell into the top third of the distribution

Table 1

RELATIONSHIPS BETWEEN TASK CHARACTERISTICS AND EMPLOYEE REACTIONS

Employee Reactions	Variety	Autonomy	Task Identity	Feedback
Level of internal motivation	.26*	.32*	.06	.37*
Job involvement	.35*	.34*	.20*	.40*
General job satisfaction	.31*	.51*	.34*	.37*
Satisfaction with the work itself	.37*	.51*	.39*	.35*

*p<.05; N = 104.

Table 2

MODERATING EFFECTS OF HIGHER-ORDER NEED STRENGTH

Dependent Variable	Variety		Autonomy		Task Identity		Feedback	
	High Strength	Low Strength	High Strength	Low Strength	High Strength	Low Strength	High Strength	Low Strength
Level of internal work motivation	.47*	.22	.32	.15	.07	—.06	.44*	.46*
General job satisfaction	.47*	.35*	.53*	.35*	.40*	.33	.36*	.36*
Job involvement	.42*	.27	.39*	.12	.36*	.15	.52*	.30
Satisfaction with the work itself	.63*	.20	.62*	.36*	.40*	.35*	.52*	.18

*p<.05; N = 104.

and those subjects whose scores fell into the bottom third of the distribution. All differences are in the predicted direction except for the relationships between feedback and level of internal work motivation, and between feedback and general job satisfaction. Therefore, it appears that subjects with strong higher-order need strength do respond more positively to the degree to which the job is enlarged than do subjects with weak higher-order need strength.

DISCUSSION

The above findings indicate that the results of job enlargement studies conducted in industrial settings generalize to the corrections institution. Correctional personnel respond more positively to a job that offers them skill variety, autonomy, task identity, and feedback than they do to a job that is perceived as dull and monotonous. From an administrative perspective, this more favorable response may ultimately translate into reduced rates of absenteeism and turnover, and into enhanced levels of job performance.

The results further indicate that an employee's desire for the fulfillment of higher-order needs influences his reactions to his job. The correctional employee who is searching for such job outcomes as recognition, achievement, and advancement is particularly sensitive to attempts at job enlargement. In fact, one might anticipate an institution whose staff is composed of a preponderance of individuals striving for the fulfillment of higher-order needs to experience exceedingly low levels of morale *unless* employees are offered enlarged jobs.

Previous research suggests that a well-educated, rural staff is more likely to be desirous of the fulfillment of higher-order needs than a less educated, urban staff (Hulin and Blood, 1968; Aldag and Brief, 1974; Wanous, 1974). Thus, it would appear that the administrator of a predominantly well-educated and rural staff should pay special heed to the potentials of job enlargement.

CONCLUSION

As the preceding data indicate, job enlargement would serve a useful function for correctional employees, particularly for those employees who exhibit a strong desire for the fulfillment of higher-order needs. In addition to the personnel and managerial arguments for job enlargement, a strong case can be made on the basis of theoretical considerations affecting institutional programming. The first of these considerations is in the nature of the relationship existing between custodial and rehabilitative personnel. For many years authorities in the field of corrections have been pointing out the ill effects that arise from viewing custody and treatment as two different and unrelated functions (President's Commission, 1967). Certainly the preponderance of evidence favors viewing all personnel as treatment personnel (Cressey, 1960: ch. 4; National Advisory Commission, 1973: chs. 13-14). One management response to accomplish this end might be to so redefine the structure of tasks within the organization that the enlarged jobs would encompass both functions.

Another consideration buttressing the argument for job enlargement is that of general systems theory (Munro, 1971). Whether or not the administrator recognizes it as such, the correctional institution is an open system from both a managerial and a programmatic point of view. Enlarging the jobs of correctional personnel would be one method of assisting the institution in conforming to environmental reality.

The data in this paper support the position that job enlargement enhances motivation and satisfaction. In this particular case, a good personnel practice also makes excellent program sense by recognizing the openness of the correctional institution and by overcoming the therapy-custody dichotomy in staffing.

Notes

1. For a summary of the literature on this point, see Applewhite (1965).
2. For an extended discussion of job enlargement, see Guest (1957).

References

Aldag, R. J., and Brief, A. P. (1974). "Moderators of affective responses to task characteristics." Paper presented at the tenth annual Southeastern Conference of the Institute of Management Sciences, Miami Beach.

Applewhite, P. B. (1965). *Organizational Behavior.* Englewood Cliffs, New Jersey, 6-35.

Brief, A. P., and Aldag, R. J. (1974). "Affective responses to job characteristics." Paper presented at the Southeastern American Institute Decision Sciences Meetings, Columbia, South Carolina.

Cressey, D. R. (1960). "Limitations on organization of treatment in a modern prison." In *Theoretical Studies in Social Organization of the Prison.* New York: Social Science Research Council.

Guest, R. H. (1957). "Job enlargements — A revolution in job design." *Personnel Administration* 20:9-16.

Hackman, J. R. (1974). *Scoring Key for Yale Job Inventory.* New Haven: Yale University Department of Administrative Sciences.

Hackman, J. R., and Lawler, E. E. (1971). "Employee reactions to job characteristics." *Journal of Applied Psychology* 55:259-86.

Hulin, C. L., and Blood, M. R. (1968). "Job enlargement, individual differences, and worker responses." *Psychological Bulletin* 69:42.

Joint Commission on Correctional Manpower and Training (1969). *Final report: A Time to Act.* Washington, D.C.: Government Printing Office.

Lawler, E. E., and Porter, L. W. (1969). "The effect of performance on job satisfaction." In *Readings in Organizational Behavior and Human Performance,* L. L. Cummings and W. E. Scott (eds.). Homewood, Illinois: Richard D. Irwin, Inc., 283.

Munro, J. L. (1971). "Towards a theory of criminal justice administration: A general systems perspective." *Public Administration Review* 31:621-31.

National Advisory Commission on Criminal Justice Standards and Goals (1973). *Corrections.* Washington, D.C.: Government Printing Office.

President's Commission on Law Enforcement and Administration of Justice (1967). *Task Force Report: Corrections.* Washington, D.C.: Government Printing Office, Ch. 5.

Smith, P., Kendall, L., and Hulin, C. (1969). *The Measure of Satisfaction in Work and Retirement.* Chicago: Rand McNally.

Turner, A. N., and Lawrence, P. R. (1965). *Industrial Jobs and the Worker.* Boston: Harvard University Graduate School of Business Administration.

Wanous, J. P. (1974). "Individual differences and reactions to job characteristics." *Journal of Applied Psychology* 59:616-22.

Chapter 18
Guard Unions: The Search For Solidarity*

Joan Potter

"That jerk! They should keep him in jail forever," shouted a guard in one of New York's maximum-security prisons during an interview last spring.

The guard was not referring to a mass murderer, a drug pusher or a child molester. He was talking about the head of his union, which had recently ended a 16-day walkout at the state's 33 prisons to protest a tentative contract agreement. As a result of the illegal strike, the union leader had been jailed and a settlement had finally been reached. But some officers thought they had been sold out.

Since the officers did win salary increases and better benefits, and since almost all the guards walked off the job when their union leaders told them to, the disaffection expressed by the man quoted above might seem puzzling.

But when looking at problems of correction-officer unions, one must accept the fact that prison-guard unionists are different because many of the issues that anger them are different. In the case of the New York strike, "it was not a strike over economic issues, it was a strike over deep, long-standing issues that have never been dealt with," said a spokesman for the state's Office of Employee Relations. "There is one big difference in correction-officer unions," he added. "The labor-management relationship has a third component — the prisoners." The rights and privileges that the prisoners have gained in recent years, and the rights and status that the guards feel they have lost have often become the focus of unrest. The problem for labor negotiators is that this unrest is not readily amenable to conventional collective bargaining.

During the last ten years, there have been dozens of strikes, job actions, work slow-downs and other signs of militancy among prison guards. Most of these actions have occurred in northeastern states where guards have been unionized for a long time. But the practice of expressing discontent on the picket line is spreading to the South, Southwest and West as guards in those regions become more organized.

Research for the California portion of this article was done by Contributing Editor Rob Wilson.

* Copyright 1979, Criminal Justice Publications. Reprinted with permission from *Corrections Magazine*, Vol. 5, No. 3.

Analysts of the prison-guard labor movement are inclined to psychological explanations for some of the new militancy. Labor actions, they say, often represent something more than demands for higher pay and benefits. They are often protests against disturbing social changes by lower-middle-class people whose jobs are regarded with contempt not only by prisoners and prison reformers, but by the public at large. Increasingly, too, guards are angry at the push by increasingly distant — and, in their view, arrogant — administrators to expand academic, vocational and other programs in the prisons.

Many correction officers also feel that recent court decisions that mandate better prison conditions or add to inmates' rights have made the job of custody and security much more difficult. Officers often repeat two familiar complaints: "The courts are running the prisons," and "The inmates are running the prisons." Court decisions such as those extending inmates due-process rights during disciplinary proceedings, and administrative decisions establishing inmate-grievance mechanisms, have particularly disturbed correction officers.

While the frustration of prison guards has been building for a long time, it is only in recent years that large numbers of guards have begun to join unions and use tactics such as strikes and sick-outs.

The union that represents the largest number of correction officers throughout the country is the American Federation of State, County and Municipal Employees (AFSCME), which counts among its members more than 50,000 correction officers in at least 15 states, including New York, Massachusetts, Connecticut, New Jersey, Illinois, Wisconsin and Rhode Island. There are also scattered groups of guards who belong to the Service Employees International Union, the International Brotherhood of Teamsters, state employees associations and other organizations.

New York and Massachusetts have very militant guard unions. Even more aggressive are the guards who work in the New York City detention facilities on Rikers Island; several times a year the Rikers Island guards strike or stage other job actions to protest their working conditions. Massachusetts has had a number of strikes in recent years, the most recent a two-and-a-half-day strike at Walpole prison and a one-day walkout at the Framingham institution last spring.

More than 100 officers walked out of Graterford prison in Pennsylvania after several guards were suspended. In California, at the same time, several thousand employees of the Department of Corrections and the California Youth Authority participated in a three-day sick-out that was sanctioned by the California State Employees Association. This was the first job action by correction officers in the history of the California Department of Corrections.

In Illinois, the threat of a strike was enough to force the warden to beef up security at the Pontiac prison. In July 1978, a riot there left three guards dead before the prison could be locked down. The prisoners went to court seeking an end to the lockup. "We said that if the judge took the prison off deadlock our people would walk off the job," says Steve Culen, a leader of the local guards union. The judge did not lift the lockdown, and the Department of Corrections adopted some of the security measures the union had demanded.

Other Illinois prisons have also had labor troubles. A three-day strike at the Stateville prison in November 1977 resulted in the firing of about 80 officers.

In Ohio, where correction officers are represented by a number of unions, there have been ten strikes since 1969, including one that lasted 17 days. Much of the unrest started because guards at the old Columbus penitentiary didn't want to move to the new Lucasville facility, in southern Ohio, after the Columbus prison was closed, according to the corrections department's personnel administrator, Lowell Ridenour. The Columbus prison has since reopened due to overcrowding in the system. Two years ago, guards there walked out in a dispute over salaries and working conditions. Twenty of the most active pickets were fired.

Activism by prison guards is really a phenomenon of the past ten years. Until the 1960s, the labor organizations to which guards belonged were nothing more than social or fraternal organizations. These groups offered members some insurance benefits, but were generally not politically active. According to a study of prison-employee unionism by John M. Wynne, Jr.,* the first prison-guard union to enter into formal negotiations with an employer was New York City's Correction Officers' Benevolent Association. "In the late 1950s," the study reports, "this organization represented its membership in negotiations with the city on a broad range of contract issues, including wages. But such occurrences were unusual at the time. The movement toward unionization and collective bargaining for correctional employees did not grow strong until the 1960s."

The unions have gained power by trying to break down the "old-time type of prison where the warden was a hero figure to the men," says Robert Montilla, director of a research project on prison-guard unions at the American Justice Institute in Sacramento, Calif. The unions, Montilla adds, sought to destroy the belief "that management are nice guys to be trusted." By undermining that trust, the unions could shift the loyalty of the guards toward them and could encourage them to want

---

* Editor's note: 1. J. M. Wynne, Jr. *Prison Employee Unionism: The Impact on Correctional Administration and Programs.* Washington, D.C.: U.S. Department of Justice, 1978.

2. See also: J. B. Jacobs & N. M. Crotty, *Guard Unions and the Future of the Prisons.* Ithaca, New York: New York State School of Industrial & Public Relations, 1978.

"somebody who would stand up and talk to management the way they should be talked to."

Guard organizations are weakest in those states, most of which are in the West and Southwest, where collective bargaining by the state and its employees is forbidden by law or by the state constitution.

In Texas, for instance, wages for guards and other public employees are set by the legislature, said Dean Hamm, assistant personnel director for the Department of Corrections. If Texas guards have a complaint, Hamm said, there is an in-house grievance procedure. If they are not satisfied with the resolution of the complaint, Hamm said, "there's not much they can do about it."

Even in states where correction officers' organizations have full union status, they are usually forbidden by law to take the action most likely to get some movement out of state officials: the strike. But public employee unions, especially teachers unions, routinely ignore anti-strike laws, and sometimes do so with impunity. Often, when there is a strike of public employees, part of the ultimate settlement is "amnesty" for those who broke the law by walking off the job.

This, however, will apparently not be the case with the New York guards. In late July, the Department of Correctional Services notified 120 guards that they would be subject to disciplinary action as a result of the strike; it will seek to dismiss 63 of them.

Judges have been reluctant to impose the huge fines that often could be imposed on the unions after strikes, since such fines would effectively put the organizations out of existence. After the 16-day strike by New York guards last spring, a state judge fined AFSCME Council 82 $2.55 million, the largest fine ever imposed on a public employee union. But in July the judge reduced the fine to $220,000, with the proviso that it would be raised again by $1 million if there was any kind of union-sanctioned job action or strike while the $220,000 was being paid. (The judge allowed Council 82 to pay the fine over 32 months.)

The most recent data indicate that about half of state corrections departments are operating under some form of labor agreement with correction officers. There are three different types of bargaining:

• "Meet-and-confer." This is the process often used in states where collective bargaining is not allowed. It consists of a series of meetings between administrators and union representatives to discuss such matters as working conditions and benefits. There is usually no mechanism for impartial resolution of disputes, and no contracts are written. The California corrections department operated under this procedure until a collective-bargaining law was passed last year.

• "Non-wage collective bargaining" allows formal bargaining on all issues except salary scales.

- "Comprehensive collective bargaining" consists of formal bargaining on all employee matters.

In all states where there is collective bargaining, the negotiations are not carried on directly between union officials and prison administrators. Negotiations are instead conducted by a third state agency, often called the "office of employee relations." Since so many of the non-salary issues under negotiation require some expertise in corrections, the outside negotiators must confer extensively with prison administrators.

State offices of employee relations, in addition to negotiating contracts, are also often a step in the appeal process for employee grievances. And if the issue cannot be resolved at that level, it may have to be referred to an outside arbitrator or fact-finder.

Correction officer labor leaders often object to the intercession of outsider negotiators. "I'm not sure that anyone who has not worked within prison confines can understand what officers put up with every day in a closed society," said Hollis Chase, the executive director of AFSCME Council 82 in New York.

In contract negotiations and grievance procedures, there are certain issues that are brought up repeatedly. Union leaders, negotiators and corrections administrators around the country say that, aside from money and safety, the issues that cause the most concern are "job bidding" based on seniority, and the increase in programs for prisoners.

In New York State, job-bidding based on seniority was one of the issues in the last contract negotiations. According to Jack VanDeCar, the director of manpower management for the department, the current bidding system "causes officers to bid away from inmate contact jobs. As a result, the junior officers, the least experienced, have to deal with inmates. We have a lot of officers who bid jobs who don't meet the qualifications. It takes a lot of balls for us to say, 'You can't have this job because you can't do it.' Then they file a grievance. It is said that before bidding all the plum jobs went to the friends of the superintendent, but now we are unable to pick the right man for the job or remove a poor one."

The New York union head, Hollis Chase, sees things differently. "I feel senior officers should be able to bid the jobs they want due to their years of experience, he said. "Everyone is trained to be a correction officer." Because New York guards are on probation for their first year, Chase said, "if a fellow is not fit for the job, they have a year to get rid of him."

In Massachusetts, only the prisons at Walpole and Concord have retained seniority job-bidding for vacant posts (it is called "job pick" in their contracts). Walpole's superintendent, Fred Butterworth, says his most serious problems is that he "cannot place officers in the proper jobs." The other major prisons in Massachusetts have "job pick" only for shifts and days off.

In Illinois, though the union doesn't like it, the contract calls for seniority bidding on shifts and days off but not on job assignments. "I find bidding for assignments is a means to do away with favoritism or punishment," said Steve Culen of AFSCME Council 31, which represents guards in Illinois state prisons. "Here, if they didn't like you at Stateville they'd send you to Joliet."

In Connecticut, seniority was one of the issues in a three-day strike in 1977, according to union representative Michael Ferruccio. In their current contract, Connecticut officers are allowed to bid for shifts and transfers on a seniority basis. Before, Ferruccio said, "employers used shift changes as a form of discipline and they also made punitive transfers."

The increase in academic, vocational and therapeutic programs for inmates is also an issue with many correction officer unions. They worry about outside teachers and volunteers bringing in contraband and becoming advocates for prisoners. New York's VanDeCar says: "There is a great deal of resentment of volunteer programs where officers feel the people coming in tend to disrupt the operation of the facilities. They often don't like the people who come in. They think of them as do-gooders and liberals."

In Massachusetts, guards are resentful of counselors, social workers and other treatment personnel who, according to Michael McLaughlin, president of the Walpole correction-officer local, "are making decisions about inmates and gaining control." The prisoner-classification boards in Massachusetts are composed of three civilians and two officers. If a prisoner feels he was treated unfairly by the board, McLaughlin said, "he takes it out on an officer. I think all civilian employees should have been officers at one time." (This is, in fact, a requirement in some states, including California.)

Overall, what has been the impact of correction-officer unionism? In a study of guard unions, Cornell University law and sociology professor James B. Jacobs concludes that the redistribution of organizational power brought about by collective bargaining "has brought the guards more job security, more control over their work assignments, and more say in decision-making at all levels." This redistribution of power, he says, "has ended the autocratic rule of the warden and the custodial elite." Jacobs does not feel that seniority-based "job-bidding" inevitably undermines the corrections administration nor does he think that unions are necessarily opposed to prison reform.

In his experience, said Jacobs in a recent interview, negotiators in offices of employee relations in various states are sophisticated and intelligent, with interests that go much beyond corrections. "They have to worry about the entire state," he noted. When correction officers complain about the decisions of the courts or of their union leaders, Jacobs said, it is not a true expression of their feelings, but "the normally exaggerated rhetoric of day-to-day political discourse."

Robert Montilla, who studied prison guard unions and prepared a management guide for correctional administrators, feels the demands of correction-officer unions could be detrimental to the management of the prison. "Correction officers with the power of a union are able to exert some of their power over other interests in a prison," he said in an interview. "They may say they will not go along with new programs unless a number of new officers are added, and they can sometimes defeat a program. If inmates are not allowed to have programs with outsiders they will turn inward and make the prison harder to run." Increasingly, Montilla added, correction officers are turning toward more powerful national unions. "They are dumping state associations in favor of national unions which do seem to be able to deliver what the correction officers want," he said.

Mark Corrigan, a corrections consultant and former deputy commissioner of the New York Department of Correctional Services, said he did not think collective bargaining had "worked that well in terms of improving the system." It had, he said, raised correction officers' pay to respectable levels, and it represented "the beginning of a process where labor and management talk." But, he added, "as a regular ongoing communication process not only at contract time I don't think it's worked well." Although the principal demand of correction officers appeared to be money, Corrigan said, "their needs are greater. They need training, political support and a definition of their functions." It is the responsibility of management, Corrigan said, to maintain regular, formal communication with correction officers. For example, the administration should not "dump an inmate program into the system without making the guards a part of it." Improved training is needed, he said, "so security people can grow at the rate of the rest of the system. As you change the system you have to change the nature of security as well."

To take a close look at prison-guard unions, *Corrections Magazine* visited institutions in three states — New York, Massachusetts and California.

NEW YORK: "I'M VERY BITTER"

The first statewide prison guard walkout in New York's history began last April 19 and dragged on for 16 days. The walkout was marked by incidents of violence by striking guards, a takeover of the prisons by the National Guard, and remarkably peaceful behavior by the state's 21,000 prisoners. Although there had been sporadic job actions by independent groups and locals over the years, this was the first general strike sanctioned by the statewide union. The highest number of officers off the job on a given day was 6,832, out of a total of about 7,400, according to Hollis Chase of AFSCME Council 82.

AFSCME's association with New York's guards began 26 years ago, when the union first attempted to organize correction officers. The first local was established in 1953 at Sing Sing prison. By mid-1955, locals had been formed in all of the facilities. Yet, according to Cornell's James Jacobs, membership in AFSCME grew slowly during the early years. By the end of 1965, Jacobs reports, less than 30 percent of the state's guards were organized. During that early period, the union concentrated on gaining higher salaries and benefits for its members. Complaints about working conditions were discussed in labor-management sessions with corrections department officials. According to Chase, "some conditions were corrected in this way, but for others we were given only lip service."

The decisive event for New York's prison guards was the passage, in 1967, of the Public Employees' Fair Employment Act, known as the Taylor Law, which gave all public employees the right to bargain collectively. The Taylor Law also retained the previous prohibition against strikes by public employees, and provided for such penalties as a fine of two days' pay for each day on strike and the suspension of "dues checkoff" privileges (where the state automatically deducts union dues from paychecks and turns them over to the union).

The first contract between the state and the correction officers under the new collective bargaining law was signed in 1970. The present contract is the fifth since the law was passed. The guards have had an "agency shop" since a Taylor Law amendment in 1977. Under this provision, guards who are not union members have a fee equal to union dues deducted from their paychecks.

The walkout over this year's contract started after the state refused to resume negotiations on a tentative three-year contract agreement reached early in April. The union had agreed to a seven-percent salary increase during the first year, but was dissatisfied with some of the conditions attached to the second year, such as the inclusion of salaries and seniority as contract "reopeners."

On the second day of the strike, Gov. Hugh Carey mobilized the National Guard to staff the prisons. The strikers defied a back-to-work order issued by a state court and, on the ninth day, the union head, Hollis Chase, was jailed.

When the strike ended and the new contract was finally ratified, it included, in addition to the seven-percent first-year increase, raises of from 3.5 percent to seven percent in the second and third years and training stipends of $300 in the first year and $200 in the second year. The settlement also included additional pay for pre-shift briefings. Under the new contract, the pay for the 12-week training period is $11,348; salaries for newly hired officers are $13,461; the maximum salary after 15 years is $16,860.

But at least the first year's increase will be nullified because the state is applying the Taylor Law and docking the guard 16 days' pay in addition to the 16 they lost during the strike. But many of the union leaders and officers interviewed said that their strike had been as much a general protest against the prison system and the way it treats them as it had been about wages. "The fines very well could be as big as the salary increase," said Hollis Chase, "but you have to take into consideration all of the feelings of the people who did what they did. Are they talking monetarily or are they talking about the dignity they may have gained taking the boss on the way they did?"

"The salary package wasn't that difficult," said a spokesman for the governor's office of employee relations. The real issues — the ones that did not come out at the bargaining table — were those that have to do with the basic question of the role of the correction officer in society and in the corrections department, he said. Such issues, he added, "go far beyond the standard labor-management relationship and either haven't been dealt with enough or not at all."

Many rank-and-file correction officers would probably agree. Their reactions to the strike, once it had ended, were emotional and uneven. "I'm very bitter," said one veteran officer. "Only new employees got any benefits."

Yet, the same officers who were expressing their bitterness and discontent claimed they were glad they had persevered in their walkout. "We kept our dignity," one said. "We were out 99 percent," said Valentine Kriele, a 20-year veteran and the president of the union local at Coxsackie Correctional Facility, a maximum-security prison near Albany. "We were united. The officers got what they wanted. They got their dignity and they got their respect."

All this talk of dignity, though, raises questions in the minds of observers who saw striking guards at some prisons throwing rocks at National Guard vehicles, and brandishing pistols and shouting insults at prison visitors. But even those in the corrections department whom the officers have opposed are sometimes sympathetic to the stress of their jobs. Lewis Douglass, who was second in command to the former commissioner, Benjamin Ward, and is now a judge, noted that Council 82 was "a tough union, a hostile union." The officers, he added, "have taken a very bad rap over the years, so naturally they're hostile to people like me. Nobody has acknowledged how tough their jobs are. They're caught in a no-win position. People want them to be in control and they also call them racist brutes who beat up inmates."

In recalling former Commissioner Ward, a black former police officer who resigned in the summer of 1978, union chief Chase said: "We had our differences. We felt he was inexperienced with running a state prison system on a day-to-day basis. He was, in our opinion, anti-union. He felt any time the union voiced opinions or objections, we were interfering with his running the prisons." Yet even some experienced prison wardens resent advice from the union, Chase said. "We still have certain superintendents who want to run their co-called castles and don't want any interference. The majority have come through the ranks, but some people forget where they come from and look down their noses at people who are where they used to be."

In fact, said Chase, the union "is always at odds with the department of corrections. We have feelings about the people who head the department and handle grievances. Ninety-five percent of our grievances are denied. Management doesn't think things are wrong that we think are wrong."

The director of manpower management for the Department of Correctional Services, Jack VanDeCar, disputed Chase's claims. The union, he said, does not count the complaints that have been settled internally without an official filing of grievances. In addition to sitting in on contract negotiations and handling grievances, VanDeCar and his staff also become involved in disciplinary charges against officers. Most charges, he said, are based on the abuse of sick time, tardiness and excessive absenteeism. Occasionally, there are charges of misuse of a firearm, bringing in contraband or allowing an escape. Guards are rarely charged with assaulting inmates, VanDeCar said, but if the charges are proven the officers can be dismissed.

Recently, VanDeCar said, Council 82 was charged by individual officers with failing to represent them properly in disciplinary procedures. "The union will defend an officer in any case now," VanDeCar said. "And no matter how much the officers may complain about the union, I'm sure the majority of them run to the union when they get into trouble."

MASSACHUSETTS: GIVING AWAY THE SYSTEM

On the cover of the April issue of the *Bay State Employee,* a publication of AFSCME Council 93, there was a picture of a disgruntled-looking correction officer holding a portable television set. "TV Violence at Walpole" announced a caption beneath the picture, referring to the 650-inmate maximum-security prison outside of Boston. Correction officers had staged a two and a half day strike there over safety conditions in Block 10, a dismal, filthy 60-cell segregation unit where prisoners from facilities all over the state are sent for serious disciplinary infractions.

The strike was set off when a Block-10 prisoner, according to a union spokesman, threw a mixture of cleaning fluid and excrement into the eyes of a guard. Also, according to the striking officers, some prisoners in Block 10 had used antennas from portable television sets and radios as weapons against the guards. As a result of the walkout, radios and television sets were taken out of the cells on Block 10; some were removed permanently.

Those Block-10 inmates who were considered the most troublesome were moved into the lower tier of the two-story unit, and inmates were required to be handcuffed before they were taken out of their cells for showers or visits, both of which happen infrequently.

The strike was the latest in a long series of disruptions, job actions and walkouts at Walpole and other Massachusetts prisons.

Correction officers in Massachusetts date the beginning of their problems to January 1972, when reformer John O. Boone was named commissioner of corrections. Boone was publicly critical of correction officers and sympathetic to inmates, particularly in his liberal furlough program and his support of inmate organizations. "The officers came to believe that they had no support to enforce regulations," recalled Larry Meachum, the present commissioner. "The senior officers did not require junior officers to do their job. Attendance started to drop and there was an abuse of sick leave. The officers became more vocal and got contract concessions. The system was given away on two levels — to the officers and to the inmates."

Things got so bad, recalled the present Walpole superintendent, Fred Butterworth, that guards even refused to enter the cellblocks. "Prior to 1972 I was always proud to go to work and enjoyed going to work," says Red Taylor, who was a guard for 19 years and now works full time for Council 93. "After 1972, I couldn't say the same. There was such a drastic change in working conditions that came about when the department placed emphasis on treatment at the expense of security." Boone, who is now the urban affairs director of a Boston TV station, blamed his problems partly on the union. "They would like anybody who would give them absolute control over the prisoners," he said. He also blames his troubles on the temper of the times. "I came here at the height of the civil rights movement and behind Attica," he recalled. "All prisons were in a turmoil."

After 17 months of sometimes violent unrest among both inmates and guards, Boone was fired by Gov. Francis Sargent and replaced by Frank Hall, who had been a prison official in North Carolina. Hall, who is now the head of New York's Division for Youth, says the relationship between the guards and the department improved during his tenure. When he entered the department, "it was a war zone," Hall recalled. But by the time he left, "management could sit down from a position of strength and meet with the union. It was not like a few years back when the department had to do whatever the union wanted." Hall said he had "kept a fairly open door and was reasonably receptive to sitting down with people to look at problems."

Not everyone agrees with Hall's appraisal. The department's relationship with the guards during Hall's tenure was only "bearable," according to one central staff member. The current president of the Walpole local, Michael McLaughlin, said Hall was "far more subtle" than Boone, but did not like correction officers and was "not in tune with safety and security." In fact, said Red Taylor, "the correction officer's lot has not improved" since the bleak days of 1972.

One real change, however, was the advent of collective bargaining for public employees, instituted by law in Massachusetts in 1974. Correction officers signed their first statewide contract with the department on July 1, 1977. Before then, salaries and benefits were determined by the state legislature, and agreements on conditions and job bidding were made with individual superintendents. Even before 1977, all but two local correction officer organizations had become affiliated with AFSCME. In 1977, these two, Norfolk and Bridgewater, voted to join AFSCME, and Council 93 became the bargaining agent for all 1,800 correction officers in the state. (The council also represents 48,000 other Massachusetts public employees including hospital and mental health workers.)

The 1977 contract, which was for three years, raised starting salaries from $10,778 to $11,078. But officers hired after July 1, 1977, lost their right to "step" raises — automatic increases computed according to seniority. This could mean a difference of as much as $1,800 a year to someone hired after that date, according to Jeff Bolger, the Department of Correction's labor relations specialist.

Today, even with a total representation by AFSCME, there are substantial differences between locals. Walpole had always been the most strife-ridden institution, and the local there, according to Meachum, "has a tendency to walk rather than talk." Some observers place part of the blame for the dissension on the local's president, Michael McLaughlin, whom one administrator called a "publicity-seeking hothead." McLaughlin, though, said management "put us on strike 16 days from August 1977 to March 1979." Most of the walkouts, he said, involved safety issues. He claimed that 39 officers were stabbed or beaten in Block 10 between last January 1 and March 25.

Those inmates who are considered the most troublesome in the state live on the lower tier of Walpole's Block 10, which consists of two units of 15 cells facing a wall that is layered with food, garbage and feces that have been thrown at it over the years. One day last June, the four-foot walkways between the cells and the walls were covered with piles of paper, garbage and other nondescript objects. On one walkway, a small fire was burning a pile of papers. A barred gate at the end of each tier was kept locked. On the other side of the gate, two guards loitered, occasionally trading insults with the prisoners. One guard wore his shirt completely unbuttoned with his bare chest on view to both prisoners and visitors. Block 10 prisoners are reviewed every 90 days; it is possible for a prisoner to stay there as long as three or four years.

The rest of Walpole is divided into two sections. Section A houses medium-security men who are allowed to work and attend programs. The blocks are clean and one has even been decorated with paintings of climbing vines and flowers. Section B houses maximum-security men who are allowed to work only in the blocks and corridors and who have no access to programs. The three-tiered cellblocks in Section B are dirty and garbage-littered and the walls are covered with splotches and stains. The atmosphere is chaotic and oppressive. A recent lawsuit filed in federal court by Walpole prisoners against the Department of Correction asked that the prison be made fit for habitation and that programs and work be offered to prisoners in the maximum-security section. According to Judy Stalus, a lawyer with Massachusetts Correctional Legal Services, which is representing the inmates, "the guards are a major part of the problem at Walpole. Commissioners, historically, have never really tried to take control of Walpole from the guards. They didn't care about the prisoners but they didn't care about the guards either. That affects the way people feel about their jobs and influences the whole system."

Conversations with line officers in two Massachusetts prisons lend support to Stalus's assessment. Rank-and-file guards feel alienated from both the prison administration and the union leaders. "I have no use for the union," said a Walpole guard. "They don't represent us. The leaders get what they want." An officer in Walpole's maximum-security section said: "Safety is the main concern. We talk to the union and nothing happens. We need better management."

A guard at Norfolk prison, a 730-inmate facility which houses many long-termers, was even more emphatic. "I think they ought to throw out collective bargaining," he said. "We used to be our own little union. I don't think [Council 93] can effectively bargain for correction officers when they represent 50,000 people. In the last negotiation we were sold down the river."

Another officer reminisced about the past, when the warden really ran the prison. "In the old days, the superintendent used to maintain supervision of officers and inmates," he said. Now, he went on, "superintendents and commissioners come and go, and the prisons are controlled by court decisions that favor inmate rights." "I prefer a strong independent local," said one Norfolk officer, "but maybe under collective bargaining we will need a big union. We lost step raises in the last contract. We'll see what happens next time."

Norfolk's superintendent, William Callahan, is one of two Massachusetts superintendents who came up through the ranks. (The other is Walpole's Butterworth.) Norfolk has a less volatile prisoner population than Walpole and a more relaxed atmosphere, but the remains of a rash of dormitory fires are still in evidence. Callahan said he has few problems with the union because the executive board of the Norfolk local tries to work out officer grievances before they are taken to him. "Here at Norfolk the executive committee was known to do some filtering before they went in to the boss," he said. Perhaps other locals are more militant, Callahan said, "because of the composition of the executive board. Maybe people here don't have the same blind aspirations as people on other executive committees."

CALIFORNIA: THREE-WAY BATTLE

In California, where a collective-bargaining law was passed last year, the major union activity during the summer was the competition between the three organizations that are vying to represent the 13,000 employees of the state Department of Corrections and California Youth Authority.

The new law stipulates that only one union can represent each public employee bargaining unit. The units, one of which will probably include most correctional employees, will be established by the state Public Employee Relations Board. State workers will not vote for the union of their choice until the board completes its work at the end of the year.

Meanwhile, state employees must continue to depend on the largesse of the legislature and the governor. And some of them, including correction officers, are already getting more militant in anticipation of their new status. In April, prison guards across the state staged a sick-out to express their dissatisfaction with a proposal by Gov. Jerry Brown to raise their pay 16 percent — eight percent last July 1 and eight percent more on Jan. 1. The action was a little premature, since the legislature rejected Brown's plan and instead awarded state employees, including the guards, a flat 14.5 percent pay increase retroactive to last Oct. 1.

The April job-action actually had more to do with union politics than with Brown's salary proposal. Three unions — the California Correctional Officers Association (CCOA), the California State Employees Association (CSEA) and the International Brotherhood of Teamsters — are competing for the loyalty of the correctional workers in anticipation of the union election. The CSEA is leading the race; it claims 4,500 correctional workers as members. The CCOA claim about 2,500 and the Teamsters only 600. The CSEA supported the action while the other two unions did not.

The sick-out involved an estimated 1,020 to 4,000 employees of the Department of Corrections and the Youth Authority (the lower figure was the state's estimate; the larger was the CSEA's.) The action was the result of a grass-roots movement among corrections employees who were members of several different employee organizations.

According to Ken Brown, an executive of the CCOA, the job action damaged negotiations with the governor's office. "We felt the manner of approach was only negative," Brown said. "It's inconceivable to us that you first strike, then sit down at the bargaining table. There's nothing wrong with the idea of a job action, but it's the last resort."

Florence Gardner, a correction officer at the California Institution for Women at Frontera and one of the organizers of the action, said, however, that the sick-out was long overdue and was a complete success. "You can't hold back a mass of people when they're angry," she said, "and you can't fight for something after the fact. You've got to do it when it's happening."

According to Gardner, a majority of the correction officers believe they are "being blatantly shafted" by the governor. They feel, she said, that they face the highest stress, the worst conditions and the lowest pay of any criminal justice group in the state. With no new facilities foreseen in the immediate future, and some prisons already doubling up inmates, the officers see conditions deteriorating in the coming year. At the same time, they see already lagging salaries possibly being frozen while the cost of living soars. Besides money, the officers are concerned with questions of safety and custodial equipment.

The competition between the three organizations, according to Donald Novey, a correction officer at Folsom prison and a CCOA official, has created "a mud-slinging, rotten affair over salaries. You've got three major unions cutting throats, and the poor officer in the middle is going to get screwed."

Each of the three organizations is offering different benefits to corrections employees. According to Robert Bark, director of the CSEA, "One of our main features is that we are large. We have the capital to make collective bargaining work." The union has a staff of six full-time lobbyists and attorneys and a five-member field staff. The Teamsters union, although numerically weak among corrections employees, has the power of its national organization behind it, and offers professional organization teams for local job actions.

The CCOA claims that its main strength is its specific focus on correctional problems. "We won't be diluted in terms of determining issues," said Ken Brown. "We won't have to consider anything else beyond the needs of the correction officers. We'll have less conflict of interest."

As the three major unions compete for members, a number of smaller employee organizations have banded together to oppose the collective bargaining law. One of them, the Public Employee Service Association, is suing the state, challenging the constitutionality of the statute. The legal basis of the lawsuit, which is supported by the state Attorney General's office, is that the California constitution states specifically that the State Personnel Board has authority over the setting of wages and salaries.

The new collective-bargaining law, according to Talmadge Jones of the Attorney General's office, circumvents the intent of the framers of the state constitution. "They clearly wanted the spoils system out of the state government," he said. The old system was based on a civil-service merit scale, with salaries set by the personnel board. "The legislature has had the power to make the pie," Jones said, "but the personnel board cuts it up." By putting that power in the hands of unions and the governor, Jones said, the law "politicizes what was intended to be a non-political system, and there is no question that this gives the governor much more power."

According to Best, the new provisions remove the choice of representation that correctional employees used to have. Before, he said, the smaller groups survived because of an automatic dues check-off system. "Under the new law," he said, "they lose that. Either you declare yourself a labor association and get in and fight, winner take all, or you agree to withdraw and become a little social club."

Best said there were many employees who belonged to several organizations and wanted to continue to belong to them. "They would rather be represented by a tight group of people who they work with daily," he said, "and not be sucked into a very large, very remote professional labor organization where they see themselves getting lost."

Chapter 19
A Bill of Rights for the Correctional Officer*

Stanley L. Brodsky

Demands are increasingly made by many segments of the American population in the forms of legal actions, informal requests, and organized political activity. Public attention has been drawn to advocates of women's rights, of rights of Blacks and Chicanos, rights of homosexuals, rights of college students, and of rights of welfare recipients.

In this medley of loud demands, the legal rights of accused persons and convicted offenders have been in good voice. The tune includes themes related to the charging process, adjudication, right to counsel, freedom from self-incrimination, and illegal search and seizure. Any correctional administrator will attest to a continuation of such legal concerns after imprisonment. Inmates individually, as well as in class actions, are submitting writs and filing suits at an unprecedented pace.

Law enforcement personnel have had a similarly vocal expansion of demands for rights, privileges, and status. The development of police strikes, organized political activities, police unions, and the occasional emergence of police commissioners as mayors of large cities reflects this pattern.

I strongly approve of these developments. I feel that offenders, police, and other groups who have grievances should actively seek redress through existing legal structures, as well as through informal negotiations. We should note that correctional officers have been underrepresented in this increasing dialogue for occupational welfare and rights. The purpose of this article is to propose a set of rights for correctional officers.

The rights on which this article will focus are not legal rights; rather they are organizational and interpersonal rights of officers. While such rights would be difficult to substantiate in a constitutional or statutory sense, they are rights applicable toward development of maximum effective functioning within the job demands.

Right No. 1: *A Piece of the Action.*—A military hierarchy of command often exists in correctional facilities. In this hierarchy, information

---

* Reprinted with permission from *Federal Probation* Vol. 38, No. 4 (1974). The author is indebted to Myrl Alexander for his thoughtful comments on an earlier draft of this article.

and communication patterns flow in one direction. That direction is down, from the top of the hierarchy to the front line staff at the very bottom. This is an undesirable procedure for two reasons.

First, there are perspectives and experiences correctional officers have to contribute from their direct contact with the offenders. These perspectives represent important information sources upon which relevant decisions should be made.

Secondly, it is uncomfortable to be swept along in a process over which one has no control. And just as individuals generally should have an opportunity to participate in decisions that affect their welfare, active participation will make correctional job functioning more meaningful and responsible.

Correctional officers should serve on boards, committees, and decision-making structures at all levels within penal institutions. These include evaluation meetings, disciplinary actions, classification and parole boards and administrative and treatment staff meetings. Such communications and activities lead to a sense of mutual respect among staff, which is not achieved in any organization that insists on personnel keeping their mouths shut and saying "yes sir."

I recently visited a prison in which a new warden was being selected. Not only was there no participation by institutional personnel in the selection process, but the actual method of selection was maintained as a secret. Correctional officers should have a representative body who would meet with warden candidates and at the least would submit advisory recommendations.

It is difficult to say whether what is good for the spider should be good for the fly. However, if all individuals should have an opportunity to participate in decision making related to their welfare, a logical implication is that the same privilege should be allocated to inmates. Thus almost all boards and committees in prisons and all decision making — including warden selection — should have inmate participation and representation.

Right No. 2: *Clearly Defined Roles and Loyalties.*—This is a time at which the goals of correctional institutions are changing. Exclusively custodial institutions are adopting ideologies of reintegration of offenders into communities and prisons as agents of positive behavior change. As a result several messages may be given to employees as well as inmates. The officer is sometimes perceived as being a personal counselor to whom inmates can turn in times of need. At the same time he must be a firm symbol of authority who will encourage by example and by punitive action appropriate societal behaviors. Such conflicts can and do occur.

New job terminologies that are coined may exacerbate these conflicts. For example, new job descriptions have emerged in North Carolina of correctional treatment officer and in the State of Illinois Security Hospital of security therapist.

It is important that officers have a clearly defined set of roles and priorities, and that in their dealings with inmates these loyalties, responsibilities, and roles be explained. Thus, there would be no presenting of self under false guises.

For example, it is incorrect that a major goal of a prison is to produce happy prisoners. This simple statement may reduce considerable role conflict in officers. We might also ask, is the role of the prison to have happy officers? Again I suggest that the answer is no. However, in both cases having relatively satisfied officers and relatively satisfied inmates is an expected byproduct of meeting other goals in reasonable and effective ways.

Is it true an inmate would not confide in an officer or seek counsel and help if he knew the officer might communicate the conversation to the administration? This is true for a small number of inmates. However, if there is a sense of trust and interpersonal comfort in speaking to the officer, most inmates would speak freely and openly. The same judgment deficit that caused many inmates to get into trouble — that is, not planning ahead into the consequences of their actions — prompts inmates to discuss potentially troublesome matters with correctional personnel they do trust.

Right No. 3: *Education and Training Relevant to Job Activities and Career Development.*—Too many training programs for correctional officers are cursory, superficial, or consist of a training officer reading from a book of regulations. There is no reason to believe that a person without any correctional background will automatically be a good correctional officer. Nor is it reasonable to believe that he will acquire appropriate job behaviors simply as a result of, on-the-job experience. He is entitled to training that defines goals and prepares him to have "a piece of the action." Such minimal training rehearses and emphasizes appropriate behavior through role-playing, positive experiences, and high exposure to troublesome situations and their solutions.

A part of this preparatory process is continuing education, and career and personal development, in a system that values these characteristics. The correctional officer should be entitled to an optimal opportunity to develop his potential, and to maximize the constructive use of his talents. The encouragement of this personal improvement, through higher education or through a variety of other developmental experiences, will be accompanied by parallel improvement and growth in the agency.

Right No. 4: *Differential Assignments Related to Skills and Abilities.*— A major development in psychological research on prisons is that different inmates respond selectively to different types of officers. This basic principle is that correctional officers should be placed with the types of inmates or in the types of positions that fit best. There are some officers who are most comfortable and effective when having minimal interpersonal contact with inmates, as a result of temperament, background, or opinions. In such cases, these individuals ought to be opening and closing gates or working in isolated towers. There are others, by virtue of their high interpersonal effectiveness, who should be in situations of maximum impact with selected groups of inmates.

We know that inmates are highly variable, and it is faulty to speak of offenders as if they were alike. In the same sense it is false and unreasonable to think of correctional officers as if they were cast in the same mold. There is as much variability and difference in officers as in any other segment of the population. The Camp Elliott Study, the R.F.K. Youth Center experience, and the California Community Treatment Project have all demonstrated that the interaction between offender types and correctional officer types is more effective in producing desired behavior changes than either factor alone. We should also note that assigning officers to work with a relatively homogeneous group of prisoners makes the officers' role definition much clearer.

Right No. 5: *Informed Behavioral Science Consultation on Managing People.*—Much correctional work is private; that is, it involves unobserved one-to-one interpersonal transactions between an officer and an inmate. And there are a number of problem inmates in every prison. As officers have difficulty in relating to or supervising such prisoners, they are entitled to have expert consultation. Expert advice, however, does not come out of a vacuum. The notion of *informed* behavioral science consultation carries with it the belief that the behavior consultant will have direct knowledge and awareness of correctional officer tasks, perceptions, and situations. Pious lectures or unrealistic treatment suggestions are not part of this consultation process. Rather, good consultation makes the correctional officer a more effective manager of people through an on-site education process.

Many consultants have attempted this through meeting weekly with small groups of correctional officers. Cases with positive results have been discussed as well as problem cases. Opinions are shared and the consultation process is typically a two-way learning experience.

Right No. 6: *The Development of Professionalism.*—Professionalism indicates specialized sets of knowledge and skills as well as the acquisition of high status. This notion of professionalism has been contagious among police departments. It is time that correctional officers acquire the objectivity, the pride, status, and skills of a professional group. This sense of pride is strongly and much needed at a time that attacks on correctional officers by the public and the press often put officers in defensive positions. It is out of the security of professionalism that officers can face difficulties within and without the institution in a non-threatened, constructive, and positive manner.

CONCLUSION

These are not inalienable rights nor are they rights in the sense of the Constitutional Bill of Rights. However, they represent a series of critical steps and occupational landmarks for development of correctional officers. Most persons do not go into corrections work for altruistic reasons or because of the nature of the work itself. Rather they enter because of a need for employment or job security reasons. Once they have entered, it is incumbent upon administrators and upon the officers themselves to carefully consider what they are doing and where they are going. The present list of occupational rights represents one such set of considerations.